CW00494743

Trade Law Experienced:
Pottering about in the GATT and WTO

From Marie-Christine, William, Hendrik and Emilie,
who would like to add a footnote:

"It kept him blisfully (sic) busy burning midnight oil on
what hopefully is not entirely a chronicle of wasted time."

Trade Law Experienced:
Pottering about in the GATT and WTO

Jacques H.J. Bourgeois

Published 2005 by Cameron May Ltd
17 Queen Anne's Gate, London SW1H 9BU, UK.
Tel: +44 (0)20 7799 3636 Fax: +44 (0)20 7222 8517
email: enquiries@cameronmay.com
Website: http://www.lexmercatoria.org

ISBN: 1 905017 03 0

Printed and Bound in Great Britain by DBL

TABLE OF CONTENTS

1. "SUBSIDIARITY" IN THE WTO CONTEXT FROM A LEGAL PERSPECTIVE

Discussing the possible role of the "subsidiarity" concept in the WTO borrowed from EC law, may appear as a typical academic exercise at odds with the reality of an organisation whose "legislative" capacity is in fact very limited. The WTO is a "Member-driven" organization and a consensus on new rules is particularly difficult to reach. The Members may be expected to ensure that the obligations they enter into and become WTO law only by consensus will be strictly limited to what can only be achieved in and by the WTO. Yet, in practice, the negotiation process could lead WTO Members to agree on rules that would deserve to be subjected to a "subsidiarity" test before they are adopted.

I.   INTRODUCTION

In one of his books, *The World Trading System*, John Jackson referred to some of the implications of interdependence. "When economic transactions so easily cross national borders, tensions occur merely because of the differences between economic institutions as well as cultures ... Even morally sensitive entrepreneurs find their effective power enhanced when they can move activity quickly from one nation to another. Governments, by contrast, find themselves increasingly frustrated by effective evasion of their regulatory powers. Furthermore, governments find that actions of other governments can cause them great difficulties." (pp. 4-5*)*

These remarks made in 1989 still are relevant today. One might add that as a result of the growing interdependence and the broadening scope of the WTO regulatory scheme, the scene of international economic policy making is nowadays characterized by more drama and by the added presence of actors other than entrepreneurs and governments.

Canada and France and other countries that support them consider that there should be a culture "carve out" in the WTO system. Environmentalists fear that precedence taken by WTO trade rules over national rules designed to protect the environment put environmental policies in jeopardy. Humanitarian NGOs, such as *Médecins Sans Frontières*, take the view that the TRIPs Agreement unduly prevents developing country WTO Members' access to essential pharmaceutical products at affordable prices. Trade unions in developing country WTO Members and policymakers supporting them are calling for labor standards to be adopted by the WTO or for ILO standards to be enforced through the WTO, alternatively for the possibility of denying trade benefits to products originating in WTO Members that do not comply with such standards.

It is conceivable that some of these policy issues having worldwide implications are dealt with by the WTO and that the political trade-offs between these policies and the policies underlying the current WTO regulatory scheme are made at the WTO level. In view of the considerable political difficulties that stand in the way and also because it may be appropriate to think about whether what is achievable at the WTO level should necessarily be aimed for, the question arises whether the concept of "subsidiarity" developed by the European Community might be introduced in the WTO regulatory scheme.

II. "SUBSIDIARITY" IN THE EUROPEAN COMMUNITY CONTEXT

A. Some General Points[1]

Part One of the Treaty establishing the European Community[2] (hereinafter: the EC), entitled "Principles" contains Article 5 as inserted in the Treaty on European Union of February 7, 1992, better known as the Maastricht Treaty.[3]

The relevant part of this Article 5 reads as follows:

"In areas which do not fall within its exclusive competence, the Community shall take action, in accordance with the principle of subsidiarity, only if and in so far as the objectives of the proposed action cannot be sufficiently achieved by the Member States and can therefore, by reason of the scale on effects of the proposed action, be better achieved by the Community."

The subsidiarity principle is not a new concept. In the EC context, it has already appeared in the 1976 *Tindemans Report in the European*

---

[1] *Note on terminology:* reference is made to the European Community rather than to the European Union. The latter one has no legal capacity. The principle of subsidiarity applies in the framework of the Treaty establishing the European Community, not in the framework of the Treaty on European Union dealing with the Common Foreign and Security Policy and Cooperation in the Fields of Justice and Home Affairs.

[2] The consolidated version of the Treaty establishing the European Community is published i.a. in the Official Journal of the European Communities (hereinafter: OJ) 1997 C 340/173.

[3] Published in OJ 1992 L 224/1.

Union,[4] and in the 1977 *McDougall Report on the Role of Public Finance in European Integration*[5] and in the 1989 *Delors Report for the Study of Economic and Monetary Union*.[6] There also is a precedent for it in Article 130 R(4) prior to its amendment by the Amsterdam Treaty,[7] which was inserted in the Treaty establishing the European Economic Community by the so-called Single European Act of 28 February 1986.[8]

By its insertion in Part One of the EC Treaty, the subsidiarity principle has been given the status of a central principle having general application.

As evidenced by a considerable amount of legal writing, the subsidiarity principle as formulated in the EC Treaty raises a number of interpretative questions.

Three points at least are relatively clear.

First, before the subsidiarity principle comes into play, there has to be a finding by the EC that action is required to achieve some aim of the EC Treaty and that the EC has the necessary powers to take such action.

Second, the subsidiarity principle does not apply to areas falling within the EC's exclusive powers. There are certain areas with respect to which the Court of Justice of the European Communities (hereinafter: the ECJ) expressly recognized the existence of exclusive EC powers resulting from the EC Treaty itself (e.g. trade policy) or resulting from the exercise by the EC of concurrent powers. Not surprisingly there are grey areas.[9] This makes at any rate clear that the subsidiarity principle in the EC context concerns the relationship between the EC and its Member States; it is not a principle designed to regulate governmental action as such - be EC or Member State action - to further the aims of the EC Treaty.

Third, the subsidiarity principle as used in the EC context is to be distinguished from the proportionality principle set out in the third paragraph of Article 5 of the EC Treaty, stating that any action by the EC

---

[4] *Bull CE* Suppl. 1/76.
[5] *EC Commission* (Brussels-Luxembourg, 1977).
[6] OOPEC, Luxembourg, 1989.
[7] Published in OJ 1997 C 340/145.
[8] Published in OJ 1987 L/169/1.
[9] *See* e.g. European Commission, *Communication on the Subsidiarity Principle*, Bull. EC 10-1992, 121 stating that there is exclusive competence where the EC has a duty to act. *See also* European Commission, *Report to the European Council on the Application of the Subsidiarity Principle*, COM (94) 533, 3.

must not go beyond what is necessary to achieve the objectives of the EC Treaty. Simplifying one could say that the subsidiarity principle concerns the "whether" of action by the EC opposed to action by EC Member States, while the proportionality principle applies subsequently and concerns the "how far" of action by the EC.

In view of the question of its possible relevance in the context of the World Trade Organization (hereinafter: the WTO), two other points should be underlined.

First, for the subsidiarity principle, designed to indicate who should do what, to work there must be agreement on objectives in the first place. Such agreement is to be found in the EC Treaty itself or is to be worked out by the EC policy-making bodies.

Second, the subsidiarity principle as formulated in Article 5 of the EC Treaty must be read in the context of the EC Treaty. The text of Article 5 which refers to a situation where the objectives of the proposed action cannot be sufficiently achieved by the Member States makes this clear. The drafters of the Maastricht Treaty, by which the subsidiarity was inserted in the EC Treaty, contemplated action by EC Member States as an alternative for action by the EC. Where the EC refrains from acting pursuant to this principle, this does not imply that EC Member States have no duty to act. Not only the EC but also Member States are bound to further the aims of the EC Treaty. The European Council has taken the view that "where the application of the subsidiarity test excludes Community action, Member States would still be required in their action to comply with the general rules laid down in Article 5 [now Article 10] of the Treaty".[10] Thus, if the EC finds in a given case that in line with the subsidiarity principle the pursuit of one of the aims of the EC Treaty does not require action by the EC, it is then incumbent on EC Member States to take the appropriate action.[11]

[10] *Conclusions of the Presidency, European Council Meeting of December 1992*, Bull. EC 12-1992, 14. Article 10 states: "Member States shall take all appropriate measures, whether general or particular, to ensure fulfillment of the obligations arising out of this Treat or resulting from action taken by the institutions of the Community. They shall facilitate the achievement of the Community's tasks. They shall abstain from any measure which could jeopardize the attainment of the objectives of this Treaty."

[11] *See*, however, N. Bernard, *The Future of European Economic Law in the Light of the Principle of Subsidiarity*, (33) CML Rev. 633 (1996) who accepts that Article 3.b (now Article 5) of the EC Treaty raises the expectation that, in the absence of Community action, Member States should act but considers that this expectation is not a positive, legally enforceable duty. According to this author, failure of a Member State to act would however justify the adoption of binding EC measures (at 652). Does this not defeat the purpose of subsidiarity?

B.   How to Implement "Subsidiarity"

It is obvious that, as formulated in Article 5 of the EC Treaty, the subsidiarity principle needs to be clarified in order to be implemented.

At its Edinburgh meeting of December 1992, the European Council endorsed the following guidelines to be used in examining the criteria set out in Article 3.b (now Article 5) of the EC Treaty, i.e. the objectives of the proposed action cannot be sufficiently achieved by Member States' action; they can be better achieved by EC action:

- The issue under consideration has transnational aspects which cannot be satisfactorily regulated by action by EC Member States; and/or

- action by EC Member States alone or lack of EC action would conflict with the requirements of the EC Treaty (such as the need to correct distortions of competition or avoid disguised restrictions on trade or strengthen economic and social cohesion) or would otherwise significantly damage EC Member States' interests; and/or

- the Council of the European Union must be satisfied that action at EC level would produce clear benefits by reason of its scale or effects compared with action at the level of the EC Member States.

In a further paragraph the guidelines state that the reasons for concluding that an EC objective cannot be sufficiently achieved by the EC Member States but can be better achieved by the EC must be substantiated by qualitative or, whether possible, quantitative indicators.[12]

The European Commission has attempted to find an objective basis for the criterion that EC action would produce clear benefits by reason of its scale or effects. It has devised two tests: The first is "comparative efficacy": Do EC Member States have the necessary means and resources? The second one is "added value": i.e. assessing the efficacy of Community action, its scale, the transnational problems, the cost of inaction, critical mass.[13]

---

[12] *Conclusion of the Presidency, supra* n. 9 at 14–15. These guidelines are now in substance incorporated in Protocol No. 30 to the EC Treaty on the Application of the Principles of Subsidiarity and Proportionality (*see* consolidated text of the EC Treaty as published in OJ 1997 C173).

[13] European Commission Communication, *supra* n. 8.

There are areas in which an assessment of scale and effect of EC action are controversial to say the least. How can one judge the scale and effect of, say, a measure designed to improve consumer protection, or the health and safety of workers?[14]

This illustrates the point made in the legal literature about the mainly political nature of the subsidiarity principle, which makes it less amenable to judicial review. Yet – for the purposes of analysing its relevance in WTO context – it should be pointed out that in the EC system action by the EC is subject to judicial review by the ECJ and by the Court of First Instance of the EC, either in direct appeals or in so-called "preliminary questions" submitted by EC Member States courts to the ECJ. The final arbiters of the EC political bodies' compliance with the subsidiarity principle are the EC courts.[15]

C. The Implementation in Practice

A review of the 1995 European Commission *Report on Better Law-making*[16] shows several things.

First, "subsidiarity" appears not only to be a question of the level (EC or EC Member States) at which action should be taken; it also involves the question whether there are, on the EC level, alternatives to legislation. Three examples are cited in the report. On accounting standards greater use is to be made of the Accounting Directives Contact Committee with a view to making financial information more readily comparable before proposing new legislation. In the field of environment policy the European Commission is studying whether and, if so, how voluntary agreements with industry on the environment ought to be envisaged. In the field of social policy, the EC Treaty provides possible alternatives to legislation in the form of agreements between the two sides of industry, of which there now are numerous examples establishing EC-wide works councils. One may wonder whether this is not "proportionality" rather than "subsidiarity".

---

[14] D. Cass, *The Word that saves Maastricht? The Principle of Subsidiarity and the Division of Powers within the European Community,* (29) CMLR 1107 at 1132 (1992).

[15] So far the subsidiarity principle has come up in three cases: *Bosman* (1995) ECR 1-5041, in which the ECJ held that "the principle of subsidiarity ... cannot lead to a situation in which the freedom of private associations to adopt sporting rules restricts the exercise of rights conferred on individuals by the Treaty" (para. 81); in the *Working Time Directive case* (1996) ECR 1-5793, the ECJ construed the argument of the UK based on the subsidiarity principle as concerning the need for EC action (para. 55); in the *Deposit-Guarantee Schemes Directive case* (1997) ECR 1-2441 Germany did not claim that the Directive infringed the principle of subsidiarity but only that the EC legislature failed to give reasons substantiating the compatibility of the EC action with that principle (para. 24).

[16] Doc. CSE (95) 580.

Second, as appears from the first point, the borderline between "subsidiarity" and "proportionality" is not always easy to draw. Under the heading "proportionality" the European Commission refers to cases in which it proposed to use "framework instruments that leave Member States as much latitude as possible". This pertains more to "subsidiarity".

Third, "subsidiarity" does not only concern new legislation. In its 1995 report, the European Commission refers to 61 legislative proposals it withdrew in 1995. Interestingly, in some cases the withdrawn legislative proposal is replaced by a non-binding EC act, e.g. on zoos there will be a recommendation, or by a less detailed act, e.g. on take-over bids the European Commission announced that it would limit itself to propose a framework directive.

In practice, the "black and white" analysis that the subsidiarity principle appears to imply does not always work. Real life is more complex than that. Two examples going in opposite directions may illustrate the point.

One of the traditional lines of division of responsibilities and tasks between the EC institutions and EC Member States has to do with the fact that for matters coming within the scope of their powers the EC institutions are making rules and the EC Member States are applying them. As one author pointed out,[17] the subsidiarity principle is anchored in the very structure of the EC administration. This implies i.a. that private parties rely essentially on EC Member States courts to enforce their rights under EC law and that these courts, while enforcing EC law, apply their national procedural rules. EC Member States are very reluctant to agree to EC rules that interfere with the organization of their judicial system and their autonomy on matters of procedural law. Yet, there are instances in which the Council of the European Union enacted rules requiring EC Member States to amend national procedural rules as all EC Member States were convinced that the effective implementation of the relevant substantive EC rules made this inevitable.[18] There also are instances in which the ECJ was led into filling the gaps between private parties' rights under EC law and their enforcement by national courts.[19]

[17] J. Mertens de Wilmars, *Du bon usage de la subsidiarité*, (1992) Revue Du Marche Unique Europeen 193 at 194 (No. 4).
[18] For example, EEC Directive of 25 February 1964 on coordination of special measures concerning the movement and residence of foreign nationals which are justified on grounds of public policy, public security or public health (OJ 56/1964); EC Directive of 21 December 1989 on the coordination of the laws, regulations and administrative provisions relating to the application of review procedures to the award of public supply and public works contracts (OJ L 395/1989).
[19] For example, for a description of some of the gap filling by the case-law in this respect see W. Van Gerven, *Bridging the Unbridgeable: Community and National Tort Law after Francovich and Brasserie* (45) ICLR 507 at 513-16 (1996).

The second example concerns approximation of EC Member States technical regulations. Under the so-called "new approach" taken in 1985, the EC generally refrains from attempting to harmonize EC Member States technical regulations by enacting EC-wide technical regulations. Since then EC legislation in this field is broadly limited to laying down EC-wide essential requirements with which products must comply. Technical specifications on the basis of which industry can manufacture so that products fulfil such requirements are preferably worked out by private European standardization bodies. Compliance with such technical standards is voluntary. Where products comply with such technical specifications, there is a presumption that those products meet the essential requirements laid down in EC rules. EC Member States must accept them, except where they can rebut this presumption.[20] This may be the subsidiarity principle applied *"avant la lettre"*. It is, however, subsidiarity to a certain extent only: the EC has refrained in part from acting. It should be borne in mind that this new approach came about following *Cassis de Dijon*,[21] a judgement in which the ECJ has introduced a form of "mutual recognition" by requiring that a product lawfully produced and marketed in an EC Member State under the law of that EC Member State must be accepted by another EC Member State, except where this EC Member State shows that the refusal of the product is justified by some mandatory requirement of its own legislation.

III. RELEVANT ASPECTS OF THE EC SUBSIDIARITY PRINCIPLE IN THE WTO CONTEXT

A. Subsidiarity as such

The type of arguments that led to the insertion of the subsidiarity principle in the EC Treaty can up to a point also be made in the WTO context. With respect to the WTO arguably the same issues arise as those dealt with by the EC subsidiarity principle: can the objectives of a WTO action be sufficiently achieved by Members' action? Can they be better achieved by WTO action?

Some examples in which "subsidiarity" type arguments could have been made come readily to mind. In a series of agreements resulting

---

[20] For an analysis, see P.J. Slot, *Harmonisation* 21 E.L. Rev. 378 (1996).
[21] (1979) ECR 649; for a good comment *see* P. Oliver, *Free Movement of Goods in the European Community*, 3rd ed. 92–93 (Sweet & Maxwell, London 1996); for its policy consequences *see* Commission Communication (OJ C 256/80).

from the Uruguay Round there appear clauses which go in "the nooks and cranies" of Members' internal systems. Suffice it to mention two examples.

Clauses of the Agreement on Trade-related Aspects of Intellectual Property Rights dealing with enforcement of intellectual property rights lay down far-reaching obligations in the area of national procedural rules.[22] The Agreement on Subsidies and Countervailing Measures prohibits a series of subsidies and for another series of "actionable subsidies" imposes on Members the duty to withdraw the subsidy or to remove its adverse effects.[23] In doing so, this Agreement obviously touches on an essential instrument of national policy.

These developments can be explained by some of the factors which led in the EC framework to action that the subsidiarity principle is now designed to moderate. The "reefs" theory comes inevitably to mind: as traditional barriers to trade fade away, other obstacles that were always there make their impact increasingly felt.

In addition, the considerable increase of trade in goods and in services and of FDI make more apparent the tensions between the WTO regulatory scheme and series of economic and social policies that remain national. The *Shrimps*[24] and *Hormones*[25] cases are some of the better known examples. The discussions leading up to the Seattle WTO Ministerial Conference and the events in Seattle have revealed many other areas of perceived tensions.

B.   Subsidiarity and Proportionality

As evidenced by the EC experience the dividing line between "subsidiarity" and "proportionality" is not always easy to draw in practice. Theoretically, however, in the EC context, "proportionality" has more to do with the action of the EC as legislator *vis-à-vis* private parties and less with the relationship of EC–EC Member States. By contrast to the multipolar EC context, the WTO context is so far a bipolar one, private

---

[22] In particular, Articles 42 to 50. WTO, *The Results of the Uruguay Round of Multilateral Trade Negotiations. The Legal Texts* 365 (Geneva, 1995).

[23] In particular Articles 3 and 7.8; *ibid.* 264.

[24] WTO Appellate Body Report in *United States – Import Prohibition of Certain Shrimp and Shrimp Products*, adopted October 12, 1998, WT/DS58/AB/R.

[25] WTO Appellate Body Report in *EC – Measures Concerning Meat and Meat Products (Hormones)*, adopted January 16, 1998, WT/DS26/AB/R.

parties are only involved and concerned via Members. Consequently, the distinction made in the EC "constitution" between "subsidiarity" and "proportionality" might not be appropriate nor necessary in the WTO context. Put otherwise, in the WTO context "subsidiarity" should mean not only that action be taken at WTO level if the objectives of such action cannot be sufficiently achieved by the Members on their own but also that action by the WTO must not go beyond what is necessary to achieve the objectives of the WTO Agreement.

Two series of questions should be examined. *First,* should the subsidiarity and the proportionality principles be transplanted in the WTO context, in other words, is there a need for them? What are their possible functions? *Second,* if so, could they work in the WTO context without jeopardizing the pursuit of the WTO's aims?

C.   Possible Functions of the Subsidiarity Principle in the WTO Context

At first blush, *two* possible functions of the subsidiarity principle may be distinguished.

First, this principle can be a tool to control the flood of rules. In the EC the fashion enjoyed by the subsidiarity principle can be explained in part by a reaction against the EC's tendency to enact detailed rules. It should be noted in passing that this is less the result of activism by the European Commission than of conduct of EC Member States. Proposals by the European Commission may be prompted by EC Member States reacting to pressure from their public opinion whose perception of what the EC should regulate does not always coincide with what politicians consider to be the proper task of the EC. The British citizen expects to be protected by EC rules when acquiring a time-share in an apartment in Spain. Animal friends in several EC Member States consider it an obvious EC responsibility to impose decent conditions for transporting animals across intra-EC borders. Moreover, over-detailed regulation may also result from the decision-making in the Council of the European Union where EC Member States, which may not always trust each other, want to be sure that there are no loopholes from which other EC Member States could take advantage, or from Members of the European Parliament who occasionally want to change a piece of legislation into a Christmas tree. It is doubtful whether the same phenomena occur in the WTO.

Second, the subsidiarity can also be a tool to limit the substantive scope of action. In the EC where in practice there is an increased recourse to qualified majority decisions, the subsidiarity principle also performs a protective function for EC Member States which are outvoted. The WTO on the other hand "shall continue to practise the decision-making by consensus followed under GATT 1947".[26] Would enshrining the subsidiarity principle in the WTO be of any help to a Member forced into not blocking a consensus?

There is, however, a third function that the subsidiarity principle could perform in the WTO context. There is not much scope for "rule-making" by the WTO itself as an international organization even by consensus. "Rule-making" in the WTO will more often than not take the form of WTO-implementing and WTO-side agreements entered into by the WTO Members, as happened under the GATT 1947. This means that before they can accept to be internationally bound by such agreements entered into in the WTO framework, many Members must go through national, mostly parliamentary, procedures and obtain some form of approval, assent or consent. This has certain implications.

One of them is that negotiations have to be simultaneously held on two fronts: with the other WTO Members and with national bodies. Another implication is the risk that what has been tentatively agreed at the international level is subsequently put into question at national level, which forces negotiators to return to the negotiating table. A third one is that, when approving WTO implementing and WTO side agreements, national bodies will decree that these agreements have no direct application in national legal systems, i.e. that they cannot be enforced as such by national courts, or that they do not take precedence over national law, meaning that existing or subsequent national legislation conflicting with WTO-implementing or WTO-side agreements sets these agreements effectively aside [27] Whether this makes sense can be left aside here.[28] It is a fact and it is doubtful that the situation would change in the foreseeable future.

---

[26] Marrakesh Agreement Establishing the World Trade Organization, Art. IX(1); *loc. cit.* n. 21 at 6.

[27] For a perceptive analysis of the underlying policy considerations, *see* John H. Jackson, *Status of Treaties in Domestic Legal Systems: a Policy Analysis*, (86) AM. J'L INT'L L 310 (1992).

[28] For a critique of the Council of the European Union's decreeing that the WTO agreement may not be invoked by private parties, *see* P. Mengozzi, *The Marrakesh DSU and its Implications in the International and European Level* in J. Bourgeois, F. Berrod, E. Gippini Fournier (eds) THE URUGUAY ROUND RESULTS. A EUROPEAN LAWYERS' PERSPECTIVE 115 at 124–131 (E.I.P., Brussels, 1995); for a defense, *see* C.W.A Timmermans, *The Implementation of the Uruguay Round by the EC, ibid,* at 501.

One may wonder whether the inclusion of the subsidiarity principle in the WTO Agreement would not give national governments and parliaments some kind of insurance against the risk they perceive that the WTO would encroach on national sovereignty. This could persuade them to lengthen the leash on which they keep WTO negotiators. This could conceivably also contribute to a change of attitude with respect to direct application of WTO rules.

A first question is whether the subsidiarity principle seen as a device to allocate responsibilities and tasks between the WTO and its Members could work in the WTO context.

One should bear in mind that in contrast to the EC the WTO is composed of Members at very different stages of economic development, having diverging interests and stakes in the operation of the WTO and with starkly contrasting approaches to the aims of the WTO Agreement. Could the subsidiarity principle operate without there being an agreement on objectives?

Another question is whether the subsidiarity principle could work in the WTO context without jeopardizing the pursuit of the WTO's aims. This question is relevant in that the subsidiarity principle as formulated in Article 5 of the EC Treaty is designed to establish a better balance between EC action and EC Member State action, it is not meant to be a recipe for non-action. If the WTO would refrain from taking action pursuant to subsidiarity principle, there is no obligation on individual Members to take action on their own to further the objectives of the WTO. It would consequently appear that transposing the EC subsidiarity principle to the WTO context would effectively mean putting some of the WTO objectives on hold or achieve a better balance between the underlying WTO policies and national policies. This may not necessarily be a bad thing. One should only be aware of it. This could be avoided if the WTO Agreement were to include a form of "WTO loyalty" clause whereby Members accept the duty to abstain from any action that would put the aims of the WTO in jeopardy and the duty to take measures to further these aims. It is, however, doubtful that such a clause, which goes beyond accepted principles of international law, as "good faith", would ever be accepted by WTO Members.

A third question relates to the implications of the way in which compliance with the subsidiarity principle would be enforced.

As policy guideline, this principle would play mainly a role in the negotiating process. It could be of some help to Members that would be put under pressure by other Members not to block a consensus. In contrast to the EC, however, in the WTO there is no final arbiter to whom such a Member could turn to challenge the finding of the other Members that a WTO action complies with the subsidiarity principle: the rules of the WTO Dispute Settlement Understanding apply to the conduct of individual Members under WTO rules, they are not designed to review the conduct of the WTO itself.

Yet, it would play a role in interpreting WTO rules against which WTO Members' measures are reviewed in dispute settlement proceedings. It would provide a useful tool to strike a proper balance between WTO rules and their aims and purpose, on the one hand, and national measures and their aims and purpose, on the other hand.

In addition, if this principle were to be inserted in the WTO Agreement, it could arguably be used by national courts to review the legality of WTO rules. The enforcement of WTO rules would vary between Members as the subsidiarity principle would be interpreted differently by various Members' national courts. By contrast, in the EC system Member States courts may only set aside EC rules as contrary to the subsidiarity principle or the proportionality principle following a ruling of the ECJ to the effect that such rules are invalid on such ground. However, currently in practically all states that are WTO Members, courts do not recognize direct application of WTO rules and/or consider that national legislation takes precedence over WTO rules anyway. Enshrining the subsidiarity principle in the WTO could add another rationale for not enforcing WTO rules.

It could also lead to subjecting the national "adoption", "approval", "incorporation", "reception", or terms to that effect, of WTO rules to a review designed to verify whether these WTO rules comply with the subsidiarity principle with the possible result of sending the WTO rules back to the negotiating table.

On the other hand, these obvious disadvantages may be counterbalanced by certain advantages. The presence of the subsidiarity principle could be some sort of ultimate safeguard against the risk that WTO rules would in the event of conflict override national policies in fields not regulated by the WTO, both in the WTO political decision-making process and in WTO dispute settlement proceedings. The possibility for national courts to review WTO rules against the WTO subsidiarity principle could entice these courts to accept that WTO rules can be relied upon by private parties. Making it possible for national parliaments or other bodies to verify whether the WTO subsidiarity principle is complied with would at least have the merit of improving the democratic control over the WTO rule-making, thus contributing to better acceptance of WTO rules and to improving their effectiveness.

Tentative Conclusions

This brief review of the possible role of the subsidiarity principle, in its wider sense including the proportionality principle, in the WTO context raises a series of questions that are not easily answered.

From the point of view of the WTO rule-making process, there seem to be less need for it than in the EC context and it may be a convenient excuse for putting the pursuit of the WTO aim on hold.

While adding additional complications to an already complicated rule-making process, the subsidiarity principle would probably be perceived by governments and parliaments as some insurance that their negotiators would not be led into accepting at the negotiating stage draft WTO rules that would be excessively burdensome.

The inclusion of the subsidiarity principle in the WTO Agreement could result in a review of compliance of WTO rules with such subsidiarity principle and justify blocking their "adoption", "approval", "incorporation" or "reception" at national level. Paradoxically, however, this could contribute to better acceptance of WTO rules and improve their effectiveness.

In the WTO context, it would be a legal principle regulating the Members' rule-making within the WTO without a final arbiter in the event the Members disagree on its application. It would however be relevant in dispute settlement proceedings for the purpose of interpreting WTO rules.

2. INTERNAL MORALITY OF WTO LAW

I.   INTRODUCTION

In the early years of the European Economic Community, Guy Schrans produced an essay in which he analyzed the European Economic Community legal system from the angle of the "morality" of the law[1]. He borrowed the concept of "morality" from Lon Fuller.[2] The *internal morality* of law relates to the requirements which determine the efficacy of the legal system itself. The *external morality* of law expresses the substantive aims of the law, i. e. the external values which a legal system is designed to serve, such as justice, equity, solidarity, economic efficacy and protection of individual rights.

The present essay is an attempt to subject the WTO legal system to the same type of analysis with respect to some requirements of the internal morality of WTO law only. As will be seen, it raises more questions than it provides answers. Two introductory comments are called for: a first one about the limits of such analysis, a second one about the sources of the internal morality standards.

A.   The limits of this exercise

There are clearly limits to the appropriateness of such analysis. The various morality standards designed by Fuller refer to national legal systems. Their extrapolation by Schrans to the European Community legal system was an important step which was justified by characteristic features of the Treaty establishing the European Economic Community and by the case-law of the EC Court of Justice interpreting this Treaty.

Caution should be exercised when comparing the EC and the WTO and, above all, when drawing normative consequences for the WTO from such comparison. It is true that quite a few of the issues increasingly facing the WTO, in particular the conflicts, be they actual or perceived, between trade and non-trade values, are issues with which the EC has been confronted and is dealing. The EC started off, not unlike the GATT, with a scheme of negative integration set out in treaty obligations.

---

[1] G. Schrans, "The Instrumentality and the Morality of European Economic Law", in: W. J. Ganshof van der Meersch, *Miscellanea*, 1972, 382– 432.
[2] L. Fuller, *The Morality of Law*, 1964.

However, from the beginning the EEC Treaty contained commitments relating to common policies in a limited number of areas. Moreover, successive constitutional amendments have granted new powers to the EC legislative body with an expanding involvement of a directly elected European Parliament. By enlarging the scope of the positive integration scheme, these amendments create the possibility to adopt at EC level policies designed to support the operation of the negative integration scheme and to strike a balance between the interests served by such scheme and other societal interests. Furthermore, under the EC Treaty, the mandate of the EC Court of Justice is to "ensure that in the interpretation and application of this Treaty the law is observed" (Art. 220 EC Treaty). The expansive interpretation of the EC treaty obligations by the EC Court of Justice, largely followed and supported by EC Member States courts, is to be seen in an institutional framework in which there is relatively effective legislative body, allowing for a dialectic between that body and the judiciary.

In contrast, WTO "legislation" remains a process of negotiations between Members based on consensus. The "legislative" body is far from being effective. As matters stand there is a deficit in international governance.[3] The WTO could take on additional tasks and strike the proper balance between trade liberalization and other values. However, in its present form, it cannot responsibly assume a larger mandate.[4] Under Article 3.2 of the Understanding on Rules and Procedures Governing the Settlement of Disputes (hereinafter: DSU), the mandate of the "judicial" bodies is limited to review Members' compliance with their obligations under the covered agreements, whereby panels and the Appellate Body are "to clarify the provisions of these agreements in accordance with the customary rules of interpretation of public international law".

It may be argued that, while in the case of the EC rules internal morality requirements are relevant at EC level since EC rules may be directly applicable and may be relied upon by private parties, with respect

---

[3] According to Pascal Lamy, "until the WTO amounts to an effective instrument of world governance, questions of legitimacy will, by definition, tend to take a back seat with a weak WTO on the side", *Harnessing globalization: do we need cosmopolies*, speech at the LSE, 1 February 2001 (http://europa/eu. int/comm/trade/speeches_articles/spla45_en. htm).
[4] See the penetrating analysis of, and proposals put forward by, M. C. EJ. Bronckers "More Power to the WTO?", JIEL (2001), 41 *et seq.*

to WTO rules the internal morality is more likely to be relevant in the national legal systems where Members implement WTO rules than at WTO level. According to the EC Court of Justice the (E)EC Treaty has established "a new legal order for the benefit of which the states have limited their sovereign rights, albeit within limited fields, and the subjects of which comprise not only the Member States but also their nationals", [5] EC law having "an authority which can be invoked by [Member State] nationals before [national] courts and tribunals".[6] In contrast, as pointed out by a WTO panel, "[n]either the GATT nor the WTO has so far been interpreted by GATT/WTO institutions as a legal order producing direct effect. Following this approach, the GATT/WTO did not create a new legal order the subjects of which comprise both Contracting Parties or Members and their nationals".[7] One might add that a Swiss proposal tabled during the Uruguay Round designed to ensure that the resulting agreements would be capable of having direct effect or some equivalent status in the national law of all participants was rejected by most big players in the negotiations and dropped.[8]

However, internal morality is also relevant for States as WTO Members. The argument that WTO rules are adopted on the basis of consensus and that a Member ought not to be admitted to subsequently complain may be right in strictly legal terms. However, the legitimacy of a legal system depends in great part on the system's perceived fairness and, in turn, the effectiveness of the system depends on its fairness as perceived by its constituent members.[9]

Another argument is that WTO rules are one thing and national legal systems in which WTO rules are implemented are another thing: internal morality requirements in so far as they concern private parties are thus a matter for national legal systems. But what if a Member enters in conflict with its WTO obligations where in implementing WTO rules

---

[5] *Firma Molkerei-Zentrale Westfalen Lippe GmbH v HZA Paderborn,* [1968] ECR 143 *et seq.* (152).
[6] *NV Algemene Transport – en Expeditieonderneming van Gend en Loos* v. *Nederlandse administratie der belastingen* [1963] ECR 1 *et seq.* (12).
[7] *United States – Sections 301-310 of the Trade Act of 1974,* 22 December 1999, para. 7.72.
[8] P. J. Kuijper, "The New Dispute Settlement System: the Impact on the Community", in: Bourgeois, Berrod, Gippini-Fournier (eds), *The Uruguay Round Results, A European Lawyers' Perspective,* 1995, 87 *et seq.* (106).
[9] Th. Cottier and K. N. Schefer, "Good Faith and Protection of Legislative Expectations in the WTO", in: M. Bronckers and R. Quick (eds), *New Directions in International Economic Law,* 2000, 47 *et seq.* (57).

that Member complies with internal morality requirements of its own legal system? For example in the proceeding under Article 21.5 of the DSU in Brazil – Export Financing Program for Aircraft, Brazil claimed that it could continue to make payments of export subsidies pursuant to commitments entered into before the entry into force for Brazil of the Agreement on Subsidies and Countervailing Measures.[10] Both the Panel and the Appellate Body were of the view that any private contractual obligations, which Brazil may have under its domestic law, were not relevant to the issue whether the DSB's recommendation to "withdraw" the export subsidies prohibits payments pursuant to prior commitments.[11] The Panel's and the Appellate Body's responses to Brazil's claim are legally correct. Under customary international law as codified by the Vienna Convention (Art. 27), national law cannot be invoked as justification for failure to perform international obligations. Ultimately, however, such response is not sustainable from a legal policy point of view. WTO rules should avoid conflicts with internal morality requirements of Members' national legal systems and, as the case may be, WTO rules should therefore themselves be drafted so as to comply with internal morality requirements.

B.   The sources of internal morality requirements

The internal morality comprises requirements which determine the efficacy of the legal system itself: there must be rules; these rules must be of a general nature; they must have been published; they ought not to be retroactive; they must be clear; they ought not to be contradictory; they ought not to demand the impossible; they must be constant through time; there must be a congruence between official action and the declared rule.[12]

Compliance with these requirements is first and foremost a matter of legislation. This contribution will thus examine to what extent it may be said that WTO agreements fulfill some of these requirements.

But what if WTO agreements do not fulfill these requirements, alternatively if they do not address these requirements? May general principles of law embodying some of these requirements be relied upon for the purpose of interpreting WTO rules?

---

[10] Appellate Body Report, WT/DS 46/AB/RW of 21 July 2000, paras 13 and 14.
[11] Panel Report, *ibid*, paras 6 –16; Appellate Body Report, *ibid*. para. 46.
[12] Schrans, see n. 1, 405– 406 with references to the literature.

In light of the text of Article 3.2 of the DSU, it is fairly obvious that it is not the task of WTO panels and the WTO Appellate Body to clarify international law other than the "covered agreements". Another matter is whether panels and the Appellate Body, in interpreting "covered agreements", may, or are required to, take into account other international law. WTO panels and the Appellate Body have held that "customary rules of interpretation of public international law", in accordance with which Article 3.2 of the DSU directs them to interpret "covered agreements", are to all intents and purposes Articles 31 and 32 of the Vienna Convention of the Law of Treaties[13] (hereinafter: the Vienna Convention), which are considered as codifying customary international law on the subject.[14]

Are other provisions of the Vienna Convention that embody requirements of internal morality relevant and how? For example, is Article 28 on the non-retroactivity of treaties relevant in WTO dispute settlement as a customary rule of interpretation within the meaning of Article 3.2 DSU? For example, in *Canada –Term of Patent Protection*, the Appellate Body indicates "we have endorsed this general principle of international law".[15] Moreover, does Article 3.2 DSU refer to procedural custom only or also to substantive custom? For example, in *EC –Measures concerning Meat and Meat Products (Hormones)* the Appellate Body stated that while the precautionary principle might have crystallized into a general principle of customary international *environmental* law, it is less clear whether it has been widely accepted as a principle of *general* customary international law.[16] Does this mean that, if according to the Appellate Body the precautionary principle had been accepted as customary international law, it would be relevant?

While the Appellate Body has stated that WTO law "is not to be read in clinical isolation from public international law"[17] it has so far proceeded pragmatically in an *ad hoc* fashion and has not attempted to develop a doctrine defining how and to what extent the DSU mandates or permits in interpreting WTO rules to draw on sources other than the text of WTO agreements, interpreted following the customary rules of

---

[13] 1155 UNTS Vol. 331.
[14] Starting with *US – Standards for Reformulated and Conventional Gasoline*, WT/DS 2/AB/R of 29 May 1996 at 17.
[15] WT/DS 170/AB/R of 18 September 2000, see n. 49, with references to previous reports.
[16] WT/DS 26/AB/R of 16 January 1998, para. 123.
[17] *US – Standards for Reformulated and Conventional Gasoline*, WT/DS 2/AB/R of 29 May 1996 para. 17.

interpretation, and in particular on the sources indicated in Article 38(1) of the Statute of the International Court of Justice.[18]

This question is debated in the literature. In this short essay, it is not possible to do justice to all writers. Mavroidis and Palmeter are of the view that the terms of Article 38(1) of the Statute of the International Court of Justice are effectively brought in WTO dispute settlement by Articles 3.2 and 7 DSU.[19] But, does "customary rules of interpretation" in Article 3.2 DSU include the sources of international law referred to in the Statute of the International Court of Justice? Does Article 7 DSU, which refers to "covered agreement or agreements", open up the possibility to draw on other sources where these agreements do not explicitly refer to other international agreements? Others writers are more doubtful.[20]

One possibility is to rely on Article 31.3(c) of the Vienna Convention citing among the rules of interpretation "any relevant rules of international law applicable in the relations between the parties". This opens up a series of questions: what rules of international law? What rules are relevant? Which ones are "applicable in the relations between parties"? Which parties: the parties to the dispute? Some WTO Members? All WTO Members? Behind these technical legal questions lurks another more fundamental legal policy question: to what extent is this a matter to be left to the dispute settlement rather than a matter to be regulated by the WTO "political" bodies? Marceau concluded from her probing analysis that there remain significant doubts about the appropriateness of dealing with an important issue such as the interface between trade and environmental policy through the development of *ad hoc* rules and noted that WTO adjudication bodies lack the democratic accountability of national governments and, arguably, also the capacity to mediate between complex trade, development and environmental issues. According to Marceau, the proper way is for Members to agree on further rules on

---

[18] See http://www.icj-cij.org/icjwww/ibasicdocuments/ibasictext/ibasicstatute.htm.
[19] P. Mavroides, D. Palmeter, *Dispute Settlement in the World Trade Organization. Practice and Procedure*, 1999, 36; *acc* Bronckers, see n. 4, 59; M. Garcia-Rubio, *On the Application of Customary Rules of State Responsibility by the WTO Dispute Settlement Organs*, 2001, 46; with respect to the principle of good faith of Article 31 of the Vienna Convention, Cottier and Shefer, see n. 9, 60 criticizing the Appellate Body for denying its applicability in violation complaints.
[20] For example, P. Mengozzi, "The WTO Law: an Analysis of its First Practice", in: P. Mengozzi (Ed.), *International Trade law on the 50th Anniversary of the Multilateral Trade System*, 1999, 3 *et seq.* (15); G. Marceau, "A Call for Coherence in International Law – Praises for the Prohibition Against 'Clinical Isolation' in WTO Dispute Settlement", JWT 33 (No. 5, 1999), 87; J. Trachtmann, "The Domain of WTO Dispute Resolution", Harvard Int'l LJ 40 (1999), 333 *et seq.* (341).

trade and environment.[21] Such conclusion applies equally to the interface between trade and other policies. These considerations belong to the external morality of WTO law. It is submitted that they are also relevant for the internal morality of WTO law.

II.   THERE SHOULD BE RULES

The debate about norms versus procedures goes back to the early years of the GATT, procedures referring to a system in which, when an issue arises, it should be resolved on *ad hoc* basis by negotiations. The emphasis has unquestionably shifted towards a system based principally on norms: the corpus of GATT rules has progressively grown as a result of successive rounds of multilateral trade negotiations culminating in the establishment of the WTO Trade Organization, characterized as a "rule-based system" with an improved system of dispute settlement designed as "a central element in providing security and predictability to the multilateral trading system" according to Article 3.2 DSU.

One of the deficiencies of the WTO legal system is its very cumbersome rule-making process. It takes so much time before new rules are created and existing rules are adjusted, so much that Members may be tempted to resolve policy issues by initiating dispute settlement proceedings. It should be possible to improve the rule-making process. One of the ways could be to mandate the various functional committees to work out guidelines and recommendations. Such guidelines and recommendations are normally only pseudo-legislation, They would at least have the merit that policy issues are addressed where they should be, i.e. the "political" bodies of the WTO.

In addition, as is the case for economic law in national systems, in many instances because of its very nature, the subject matter cannot be regulated by precise and rigid rules, recourse to economic concepts is unavoidable and, although parameters and factors to be verified and taken into account can be, and are, set forth, the ultimate assessment is a discretionary one.

There are a number of instances where such assessment is entrusted to WTO bodies.[22] However, as a rule, this is left to national

---

[21] Ibid at 139.
[22] See for example, the function of the Committee established under the Agreement on the Application of Sanitary and Phytosanitary Measures (Art. 12); the "recommendations" which the Textiles Monitoring Body may address to Members under the Agreement on Textiles

Continues

authorities. The implementation of WTO rules, involving economic assessments, by national authorities may very well lead to outcomes that differ according to Members. WTO rules are not meant to bring about a single worldwide economic area in which distortions of competition are eliminated. In addition, decentralized implementation of WTO rules is the only realistic, politically acceptable and, probably, wisest solution. Different outcomes of economic assessments are its normal consequence. One cannot have its cake and eat it.

Particularly with respect to economic assessment on the basis of which trade policy measures such as antidumping and countervailing duties and safeguard measures are adopted, in the course of the Uruguay Round and subsequently Members have made clear that such economic assessments by national authorities ought not to be reviewed in dispute settlement proceedings under the motto "no *de novo* review". One of the objections to the inclusion of competition rules in the WTO system is the application of the DSU which, it is feared, would lead to reviewing the assessment by national authorities of complex economic factors.[23] The record so far shows, however, that WTO panels have quite rightly not attempted to second guess national authorities and have limited themselves to verify whether the findings of national authorities were supported in fact and whether in view of apparently conflicting findings of fact the conclusions reached were adequately explained.[24]

III.   GENERALITY OF THE RULES

In national legal systems the requirement of the generality of the rules means that rules should operate impersonally and apply to general categories of persons. Translated in WTO terms, this requirement means that WTO rules should treat WTO Members equally and apply to general categories of WTO Members. It finds its concrete expression in the many

---

...and Clothing; "responsibilities" may be assigned under the Agreement on Technical Barriers to Trade or by the Members to the committee established under this agreement (Art. 13.1); the committee established under the Agreement on Subsidies and Countervailing Measures may make "determinations" (Art. 27), "give departures" to Members in the process of transformation from a centrally planned into a market, free enterprise economy (Art. 29.4); the surveillance functions of the committee established under the Agreement on Safeguards (Art. 13).

[23] For example, (US) International Competition Policy Advisory Committee, Final Report (2000) at 278 (http://www.usdoj.gov/atr/icpac/finalreport.htm).

[24] For example, in one particular area, J. H. J. Bourgeois, "GATT/WTO Dispute Settlement Practice in the Field of Anti-Dumping Law", in: E. U. Petersmann (ed.), *International Trade Law and the GATT/WTO Dispute Settlement System*, 1997, 285 *et seq.* (299–300).

provisions that apply the standards of most favoured nation treatment and of national treatment, which are obligations resting on Members.

This requirement is *prima facie* straightforward. It raises, however, some fundamental questions.

First, do the obligations expressing this requirement go beyond equal treatment in the formal sense, i.e. may, alternatively should, Members treat certain other Members unequally to the extent that these other Members are in an unequal situation, thus according them substantive equality? There are some precedents along this line, such as the clauses on special and differential treatment for developing country Members and the Tokyo Round Decision on tariff preferences for developing countries.

Second, does this requirement go beyond de *jure* discrimination? For example, in trade in products should WTO rules address the negative impact of product differentiation - which is formally non–discriminatory - on the conditions of competition of the imported product? If so, should the concept of like product be extended to competing products and how should the WTO then take account of the legitimate purposes of product differentiation by WTO Members? Is this a matter for interpretation, or does this require amending the rules?[25]

IV.   NO RETROACTIVE RULES

Retroactivity of rules is often used under two distinct meanings. It may mean that a new rule applies to an act performed, a transaction entered into or a situation occurring, and whose effects ceased, before the new rule was enacted. It may also mean that a new rule applies to such act, transaction or situation, whose effects continue after the new rule was enacted. In this second meaning, there is immediate application of the new rule to the continuing effects of the act, transaction or situation rather than retroactive application of the new rule.

A second distinction ought to be made between retroactivity of legislation and retroactivity of the judicial process.

---

[25] For these and other questions, see Th. Cottier and P. Mavroidis, "Conclusions", in: Th. Cottier and P. Mavroidis, *Regulatory Barriers and the Principle of Non-Discrimination in World Trade Law*, 2000, 389 *et seq.* (390–391).

A. WTO "legislation"

More often than not, the various agreements that form part of the Marrakesh Agreement establishing the WTO do not specifically address their application in time. Generally, their entry into effect is determined by Article XIV of the Marrakesh Agreement. Some agreements provide that all or certain obligations are to be complied with at a later date, [26] others provide for transitional periods either for all Members[27] or for developing country Members.[28]

None of the agreements can be considered as containing genuinely retroactive rules and most of them are intended to create obligations for WTO Members to act or to abstain from acting with respect to future acts, transactions and situations. This is in line with each Member's general obligation to "ensure conformity of its laws, regulations and administrative procedures with its obligations as provided in the annexed Agreements" set forth in Article XVI.4 of the Marrakesh Agreement. Normally, the necessary amendments to such laws, regulations and administrative procedures are designed to operate *ex nunc*.

Some agreements contain express provisions addressing their application to old acts, transactions and situations whose effects continue under the new rule.

The Agreement on Implementation of Article VI of the GATT (the Anti-dumping Agreement) provides that it applies to investigations and reviews of existing measures, initiated pursuant to applications (i.e. complaints by the domestic industry) which have been made on or after the entry into force for a Member of the WTO Agreement (Art. 18.3). Thus, by implication, the old rules continue to apply to investigations initiated pursuant to complaints filed before the entry into force of the new Anti-dumping Agreement. The Agreement on Subsidies and Countervailing Measures contains the same provision (Art. 32.2). Understandably legal certainty required to define a point in time for the application of the new rules that took account of pending investigations. Regretfully, no effort was made to distinguish between new rules whose application would

---

[26] Agreement on Trade-Related Investment Measures, Art. 5.2; Agreement on Subsidies and Countervailing Measures, Art. 28; Agreement on Trade-Related Aspects of Intellectual Property Rights (TRIPs Agreement), Art. 65.1.

[27] Agreement on Rules of Origin, Art. 2.

[28] Agreement on Subsidies and Countervailing Measures, Art. 27; TRIPs Agreement, Art. 65.2; the same goes for country in transition Members, Art. 65.3; for least-developed country Members, Art. 66.

have required to re-do the investigation and new rules that could apply without further ado to pending investigations.

The Agreement on Safeguards does not contain the same or a similar provision presumably because there are no old WTO rules on safeguard investigations. It does not address the issue whether those Members that carried out investigations under Article XIX GATT 1947 must comply with the Agreement on Safeguards for investigations pending at the date of entry into force of this agreement. There is only an obligation to terminate at certain dates safeguard measures that were in existence on the date of entry into force of the WTO Agreement (Art. 10).

The more interesting provisions appear in the Agreement on Trade-Related Aspects of Intellectual Property Rights (hereinafter: the TRIPs Agreement). A first one states that the Agreement does not give rise to obligations "in respect of acts which occurred before the date of application of the Agreement for the Member in question" (Art. 70.1). A second provision states that, except as otherwise provided for in the TRIPs Agreement, this agreement gives rise to obligations "in respect of all subject matter existing at the date of application of this Agreement for the Member in question, and which is protected in that Member on the said date or which meets or comes subsequently to meet the criteria for protection under the terms of this Agreement" (Art. 70.2). There are other provisions of the same kind in the TRIPs Agreement, which are left aside here.

Articles 70.1 and 70.2 gave rise to a dispute between the US and Canada in *Canada –Term of Patent Protection*.[29] With effect from 1 October 1989, Canada had brought the term of protection from seventeen years from the date of grant of a patent to twenty years from the date of filing of the application for a patent. A subsequent amendment of the Canadian legislation provided that the old rule of seventeen years terms of protection was maintained for patent applications filed before 1 October 1989. The WTO law issue was whether, as Canada claimed, the TRIPs obligation to grant a term of protection of twenty years (Art. 33) did not apply by virtue of Article 70.1 where the act, i.e. either the filing of the application for a patent or the granting of a patent, occurred before the date of application of the TRIPs Agreement for Canada. Both the Panel and the Appellate Body agreed that Article 70.1 applies to such "acts", which occurred before the entry into force of the TRIPs Agreement. They found, however, that

---

[29] Panel Report, WT/DS 170/R of 5 May 2000; Appellate Body Report, WT/DS 170/AB/R of 18 September 2000.

Article 70.2 applies to inventions protected by patents resulting from such acts, i.e. the basis of applications filed before 1 October 1989, on the ground that such inventions are "subject matter existing ... and which is protected" within the meaning of Article 70.2. In reaching this conclusion, the Panel made the point that the protection accorded to patents that had been applied for before 1 October 1989 is a "situation which has not ceased to exist" at the date the TRIPs Agreement entered into force.[30] The Appellate Body observed that if the phrase "acts which occurred" were interpreted to cover all continuing situations involving patents which were granted before the date of application of the TRIPs Agreement, Article 70.1 would preclude the application of virtually the whole of the TRIPs Agreement to rights conferred by the patents arising from such "acts".[31]

As interpreted by that panel and the Appellate Body, Article 70.1 of the TRIPs Agreement offers a good example of a provision excluding expressly retroactive application of WTO rules, while Article 70.2 is an example of application of a new rule to the continuing effects of an act accomplished under the old rule. This solution establishes a proper balance between the principle that rules ought not to be retroactive and the principle that new rules which are supposed to be better ought to apply fully and forthwith.

B.   The WTO dispute settlement process

The retroactivity issue in the WTO dispute settlement has several aspects. The first one concerns the relevance of customary international rules on the time factor in interpreting WTO rules. The second one deals with the temporal effect of interpretations of WTO rules. The third one relates to the effect in time of remedies.

On the first aspect of the issue there have been several cases in which panels and the Appellate Body referred to Article 28 of the Vienna Convention according to which, absent a contrary intention, the provisions of a treaty do not bind a party in relation to any act or fact which took place or any situation which ceased to exist before the date of entry into force of the treaty with respect to that party.[32]

---

[30] Panel Report, *ibid.* para. 6.41.

[31] Appellate Body Report, *ibid.* para. 59.

[32] Reports of the Appellate Body, *Brazil –Measures Affecting Desiccated Coconut*, WT/DS 22/AB/R of 20 March 1997, para. 15; *EC –Regime the Importation, Sale and Distribution of Bananas*, WT/DS 27/AB/R of 25 September 1997, para. 235; *Canada - Term of Patent Protection*, WT/DS 170/AB/R of 18 September 2000, para. 71.

In *EC–Regime for the Importation, Sale and Distribution of Bananas,* the EC referred to Article 28 of the Vienna Convention and claimed that the Articles II and XVII of the General Agreement on Trade in Services (hereinafter: the GATS), which entered into force on 1 January 1995, did not apply to its import licensing regime enacted in 1993. The Panel disagreed with the EC's interpretation of Article 28 of the Vienna Convention and stated that it examined only "actions which the EC took or continued to take, or measures that remained in force or continued to be applied by the EC and thus did not cease to exist after the entry into force of the GATS".[33] It added that "the EC measures at issue may be considered as continuing measures, which in some cases were enacted before the entry into force of the GATS but which did *not* cease to exist after that date (the opposite of the situation envisaged in Article 28)".[34] In *Canada –Term of Patent Protection* the Appellate Body sought in Article 28 of the Vienna Convention a confirmation of its interpretation of a WTO rule that addressed the application in time, i.e. Article 70 of the TRIPs Agreement, as it did in *Brazil –Desiccated Coconut* with respect to Article 32.2 of the Agreement on Subsidies and Countervailing Measures. In contrast, the GATS relied upon in *EC –Bananas* did not contain a similar rule. Interestingly, on appeal, the EC did not contest that reliance could be had on Article 28 of the Vienna Convention but argued that the Panel erred in its interpretation of Article 28. This being said, the principle implied in that article, i.e. that the new rule applies to continuing effects of acts done, transactions entered into and situations occurred under the old rule, makes sense.

The second aspect of the issue of retroactivity concerns the temporal effect of interpretations of WTO rules. According to the DSU, the function of the WTO dispute settlement is to "clarify the provisions of [the covered] agreements". Consequently, when a panel or the Appellate Body interprets a WTO rule, this interpretation concerns the rule as it is and as it has always been. In some legal systems in certain cases affecting a potentially large category of persons, courts may rule that their interpretation applies to the litigation at hand and to future litigation and may not be relied upon with respect to past acts, transactions or situations. So far, this particular aspect of retroactivity has not been argued in WTO disputes. This may be linked to the way in which the DSU appears to deal with the next aspect of retroactivity.

---

[33] For example, Panel Report WT/DS 27/R/USA of 13 June 1997, para. 7. 308. On appeal, the Appellate Body declined to enter into the merits of this issue. It considered that the Panel's finding of continued existence was a factual finding. Appellate Body Report, para. 237.
[34] *Ibid.,* at fn. 797.

The third aspect of retroactivity in the judicial processes relates to the effect of remedies in time. Assuming that the ILC Draft Articles on State Responsibility can be considered as codifying customary law, a State that has committed an illegal act has two obligations: the obligation to stop the illegal act and the obligation to provide reparation to the injured party.[35] Reparation may be restitutio in integrum, i.e. reestablishment of the status quo ante, restitution by equivalent, i.e. compensation, satisfaction and/or guarantees for non-repetition. Article 37 of the ILC Draft, however, gives precedence to other rules of international law relating specifically to an internationally wrongful act whose legal consequences they determine.

The question is whether the WTO DSU does contain specific provisions dealing with the issue of remedies that would take precedence over customary international law. This question is disputed.[36] The discussion about whether WTO remedies are prospective only or also retrospective focuses on Article 19 DSU, according to which a panel or the Appellate Body "shall recommend that the Member concerned bring the measure [found to be inconsistent with a covered agreement] into conformity with that agreement" and, furthermore, that a panel or the Appellate "*may suggest* ways in which the Member concerned *could* implement the recommendation" (emphasis added). It seems clear that Article 19 was inserted in the DSU as a reaction of a number of WTO Members against GATT panel reports in the area of antidumping and countervailing duties recommending *ex tunc* remedies, i.e. revocation and reimbursement. It should be noted that these panels relied implicitly or explicitly on the ILC Draft Articles and could arguably do so absent contrary provisions in GATT law.

The issue was squarely faced by the Article 21.5 DSU Panel in *Australia –Subsidies Provided to Producers and Exporters of Automotive Leather,* which examined whether the action taken by Australia implementing an earlier recommendation that the Australian export subsidies schemes be withdrawn was adequate.[37] Relying on the Vienna Convention[38] and on the "effectiveness" of the remedy,[39] the Panel considered that retroactive remedies can very well exist within the WTO

---

[35] Art. 41 and 42 UN GA Doc. A/CN. 4/L 528/Add. 2 of 16 July 1996.
[36] For a comprehensive treatment, see P. C. Mavroidis, "Remedies in the WTO Legal System: Between a Rock and a Hard Place", EJIL 11 (2000), 763–813.
[37] WT/DS 126/RW of 21 January 2000.
[38] *Ibid,* paras 6.25 *et seq.*
[39] *Ibid.* para. 6.35.

legal system. It rejected the US argument that Article 19(1) DSU, even read in conjunction with Article 3(7) DSU, requires the limitation of the specific remedy provided for in Article 4(7) of the Agreement on Subsidies and Countervailing Measures to purely prospective action.[40]

Unquestionably, there are good policy arguments in support of the Panel's finding - retrospective remedies are probably the only way to counteract "hit and run" practices and are a deterrent against potential violators. But does this, as Mavroidis argues, justify this finding?[41]

The Panel's interpretation was strongly criticized by a number of WTO Members in the DSB which considered it contrary to the intention of the drafters of Article 19 of this DSU.[42] There was no appeal as Australia and the US reached a settlement, involving i.a. the repayment by the beneficiary of the subsidy of AU$ 7. 2 million over 12 years.[43]

V.   CONGRUENCE BETWEEN OFFICIAL ACTION AND DECLARED RULE

In the WTO legal system, discrepancies between the rule as declared and official action could occur at two levels. First, at the WTO level where a subordinate body would derogate from the WTO agreement which it is called upon to administer. Second, at national level where a Member would fail to take measures which, according to Article XVI: 4 of the Marrakesh Agreement, it is required to take to "ensure the conformity of its laws, regulations and measures with its obligations as provided in the annexes Agreements".

(a) The more obvious way to maintain or to re-establish congruence between the rule as declared and official action, is to bring this action in line with the rule.

At the first level, the instances in which subordinate bodies may make findings and issue recommendations are few and far between. Preventing discrepancies should normally be the task of either the General Council or the Council for Trade in Goods. Whether action by subordinate

---

[40] *Ibid.* para. 6.31.
[41] See n. 36, 790.
[42] WT/DSB/M/75, paras 5 *et seq.*
[43] "US and Australia Reach Accord in Dispute over Leather Subsidies", International Trade Re porter 17 (No. 25, 22 June 2000), 964.

bodies can be reviewed in dispute settlement proceedings is an open question. Unlike for example in the EC legal system, the WTO dispute settlement system is not specifically designed to review WTO measures. In *India –Quantitative Restrictions on Imports of Agricultural Textile and Industrial Products,* India challenged the competence of the Panel to make findings on BOP restrictions, i.a. on the ground that such findings could lead to conflicts between a panel report and the BOP Committee. The Panel rejected the argument noting that it would take the conclusions of the BOP Committee into account.[44] The Appellate Body upheld the Panel's interpretation. It rejected India's institutional balance argument and expressed its conviction "that, in considering the justification of balance-of-payments restrictions, panels should take into account the deliberations and conclusions of the BOP Committee".[45] The interesting question is what would happen if a Member were to claim and show that the BOP Committee conclusions were patently wrong?

At the second level, the potential for discrepancy between a WTO rule as declared and official action of a Member is the greatest. So far in the WTO system, there is no genuine preventive machinery against such discrepancies.[46] The main corrective machinery is the dispute settlement mechanism.

A dispute may only be initiated in case of "nullification or impairment" of a benefit accruing to the complaining party or where the attainment of any objective of the agreement is being impeded not against a breach as such.[47] However, sanctioning a practice developed under GATT 1947, the DSU provides in its Article 3.8 that in cases of infringement of an obligation, the action is considered *prima facie* to constitute a case of nullification or impairment and that there is normally a presumption that a breach of rules has an adverse impact. In practice, this presumption is so difficult to rebut that breaches of rules are equipollent to nullification or impairment. A finding by a panel or the Appellate Body adopted by the DSB that a WTO rule has been breached should normally put an end to the discrepancy between the rule as declared and official action. As the DSU states in its Article 3.7, absent a solution mutually acceptable to the parties in dispute, the first objective of the dispute settlement mechanism

---

[44] WT/DS 90/R of 6 April 1999, para. 5.90.
[45] WT/DS 90/AB/R of 23 August 1999, paras 80–109.
[46] E.g. contrast on balances of payment restrictions GATT rules (Art. XII and the 1994 Understanding on the Balance-of-Payment Provisions of the GATT 1994) and the old EC rules (Art. 109 and 110).
[47] Art. XXIII. 1 GATT 1994; Art. 64 TRIPs referring to Art. XXIII GATT 1994.

is usually to secure the withdrawal of the measures concerned if found to be inconsistent with any of the covered agreements. The DSU provides, however, as last resort, for countermeasures, subject to authorization by the DSB. The drawbacks of countermeasures are well known. Countermeasures by a successful complainant Member are unlikely to force a large respondent Member to comply. Moreover, countermeasures are trade restricting. Lastly, in the Member failing to comply with its obligations countermeasures affect mostly a sector of the economy other than the sector benefiting from that Member's measure in breach of a WTO rule. When reviewing the DSU, Members should consider other measures to bring about compliance, such as financial penalties or suspension by the successful complainant Member vis-à-vis respondent Member of the same obligation which the respondent Member breached.

(b) Discrepancies between the rules as declared and official action may also result from fundamental changes in socio-economic premises of the rule or in the values that the rule is designed to protect. In national legal systems, the congruence is then re-established by bringing the rule in line with such changes. This is done either by courts interpreting the rule, taking into account such changes, or by the legislative body amending the rule. In this respect, the WTO legal system finds itself in a catch-22 situation. On the one hand, the Members have declared in Article 3.2 DSU that the dispute settlement process "cannot add or diminish the rights and obligations provided in the covered agreements" and in Article 3.9 DSU that its provisions "are without prejudice to [...] authoritative interpretation of the provisions of a covered agreement" by the political bodies of the WTO. The Marrakesh Agreement states in its Article IX. 2 that the Ministerial Conference and the General Council shall have the exclusive authority to adopt interpretations of this Agreement and the Multilateral Trade Agreement. Panels and the Appellate Body are thus expected more than national courts, to rely on interpretation methods based on text and context rather than on systemic and functional arguments which would allow to take account of changed socio-economic premises. On the other hand, partly as a result of this, Members can rely less on general standards (as opposed to specific rules) than when they make law domestically.[48] This would not matter too much if those more specific rules could be amended and within a reasonably time frame by the "political" body of the WTO, i.e. the Members. This, however, it not the case.

---

[48] See J. H. Jackson, "Dispute Settlement in the WTO: Emerging Problems", JIEL 1 (No. 3, 1998), 329 *et seq.*, (346–347).

To escape this dilemma, Members should agree on different systems of rule making in which only general rules would be adopted through the normal decision-making process and implementing rules would be adopted by a less cumbersome decision-making process. Failing this, only second best solutions are available or could be contemplated, at least where one or several Members consider that they can no longer comply with the rules as they are. First, the Member(s) in question could seek a waiver, which according to Article IX. 3 of the Marrakesh Agreement may be decided for any WTO obligation by a three fourths majority of the Members. There is another possible second best solution[49] that could be considered in a review of the DSU: where a Member considers it cannot comply and whose measures have been found inconsistent with a WTO rule on a dispute settlement proceeding, it should be able to keep its WTO inconsistent measures, provided that it pays to other Members affected by these measures compensation the amount and the modalities of which should be determined by the DSB.

VI. CONCLUSION

The very fact that it may be worth examining whether the WTO legal system complies with certain requirements of internal morality evidences the considerable achievements of the rule-based system established by the Marrakesh Agreement. This brief review highlights certain deficiencies in the rule-making process. In order to operate satisfactorily a rule-based system must be capable of producing rules and amending them in a timely fashion. As it stands, the WTO rule-making process does not. Members need to address this issue. This brief review also points to certain open questions and to some of the unresolved systemic issues Members should deal with in order to improve the efficacy of the WTO legal system, which in turn conditions the proper application of its rules and protects their operational functions in a market economy.

---

[49] This is only a second best solution contrary to the views expressed by A. Sykes, "The Remedy for Breach of Obligations under the WTO Dispute Settlement Understanding: Damages or Specific Performance" in: Bronckers and Quick, *op. cit. supra* n. 9, 347.

3. SOME REFLECTIONS ON THE WTO DISPUTE SETTLEMENT SYSTEM FROM A PRACTITIONER'S PERSPECTIVE

This brief article deals with some discrete aspects of the WTO dispute settlement system as it stands. Some of them are currently discussed in the difficult and drawn-out review of the WTO Understanding on Rules and Procedures Governing the Settlement of Disputes, mandated by the 2001 Doha Ministerial Declaration launching the current round of multilateral trade negotiations. Others, of a procedural nature, do not seem to have caught the attention of delegates to the Special Session of the WTO Dispute Settlement Body.

ABSTRACT

This brief article advocates the establishing of a standing or standing WTO Dispute Settlement panels. It also draws the attention to some deficiencies of a procedural nature, i.e. on standing, preliminary rulings, scope of disputes, judicial economy and appeals, and review of factual findings on appeal. It suggests improvements and raises the question whether interim relief should be provided.

I.   INTRODUCTION

The purpose of this contribution is simple and modest: it is to explore whether (and how) it is possible to improve the WTO dispute settlement system on some discrete points.

The items that, from a practitioner's perspective, ought to be put on the improvement agenda[1] can be grouped together under two headings: panels and procedural matters.

II.   PANELS

The following comments are not meant as a criticism of the way WTO panels have so far handled the tasks assigned to them. From a technical point of view, panels have generally done a good job, taking into account: the complexities of some cases; the legal imperfections of the rules to be interpreted and applied; the length of the submissions of

---

[1] A series of interesting papers on the theme 'The Role of the Judge. Lessons for the WTO' were submitted and discussed at the 2000 World Trade Forum under the chairmanship of Thomas Cottier and Petros Mavroidis. They will not be quoted here at the authors' request. These papers and the comments will be published in the course of 2001, as *The World Trade Forum, Vol. 3*, in the *Studies in International Economics*, by the University of Michigan Press.

parties; and the time constraints within which they are required to come up with their findings and recommendations. There is, however, room for improvement.

A. Appointment

The present system, characterized by a case-by-case selection in which the WTO Secretariat (the Director of the Secretariat's Legal Affairs Division and the Director of the Secretariat's Division in charge of the matter in dispute) proposes panelists to the parties, has reached its limits.

The actual procedure is rather clumsy. Before it selects the panelists it proposes to the parties, the Secretariat will "sound the parties out" about a number of panelists. In its quest for the right candidates, the Secretariat usually takes account of the fact that it must keep panelists "in reserve" in the event that parties fail to agree and the Director General is called upon to appoint the panelists. Parties then make sometimes frantic inquiries about the personality, the quality, and the views of the candidates. While Members are not supposed to oppose nominees of the Secretariat "except for compelling reasons",[2] at the informal stage each party manoeuvres to have panelists named whom it hopes will be favorable to its views. At the formal stage, it is not uncommon that, pursuant to Article 8.7 of the DSU, the Director General has to cut the Gordian knot in consultation with the Chairman of the DSB and the Chairman of the relevant Council or Committee. This is all the more useless because, at least in this author's personal experience, no party ever subsequently attempted to influence "its" panelist in the course of the proceeding. Parties will often resist the nomination not only on the basis of the nationality of the other party, as they are entitled to do under Article 8.3 of the DSU, but also on the basis of the nationality of all WTO Members of a given trade block. In addition, although the list of potential panelists now also includes academics, more often than not current or former members of delegations to the WTO are selected. While the cost of the panelists in government service is borne by their governments, in view of the less than adequate remuneration of panelists, others are reluctant to serve. As a result of this and the growing number of disputes, the difficulties of constituting panels are increasing. Certain Members are now supplying a disproportionate number of panelists.[3] All this takes time and prevents the parties from focusing on the preparation of their case.

[2] DSU Art. 8.6.
[3] D. Steger, "Overview of WTO Dispute Settlement". Address at the 1998 Conference of the World Trade Law Association (leaving mainly panelists from New Zealand and Switzerland); B. Janseo, "Selected Problem Areas in the Course of a Dispute Settlement Procedure" in A. Pérez van Kappel and W. Hensel (eds), *Free World Trade and the European Union*, 59 at 60 (Vol. 28, Publications by the Academy of European Law in Trier, Bundesanzeiger, 2000), (adding panelists from Australia and Latin American countries).

Preferably, panelists should be selected outside the 'Geneva Club' of current or former members of delegations to the WTO. Members of the 'Geneva Club' may or may not have an institutional bias. Some former members of delegations would probably decline to serve as panelists but for their sense of loyalty vis-à-vis the institution. It is, however, important to avoid the perception of an institutional bias, especially now that an increasing number of disputes touch on interests that are not purely trade. It is true that outside of the "Geneva Club", experts on WTO law and policy are few and far between. But should panelists necessarily be experts in WTO law and policy? When they were appointed, most members of the Appellate Body were not particularly well-versed in WTO matters. This did not prevent them from dealing very professionally with the issues of WTO law submitted to them.

B. Standing panel(s)

1. The pros and cons

There are arguments in favor of establishing a standing panel or panels. Whether one should establish one single standing panel functioning in divisions, as in the case of the Appellate Body, or whether one should establish several standing panels is left aside here. A standing panel would avoid the current clumsy time-consuming process of constituting panels on a case-by-case basis. It would enhance consistency in the interpretation of the rather complex WTO body of rules. It would permit coordination between the various divisions of the standing panel or, as the case may be, between the various standing panels, along the lines of the collegial functioning of the Appellate Body divisions.

There are also arguments against a standing panel. The first one seems to be that the current system allows for a broad representation of the WTO membership. In practice, however, the *ad hoc* selection does not achieve this result. The second argument is that parties to the dispute have a measure of confidence and trust when they have a say in the selection of panelists. Both of these arguments could also be advanced against the standing Appellate Body. Yet, as far as this author is aware, assuming that these arguments have been put forward when the proposal of a standing Appellate Body was put on the table, hardly anybody would now see these as convincing arguments in the case of the Appellate Body. The third argument is that the number of standing panelists would have to be high on account of the need to have panelists available that have expertise relevant to the various covered agreements. This argument is hardly convincing. At present there does not seem to be a particular effort to select panelists that are experts in agriculture, government procurement, health, subsidies, technical rules, etc. Moreover, so far specific expert panelists are contemplated only for disputes under GATS regarding particular service sectors.[4] The reasons why panelists should have specific expertise are not obvious. The panel's task is not to reassess economic, social, or technical merits of the measures in dispute. If panels need expert technical advice, they may consult experts. They are currently making use of this possibility. They may also request an advisory report from an expert review group,[5] although they have not done so, so far.

2. *Other aspects*

For the purpose of selecting the members of the standing panel, there is no need to reinvent the wheel. The model used to select the first members of the Appellate Body has worked well. On the basis of some broad criteria agreed upon by the WTO membership, a high-level representative selection committee[6] should review the applications submitted by the Members, interview candidates, and make recommendations. It would be wise to also seek the views of practitioners.

There is every reason why the status of the standing panel members should be regulated in the same fashion as that of the Appellate Body members. First, the availability at all times and at short notice is an obvious requirement. It should be borne in mind that as the experience of the Appellate Body shows, the number of weeks spent on WTO work may be much higher than anticipated. Second, they should be unaffiliated with any government. If a standing panel member were affiliated with a government, parties would have to be given the opportunity to object to that member being on the division dealing with the dispute. One of the advantages sought by having a standing panel would be lost. Third, they should be subject to rules on conflict of interest avoidance.[7]

Their remuneration should be adequate enough to enable high quality applicants to constantly be available for proceedings in which

---

[4] Decision on Certain Dispute Settlement Procedures for the General Agreement on Trade in Services, §4.

[5] DSU Art. 13.2.

[6] In the case of the initial composition of the Appellate Body, the selection committee was composed of ambassadors under the able chairmanship of Ambassador Kenyon.

[7] Panelists are also subject to the Rules of Conduct for the Undertaking on Rules and Procedures Governing the Settlement of Disputes (WT/DSBRC/1 adopted by the DSB on 3 December 1996). For a comment: G. Marceau, "Rules of Ethics for the New World Trade Organization Dispute Settlement Mechanism", 32(3) JWT 57 (1998).

panels no longer have the possibility, as they had under the old system, to set time-lines taking account of the availability of panel members.

III.   SOME PROCEDURAL MATTERS

Although the Appellate Body has endeavored to fill lacunae, there is an obvious need for working procedures of panels. Currently, each panel adopts some working procedures that cover only very partially the potential procedural issues that may arise. More often than not panels have to deal, in an *ad hoc* fashion, with such issues raised by parties. Many such issues are genuinely relevant from a systemic point of view and are important from a due process point of view. Yet, panels do not always show much sympathy to parties raising procedural issues. They occasionally perceive these issues as devices used by parties to prevent the panels from dealing with substantive issues and have a tendency to treat procedural objections with benign neglect.

A.   Standing

The issue of whether a complainant WTO Member is entitled to have a WTO panel to deal with its complaint is well known.

It was extensively argued in *EC – Bananas III*. Before the Panel, the EC challenged the standing of the US on the grounds that the US did not export bananas and had, consequently, no legal interest. The Panel rejected this on a number of grounds. On appeal, the Appellate Body rejected the EC's reliance on the case law of the ICJ and deduced from Article XXIII of the GATT and Article 3.7 of the DSU that it is up to the WTO Member concerned to decide for itself to start an action.[8] It added that the US did, in fact, have a potential export interest in bananas as a producer and that the US internal market could be affected by the EC measures.[9] The Appellate Body concluded that the factors it identified, taken together, were enough to give the US the right to bring claims in that case but added that this did not mean that "one or more factors we have noted in this case would necessarily be dispositive in another case".[10]

While one may understand the underlying legal policy argument – i.e. as the masters of the WTO Agreement, WTO Members have an

---

[8] *EC –Regime for the Importation, Sale and Distribution of Bananas*, WT/DS 27/AB/R, adopted 25 September 1997, para. 135.
[9] Id, para. 136.
[10] Id, para. 138.

interest *per se* in its correct interpretation – the legal reasoning is hardly persuasive. The summary rejection of the ICJ's case law is all the more surprising because, as in national systems there is also generally some legal interest test. It may be argued in support of the Appellate Body's interpretation that the DSU does not require injury to be shown. This may be true, but nullification and impairment remains a requirement and a violation of a WTO provision is generally a rebuttable prima facie case of nullification and impairment.

However, the added reference made by the Appellate Body to the potential US interest, and its conclusion, do leave the door open. Quite rightly so. There are cases where one wonders why a complainant WTO Member should be permitted to bring the claim at all. Suppose WTO Member A challenges an antidumping duty imposed on its imports into WTO Member B, on the grounds that Member B established a 40 percent dumping margin, whereas a calculation consistent with the WTO Antidumping Code would have resulted in a 20 percent dumping margin. However, suppose Member B applies the "lesser duty rule" and imposed a 10 percent duty sufficient to remove the injury. Thus, even if the panel were to find Member A's argument to be correct, the antidumping duty imposed by Member B and challenged by Member A would stand and the claim would be inoperative. Such a complaint should be declared inadmissible.

If Member A wants to challenge a mandatory rule of Member B, requiring its authorities to calculate dumping margins in violation of the WTO Antidumping Code, that Member may do so. One may wonder whether it matters that the Member takes the wrong avenue. This author believes that it does. Procedural rules are there to ensure legal certainty and orderly treatment of cases. *Electa una via, altra non datur*.

B.   Preliminary rulings

Panels have occasionally dealt with certain issues by way of pre-liminary rulings.

There is one issue, however, about which there have been no preliminary rulings so far. As is well known, it is incumbent on the complainant Member to make a prima facie case. If the respondent Member is of the view that the complainant Member failed to make such a case, a panel should be prepared to make a preliminary ruling on an objection put forward by the respondent Member to that effect. Where a panel refuses to do so, the respondent Member finds itself in a catch-22 situation. Either respondent maintains its position and does not put forward affirmative defenses. In this case, if the panel finds in the end that the complainant made a prima facie case, the panel will draw inferences from the respondent's failure to put forward affirmative defenses.[11] Or, respondent wants to play it safe and puts forward affirmative defenses: in this case, respondent helps complainant to make its case. A preliminary ruling on whether the complainant Member made out a prima facie case would thus serve justice. It would not be out of line with the Appellate Body's view, that a panel should be allowed to make preliminary determinations on such matters as its jurisdiction and fact finding based upon the initial written submissions of the parties.[12]

C.   Scope of the dispute

Through case law, it has been made clear what the "matter" is and what "claims" and "arguments" are.[13] Moreover, it is now well established that Article 6.2 of the DSU requires that the claims, but not the arguments, be specified sufficiently in the request for the establishment of a panel. Arguments set out in the request may be progressively clarified in the course of the proceeding.[14] However, a panel's jurisdiction is limited by the terms of reference, for example it may not go beyond these terms and examine whether the measure complained of is in violation either of other covered agreements or other provisions of the covered agreement referred to in the terms of reference.[15]

The panel's role and, indirectly, the nature of the dispute settlement proceeding remain to be further clarified. In a number of cases, the Appellate Body has stressed the panel's investigative role. It has noted the "comprehensive nature" of the panel's authority to seek information suggesting that panels have "significant investigation authority".[16] It has also taken the view that a respondent party is under the obligation to comply with a panel's request to provide information relating to measures

---

[11] The issue arose in *Canada – Measures Affecting The Export of Civilian Aircraft* (Panel Report WT/DS 70/R adopted 14 April 1999; Appellate Body Report WT/DS 70/AB/R adopted 2 August 1999).

[12] For example, *EC – Bananas III* above n. 8 para. 144; *India – Patent Protection for Pharmaceutical and Agricultural Chemical Products*, WT/DS 50/AB/, adopted 19 December 1997, para. 95.

[13] *Brazil – Measures Affecting Desiccated Coconut*, WT/DS22/AB/R, adopted 20 March 1997, at 22.

[14] *EC – Bananas III*, above n 8.

[15] *Japan – Taxes on Alcoholic Beverages*, WT/DS 8/R, adopted on 11 July 1996, para 6.5.

[16] *Japan – Measures Affecting Agricultural Products*, WT/DS 76/AB/R, adopted 19 March 1999, paras 12–129.

that the complainant party is challenging.[17] This, however, does not mean that it is for the panel to make the complainant's case on the basis of its investigations. In *Japan –Varietals*, the Appellate Body held that the Panel could not use the scientific evidence of experts (whom it appointed) for a finding of inconsistency in the event the complainant Member itself had not first established a prima facie case of inconsistency based on specific claims asserted by it.[18] It is submitted that this is the proper solution. Another solution would turn a dispute settlement system which is essentially adversarial into an inquisitorial one. The former solution should be included as a rule in panels' working procedures. Admittedly, as the *Canada –Aircraft* case shows, the line is not always easy to draw in these situations.

A related question is whether a panel, and, as the case may be, the Appellate Body may (and ought to) raise on their own motion issues of general interest not addressed by the parties. Pierre Pescatore made an eloquent plea along these lines, arguing that this is a necessary corrective to the predominance of bilateralism in the dispute settlement which creates a structural imbalance in the framework of an essentially multilateral system of rules.[19] This point would merit an extensive discussion. It touches on the proper function of the dispute settlement system and the mandate of panels and the Appellate Body under the DSU. At any rate, from a practitioner's perspective, issues raised ex officio by panels or the Appellate Body raise significant practical problems. It already is quite a challenge to seek, in the short time available, government's instructions, often requiring input from several Ministries and agencies, on questions put by and to the parties in the course of the proceedings. If an issue of general interest were then suddenly raised, it is highly doubtful that parties would be able to adequately define their position in a timely fashion. In these circumstances, it hardly seems fair that an issue raised ex officio should be permitted to influence the outcome of the proceeding. It is submitted that Pescatore's concern could, to some extent, be taken into account without upsetting the whole apple cart. A panel or the Appellate Body could indicate in an *obiter dictum* that they have identified such an issue but that, as it has not been put to them, they do not address it.

---

[17] *Canada –Aircraft* (AB Report), above n. 11, para 187ff. In support of that view, the AB went as far as considering that Article 13.1 of the DSU providing that "a Member *should* respond [...] to any request by a panel for such information as the panel considers necessary and appropriate" as expressing a *duty* for Members (para. 187)!
[18] *Japan –Varietals*, above n. 16, para. 130.
[19] "Free World Trade and the European Union - The Reconciliation of Interests and the Revision of Dispute Resolution Procedures in the Framework of the WTO", in A. Pérez van Kappel and W. Hensel, 9 at 16, above n. 3.

D.   Judicial economy and appeals

When a panel, invoking "judicial economy", disposes of a matter submitted to it by dealing with one or more claims and leaving other claims aside, it may (and does) happen that the Appellate Body reverses the panel's finding on the claim or claims it dealt with. In such cases, taking implicitly the view that it has no remand authority, the Appellate Body deals with the claims left aside by the panel,[20] albeit that the Appellate Body does so on the basis of the factual record before the panel.

Arguably this is not the proper method of resolution. There are at least two good reasons for the Appellate Body to refrain from taking up an issue which has not been dealt with by a panel. First, when taking up an issue left aside by a panel, the Appellate Body will either deal imperfectly with it, if it considers that it may not review issues of fact or step beyond the limits of its mandate. Second, by taking up an issue that the panel should have addressed, the Appellate Body in fact deprives the parties of their right of appeal.

The Appellate Body should limit itself to determine only that the panel erred in failing to make a finding, or that the panel's analysis was incomplete and send the matter back to the DSB. The DSB could then reconvene the original panel or establish another panel. It has been argued that the Appellate Body has no remand authority. This is not persuasive. The DSU is silent on this point. If the Appellate Body were to send a case back to the DSB it would not be acting out of line with the common practice in many jurisdictions. Moreover, the negative aspects of the current solution outweigh the interpretation of the DSU: that the Appellate Body has the prerogative to send the case back to the DSB so that the proceeding can be completed by a panel in compliance with the system set up by the DSU

E.   Review of factual findings on appeal

The appeal is limited to issues of law covered in the panel report and legal interpretations developed by the panel.[21] The distinction between fact and law occasionally raises problems in most appellate systems, which

---

[20] *US –Standards for Reformulated and Conventional Gasoline* (WT/DS 2/AB/R adopted 29 April 1996); *Canada – Certain Measures Concerning Periodicals* (WT/DS 31/AB/R, adopted 30 July 1997), 23-24; *EC – Measures Affecting the Importation of Certain Poultry Products* (WT/DS 69/AB/R adopted 13 July 1998), para. 156
[21] DSU Article 17.6.

then try to cope with it through various techniques. One of the problems is whether (and, if so, when) an appellate body, whose jurisdiction is limited to questions of law should step in to correct an error of fact of the lower adjudication body.

In *Australia – Measures Affecting Importation of Salmon*,[22] the Appellate Body explained that "credibility" and "weight" to be ascribed to fact is a matter for a panel, subject to Appellate Body review, where the panel's consideration of the facts is so flawed as to amount to a failure to conduct an "objective assessment" of the facts as requested by Article 11 of the DSU. However, the case law of the Appellate Body so far is unclear on what is a failure to conduct an "objective assessment". This becomes apparent when one examines the *EC Hormones* alongside the earlier *Canada - Periodicals* Appellate Body reports.[23]

Regardless of the theories underlying the Appellate Body's function in the dispute settlement system, from a practitioner's point of view, a perfectly honest manifest error of fact made by a panel on a crucial point on which the outcome of the case depends, also should be reviewed by the Appellate Body. It would certainly be exceedingly difficult to persuade the losing party that the result of the WTO dispute settlement proceeding – that would allow such an error to stand – should be complied with.

F.   Should there be interim relief?

Even with the introduction of the time-limits for every step in a WTO dispute settlement proceeding, quite some time may elapse before the final resolution of a dispute, in particular when one takes account of possible Article 21.5 DSU disputes that may also involve the Appellate Body.[24] In addition, it is generally considered that recommendations and rulings of the DSB are prospective in that the WTO Member's duty to comply concerns the future.

---

[22] WT/DS18/AB/R adopted 20 1998, paras 264–67.

[23] See M. Bronckers and N. McNelis, "Fact and Law in Pleadings before the WTB Appellate Body". (1999) *Int'l T. L. R.* 118; cf. M. Lugard, "Scope of Appellate Review: Objective Assessment of the Facts and Issues of Law", *J. Int'l Econ. L.* 323 (1998).

[24] For example, in *Brazil – Export Financing Program for Aircraft*, Canada requested consultations on 18 June 1996, the request for establishment of a panel was made on 10 July 1998, and the Appellate Body's report in the Article 21.5 proceeding was adopted on 21 July 2000.

In certain cases, as a result of both of these elements, a WTO dispute settlement proceeding may be tantamount to closing the stable door when the horse has bolted.[25] This may not be entirely in line with the function of the WTO dispute settlement system which, according to Article 3(2) of the DSU, "serves to *preserve* the rights and obligations of the Members under the covered agreements".

It can be left aside here whether the purely prospective nature of WTO remedies is consistent with customary public international law[26] and, if not, whether the DSU is to be interpreted as having set aside such customary public international law. It is at any rate doubtful that WTO Members would find retrospective remedies acceptable.[27]

In light of this, a case can be made for interim relief, for which there are a number of precedents in international dispute settlement systems.[28] Basically, such interim relief should be designed to preserve provisionally the status quo and should be available only under certain conditions. The requesting parry must make a prima facie case on the merits. It must be found that the continuation of the measure complained of causes irreparable harm. Moreover, it would be appropriate that the panel assess whether the balance of interests justifies interim relief.

IV.   CONCLUSION

The practical difficulties of the current selection of panelists and the need for consistency in the interpretation of the complex body of WTO rules justify the establishment of a standing WTO panel or panels. A

---

[25] See the cases referred to by G. A. Cavallier, "A Call for Interim Relief at WTO Level. Dispute Settlement and International Trade Diplomacy", 22(2) World Competition, 103-39 (1999).

[26] To the extent that it reflects customary international law, the Draft Convention on the Responsibility of States provides that the injured state is entitled to obtain from the state which has committed an internationally wrongful act restitution in kind, that is the re-establishment of the situation which existed before the wrongful act was committed, subject to a number of provisions.

[27] *Australia – Subsidies Provided to Producers and Exporters of Automotive Leather – Recourse to Article 21.5 of the DSU by the US*, (WT/DS 126/RW adopted 21 January 2000) the Panel considered that "withdraw the subsidy" meant repayment in full of the subsidy granted (para 6.48). Although the Panel pointed to Article 4.7 of the SCM Agreement as "a special or additional rule or procedure on dispute settlement" (para. 6.41), the finding caused quite a commotion. Neither Australia, nor the US appealed. They reached a settlement, involving, i.a. repayment by the beneficiary of part of the subsidy (International Trade Reporter, Vol. 17, no. 25, at 964).

[28] See the precedents mentioned by Cavallier above, n. 25.

number of procedural issues ought to be clearly regulated. Both series of items need to be addressed. The issues of substance which WTO Members throw in the lap of the WTO dispute settlement system are too important to be treated by *ad hoc* panels and under procedural arrangements that are often imprecise. The results of these arrangements are often that issues are left to be resolved as they come up and thus do not provide the required legal certainty.

Moreover, a system operating with strict deadlines needs to go hand in hand with clear and comprehensive procedural rules. Even though the six months between the establishment of a panel and the circulation of the report to the Members is often exceeded, the nine months maximum period is, in certain cases, quite a challenge for parties and panels.

4. GATT/WTO DISPUTE SETTLEMENT PRACTICE IN THE FIELD OF ANTI-DUMPING LAW

I.   INTRODUCTION

Do dispute settlement proceedings in the anti-dumping field merit a separate contribution to this book? An analysis of the panel reports and their fate suggest an affirmative answer. Hudec has referred to the high percentage of legal failures in antidumping and countervailing duties cases – i.e. when complaints filed "have been terminated for negative reasons" – their low rate of settlement and their sharp increase. He explains this phenomenon by "the typical arbitrariness of anti-dumping and countervailing duties criteria" and "the legal rigidity of the measures once taken".[1] Petersmann mentions other aspects: "blockage" of the adoption of panel reports, political interference into the dispute settlement process, *US* attempts to limit the "standard of review" and to "explicitly legalize protectionist abuses of anti-dumping laws".[2] The subject matter of the disputes brought before panels was thus rather controversial and prompted litigants to search for, and put forward, as many legal issues as possible.

Mainly procedural issues are addressed in this chapter. In an area where facts and law are as interwoven as in anti-dumping, examining also the extent to which dispute settlement proceedings have interpreted substantive provisions of the Tokyo Round Anti-dumping Code would require analysing the often complex fact situations and would thus best be considered in the framework of a review of the substantive rules of the Anti-dumping Code. In addition, some comments are made on the question whether and how the new WTO Anti-dumping Agreement has dealt with some of these issues.

This chapter is not intended to be exhaustive. It deals only with issues in dispute settlement proceedings that the author considers the more important ones. Moreover, the chapter is intended to be descriptive rather than prescriptive.

---

[1] R. Hudec, *Enforcing International Trade Law: The Evolution Of The Modern Gan Legal System*, Butterworth, Salem NH., 1993, 354.
[2] "The Dispute Settlement System of the World Trade Organization and the Evolution of the GAIT Dispute Settlement System since 1948", 31 *CMLR* 1157 at 1204 (1994).

II.   STANDING

The term "standing" has not been referred to by panels on anti-dumping matters. It is used here for the purpose of examining whether a party must demonstrate an interest in lodging a complaint and, if so, what sort of interest. Technically, this is to be distinguished from the question as to whether there is a dispute, i.e. whether parties disagree as to the interpretation and application of rules.

From his review of the GATT dispute settlement practice on this point Hudec concludes that panels have effectively considered that a complaining contracting party had a legal interest to have the GATT rules complied with, provided it showed that the measure complained of had distorted the equal competitive opportunity available to it.[3] Kuijper draws from his review of the practice the impression that contracting parties still regard some kind of damage to their own interests or rights a "processual requirement".[4]

In the anti-dumping field, the issue was raised as a preliminary objection by the EC in *EC – Anti-dumping Duties on Audio Tapes in Cassettes Originating in Japan*[5] (hereinafter: *Audio Tapes*). The EC noted that even if the panel were to find that, as Japan had claimed, Article 2 of the Tokyo-Round Anti-dumping Code had been breached and that the calculation of the dumping margin was wrong, this could have had no impact whatsoever on the anti-dumping duty, which was 49% lower than the dumping margin. The EC argued that in the circumstances Japan had no legal interest in obtaining a ruling that the dumping margin had been incorrectly calculated. The EC acknowledged that, where a complaining party established a violation of a provision of the GATT or of a GATT agreement, the action complained of was considered *prima facie* to give rise to nullification or impairment. The respondent party could, however, debut the presumption by showing that no trade effects resulted from the action complained of. According to the EC, the complaining party must demonstrate that the action had at least a potential impact on the complaining party.[6] The EC was thus effectively asserting that there is no *actio popularis* in the GATT dispute settlement.

---

[3] R. Hudec, see note 1 above, at 268– 269
[4] P. J. Kuijper, "The Law of GATT as a Special Field of International Law", XXV Neth. Yb'k Int'l L 227 at 240(1994).
[5] ADP 136 of 28 April 1995.
[6] *Audio Tapes*, paras 47, 49 and 50.

Referring to *US —Taxes on Petroleum and Certain Imported Substances*[7] (hereinafter: *Superfund*), the panel observed that previous panels had treated breaches of rules as an irrebuttable presumption of nullification or impairment and, assuming *arguendo* that the presumption could be rebutted, had not considered the absence of trade effect as a sufficient rebuttal. The panel noted that the EC had not submitted calculations of its own to contradict Japan's calculations purporting to show that, with respect to one exporter, correct calculations could have led to a dumping margin lower than the anti-dumping duty imposed. The panel concluded:

> "that, assuming *arguendo* the presumption of nullification or impairment arising from an inconsistency with the Agreement was rebuttable, and that a demonstration of the absence of adverse trade effects could constitute sufficient rebuttal, the EC had not rebutted the presumption that the measures claimed by Japan to be inconsistent with the Agreement had caused nullification or impairment in this case".[8]

Rather than considering that "legal interest" coincides with *prima facie* nullification or impairment, the panel effectively ducked the "legal interest" issue. It – probably wisely – left aside the whole question as to whether the presumption of nullification or impairment resulting from a breach of the rules was rebuttable, and rejected the EC's preliminary objection on the ground that the EC had not rebutted the presumption that the allegedly wrong calculation of the dumping margin had caused the anti-dumping duty to be inconsistent with the Anti-dumping Code. The panel appears to have required that, in order to rebut the *prima facie* nullification or impairment resulting from a breach, the respondent party must do more than provide *prima facie* evidence to the contrary; the respondent party must fully demonstrate that there is no nullification or impairment. The question is whether this can still be considered as being part of a *preliminary* objection.

The *Audio Tapes* report and previous reports to which it refers call for two comments. First, a WTO member may have an interest without there being any actual impairement or nullification of its benefits. There may be many reasons why member A might not want to challenge

---

[7] BISD 34 S/36 paras 5.1.7, 5.1.9.
[8] *Audio Tapes* panel report, para. 345.

member B's anti-dumping measures that affect its exports, but member C might want to pre-empt future action by member B affecting its interests or in order to safeguard its legal position on an issue that could be held against it at a later stage.[9] It is true that member C could request explanations from member B in the course of the periodic review by the Committee on Anti-dumping Practices of measures taken by members and it could criticize them. This does not, however, lead to a ruling by that Committee that would be a substitute for a dispute settlement proceeding. In addition, every WTO member has arguably a general interest in ensuring compliance with the Anti-dumping Code. As the WTO does not have the right to initiate itself dispute settlement proceedings in the general interest of its members, it could be argued that individual members should be entitled to act in the general interest.

On the other hand, one should bear in mind that part of the mandate of panels now is explicitly and generally to interpret the relevant provisions of the Anti-dumping Agreement "in accordance with customary rules of interpretation of public international law". Whether this also applies to the *ius standi* of a complaining member is uncertain. One could argue that this reference to customary international law in the new Anti-dumping Agreement does not apply to the issue of standing, which is not dealt with in the specific dispute settlement provisions of this Agreement. Similar language appears, however, in the DSU, albeit that it is much less strongly worded (Article 3(2)). Assuming that indeed customary international law applies, regard should then be had to the case law of the ICJ. It is worth mentioning that in the *Northern-Cameroons* case,[10] the ICJ held that there must be:

> "concrete cases where there exists at the time of the adjudication an actual controversy involving a conflict of legal interests between the parties. The Court's judgment must have some practical consequences in the sense that it can affect existing legal rights or obligations of the parties, thus removing uncertainty from their legal relations".[11]

---

[9] See, for example, the arguments put forward by the EC to justify its intervention in *US – Restrictions on Imports of Tuna II*, DS 38/R of 11 February 1994.

[10] Case concerning the Northern Cameroons *(Cameroon v. United Kingdom)*, preliminary Objections. Judgment of 2 December 1963 : ICJ Rep. 1963. 15.

[11] For an analysis of this ICJ opinion and other opinions, see P. Van Dijk., *Toetsing van overheidshandelen door de nationale en internationale rechter en het vereiste procesbelang*, Tjeenk Willink, Zwolle, 1976, 227–234.

From a policy point of view, one obvious comment is that the issue of standing has implications for WTO dispute settlement in general. In light of the fundamental change in the dispute settlement procedure resulting from the "negative consensus" required to block panel reports and in view of the disappearance of the conciliation stage "filter", it would probably be wise for panels to continue to require that complaining members demonstrate some personal legal interest by showing lost trade opportunities. This appears logical in view of the available remedy in the event that the respondent member does not comply, i.e. compensation equivalent to the lost trade opportunities. This also seems advisable as in the absence of such requirement complaints resembling *"recours dans l'intérêt de la loi"* are more likely to lead to abstract rulings and thus to interpretations that may "add to or diminish the rights and obligations provided in the covered agreements" which, according to Article 3(2) of the DSU, rulings and recommendations of the DSB are not supposed to do.

III.   CONSULTATION AND CONCILIATION AS PRELIMINARY STEPS

The Tokyo Round Anti-dumping Code stated that a party that considered that any benefit accruing to it under the agreement was being nullified or impaired, could request consultations with the party or parties in question with a view to achieving a mutually satisfactory resolution of the matter (Article 15(2)). If the complaining party considered that the consultations had failed to achieve a mutually satisfactory solution of the matter, it could refer the matter to the Committee on Anti-Dumping Practices for conciliation (Article 15(3)), which was required to conduct a detailed examination of the matter (Article 15(5)).

These provisions have raised a number of interpretative questions, including whether consultation and conciliation were mandatory preliminary steps and whether claims had to be aired at the consultation and conciliation stages before being considered properly by a panel. These questions were dealt with in *US – Imposition of Anti-dumping Duties on Imports of Fresh and Chilled Atlantic Salmon from Norway*[12] (hereinafter : *Salmon*). As to the first question, the panel relied on the text of Article 5 which uses consistently throughout its various paragraphs the term "matter" and on he purpose of the consultation and conciliation stages; it concluded that:

---

[12] ADP/87 of 30 November 1992. They arose also in *Audio Tapes*, see note 5 above, and were dealt with similarly.

"... the Agreement provided that before a party to a dispute could request a panel concerning a matter, the parties to the dispute had to have been given an opportunity to reach a mutually satisfactory resolution of the matter. This condition would not be meaningful unless the matter had been raised in consultation and conciliation".[13]

The panel thus construed consultation and conciliation as mandatory steps. It may be argued that in certain cases consultation is treated by the parties as a meaningless exercise. However, it is not because some parties do not comply with their obligation to seek "a mutually satisfactory resolution of the matter" that this step should be left out. Moreover, a number of claims are in fact withdrawn at the consultation stage.[14] Conciliation involves a detailed examination of the matter by the Committee, allows other parties to express their views and, as the case may be, to exercise peer pressure on the parties to the dispute to reach an agreed solution. It is to be regretted that the new Anti-dumping Agreement deletes the conciliation stage, while Article 5 of the DSU leaves it entirely to the parties to submit to conciliation. In view of the fundamental change brought about by the consensus to reject panel reports, mandatory conciliation would have been useful as a "filter".

In dealing with the second question before it, i.e. whether all claims had to be aired at the consultation and conciliation stages to be properly before a panel, the *Salmon* panel relied also on the text of the relevant paragraphs of Article 15 of the Tokyo Round Anti-dumping Code and on their purpose. As far as consultation is concerned the panel referred to the 1979 Understanding Regarding Notification, Consultation, Dispute Settlement and Surveillance which provided that "any requests for consultations should include the reasons therefor". As far as conciliation is concerned, the panel considered that paragraphs 3 and 5 of Article 15 of the Tokyo Round Anti-dumping Code:

---

[13] *Salmon* panel report, sec note 12 above.
[14] Hudec, see note I above, at 277 considering that 88 complaints leading to a ruling, i.e. 43%, out of 207 complaints lodged is a high percentage. One of his explanations is that defendant governments find it politically difficult to settle once a complaint is launched. If that is so, 57% settlements/withdrawals is not a bad record. From this perspective, the record in the anti-dumping and countervailing duties field is comparable: 50% of the complaints led to a ruling (at 343).

"implied that the conciliation process envisaged was one which would examine legal claims and their bases and in which each member of the Committee would be able to express its views on these legal issues. Such a process would not be possible unless the request for conciliation identified the matter and the claims composing it".[15]

The panel concluded that:

"a matter, including each claim composing that matter, could not be examined by a panel under the Agreement unless that same matter and claim had been referred to the Committee for conciliation in accordance with Article 15:3".[16]

As a result of the deletion of the mandatory conciliation stage by the new Anti-dumping Agreement, the question arises whether the panel pronouncements on the requirement that all claims have to be aired at the consultation stage in order to be properly before a panel are still good law, assuming that panels are bound by previous adopted panel reports; apparently they are. Only the mandatory conciliation stage has been deleted; and, according to Article 4(4) of the DSU, requests for consultation must now not only give the reasons for the request but also contain "identification of the measures at issue and an indication of the legal basis for the complaint".

This requirement makes sense. How can parties attempt "to obtain satisfactory adjustment of the matter" as required by Article 4(5) of the DSU or reach "a mulually satisfactory resolution of the matter" as contemplated by Article 17.3 of the new Anti-dumping Agreement in good faith at the consultation stage, if they do not put the whole matter, i.e. their claims on the table? "Good faith" is a two-way street; if the respondent party does not comment on an issue raised at the consultation stage, it cannot subsequently claim that the issue is not properly before the panel.[17] In addition, while this requirement is not tantamount to an agreement between parties that they have a dispute as usually required under classical international law, it is for each party a healthy and useful exercise to work out its claims and arguments and to exchange views on

---

[15] *Salmon* panel report, see note 12 above, para. 335. Other panels have taken a different view, *e.g.*, *EC–Member States' Import Regime for Bananas*, DS 32/R paras. 324–325.
[16] *Salmon* panel report, see note 12 above, para. 335.
[17] *United States –Anti-dumping Duties on Grav Portland Cement and Cement Clinker from Mexico*, ADP/182 of 7 September 1992., para. 5.12

them with the other party. In fact misunderstandings do arise. This is particularly the case in the area of anti-dumping where a large number of WTO members are at the receiving end of the enforcement of anti-dumping measures and have not acquired the knowledge and expertise that result from applying anti-dumping rules.

IV. THE INTERNATIONAL EXHAUSTION OF LOCAL REMEDIES RULE-CLAIMS NOT RAISED IN NATIONAL PROCEEDINGS

A. Is the Exhaustion of National Administrative and Judicial Remedies Necessary?

Whether the exhaustion of national administrative and judicial remedies is a condition for recourse to the dispute settlement system came up in dispute settlement proceedings under the Tokyo Round Anti-dumping Code. The case in which the issue was addressed in the clearest terms is the *Cement* case.[18] In that case, the US did not claim that the rule of exhaustion of local remedies applied as such, but that for an issue to be properly before a panel it should have been raised earlier during the administrative proceedings.[19] The panel, however, held that Article 15.5 of the Tokyo Round Anti-dumping Code; "did not require the exhaustion of administrative remedies, but provided that the matter examined by the panel would have to be based on facts raised in the first instance ... in the administrative proceedings in the importing country".[20] As to other provisions of the Anti-dumping Code relied upon by the US in the context of exhaustion of administrative remedies, the panel stated that they:

> "were designed to ensure that the investigating authorities in the importing country afforded adequate procedural opportunities to foreign suppliers and other interested parties to present evidence and defend their interests...but that these provisions did not establish a principle of exhaustion of administrative remedies".[21]

In the *Salmon* case,[22] the US effectively withdrew its argument based on the rule of exhaustion of local remedies. The panel was thus

---

[18] See note 14 above.
[19] *Cement* Panel Report, see note 14 above, para. 3.1.4.
[20] *Cement* Panel Report, see note 14 above, para. 5.9.
[21] *Cement* Panel Report, note 14 above, para. 5.9.
[22] See note 12 above.

able to consider that the issue of application of this doctrine to dispute settlement under the Code was not before it.[23]

Assuming that this reflects effectively the practice under the Tokyo Round Anti-dumping Code, the question arises whether this is also the position under the new Anti-dumping Agreement. In the course of the negotiations the US proposed a provision requiring the exhaustion of local administrative remedies. Their proposal was not inserted in the final text.[24] This does not mean that the negotiators must be regarded as having rejected the international rule of exhaustion of local remedies: the "exhaustion of administrative remedies" sought by the US concerned more the scope and standard of review than the international law rule. The question is thus not expressly addressed in the new Anti-dumping Agreement and has been left open. There are two new provisions, which appear relevant.

First, the Anti-dumping Agreement lays down the obligation to maintain judicial, arbitral or administrative tribunals or procedures for the purpose, *inter alia*, of the prompt review of administrative actions relating to final determinations and reviews of determinations (Article 13). Second, the new Anti-dumping Agreement requires panels to interpret the relevant provisions of the Agreement "in accordance with customary rules of interpretation of public international law" (Article 17.6(ii)).

P. J. Kuijper draws from the new obligation to provide for judicial review of actions under the Anti-dumping Agreement the conclusion that the drafters must have intended that the rule of exhaustion of local remedies apply.[25] In addition, referring to the *Interhandel* case,[26] he argues that the rule of exhaustion of local remedies is a well-established rule of customary international law, which applies not only in cases of espousal of private claims by the State in the context of classical diplomatic protection, but also when rights derived by individuals from treaties are at stake. For this latter view, he seeks support in the *ELSI* case.[27] P. J.

---

[23] *Salmon* Panel Report, see note 12 above, para. 348.

[24] M. Koulen. "The New Anti-dumping Code through its Negotiating History", J. H. J. Bourgeois, F. Berrod and E. Gippini-Fournier (eds). *The Uruguay Round. A European lawyers' Perspective*, E.I.P., Brussels, 1995, at 185.

[25] P.J. Kuijper, "The New WTO Dispute Settlement System: the Impact on the Community". J. Bourgeois, F. Berrod and E, Gippini-Fournier, see note 24 above, at 107.

[26] ICJ Rep., 1959. at 27.

[27] ICJ Rep., 1989, 15; P. Mengozzi argues that this opinion refers to classical international law and that this principle is inapposite in the context of the new international trade law. "The Marrakesh DSU and its Implications on the International and European Level". J. Bourgeois, F. Berrod and E. Gippini-Fournier, see note 24 above, at 123.

Kuijper recalls that in that case the ICJ ruled that this rule of customary international law cannot be dispensed with by treaty partners by way of implication.

E.U. Petersmann on the other hand defends the view that the rule of exhaustion of local remedies does not apply. He argues that it only applies in cases of "diplomatic protection" of nationals, as distinguished from cases of "direct injury" to states, and points out that the "interest structure" of GATT law, protecting rights and obligations of governments, is different from that of the international law of aliens and of diplomatic protection. He seeks support in the Anti-dumping Agreement which sanctions the submission of disputes to the DSB even, in appropriate circumstances, against a provisional measure of the administering authority (Article 17.5).[28]

Whatever may be the merits of both views, it would seem that requiring that local remedies be exhausted before a WTO member may start dispute settlement proceedings pre-supposes either that the national anti-dumping legislation which the administering authority of the respondent WTO members enforces is in strict conformity with the Anti-dumping Agreement or that national courts may and do review the conformity of national legislation and the action taken under it with the Anti-dumping Agreement. If this is not the case, WTO law does not, as a rule, come into play before national courts. Can then the rule of exhaustion of local remedies perform its main function as described by Kuijper,[29] i.e. preventing an international conflict from arising before the State concerned has had the full opportunity to correct the action which prima facie has to be qualified as an international wrong?

B.   The Raising of a New Claim in a Dispute Settlement Proceeding

A second, related but distinct issue, is whether a complainant WTO member may raise a claim in a dispute settlement proceeding under

---

[28] See Petersmann note 2 above, at 1240–1241. Kuijper points out, however, that this provision and Article 15.3 of the Anti-dumping Code do not amount to a specific exclusion of the rule of exhaustion of local remedies as required by the ICJ in *ELSI* (see note 4 above at 234). Koulen considers that the rule of exhaustion of administrative remedies is distinct from the international law rule of exhaustion of local remedies (see note 24 above, at footnote 77).
[29] See note 25 above at 106.

the Anti-dumping Agrement where such claim had not been raised before the national investigating authorities. This issue came up in three cases under the Tokyo Round Anti-dumping Code. In *United States – Imposition of Anti-dumping Duties on Imports of Seamless Steel Hollow Products from Sweden*[30] (hereinafter : the *First Stainless Steel* case), the panel did not deem it necessary to deal with the US claim to that effect. In *Cement*[31] the US claimed that Mexico should be precluded from raising the issue of "standing" of the petitioners and the issue of cumulation of Mexican and Japanese imports, as these issues had not been raised during the administrative proceedings. The US relied on Article 6.1 of the Tokyo Round Anti-dumping Code, which, according to the US, required that all issues and arguments had to be raised before the national investigating authorities; if issues were raised in the first instance before a panel, the investigating authorities would be prevented from conducting a full investigation, and thus from considering all of the evidence and arguments required to render determinations.[32] Appearing before the panel Canada and the EC defended conflicting views on this point. According to Canada there was not any basis in the GATT practice for requiring that all issues be raised in domestic administrative proceedings if they were to be considered admissible before a GATT panel.[33] The EC took the view that if new arguments were to be admissible, panel proceedings would resemble a court of appeal where the plaintiff, i.e. the petitioner, would be absent and could not make any input. It found in Article 6 and Article 15 of the Tokyo Round Anti-dumping Code the indication that only points raised during the course of the investigation could be brought before a panel.[34] The panel rejected the US claim. It considered that: "if such fundamental restriction on the right of recourse to the Agreement's dispute settlement process had been intended by the drafters of the Agreement, they would have made explicit provision for it".[35] It viewed the EC argument based on the provisions of the Anti-dumping Code relating to national proceedings as irrelevant: according to the panel the purpose of these provisions is to ensure that foreign suppliers and other interested parties have the opportunity to defend themselves and has nothing to do with the possibility for the panel to examine claims put before it.

---

[30] ADP/47 of 20 August 1990.

[31] See note 17 above.

[32] *Cement* panel, note 17 above, para. 3.1.

[33] *Cement* panel, see note 17 above, para 4.9.

[34] *Cement* panel, sec note 17 above, para. 4.6; the EC also intervened in the *Salmon* case and look the same line on this issue (see note 12 above, para. 317).

[35] *Cement* panel see note 17 above, para. 5.9.

However, the panel added that "the matter examined by the panel would have to be based on facts raised in the first instance, in conformity with the appropriate domestic procedures, in the administrative proceedings in the importing country".[36]

In the *Salmon* case,[37] the US raised the preliminary objection that two issues raised by Norway before the panel, i.e. the standing of the petitioners to request the initiation of the anti-dumping proceeding and the allegedly incorrect comparison of an average normal value in Norway to individual prices charged by Norwegian exporters for exports to the US, had not been raised by the Norwegian respondents in the national administrative proceedings in the US; according to the US these issues were therefore not admissible in the proceedings before the panel.[38] It relied on several arguments based on the provisions of the Tokyo Round Anti-dumping Code: the exclusive authority of the national investigating authorities to gather and consider evidence and make findings of fact and law concerning dumping and injury (Article 3.6), the one-year deadline for investigations (Article 5.5), the requirement that investigating authorities make their decision based on the agency record (Article 6); the transparency and due-process requirements applying to investigations (Article 6).[39]

The panel rejected this claim on the ground that the dispute settlement provisions of the Anti-dumping Code (Article 15) did not offer any basis for refusing to consider a claim by a party in a dispute settlement merely because the subject matter of the claim had not been raised before the investigating authorities under national law.[40] The panel noted, however, that its conclusion: "did not imply that in reviewing the merits of a claim a panel should not take account of whether or not the issues to which the claim relates were raised before the investigating authorities in the domestic anti-dumping duty proceeding".[41]

The practical conclusion seems to be that the panels before which this issue was raised did consider GATT dispute settlement proceedings as quite independent from national proceedings, in the sense that they

---

[36] Ibid.
[37] See note 12 above.
[38] *Salmon* panel, note 12 above, para. 31.
[39] *Salmon* panel, note 12 above, para. 347.
[40] *Salmon* panel, note 12 above, para. 349
[41] *Salmon* panel, note 12 above, para. 350.

did not consider themselves bound to remain within the limits of the case as brought before, and dealt with by, national administrative authorities. While this is probably to be welcomed, some of the arguments put forward in support of the contrary view are not without merit and are likely to come up in another guise. This is the case more particularly for the argument based on the requirement that the administering authority make its findings on the basis of a record, which raises the question whether a panel can "go outside of the investigation" (see Section V below). This may explain the proviso in one of the panel reports that the matter would have to be based on facts raised in the administrative proceedings. This proviso reflects a provision of the Tokyo Round Anti-dumping Code according to which a panel must base its examination on "the facts made available in conformity with appropriate domestic procedures to the authorities of the importing country" (Article 15(5)), a requirement which also appears in the new Anti-dumping Agreement (Article 17(5)(ii)). However, the proviso in the *Salmon* panel report that the panel should take account of whether or not the issues were raised before the investigating authorities appears doubtful, if it meant to say that an issue must have been raised before investigating authorities. This would force exporting members to appear before national investigating authorities in order to keep the possibility to raise issues in panel proceedings.

V.   TERMS OF REFERENCE

A.   Disputes under the Tokyo Round Anti-Dumping Code

The panel's terms of reference were with minor variations standard ones, requiring the panel "to examine in the light of the relevant GATT provisions, the matter referred to the CONTRACTING PARTIES by... relating to... and to make such findings as will assist the CONTRACTING PARTIES in making recommendations and rulings as provided for in Article XXIII". These "standard terms of reference" became the norm under the 1989 Dispute Settlement Procedures Improvements to avoid the often protracted discussions about the content and drafting of "terms of reference" being an opportunity for a reluctant party to delay proceedings.

Pescatore has pointed out that this standard formula is remarkable in several respects: cases are introduced in the terms defined by the complaining party, the panel is empowered to examine the complaint in the light of "the relevant GATT provisions", which has been construed to mean also the whole GATT system, they invite the panels to propose "rulings" and "recommendations".[42]

B.   Anti-Dumping Cases

In the cases reviewed, while they had often led to many discussions before reaching the panel stage, "terms of reference" have only occasionally been a bone of contention before panels.

One such instance has been the *Salmon* case,[43] in which the US put forward as a preliminary objection the fact that several of Norway's claims were not within the terms of reference. The panel examined carefully the documents containing the request for the establishment of a panel and accepted the US argument for some claims and rejected them for others.

The panel made a more general statement that is of some interest about the "matter" referred in Norway's request for the establishment of a panel:

"… this matter consisted of specific claims stated by Norway in these documents with respect to the imposition of these duties by the United States. The panel considered that the logical implication of the definition advanced by Norway of the 'matter' before the panel was that whenever a panel was established in a dispute concerning the imposition of anti-dumping duties, such a panel could examine any aspect of the procedures followed and the determinations made…regardless of whether these aspects had been referred to in the complaining party's request for the establishment of a panel. There would then be practically no limit to the claim which could be raised before a panel without advance notice to the defending party or to third parties".[44]

In *Audio Tapes*,[45] the EC argued that the matter before the panel was defined by the terms of reference which were set out in two

---

[42] P. Pescatore, "Drafting and Analyzing Decisions on Dispute Settlement", P. Pescatore, W. J. Davey, A. F. Lowenfeld, *Handbook Of Gatt Dispute Settlement*, 3 at 12–13. Transnational Iuris Publications, Kluwer, Irvington-on-Hudson, New York/Den Haag, 1991.

[43] See note 12 above.

[44] *Salmon* panel, see note 12 above, para. 342.

[45] See note 5 above. Another case is *EEC – Regulation on Imports of Parts and Components* BISD 375/132 under Art. XXIII of the GATT and not under the Anti-dumping Code. The

Continues

documents requesting the establishment of the panel, it being under-stood between the parties that clarifications contained in an "explana-tory note" to one of these documents would be used by the panel to interpret the other documents before it.[46] The panel carefully examined these documents in order to verify whether each of Japan's claims were within the terms of reference.

In dealing with the EC's objection the panel expressed its views on the function of terms of reference providing: "the basis for each party to determine how its interests might be affected and whether it would wish to exercise its right to participate in a dispute as an interested third party".[47] From this, the panel concluded: "This ... required that the terms of reference identify not only the obligation under the Agreement allegedly violated but also the action or factual situation allegedly giving rise to an inconsistency with the Agreement".[48] The panel then applied this test to the various claims whose admissibility was contested by the EC on that ground and concluded that some of them were not within its terms of reference.

Thus, according to the *Audio Tapes* panel, standard terms of ref-erence whose content is defined by reference to the "matter" as set out in the request for the establishment of the panel imply that, for a claim to be properly before a panel, the action or factual situation allegedly giv-ing rise to an inconsistency with the Agreement must be identified with sufficient particularity.

C.   Some Comments

First, in the *Audio Tapes* case the matter had been submitted for conciliation and the parties had clarified the matter at that stage; this had been recorded in the document requesting the establishment of the panel. Under the new Anti-dumping Ageement conciliation is no longer a mandatory step. In such a situation the request for the establishment of a panel could refer to the document recording the results of the

---

...panel did not formally settle the question disputed by the parties, whether Art. VI came within the terms of reference, having decided that it did not have to address the question whether the measures were justified under Art. VI of the GATT on the ground that the EC had put Art. XX(d) of the GATT as legal basis for the measures challenged, because Art. VI did not, according to the EC, apply a basis for such measures (para.. 5.11).

[46] *Audio Tapes* Panel Report, see note 5 above, para. 22.

[47] *Audio Tapes* Panel Report, see note 5 above, para. 310.

[48] *Audio Tapes* Panel Report, see note 5 above, para. 310.

consultation as had happened in the past where the matter had not been submitted to conciliation.[49] The *Audio Tapes* panels rationale based on the function of the terms of reference still applies, albeit that now members are made fully aware of the matter at the stage of the request made to the DSB for the establishment of a panel.

Second, in the view of the *Audio Tapes* panel the terms of reference must be sufficiently precise in the interest *of other* parties.[50] This should not be taken to mean that the panel considered that the clarity of the terms of reference was of no importance for the dispute settlement itself: this matter is addressed by the requirement that the matter be sufficiently defined at the mandatory consultation and conciliation stages.

Third, in the *Audio Tapes* case, the EC had recognized before the panel that Japan had advanced a point as an argument and not as a claim. The panel considered that it needed to take no further action on the EC's preliminary objection on this issue.[51] According to the panel, while claims must be defined, albeit by reference to earlier documents, in the terms of reference, arguments in support of the claim need not be. This is consistent with the panel's view that all claims must have been raised at the consultation and conciliation stages, but (implicitly) not the arguments. The question arises, however, whether the *Audio Tapes* panel's rationale is not equally valid for arguments put forward in support of claims: do not the other parties, now WTO members, need to know the parties' arguments in order to determine whether they should intervene in panel proceedings? Are not arguments, which raise interpretative questions of more interest and importance to them than claims which more often than not fail to reveal such interpretative questions?

VI.   SCOPE AND STANDARD OF REVIEW

A.   Standard of Review in General Terms

In another contribution to this book Steven Croley and John Jackson deal generally with standard of review. They make the point that the

---

[49] See *e.g. EC – Regulation on Imports of Parts and Components* where Japan had complained under Article XXIII rather than under the Tokyo Round Anti-dumping (note 45 above).
[50] This is questionable. This is also of interest to the respondent, as the *Salmon* panel emphasized (note 12 above, para. 334).
[51] *Audio Tapes* Panel Report, see note 5 above, para. 318.

controversy over the language of the standard of review provision during the GATT/WTO negotiations might at first glance seem absurd but indicate that the basic question considered reaches beyond the GATT/WTO dispute resolution process itself. They identify the underlying difficulty: on the one hand, effective international cooperation depends in part upon sovereigns' willingness to constrain themselves by relinquishing to international tribunals at least minimum powers to interpret treaties and articulate international obligations. On the other hand, nations and their citizens - and particularly those special interests within nation states who are reasonably successful at influencing their national political actors - want to remain in control.[52]

The issue of scope of review became a controversy in the negotiations of the new Anti-Dumping Agreement during the Uruguay Round and centred on what standard of review should be applied by panels in examining issues of law, especially when the agreement does not specifically address an issue and whether there should be a provision limiting the extent of scrutiny by a panel of factual issues, so as to prevent panels from engaging in a *de novo* review of such factual issues.[53]

On a more practical and technical level, the first issue can be divided into two sub-questions: first, what should a panel do when faced with a given interpretation of the Anti-dumping Agreement relied upon by a national administering authority? Second, what should a panel do when faced with the argument that a question is not regulated by the Anti-dumping Agreement? This second sub-question will be examined in section vii of this chapter. As to the second issue, obviously standard of review and scope of review are closely linked.

B.   Review of Findings of Fact

Apart from the early Swedish anti-dumping case,[54] *New–Zealand – Imports of Electrical Transformers from Finland* (hereinafter: the *Electrical Transformers* case) was the first case in which the issue was addressed. This case was brought under Article XXIII as New Zealand was not a party to the 1979 Anti-dumping Code. New Zealand argued

---

[52] See the chapter by Steven P. Croley and John H. Jackson to this book, "WTO Dispute Panel Deference to National Government Decisions. The Misplaced Analogy to the US Chevron Standard-of-Review Doctrine".

[53] Koulen, see note 24 above, 185–186 with reference to literature in footnote 78.

[54] BISD 3S/81.

that, while under Article VI a contracting party had to make a determination that material injury had been caused or threatened, it was not open to the Contracting Parties to scrutinize the manner in which a finding of injury was arrived at.[55] The panel considered that:

> "... if a contracting party affected by the determination could make a case that the importation could not in itself have the effect of causing material injury... that contracting party was entitled,... , that its representations be given sympathetic consideration and that eventually, ... , it might refer the matter to the CONTRACTING PARTIES... To conclude otherwise would give governments complete freedom and unrestricted discretion in deciding anti-dumping cases without any possibility to review the action taken in the GATT. This would lead to an unacceptable situation under the aspect of law and order in international trade relations as governed by the GATT."[56]

The panel then examined the various arguments put forward by Finland. One of them related effectively to a question of interpretation, to which the panel replied affirmatively, i.e. whether the overall state of health of the New Zealand transformer industry should provide the basis for a judgment whether injury was caused by dumped imports.[57] Another one was both of fact and law: given that the two Finnish transformers represented 1.5% of the sum of domestic production and imports or 2.5% of total imports, could the injury have been caused by, or attributed to, the imports from Finland? The panel replied negatively, as these imports "constituted an almost insignificant part in the overall sales of transformers in the period concerned".[58]

In the *First Stainless Steel* case,[59] the US raised as "a central and novel question" what the appropriate standard was by which the panel should review the determinations made by the national administering authorities. The US posited that in the absence of: "... evidence that an investigating authority deliberately acted in a way which would prejudice

---

[55] BISD 32 S/55. para. 3.10.
[56] *Electrical Transformers* Panel Report, see note 55 above, para. 4.4.
[57] *Electrical Transformers* Panel Report, see note 55 above, para. 4.6.
[58] *Electrical Transformers* Panel Report, see note 55 above, para. 4.7.
[59] See note 30 above.

the outcome of an investigation in favour of one party or was seriously negligent in the manner in which it conducted its investigation"[60] a panel, a judicial body, reviewing the results of an investigation should accord some deference to the judgment of the investigating authority. If a panel were to examine each aspect of the investigating authority's investigation, the panel would become a super-investigative authority, which would be inconsistent with the intentions of the drafters of the Anti-dumping Code.[61] The panel did not address this issue as it could dispose of the complaint without dealing with the claims on dumping and on injury.

For reasons that do not appear in the panel report, in the later *Cement* case,[62] the US did not raise the standard of review issue. This could be due to the fact that Mexico appeared to question the findings of the USITC more on legal grounds than on factual grounds. Neither did the US apparently raise that issue in the *Salmon* case.[63]

In the *Second Stainless Steel* case,[64] in reply to one of the arguments which Sweden had put forward in support of its claim that the USITC had rejected a request for review contrary to Article 9(2) of the Tokyo Round Anti-dumping Code, the US argued that a panel should refrain from re-evaluating the weight to give to the evidence. This *de novo* standard of review would exceed the proper role of a panel. The panel should only examine whether the facts reasonably supported the USITC's conclusions.[65] The panel considered that:

> "… it should examine whether the USITC determinations resulted from an objective examination of the information before the USITC and … whether the USITC had adequately explained its determination and whether the information before the USITC supported the determination".[66]

Having examined the facts before it, the panel concluded on this point:

---

[60] *First Stainless Steel* Panel Report, see note 30 above, para. 3.11.
[61] Ibid.
[62] See note 14 above.
[63] See note 12 above.
[64] *United States –Antidumping Duties on Imports of Stainless Steel Plate from Sweden* ADP/117 of 24 February 1994.
[65] *Second Stainless Steel* Panel Report, para. 113.
[66] *Second Stainless Steel* Panel Report, para. 284.

"The Panel thus found that the USITC's conclusion that there was no connection between the decline in the volume of imports since 1976 and the acquisition of a steel mill in New Castle by a predecessor of the Swedish exporter was not supported by fact. In light of this finding, the Panel also considered that the USITC erred when it stated that petitioners had provided 'no legally sufficient reason why the current levels of plate imports are the result of anything other than import relief'."[67]

With respect to other factual elements, the panel showed why it "found itself unable to determine" how they "had enabled the USITC to draw its conclusions regarding the product composition of the imports of stainless steel plate from Sweden". It stated:

"The Panel therefore was of the view that the USITC had not adequately explained its conclusions that the product composition of imports of stainless steel plate from Sweden had not been affected by the purchase in 1976 of a US steel mill by a predecessor of the Swedish exporter."[68]

It should be noted that this was one of the main reasons stated by the USITC in its decision refusing to review its injury determinations.

C.   Comments on the Cases Reviewed

First, it appears that on balance the panels did not act as "super-investigative authorities", a concern expressed by the US in the *First Stainless Steel* case, and did not engage in a *de novo* review of factual issues.[69] Second, the panels verified whether the findings of national administering authorities were supported in fact (*Second Stainless Steel* case) and whether in view of apparently conflicting findings of fact the conclusions reached were adequately explained (*Second Stainless Steel* case). This, it is submitted, is not an improper form of review in that the panels did not substitute their findings of fact to those of the national

[67] *Second Stainless Steel* Panel Report, see note 64 above, para. 311.
[68] *Second Stainless Steel* Panel Report, see note 64 above, para. 323.
[69] Acc. E. U. Petersmann, "Current Legal Problems in GATT Dispute Settlement Proceedings in the field of Anti-dumping law", Friedmann and E. J. Mestmaecker (eds), *Conflict Resolution in International Trade*. 1993, at 200; W. Davey, "The WTO/GATT World Trading System: an Overview", P. Pescalore. W. J. Davey and A. F. Lowenfeld, at note 42 above.

administering authorities. Third, only in the *Electrical Transformers* case did the panel assess a finding of fact made by the national administering authority. It reviewed the weight given by that authority to the evidence. What the panel did was verify whether the facts did reasonably support the conclusions of the administering authority. In denying this, the panel exercised what in certain jurisdictions is called "marginal control" which in view of the facts of the case was not unreasonable. Fourth, while the panels whose reports are reviewed here did not "go overboard", there remains a need for some standards of review, as in most systems where a judicial body is called upon to review findings of facts made by an administrative body.

In this respect, an attempt was made in the special dispute settlement provision of the new Anti-dumping Agreement. Article I7.b(i) reads as follows:

> "In its assessment of the facts of the matter, the panel shall determine whether the authorities' establishment of the facts was proper and whether their evaluation of those facts was unbiased and objective. If the establishment of the facts was proper and the evaluation was unbiased and objective, even though the panel might have reached a different conclusion, the evaluation shall not be overturned."

Whatever may be its substantive merits, this provision[70] does not offer much of a guideline. The second sentence does not really add anything to the first sentence. The first sentence is bound to raise interpretative problems: what does "proper" mean? Does it require a panel to verify whether the authorities had established the relevant facts? While according to Article 17(5) the matter to be examined by a panel is to be based upon "the facts made available in conformity with appropriate domestic procedures to the authorities of the importing Member", does this mean that a panel should ignore evidence adduced before it by the complaining member showing that the facts on which these administering authorities relied were patently wrong?

Moreover, it is unclear whether this provision means that panels are bound to show deference for "unbiased and objective evaluations" of facts even though they may be patently wrong.

---

[70] In E. U. Petersmann's view (see note 2 above, at 1237), this standard might be appropriate.

D. Review of Legal Interpretations

This point has not been researched in the proceedings reviewed. It should be fairly obvious that anti-dumping law (the Tokyo Round Anti-dumping Code and most national legislations) being what it is, legal interpretations by administering authorities are bound to be criticized by other contracting parties, now WTO members, all the more so since in most cases GATT/WTO law is incorporated in national law which, rather than GATT/WTO law, is applied and referred to by national administering authorities. On the other hand, the respondent contracting party/WTO member considers its competence, expertise and knowledge of anti-dumping rules to be superior to those of a panel, with the result that in the past individual contracting parties found it difficult, for this reason, to accept certain panel reports. The new Anti-dumping Agreement tries to deal with this by providing the following in its Article 17(6)(ii):

> "the panel shall interpret the relevant provisions of the Agreement in accordance with customary rules of interpretation of public international law. When the panel finds that a relevant provision of the Agreement admits of more than one permissible interpretation, the panel shall find the authorities' measure to be in conformity with the Agreement if it rests upon one of those permissible interpretations".

According to several writers, there is a contradiction between the first and the second sentence.[71] Probably, what the drafters meant to say was that panels must follow the customary rules of interpretation of public international law; however, panels must defer to the interpretation of the national authorities, if such interpretation is not totally out of line with an interpretation arrived at by using public international law methods. Moreover, as pointed out,[72] this provision might also prevent panels from ensuring uniform interpreation of the Anti-dumping Agreement. One wonders whether a reasonable interpretation of this interpretation rule would not imply making distinctions with respect to the legal quality of the provision whose interpretation is at stake (see also section VIII of this chapter "Lacunae").

---

[71] E. U. Petersmann. see note 2 above, at 1237; J. Steenbergen, "De Uruguay Ronde", 42 *Sociaal Economische Wetgeving*, 632 at 652 (1994); P. Waer and E. Vermulst, "EC Anti-dumping Law and Practice after the Uruguay Round: A New Lease of Life? ". 28 *JWT* 5 at 8-9 (1994).
[72] J. Steenbergen, see note 71 above, at 652.

VII.   SOURCES AND METHODS OF INTERPRETATION

Several writers[73] have criticized the way in which GATT panel reports use sources and methods of interpretation, while also explaining the causes of these shortcomings. Interestingly enough their criticism is essentially directed against panel reports in areas other than anti-dumping. In this author's view panels dealing with anti-dumping cases appear to have avoided the errors as to sources and methods of interpretation criticized in the literature. They followed the successive steps as codified in the Vienna Convention on the Law of Treaties[74] by examining the wording of Article VI of the GATT and/or of the relevant provisions of the Tokyo Round Anti-dumping Code, their purpose and their context. They did not have to rely on the "practice of the Contracting Parties", a method which other panels felt bound to reject.[75]

The express reference in Article 17(6)(ii) of the new Anti-dumping Agreement to customary rules of interpretation of public international law now offers specific guidance in this respect to panels and the appeals procedure enables members involved in a dispute to challenge legal interpretations developed by panels which would depart from these rules.

VIII.   THE "LACUNAE" PROBLEM

A.   Tokyo Round Anti-dumping Code Provisions

The Anti-dumping Code contains provisions that use vague concepts, probably because this was the only thing negotiators could agree on.

There also were provisions that left matters unregulated[76] because negotiators did not think of such matters or, more likely, because they

---

[73] See, *e.g.* P. J. Kuijper, at note 4 above, 229–232; E. McGovern, "Dispute Settlement in the GATT Adjudication or Negotiation", M. Hilf., F. Jacobs and E. U. Petersmann (eds). *The European Community and the Gatt,* Kluwer, Deventer, 1986, at 79–80; P. Pescatore, see note 42 above, at 22–24.

[74] 1155 UNTS 331.

[75] Criticized by P. J. Kuijper, see note 4 above, at 231–232; approved by Pescalore, see note 42 above, at 20, who considers that long-term tolerance of illegal practices does not climinate the rights and duties of contracting parties.

[76] See, *e.g.* M. Koulen, "Some Problems of Interpretation and Implementation of the GATT Anti-dumping Code", J. H. Jackson and E. A. Vermulst (eds), *Anti-dumping Law and Practice, A Comparative Analysis,* Harvester Wheatsheaf, New York, 1990, at 367.

could not reach a consensus on how to regulate them. With respect to the determination of dumping and of injury and to procedural matters certain rules were made more precise,[77] but the new Antidumping Agreement also offers examples of the use of vague concepts and of matters that are left unregulated.

A distinction ought probably to be made between vague concepts and lacunae, whether deliberate or not. When negotiators use vague concepts, they have addressed the issue. When they leave lacunae, they did not deal with an issue. The distinction might not always be easy to make, but this is no reason to avoid attempting to do so.

For panels, which are called upon to make a ruling and thus to interpret provisions, vague concepts may not be easy to deal with. As Hudec has pointed out, what he calls "flexible rules" have two serious problems for GATT. First, flexible rules invariably invite even more flexible behaviour on the part of individual contracting parties. Second, flexible rules are very difficult to administer for panels, which have extremely limited fact-finding capacity and often do not have the regulatory capacity necessary lo understand the finer points of the government regulation involved.[78] They do not, however, raise as such a jurisdictional issue which lacunae may raise, i.e. should a panel rule on a matter which negotiators did not regulate?

B. Panel Reports in the Anti-dumping Area

Regarding anti-dumping, panel reports have had their share of cases in which they were called upon to interpret vague concepts. Only two examples are mentioned here.

The *First Stainless Steel* case[79] dealt with the Tokyo Round Antidumping Code provision on initiation of investigation "upon a written request by or on behalf of the industry affected" and a footnote defining domestic industry as "the domestic producers as a whole of the like products or...those of them whose collective output of the product constitutes a major proportion of the total domestic production of those products". It interpreted these provisions as requiring that the request

---

[77] For further reading, see I. Van Bael, "The 1994 Anti-dumping Code and the New EC Anti-dumping Regulation", J. Bourgeois, F. Berrod and E. Gippini-Fournier, at note 24 above, 236–238.

[78] See note 1 above, at 265–266.

[79] See note 30 above.

must have the authorization or approval of the industry affected before the initiation of an investigation. It held, moreover, that the investigating authorities were required to satisfy themselves, before opening an investigation, that a written request is made on behalf of a domestic industry as it interpreted this concept.[80]

The *Audio Tapes* case raised the issue of how the panel should interpret the requirement of "fair comparison" between normal value and export prices in connection with the so-called "asymmetrical" approach used by the EC. The panel analysed the text of various relevant provisions and interpreted "price comparability" in light of the object and purpose of the Anti-dumping Code and considered that: "to interpret the term 'differences affecting price comparability' *per se* to exclude differences in indirect expenses would frustrate the objective of Article 2:6 to ensure a fair comparison".[81]

The panel reports in the anti-dumping field did not deal with genuine lacunae, unlike panel reports in other fields. The *Audio Tapes* case raised the question as to whether an importing party could "cumulate" dumped imports from two exporting countries when determining injury. This was a matter which negotiators of the Tokyo Round had failed to address and on which the GATT Committee on Anti-dumping Practices had been too divided to issue a recommendation or guideline. As Japan had not challenged the compatibility of cumulation itself, the panel considered that it was not called upon to interpret the meaning of "dumped imports", the terms under which "cumulation" could conceivably be brought.

C.   Whether and How Panels Should Deal with Lacunae

With respect to the GATT/WTO dispute settlement in general Petersmann seeks a solution by referring to the function of court proceedings in national systems which entail an express or implied prohibition of the *non-liquet* (i.e. issue not accessible to legal adjudication). He acknowledges, however, that such an argument might not be convincing as far as genuine lacunae are concerned.[82] Pescatore

---

[80] *First Slainlexs Steel* Panel Report, paras. 5.9 and 5.10. The adoption of this report was blocked and the Uruguay Round Anti-dumping Code, which was being negotiated at that time, now clarifies this point.

[81] *Audio Tapes* Panel Report, see note 5 above, para. 374.

[82] See note 2 above, at 1195.

criticizes the conclusions *of non-liquet* in *Uruguayan Recourse to Article XXIII*[83] by pointing out that the matter, which was the subject of negotiations in another body of GATT, remained there for the next 30 years.[84] While characterizing conclusions of *non-liquet* as legal shortcomings, Pescatore does not state that it is unlawful for panels to consider an issue as non-justiciable.

It would seem that account should be taken of the nature and characteristics of international public law. There is no need to enter here into the sort of theoretical debate about whether states may do anything that international law does not specifically forbid or states may only do what international law permits them to do: a debate well-known in matters of conflict of jurisdiction.[85] The successive anti-dumping codes are considered as being "exhaustive" in the sense that parties and now WTO members may not take measures against dumping not provided by these anti-dumping codes, e.g. by providing in national legislation additional remedies. The question remains, however, whether these codes can be considered as "sell-contained", i.e. whether lacunae may only be filled by the GATT, now by the WTO, and possibly through dispute settlement procedures.[86] Whatever may be the exact meaning of Article 3(2) of the DSU according to which "[r]ecommendations and rulings of the DSB cannot add or diminish the rights and obligations provided in the covered agreements", at least it indicates the negotiators' underlying understanding that WTO members are only bound within the limits of the various agreements.

A possible solution may lie, on the one hand, in recognizing that in the face of lacunae WTO members remain free to do as they see fit and on the other in considering that in exercising their sovereignty and in filling, on their own, the gaps, WTO members are subject to certain fundamental principles enshrined in the GATT and the WTO by which, through a "marginal" scrutiny, manifestly abusive gap-filling could be controlled.

---

[83] BISD 11 S/95.

[84] See note 73 above, at 22.

[85] See, *e.g.* W. Meng, *"Neuere Entwicklungen im Streit um die Jurisdiktionshoheit der Staaten im Bereich der Wettbewerbsbeschränkungen"*, 41 ZaöRV 469 at 470 and his references to the literature.

[86] The term used here is different from the meaning given to it in the literature: B. Simma. "Self-contained Regimes", 16 *Neth. Ybk Int'l L.* 111 (1985): L. Boisson. *Les contre-mesures dans les relations internationales économiques*, 182–186, 1992.

IX.   PROCEDURAL RIGHTS AND OBLIGATIONS

A.   Panels and Questions of Procedure

Pescatore has noted that panels have to cope quite frequently with all kinds of questions of procedure, including presumptions and rules of evidence, well beyond the directions found in the Council's Understandings on Dispute Settlement.[87] This is also the case for the DSU. Panels in the anti-dumping field appear to have dealt with most of these questions of procedure *ad hoc* in a reasonable manner. *Korea–Antidumping duties on Imports of Polyacetal Resins from the United States*[88] offers a good example. The question arose whether the panel could review the injury determination made by the Korean administering authority by reference to considerations in a document which had not been included or referred to in the public statement of reasons. The panel held that it could not take account of this document. It referred to "the requirements of an orderly and efficient conduct of the dispute settlement process"[89] and stated that:

> "[a] full and public statement of reasons underlying an affirmative determination at the time of that determination enabled Parties to the Agreement to assess whether recourse to the dispute settlement mechanism under Article 15 was appropriate and provided a basis for a delimitation of the object of such dispute settlement proceedings".[90]

It is submitted that this is a sound decision. Article 8(3) of the Tokyo Round Anti-dumping Code requires parties taking anti-dumping measures to include in a public notice "the finding and conclusions reached on all issues of fact and law considered material by the investigating authorities, and the reasons and basis therefor". Parties should not be allowed, when being subject to scrutiny from a panel, to pull out of their hat evidence which they should have shown to all parties in national administrative proceedings. The panel's approach appears to be in line with the approach one expects from any court or tribunal reviewing a decision of an administrative authority. The relevant reasons must be given when the administrative decision is taken; if in subsequent

---

[87] See note 73 above, at 26–27.
[88] ADP/92 of 2 April 1993.
[89] *Polyacetal Resins* Panel Report, at note 87 above, para. 210.
[90] *Polyacetal Resins* Panel Report, see note 87 above.

court proceedings other, additional reasons are put forward, either they are considered as inadmissible or they show that the reasons given at the time for the administrative decision were insufficient.

B.   Room for Improvement

In several cases, mostly in fields other than anti-dumping, respondent parties relied on the argument that the complaining parties had the burden of proof and panels accepted this. In certain anti-dumping cases, the issue was made more complicated as a result of an argument used by several complaining parties. According to this argument, as Article VI of the GATT permits a contracting party to impose duties in excess of bound duties and to do so on a non-most-favoured-nation basis, it is thus an exception and is as such to be interpreted narrowly; consequently the contracting party taking such exceptional measures must show in dispute settlement proceedings that the conditions in which it took them are fulfilled. Such argument was put forward in the *Cement* case,[91] the *Salmon* case[92] and in the *Audio Tapes* case.[93]

While in the *Cement* case the panel did not reach this issue, and in the *Salmon* case the panel did not address it, in *Audio Tapes* the panel did not reply in general terms to the EC's sweeping argument but considered it more narrowly in connection with Japan's claim relating to the injury determination:

> "The Panel recalled Japan's argument that the burden of proof was on the EC to prove causation and that Japan therefore was not required to prove the existence of other factors or to present the EC or the Committee [on Antidumping Practices] with a list of such factors. However, the Panel considered that Japan's argument had confused the issue of the obligations of the EC under Article 3:4 of the Agreement and the requirements placed on a Party pursuing dispute settlement by Article 15 of the Agreement.
>
> The fact that a Party was required by Article 3:4 to 'demonstrate' prior to the imposition of anti-dumping

---

[91] See note 14 above.
[92] See note 12 above.
[93] See note 5 above.

duties that dumped imports were, through the effects of dumping, causing injury did not mean that it would be sufficient for a Party pursuing dispute settlement pursuant to Article 15 of the Agreement simply to allege during the conciliation process that a Party had failed to satisfy the first sentence of Article 3:4 without identifying the action or factual circumstances alledgedly giving rise to inconsistency."[94]

The panel thus considered that Article VI of the GATT did not entail a change in the burden of proof in dispute settlement proceedings, it being understood that, when taking anti-dumping measures a party must demonstrate that the conditions arc fulfilled. According to this panel, in a dispute settlement proceeding the complaining party must show that the conditions were not fulfilled.

This is probably right as a general proposition. However, as many legal systems have recognized on the basis of various theories, there may also be a qualified duty on defendants in litigations other than criminal ones to cooperate in the resolution of the conflict.[95] This is particularly the case in the anti-dumping field in which law and facts are interwoven. In view of the fact that panels should not or may not carry out investigations *de nova*, should there not be a duty on the respondent party to make the complete record of the investigation fully available to the complaining party and the panel? In this connection it should be noted that pursuant to Article 13(1) of the DSU the investigating authorities of a respondent member are required to provide such information, but it may not be revealed without their formal authorization. It would thus seem that a panel may use it without, however, disclosing it in its report.

X.   REMEDIES

As Petersmann has pointed out, while for a number of reasons in GATT dispute settlement proceedings restitution in kind has not been requested by the complainant contracting party or recommended by

---

[94] *Audio Tapes* Panel Report, see note 5 above, para. 329.
[95] At the level of the investigation carried out by national administering authorities, this is even more important. These authorities do not have the "passive" role of an administrative tribunal but investigate themselves. An. 6 of the Uruguay Round Anti-dumping Code contains a set of rules in this respect which raise some interpretative questions on their own.

panels, the practice has been different in the field of anti-dumping and countervailing duty law.[96] Petersmann refers to the following cases: *Electrical Transformers*,[97] *Stainless Steel I*,[98] *United States –Countervailing Duties on Canadian Pork*[99] and *Cement*[100] Since then one could add the *Salmon*[101] and the *Second Stainless Steel* cases.[102]

In *Polyacetal Resins*,[103] the United States had merely requested that Korea "bring its law as applied into conformity with its obligations under the Agreement". In *Audio-Tapes*,[104] Japan requested the panel to recommend that the EC regulation imposing the definitive duties be revoked, that duties already paid be reimbursed, and even that the EC bring the relevant provisions of its legislation into conformity with the Tokyo Round Anti-dumping Code. Interestingly, the panel did not reject this request out of hand: having noted that the EC had imposed a duty that was much lower than the dumping margin found, the panel found itself unable to judge whether the EC's inconsistent methodology had any effect on the duty imposed. On that ground: "the Panel did not consider it appropriate to recommend that the Committee request the EC to revoke the Regulation imposing a definitive duty in this case".[105] It added, however, that the EC should be requested to reconsider its determination and that, if such reconsideration leads to a no-dumping finding, the EC should revoke the anti-dumping duty and reimburse the duties collected.

In the *Salmon* case,[106] Norway initially requested the panel to find that the continued imposition of anti-dumping duties was inconsistent with Article 9:1 of the Tokyo Round Anti-dumping Code. At a later stage Norway requested the panel to recommend that the US revoke the anti-dumping order and reimburse the anti-dumping duties paid. The panel did not reject this claim out of hand. It recalled that it had found that the US had acted inconsistently with its obligations under the Tokyo Round Antidumping Code, with respect to the calculation of

---

[96] E. U. Petersmann, at note 2 above.
[97] See note 55 above.
[98] See note 30 above.
[99] BISD 38 s/30.
[100] See note 17 above.
[101] See note 12 above.
[102] See note 64 above.
[103] See note 87 above.
[104] See note 5 above.
[105] See note 5 above, para. 459.
[106] See note 12 above.

the dumping margins. The panel considered that: "[i]t could not be pre-sumed that a methodology of calculating dumping margins consistent with the Panel's findings on these aspects would necessarily result in a determination that no dumping existed rather than in a determination that duties were to be imposed at a different rate".[107] It drew two conclusions from this: the US should not be requested to revoke the anti-dumping order and the US should not be requested to reimburse the anti-dumping duties.[108] Instead it held that the US should:

> "reconsider the affirmative final determination of dumping, consistent with the Panel's findings under Articles 2:4 and 2:6, and take such measures with respect to this anti-dumping duty order, as imposed on 12 April 1991, as may be warranted in the light of that reconsideration".[109]

After the panel had submitted its report to the parties on 23 October 1992, Norway wrote to the panel. In its letter of 12 November it stated *inter alia* that the panel should have recommended the revocation of the anti-dumping duty order and the reimbursement of the anti-dumping duties. In its written reply of 20 November 1992 and with reference to this particular point, the chairman of the panel noted that in contrast with previous cases relied upon by Norway the panel had not found that no anti-dumping duties should have been levied at all. He underlined that the panel had recommended that the US be required to reconsider those aspects of its determination found by the panel to be inconsistent with the Code.[110]

In the literature differing views have been put forward about whether panels may recommend, and whether the parent body (now the DSB) may decide, that the defending party apply a specific remedy.[111]

---

[107] See note 12 above, para. 596.
[108] See note 12 above, para. 596.
[109] See note 12 above, para. 597.
[110] These letters are appended to the panel report circulated as document ADP/87 of 30 November 1992.
[111] See, *e.g.* E. U. Petersmann at note 2 above, but with more qualifications in "Current Legal Problems in GATT Dispute Settlement Proceedings in the Field of Anti-dumping Law", Friedmann and Mestmaecker (eds). *Conflict Resolution in International Trade,* 1993. at 197–198; P. J. Kuijper, at note 4 above, 252 notes that such recommendations were considered nothing other than "revolutionary".

Such recommendations have at any rate proved to be rather controversial. Notwithstanding this, the specific dispute settlement provisions of the new Anti-dumping Agreement do not address this question, with the result that those of the DSU apply. According to Article 19 of the DSU, which provides that panels may "suggest" a specific way for members to bring their measures into compliance, panels in the anti-dumping field may thus "suggest" specific remedies.

It is true that implementation of such recommendations in ways "suggested" by panels raises issues under national law. However, apart from the fact that these are "recommendations" and not "rulings", and from now on "suggested" ways on how to implement a "recommendation", one wonders whether a *restitutio in integrum* would face the respondent party with an impossible task, as has been argued, as long as the way in which such "suggested" remedy is implemented is left to national law.

One should also consider that recommendations work arguably both ways. If a member follows the "suggested" way of compliance, does this not mean then that the member must be presumed to have implemented the result of the dispute settlement adequately?

XI. THE EFFECT OF DISPUTE SETTLEMENT DECISIONS IN NATIONAL PROCEEDINGS

The question briefly addressed here concerns the legal effect in national proceedings of panel reports adopted by the WTO DSB. Is there a legal duty for a WTO member to "apply directly" such panel report, i.e. does the WTO Agreement require WTO members to grant "direct effect" to DSB rulings, to enable private parties to rely on such rulings in national courts and such national courts to set aside national rules and measures that are inconsistent with such rulings?

This question is related to another question: does the WTO Agreement entail such duty for the Agreement itself? It seems indeed logical to conclude that if a state is not bound by an international treaty to apply that treaty directly, that state is not bound either to "apply directly" international jurisprudence relating to that treaty. Writers disagree about whether the status and effect of an international treaty within national systems are matters governed by international law or national law. This question may be left aside here, as few would doubt that the GATT and now the WTO Agreement do not address their status and effect in the legal systems of contracting parties and the WTO members. While under Article XVI(4) of the WTO Agreement each member is bound to "ensure the conformity of its laws, regulations and administrative procedures with its obligations as provided in the annexed Agreements", the WTO Agreement leaves it to each member to determine how this obligation is to be complied with.

As far as DSB rulings in the anti-dumping field are concerned, in particular where such rulings are accompanied by recommendations and "suggested" remedies, this means that a member does not violate an international law obligation if a private party may not rely on a DSB ruling and a recommendation in a national court, e.g. for the purpose of seeking repayment of anti-dumping duties found to be WTO-illegal by the DSB. Under international law the only means to seek compliance with such ruling and its implementation as suggested in recommendations of the DSB is the remedy at the disposal of the complaining member faced with a less than adequate implementation, i.e. recourse to Article 21 of the DSU. Whether this will have a practical effect for private parties concerned is doubtful: the complaining member may not insist on a *ex tune* implementation and the respondent member may prefer to offer compensation over, for example, re-opening an anti-dumping investigation or repaying the anti-dumping duties collected. Whether this is good or bad from a WTO policy point of view is left aside here.

It should be noted that under certain national systems, the situation may be different depending on the degree to which such national systems "apply directly" the new Anti-dumping Agreement. In some of them the situation is clear, e.g. in the US system where the implementing legislation "trumps" the Agreement. In other systems the situation is unclear. This is the case for the EC. On the one hand, under the case law, compliance with the new Anti-dumping Agreement can be enforced in the EC through the courts. In adopting the new EC anti-dumping regulation the EC made clear that it "intended to implement a particular obligation entered into within the framework"[112] of the WTO: the Preamble of that Regulation refers to the new Anti-dumping Agreement and states that it is appropriate to amend the existing EC rules in the light thereof.[113] On the other hand, the EC Decision on the conclusion of

---

[112] This is one of the circumstances in which the Court of Justice of *the* European Communities may recognize "direct effect" to GATT rules. See, *e.g.* judgment of 5 October 1994 (*Germany v. Council*) [1994] ECR 1-4973.

[113] Regulation (EC) No. 3284/94 (*Official Journal*, 1994, L/349/1).

the Uruguay Round agreements states explicitly in its Preamble that the WTO Agreement, including the Annexes thereto, "is not susceptible to being directly invoked" in EC or member states courts.[114] Apart from this uncertainty, one of the traditional grounds on which the Court of Justice of the European Communities relies to exclude the "direct effect" of GATT rules, i.e. "the great flexibility of its provisions", is hardly available where DSB rulings and recommendations are concerned.

XII.   SOME TENTATIVE CONCLUSIONS

A.   Difficult Tasks for the Panels in the Proceedings Reviewed

There were many difficulties for the panels involved in the proceedings reviewed. First, leaving aside the conflicts between the underlying economic and policy interests, they had often to deal with claims and arguments that raised issues relating to the consistency with the Anti-dumping Code not so much of anti-dumping measures complained of but of national anti-dumping legislations and regulations. In this regard, the GATT system did not operate satisfactorily. On the one hand, there appears to be a consensus that panels are as a rule not supposed to propose rulings on national antidumping legislations; panels have at any rate tried to avoid such rulings. On the other, the review by the GATT Committee on Anti-dumping Practices of national legislations has often been perfunctory: the parties that were most likely to spot potential inconsistencies with the Anti-dumping Code were more often than not themselves applying anti-dumping measures and refrained from criticizing others' legislations; other parties often realized too late what certain provisions of national legislations meant, i.e. when they were applied to their exporters. These reviews have not led to meaningful recommendations about amendments of legislations of individual parties.

Second, apart from the absence mentioned above of any guidelines on procedural matters, the panels in the proceeding reviewed were also often confronted with procedural issues on scope and standard of review about which parties had conflicting views; such views reflected specific rules and principles of their own legal system. Two examples are worth mentioning. The first example concerns the question whether, to be entertained by a panel, claims and arguments must have been raised

---

[114] Decision of 22 December 1994 (*Official Journal*, 1994, 336/1).

in national proceedings. On the US side it is probably obvious that on appeal against a decision of an administrative authority the plaintiff may not put forward claims or use arguments which were not raised in the administrative proceeding; a similar objection has been rejected by the EC courts in appeals against decisions of the European Commission on the ground that administrative proceedings and judicial ones are distinct and separate.

The second example concerns review by panels of legal interpretations of the Anti-dumping Agreement by national administering authorities. From a US perspective the argument that a panel must defer to the legal interpretation of the national administering authority is a fairly obvious one to make. From an EC perspective the opposite is true. Whether such national principles and rules should be transposed to the GATT, now the WTO, where they cannot be related to some common principles is left aside here, but this phenomenon does not make the panels' task easier and these clashes of legal philosophy explain in part the difficulty some parties had in accepting panel reports.

B.   Ad hoc Approaches and the Absence of Guidance

The record of individual panels in light of "scope of review" in most of its aspects and "standard of review" with respect of findings of fact and legal interpretations is characterized by "ad hoc" approaches. The panels are hardly to blame for it in the absence of any meaningful guidance.

Overall, however, the record appears to be satisfactory. This is particularly so, bearing in mind that the negotiators of the DSU and of the specific dispute settlement provisions of the new Anti-dumping Agreement failed to come up with much more precise guidelines than those that panels had somehow set for themselves. As far as findings of fact are concerned, the new Anti-dumping Agreement contains one guideline that purports to be more specific, i.e. restricting the possibility for panels to overturn the evaluation of facts as made by national administering authorities. Apart from the question whether this means that panels must henceforth ignore compelling new evidence, the reports examined show that panels have avoided *de nova* reviews and have at most engaged in "marginal" review of the findings of fact.

As far as review of legal interpretations is concerned, panel reports in the antidumping field have generally followed the customary rules of interpretation of public international law. To many lawyers - at least non-US lawyers –the added guideline about the "more than one permissible interpretation" appears as rather unusual since one of the points in dispute may precisely be the interpretation of the Anti-dumping Agreement. As there is likely to be disagreement between a panel and a party on whether there is more than one permissible interpretation it will have to be resolved by the Standing Appellate Body.

C.   Looking Ahead to Change?

Whether the changes in the legal context –the DSU, the limited clarifications of the substantive GATT/WTO anti-dumping rules and the specific dispute settlement provisions of the new Anti-dumping Agreement–will modify the picture referred to at the outset of this contribution is difficult to say.

Normally, the "low rate of settlement" (Hudec) and the "blockage" (Petersmann) should be a thing of the past in view of the introduction of the "negative" consensus" for the DSB. It is doubtful that the number of disputes will decrease: there has been no "rapprochement" between the conflicting views about dumping and anti-dumping; the clarification of the substantive provisions have only blunted the edges. The judge will still be needed to restore "peace in the valley".

5. IMPLEMENTING PARAGRAPH 6 OF THE DOHA DECLARATION ON TRIPS AND PUBLIC HEALTH

THE WAIVER SOLUTION

The following article offered the opportunity to test the so-called "waiver" as a solution to the perceived conflict between a provision of the WTO TRIPs Agreement and the access by developing countries to essential medicines, pending the Doha Round of Multilateral Trade Negotiations. After the publication of this article, the WTO (the TRIPs Council) adopted this solution (Decision of 30 August 2003, WT/L/540).

I.   INTRODUCTION

In Paragraph 6 of the Doha Declaration on the TRIPs Agreement and Public Health ("the Declaration"),[1] World Trade Organization (WTO) Members recognized that countries with insufficient or no manufacturing capacities in the pharmaceutical sector could face some difficulties in making effective use of compulsory licensing under the Agreement on Trade-Related Aspects of Intellectual Property Rights (TRIPs). Accordingly, they instructed the Council for TRIPs to find an expeditious solution to this problem and to report to the WTO General Council before the end of 2002.

After lengthy discussion, four options for addressing public health problems emerged and were tabled for consideration by the TRIPs Council:

–   an authoritative interpretation of TRIPs Article 30, authorizing third parties to make, sell and export pharmaceutical products without the consent of the patent holder;

–   an amendment of TRIPs Article 31, authorizing exports of medicines produced under a compulsory licence to a country with insufficient manufacturing capacities;

–   a dispute settlement moratorium with regard to the non-respect of the export restriction under Article 31(f); or

–   a waiver with regard to the export restriction under Article 31(f).

---

[1] *Declaration on the* TRIPs *Agreement and Public Health,* WT/MIN (01)/DEC/2, 20 November 2001.

This article reflects on how these approaches could properly serve the mandate under Paragraph 6 of the Declaration. Section 2 considers the problems to be addressed, and Section 3, the four available options to resolve them. After analysing in detail three of the options, Section 4 discusses the preferred waiver option before Section 5 examines briefly some practical issues related to the establishment of adequate terms and conditions to implement this solution. Section 6 concludes.

II. TRIPS AND PUBLIC HEALTH: MANUFACTURING CAPACITIES AND EFFECTIVE USE OF COMPULSORY LICENSING

A. General background: the emergence of the trips and public health issue

The magnitude of the HIV/AIDS pandemic in developing countries was not foreseen at the time of the conclusion of the TRIPS Agreement, and was one of the paramount concerns at the origin of the Doha Declaration on TRIPS and Public Health.

At the end of the 1990s, non-governmental organizations (NGOs) and civil society groups began to criticize major pharmaceutical companies manufacturing HIV therapies. The effect of patent protection on prices and access to medicines for the poorest countries was the main expressed concern. In conjunction with the dramatic development of the HIV/AIDS pandemic in Africa, both the attempt of pharmaceutical companies to challenge the TRIPs compatibility of provisions in the South African Medicines Act and the complaint brought by the United States against Brazil in challenging the TRIPs –compatibility of its use of a compulsory licensing scheme, prompted strong reactions in international public opinion.

As early as 1999, discussions took place in the World Health Organization (WHO) and the World Intellectual Property Organization (WIPO) to address the relationship between access to medicines and the TRIPs Agreement.

The African Group was first to request action at the June 2001 TRIPs s Council. This initiative launched a series of informal and formal TRIPs meetings dedicated to the issue of access to medicines in developing and least-developed countries. The outcome of the process was the adoption by the Members, at the Doha Ministerial Conference, of a Declaration on the TRIPs Agreement and Public Health.

In the first Paragraph of the Declaration, Members recognized:

"... the gravity of the public health problems afflicting many developing and least-developed countries, especially those resulting from HIV/AIDs, tuberculosis, malaria and other epidemics."[2]

In Paragraph 2, they also stressed:

"... the need for the Agreement on Trade-Related Aspects of Intellectual Property Rights (TRIPs Agreement) to be part of the wider national and international action to address these problems."

The Declaration concluded with two action items. The first directed the extension to 2016 of the transition period granted for least-developed countries with respect to the obligation to provide patent protection for pharmaceutical products.[3] On 8 July 2002, WTO Members adopted a waiver to this effect.[4] The second sought a solution to the problem of countries with insufficient or no manufacturing capacities in the pharmaceutical sector to make effective use of compulsory licensing under the TRIPs Agreement.[5] This item is still being debated and spurs the discussion in this article.

B.   The mandate of paragraph 6 of the doha declaration on trips and public health

The TRIPs Council was directed by the Members to develop an "expeditious" solution to the Paragraph 6 problem and to report to the General Council by the end of 2002. Discussions have already been going on for several months, and Members will need to reach agreement upon this solution very soon. Yet, the problem's parameters still need to be clarified.

---

[2] A related issue in reviewing the language of the Declaration is the status of the document itself as a legal and/or political document. See, *e.g.*, Frederick M. Abbott, *The Doha Declaration on the TRIPs Agreement and Public Health: Lighting a Dark Corner at the WTO*, J. Int. Econ. L., 2002, 469, at 490–504: using a paragraph-by-paragraph approach to characterizing the Doha Declaration; Christoph Herrmann, *TRIPs, Patentschutz für Medikamente and staatliche Gesundheitspolitik: Hinreichende Flexibilität?* 13 E.Z.W. 37, 2002, 42: characterizing the Declaration as an authentic interpretation intended to clarify rather than amend the TRIPs Agreement. Though we recognize this as a lively topic of debate, this article focuses narrowly on Paragraph 6 implementation options.
[3] Paragraph 7 of the Declaration, *supra*, footnote 1.
[4] Document IP/C/W/359.
[5] Paragraph 6 of the Declaration, *supra*, footnote 1.

1. A Problem in Theory until 2005

As of today, the issue raised in Paragraph 6 of the Declaration remains mostly theoretical. Developing countries that did not provide patent protection for pharmaceutical products on the date of application of the TRIPs Agreement (i.e. 2000) were granted an additional period of five years (i.e. until January 2005) to extend product patent protection to this field of technology.[6] Otherwise stated, nothing in the TRIPs Agreement prevents local companies in developing countries from producing any pharmaceutical products and offering them for sale on their domestic market or abroad prior to 2005. If the product is patented in the importing country, a compulsory licence is necessary to authorise such imports, but this is not an insurmountable obstacle. Paragraph 5(b) of the Doha Declaration on TRIPs and Public Health reminded that:

"Each Member has the right to grant compulsory licences and the freedom to determine the grounds upon which such licences are granted."

At present, countries with insufficient or no manufacturing capacity can rely on these imports to address public health problems. Among others, India does not yet provide product patents for pharmaceuticals, and may have the capacity to supply countries in need.[7] However, the situation will change substantially in January 2005.

Beginning in 2005, pharmaceuticals will become subject to patent protection in all developing countries.[8] Despite this change, developing countries will still be able to produce under compulsory licence. Also, there is nothing in the TRIPs Agreement to preclude a country with insufficient or no manufacturing capacities from importing the needed products. However, the combination of a new patent regime for pharmaceuticals and implementation of Article 31(f) of the TRIPs Agreement will modify the parameters of the problem.

---

[6] Article 65.4 of the TRIPs Agreement.
[7] Frederick M. Abbott, The *TRIPs Agreement, Access to Medicines, and the WTO Doha Ministerial Conference*, 5 *J.W.I.P.* 1, January 2002, 15, at 16.
[8] With the exception of the least-developed countries, which were granted a waiver of their obligations in this regard until 2016. After 2005, products currently available presumably can continue to be exported, as product patents will apply only on a prospective basis. This means that India will be able to continue to export all of the HIV/AIDS therapies that its companies currently market abroad.

Article 31(f) provides that a compulsory licence:

"...shall be authorized predominantly for the supply of the domestic market of the Member authorizing such use;".

While this Article contains inbuilt flexibility that allows Members to export products under compulsory licence, the expression "predominantly" limits the extent of such exports.[9]

2.   *A Defined Solution*

At this stage, it is also useful to put the solution to Paragraph 6 into perspective. The objective set forth in this Paragraph is not to find a miracle cure to all public health problems afflicting developing and least-developed countries. Whatever the solution, it will only be part of a global effort to confront the public health crisis in the developing and the least-developed world.

In the first place, the role of patents in the availability of medicines should not be overestimated. Prices can clearly be a barrier to access. Other elements, such as health infrastructure, capacity, research and development in neglected diseases, financing and political commitment play a more significant role.

Developing and least-developed countries are not yet obliged to grant patents on pharmaceuticals where protection has not been afforded in the past. As a consequence, their current problems related to access to medicines could hardly be imputed to patent systems as such. For example, most of the essential drugs listed by the WHO are in the public domain, because either they were never patented or their patents have expired.[10] In India, a country that does not allow product patents on pharmaceuticals and has a burgeoning AIDS problem, it is estimated that only 1 percent of

---

[9] According to Article 31(k), Members are exempted from this discipline only where use under a compulsory licence is permitted to remedy a practice determined after judicial or administrative process to be anti-competitive.

[10] According to some commentators, only 5 percent of the essential drugs for the treatment of human disease appearing on the WHO List of Essential Drugs are patented in any jurisdiction. See Bruce Lehman, *Patents and Health*, Presentation to the Policy Advisory Commission of the WIPO, Beijing, China, 22 May 2002, at 3; Eric Noehrenberg, *Perceived National Emergencies and Intellectual Property Rights*, Intellectual Property and Trade Issues, IFPMA, 26 February 2002, at 4. Other commentators estimate the percentage of patented essential drugs to be closer to 1 percent. See, Forum Europe Press Release, *Infrastructure the Major Obstacle to Health Care in the Developing World*, 4 June 2002.

all AIDs patients have sustained access to AIDs drugs, despite the presence of a large generic industry.[11] The pharmaceutical industry has conducted preliminary research suggesting that in Sub-Saharan Africa, as much as 99 percent of the essential drugs listed by the WHO are off-patent or were never patented.[12] Yet, one-third of all patients globally lack access to these drugs.[13]

Part of the problem is also that most pharmaceutical research and development resources are directed to produce drugs for meeting the needs of developed countries. This is no surprise, as a lack of financing for health care has prevented the emergence of developing and least-developed country markets and a lack of patent protection acts as a disincentive for research aimed at meeting the needs of these markets.

Yet, this does not explain why effective and safe medicines that have been in the public domain for many years do not reach the millions in poor countries who need them. For many of the diseases that are most endemic in poor countries, good therapies exist that were never patented or for which the patent has long since expired, and still these drugs do not get to people, resulting in millions of preventable cases of sickness and premature death.

Even in the case of the HIV / AIDS pandemic which, as mentioned earlier, brought about the political crisis at the origin of the Declaration, the role of patents in the lack of access to these drugs in Africa is contested.[14] Several experts demonstrated that the relevant drugs are not patented in most African countries and were offered by the patent owner to these countries at no cost or at significantly reduced prices.[15] Indeed, it is significant that few countries in Africa and other poor regions have taken up the offers of generic companies despite the fact that these medicines are not patented there, suggesting that a lack of political commitment, capacity or a severe shortage of financing for health care pose much more substantial barriers to access.

---

[11] Harvey Bale, *The Role of Patents in Issues of Drugs and Vaccine Innovation and Access—The Pharmaceutical Industry: Squaring the Circle*, Royal Institute of International Affairs, Chatham House, 15 March 2002.

[12] See, Forum Europe, *supra*, footnote 10.

[13] WHO, *The Impact of Essential Drugs*, available at: «http://www.who.int/medicines/ strategy/whozipl6e/ ch04.htm», last visited 14 August 2002.

[14] International Intellectual Property Institute, *Patent Protection and Access to HIV/ AIDS Pharmaceuticals in Sub-Saharan Africa*, Report prepared for the WIPO, 2000, at 52.

[15] Lehman, *supra*, footnote 10, at 11; Amir Attaran and Lee Gillespie-White, *Do Patents for Antiretroviral Drugs Constrain Access to AIDS Treatment in Africa?* 286 J. of Am. Med. Assoc. 1886, 2001.

Thus, to find a solution to the challenge of access to medicines it would not necessarily be enough to facilitate compulsory licensing for export under Paragraph 6. Generic companies operate today as suppliers of off-patent medicines, and have not generally used the compulsory licence system to get access to patented products. Their main interest lies in the rapid introduction of products after patent expiration, relying—where available—on Bolar-type exceptions.[16] Furthermore, generic companies, like their research-based counterparts, are profit-making enterprises seeking to supply well-developed markets with sufficient financing for drug purchases.

These considerations, of course, do not relieve the trips Council of its responsibilities.[17] However, they do emphasize the need to accompany a Paragraph 6 solution with indispensable measures such as global political commitment and adequate financing of health care.

III.   AVAILABLE OPTIONS TO IMPLEMENT PARAGRAPH 6 OF THE DECLARATION

Discussion of Paragraph 6 at the TRIPs Council has been particularly comprehensive. At the June 2002 meeting of the Council, approximately fifty delegations participated in the discussion. Several written contributions also added to the debate.

As of its June Meeting, the TRIPs Council had received five Communications from Members containing proposals on Paragraph 6 of the Declaration:

–   a Communication from Kenya on behalf of the African Group;[18]

---

[16] Having the right to start the process of approval of a product before the original product's patent has expired. In the United States, 35 *U.S.C.* 27.1(e), reads in part: "It shall not be an act of infringement to make, use, offer to sell, or sell within the United States or import into the United States a patented invention ... solely for uses reasonably related to the development and submission of information [regulating the] manufacture, use, or sale of drugs or veterinary biological products." The exceptions were named "Bolar" after a case judged by U.S. courts, *Roche Products Inc. v. Bolar Pharmaceutical Co.*, 733 F. 2d. 858, Fed. Cir.; cert, denied 469 U.S. 856, 1984.

[17] Statement of the European Communities representative at the June 2002 TRIPs Council, in, *Minutes of the TRIPs Council Meeting*, IP/C/M/36, para. 9, 18 July 2002.

[18] *Proposal on Paragraph 6 of the Ministerial Declaration on the TRIPs Agreement and Public Health,* Joint Communication from the African Group in the WTO, IP/C/W/ 351, 24 June 2002.

- a Communication from the European Communities and their Member States;[19]

- a Communication from the United Arab Emirates;[20]

- a Communication from Brazil on behalf of Bolivia, Brazil, Cuba, China, the Dominican Republic, Ecuador, India, Indonesia, Pakistan, Peru, Sri Lanka, Thailand and Venezuela;[21] and

- a Communication from the United States.[22]

Upon request of the Members, the WTO Secretariat prepared two Notes providing available background information on "the existence of patents in regard to diseases referred to in the Declaration on TRIPs and Public Health" and "manufacturing capacity for medicines".[23] The Secretariat also prepared, on the basis of the Communications it received from the Members, a thematic compilation of all proposals on Paragraph 6 of the Declaration.[24]

Dialogue, the contributions of the Members and the Notes of the Secretariat have greatly clarified the terms of the debate, and there appears to be an emerging consensus among WTO Members on some of the key elements of a solution. First, four options have been identified by the vast majority of the Members as having particular merit. These options, as mentioned earlier, are:

---

[19] *Concept Paper Relating to Paragraph 6 of the Ministerial Declaration on the TRIPs Agreement and Public Health,* Communication from the European Communities and their Member States, IP/C/W/339, 4 March 2002.

[20] *Paragraph 6 of the Ministerial Declaration on the TRIPs Agreement and Public Health,* Communication from the United Arab Emirates, IP/C/W/354, 24 June 2002.

[21] *Paragraph 6 of the Ministerial Declaration on the TRIPs Agreement and Public Health,* Communication received from the Permanent Mission of Brazil on behalf of the delegations of Bolivia, Brazil, Cuba, China, the Dominican Republic, Ecuador, India, Indonesia, Pakistan, Peru, Sri Lanka, Thailand and Venezuela, IP/C/W/355, 24 June 2002.

[22] *Paragraph 6 of the Ministerial Declaration on the TRIPs Agreement and Public Health,* Second Communication from the United States, IP/C/W/358, 9 July 2002.

[23] *Available Information on the Existence of Patents in Regard to Diseases Referred to in the Declaration on the TRIPs Agreement and Public Health,* Note by the Secretariat, WTO, Geneva, IP/C/W/348, 11 June 2002; *Available Information on Manufacturing Capacity for Medicines,* Note by the Secretariat, WTO, Geneva, IP/C/W/345, 24 May 2002.

[24] *Proposals on Paragraph 6 of the Doha Declaration on the TRIPs Agreement and Public Health: Thematic Compilation,* Note by the Secretariat, WTO, Geneva, IP/C/W/363, 11 July 2002.

- an authoritative interpretation of Article 30;

- an amendment to Article 31;

- a moratorium on disputes; and

- a waiver with regard to Article 31(f).

Second, Members agreed on some criteria that the solution should meet: it should be expeditious, workable, transparent, sustainable and legally secure. The following Sections analyse these options in the light of the selected criteria.[25]

The broader question of technology transfer under Article 66.2 of TRIPS was also raised by several Members in papers submitted to the Council in June.[26] But this issue is covered in Paragraph 7 of the Declaration and is not the central focus here. Two points are certain: a waiver approach to resolving Paragraph 6 issues would in no way undermine the Paragraph 7 commitment of developed countries to provide incentives to promote and encourage technology transfer to least-developed countries. Nor would a waiver approach preclude the establishment of a mechanism in the TRIPS Council to monitor Article 66.2 implementation.

A.   An authoritative interpretation based on article 30

Article 30 of the TRIPS Agreement states:

"Members may provide limited exceptions to the exclusive rights conferred by a patent, provided that such exceptions do not unreasonably conflict with a normal exploitation of the patent and do not unreasonably prejudice the legitimate interests of the patent owner, taking account of the legitimate interests of third parties."

---

[25] The four options seek to facilitate exports of cheap pharmaceutical products to WTO Members with insufficient manufacturing capacities. However, other elements of the proposals received by the WTO Secretariat appear to be directed primarily at overcoming problems of manufacturing capacity and market size so as to facilitate production under compulsory licences in countries with, at present, insufficient manufacturing capacity: see, *e.g.* Brazil *et al., supra,* footnote 21, IP/C/W/355, para. 20. These elements are not analysed below, but should under no circumstances be neglected as supplementary means to address the problem of Paragraph 6.

[26] See Brazil *et al.,* id.; African Group, *supra,* footnote 18, IP/C/W/351, para. 6(e).

This Article thus authorizes "limited" exceptions to the exclusive rights conferred by a patent, but remains silent as to what these exceptions could be. Therefore, several Members suggested that Article 30 be interpreted so as to recognize the right of WTO Members to authorize third parties to make, sell and export patented pharmaceutical products, without the consent of the patent holder, to address public health needs in another country.

1.   *Positions of Stakeholders*

A large number of developing countries consider that an authoritative interpretation of Article 30 would be the most effective solution to the problem identified in Paragraph 6. The submission by Brazil on behalf of a group of developing countries is the best illustration of this position. Important sectors of civil society and NGOs are also fervent supporters of the Article 30 solution. The shift of the European Communities with regard to this option, between the first and the second of their Communications on the issue of Paragraph 6, was thus severely criticized by NGOs.

Furthermore, the Article 30 approach is also the most contested one. Several delegations have expressed serious concern, and did not favour this solution which could ultimately undermine existing patent provisions in the TRIPs Agreement.[27]

2.   *An Unsatisfactory Solution*

Of all the options suggested so far, an authoritative interpretation of Article 30 is the least attractive and risks going further than the intended scope of Paragraph 6.

(a)   *An authoritative interpretation is not the most expeditious and workable solution*

Article IX:2 of the WTO Agreement states that the Ministerial Conference and the General Council have the exclusive authority to adopt interpretations of the Multilateral Trade Agreements. In the present case involving interpretation of the TRIPs Agreement, they would exercise their authority on the basis of a recommendation by the TRIPs Council. The

---

[27] See, *e.g.* statement of the Canadian representative to the TRIPs June 2002 Council, in IP/C/M/36, *supra*, footnote 17, para. 29.

decision to adopt an authoritative interpretation, in the absence of a consensus, would be taken by a three-fourths majority of the Members.

Article IX:2 also states that an authoritative interpretation shall not be used in a manner that would undermine the amendment provisions of Article X. In other words, an authoritative interpretation cannot add to or diminish the rights and obligations provided in the Agreement. And yet, an authoritative interpretation has almost the same legal effects as an amendment, for WTO panels and the Appellate Body are bound by this interpretation; and all Members are obliged to implement the Agreement in the light of this interpretation. In the case of an amendment, on the contrary, the revised text only applies to a Member upon acceptance of it.

As a result of these legal considerations, it is most unlikely that a consensus, or even a three-fourths majority, would be found in favour of an Article 30 solution. Several Members have expressed serious concern about the legal authority for this solution, and would under no circumstances accept this interpretation. Negotiations would, in any case, be an extended and cumbersome process.

Furthermore, as will be discussed in the next Section, implementation of Paragraph 6 of the Declaration by interpretation of Article 30 would certainly require WTO Members to modify national legislation, a prospect that should counsel against an Article 30 approach.[28] For these reasons, this solution could not be qualified as being expeditious or workable.

(b)   *An authoritative interpretation is not the most transparent or legally certain solution*

One of the arguments put forward by the Members favourable to the Article 30 solution is to avoid burdensome procedures related to the grant of compulsory licences in the exporting country. First, it should be noted that in the case of a national emergency or other circumstances of extreme urgency, requirements attached to a compulsory licence are limited and essentially consist in an obligation to notify the unauthorized use to the right holder. This notification ensures transparency and cannot be

---

[28] In an intervention at the September 2002 TRIPs Council, the representative of the Kingdom of Lesotho urged the Council to avoid solutions that could entail new obligations as "developing Members of the WTO are overwhelmed in attempting to adhere to the obligations they already have under existing provisions of the TRIPs Agreement".

considered as burdensome. Moreover, these procedures are aimed to protect the rights conferred to the patent holder who is generally entitled to compensation.

Furthermore, Article 28 of TRIPs clearly states that a patent shall confer on its owner the right "to prevent third parties not having the owner's consent from the acts of: making, using, offering for sale, selling, or importing" the patented product. The authorized manufacture of patented products for export purposes would, therefore, conflict with the normal exploitation of the patent and would unreasonably prejudice the legitimate right of the patent holder to prevent third parties from making, offering for sale and selling the patented product without authorization.[29] The mere fact that the importing country met the conditions to grant a compulsory licence does not justify the breach of the patent holder's rights in a third country. Aside from undermining the basic principle of territoriality of intellectual property rights, the Article 30 proposal would require WTO Members to amend their national legislation.

Moreover, most of the WTO Members agree that the solution to Paragraph 6 shall apply to countries where no patent system exists. In the absence of procedures related to the grant of a compulsory licence in the exporting country, the manufacture and export of patented pharmaceutical products to these patent-free zones would be subject to no limits or constraints. This is not a desirable result.

As several Members noted, there is a requirement for compensation to the patent holder on the granting or issuing of a compulsory licence, and developing and least-developed countries are usually short on resources for such purposes.[30] This is not, however, an argument in favour of the Article 30 solution. In the vast majority of cases, the poorest country will be the importing country–which obviously has less manufacturing capacities. Therefore, the burden of compensation should not fall on the importing country, but rather on the exporting country. Part of the solution would be to avoid double compensation, and to share the cost of compensation to the advantage of the importing country.[31] This is possible only if both the importing and the exporting country need a compulsory licence. Avoidance of double compensation is a technical matter that should be amenable to a quick solution among delegations.

---

[29] This is contested by the Brazil *et al.* submission, *supra*, footnote 21, IP/C/W/355, para. 9.
[30] African Group, *supra*, footnote 18, IP/C/W/351, para. 3.
[31] See developments below in Section v.4.

Some argue that an authoritative interpretation of Article 30 would be in line with the spirit of the "limited" exceptions of Article 30. However, such an interpretation of Article 30 would not conform to the ordinary meaning of the term "limited", particularly when one takes Article 31 into account. The latter Article definitively provides that "other use" without the authorization of the patent holder (i.e. a compulsory licence granted to permit a third party to use the invention) is not a limited exception within the meaning of Article 30.

According to the US proposal, Article 30 was:

"... intended to apply to statutory exceptions already provided for in many countries' laws at the time the TRIPs Agreement was negotiated, situations such as non-commercial experimental use, use aboard vessels temporarily in the territory of a Member, and prior-user rights".[32]

The United States therefore considers that the proposed authoritative interpretation of Article 30 is not a limited exception and, in addition, would both unreasonably conflict with the normal exploitation of a patent and unreasonably prejudice the legitimate interests of the patent owner. At the occasion of the June 2002 meeting of the TRIPs Council, the Brazilian delegate reacted to this US statement, and endorsed the view that the statutory exceptions mentioned by the United States were non-exhaustive examples of the acts that could be included in Article 30, but believed that the provision did not preclude an interpretation along the lines suggested by developing countries.[33] This debate is a good illustration of the legal uncertainty of an Article 30 solution.[34]

The representative of Korea at the TRIPs Council summed up these concerns by stating that:

"... the Council's reliance on Article 30 might erode the *raison d'être* of Article 31 by rendering hollow all its provisions which are designed to balance the rights and obligations of the Members concerned".[35]

---

[32] *Supra,* footnote 22, IP/C/W/358, para. 31.
[33] Statement of the Brazilian delegate at the June 2002 TRIPs Council, in IP/C/M/36, *supra,* footnote 17, para. 39.
[34] A similar problem would exist with respect to an authoritative interpretation of the word "predominant" in Article 31(f) contrary to its ordinary meaning. As mentioned earlier, an authoritative interpretation by a vote is not an appropriate way to change WTO obligations.
[35] In IP/C/M/36, *supra,* footnote 17, para. 84.

Eroding the *raison d'être* of Article 31 provisions would be an infringement of the principle of effectiveness, which has been long recognized in WTO jurisprudence. In the *United States–Reformulated Gasoline* case, the Appellate Body noted that:

> "... one of the corollaries of the 'general rule of interpretation' in the Vienna Convention is that interpretation must give meaning and effect to all the terms of the treaty. An interpreter is not free to adopt a reading that would result in reducing whole clauses or paragraphs of a treaty to redundancy or inutility."[36]

With respect to this principle, Article 30 cannot be interpreted so as to weaken the provisions of Article 31.[37]

Finally, an authoritative interpretation of Article 30 would do little to provide legal security and transparency to those countries seeking to use the solution agreed under Paragraph 6. A Member whose producer wishes to supply Paragraph 6 countries would simply take action to permit production of the needed products on an *ad hoc* basis with no notification or review by other WTO Members. Indeed, Article 30 contains no requirements for notifying the patent holder of use, for establishing particular terms and conditions, for expiration if circumstances change, or for remuneration of the patent holder. It would remain unclear whether the action taken in that Member was permissible until the conclusion of litigation involving the producer and the patent holder in that Member, or the conclusion of a dispute settlement proceeding within the WTO. The resulting legal uncertainty could undermine the commercial viability of the solution.

(c)   *An authoritative interpretation is not the most sustainable solution*

In the long run, an amendment can be changed if it appears to be harmful or does not satisfactorily address the problem raised in Paragraph 6–through another amendment procedure and modification of the revised text–but it is unclear whether an authoritative interpretation can be later repudiated. This would probably require another authoritative interpretation, and the latter in time would prevail.

---

[36] *United States—Standards for Reformulated and Conventional Gasoline*, WT/DS52/AB/R, 20 May 1996, at 23.
[37] Olivier Cattaneo, *The Interpretation of the TRIPs Agreement–Considerations for the WTO Panels and Appellate Body*, 3 J.W.I.P. 5, September 2000, 627.

This lack of flexibility could cause prejudice to the TRIPs Agreement in the long run. First, the adoption of two conflicting authoritative interpretations of the same provisions might lack legal merits and create legal uncertainty. Second, a new cumbersome and time-consuming procedure would have to be initiated, one even less likely to be supported by consensus or a three-quarters majority.

B.   Amendment to Article 31

The second option, which has been put forward by the European Communities, is to amend Article 31 of the TRIPs Agreement.[38] Indeed, the Paragraph 6 problem mainly stemmed from the restriction contained in Article 31(f). An amendment to this particular paragraph would go to the root of the problem and would be a straightforward solution within an existing legal framework.

This amendment could take different forms:

–   deleting Article 31 (f);

–   adding a new paragraph to Article 31; or

–   revising completely Article 31(f), so as as to carve out an exception to the restriction on exports of pharmaceuticals produced under a compulsory licence and needed to address public health problems in another Member.

The three options are not, however, equally likely candidates. Several Members, including the European Communities, have rejected a complete deletion of Article 31(f).[39] The Canadian delegation pointed out that Article 31(f) applied to all patents and not just to pharmaceuticals needed to address public health problems. Also, the basic principle contained in Article 31(f) is still valid, and there is:

---

[38] It should be noted that this is not the only provision of TRIPs that the European Communities seeks to amend. In the context of geographical indications the EC has proposed to extend the scope of Article 23.1 of the Agreement. "… it is proposed to remove the reference in Article 23.1 of the TRIPs Agreement to wines and spirits, and to prevent the use of a geographical indication 'identifying products of the same category' not originating in the place referred to by the geographical indication", *The Extension of the Additional Protection for Geographical Indications to Products other than Wines and Spirits,* available at: «http://europa.eu.int/comm/trade/miti/intell/intel4a.htm».

[39] In IP/C/M/36, *supra,* footnote 17, para. 10.

"... sound political rationale in respect of the territorial application of intellectual property law, national sovereignty and the need to avoid the circumvention of patent rules".[40]

An amendment would thus need to be by addition of a new paragraph to Article 31.

The African Group proposed amending Article 31 so as to expand the definition of domestic market to include regional markets, free-trade areas or customs unions.[41] This broader definition of the domestic market could contribute to economies of scale and partially solve the problem of Paragraph 6. However, it is doubtful that regional trade would suffice to solve the public health problems of countries with insufficient manufacturing capacities. Moreover, rights conferred to the parties under the TRIPS Agreement continue to apply within each free-trade area or customs union.

1. *Positions of Stakeholders*

The European Communities consider that the addition of a new paragraph to Article 31 "offers the best guarantees for a sustainable, balanced and workable solution to the problem raised under Paragraph 6 of the Doha Declaration [on TRIPs and Public Health]".[42] However, they do not exclude an agreement on a temporary arrangement, such as a waiver or a moratorium, pending the entry into force of the additional paragraph to Article 31.

Although in favour of a waiver or a moratorium approach, the United States does not exclude any proposed solution with respect to Article 31 that is expeditious, workable, transparent, sustainable and provides legal certainty.

Similarly, several developing countries in favour of an authoritative interpretation of Article 30 have declared their willingness to consider favourably an amendment to Article 31.

---

[40] *Ibid.,* para. 29.
[41] *Supra,* footnote 18, IP/C/W/351, para. 6(d).
[42] *Paragraph 6 of the Doha Declaration on the TRIPs Agreement and Public Health,* Communication from the European Communities and their Member States, IP/C/W/352, para. 5, 20 June 2002.

2. The Legal Framework

Article 71 of the TRIPs Agreement sets the procedures for reviewing and amending the Agreement. It recognizes that the TRIPs Council may undertake reviews in the light of any relevant new developments which might warrant modification or amendment of the Agreement. Problems currently encountered in developing and least-developed countries in combating HIV/AIDS and other pandemics can be treated as "new developments which might warrant modification or amendment of this Agreement."

However, Article 71.2 deals only with "amendments merely serving the purpose of adjusting to *higher* levels of protection of intellectual property rights achieved, and in force, in other multilateral agreements, and accepted under those agreements by all Members of the WTO". An amendment to TRIPs Article 31, which would consist in deleting or circumventing the obligation contained in paragraph (f), would not meet these requirements. As such, it would be governed by the rules presented in Article X of the WTO Agreement, and could not be adopted by the Ministerial Conference "without further approval acceptance process".[43]

The applicable procedure would be as follows:

– any Member of the WTO or the TRIPs Council could submit to the Ministerial Conference proposals to amend Article 31;

– within ninety days after the submission of this proposal, unless the Ministerial Conference decides upon a longer period, the Ministerial Conference shall decide by consensus, or by a two-thirds majority if consensus is not reached, to submit the proposed amendment to the Members for acceptance.

As the proposed amendment to Article 31 is "of a nature that would alter the rights and obligations of the Members", it would take effect only upon acceptance by two-thirds of the Members and, thereafter, be binding only on the Members that accept it.[44] Furthermore, of those Members that accept the amendment, changes in domestic legislation would be required. Indeed, in many Members, these steps would require approval by the legislature.[45]

[43] Article X:6 of the WTO Agreement.
[44] Article X:3 of the WTO Agreement.
[45] *Proposals on Paragraph 6 of the Doha Declaration on the TRIPs Agreement and Public Health: Thematic Compilation*, IP/C/W/363/Add. 1, at 5.

3.   *An Unsatisfactory Solution*

In light of these procedural requirements, an amendment to Article 31 is not the best way for the TRIPs Council to develop an expeditious solution to the difficulties faced by WTO Members with insufficient or no manufacturing capacities in the pharmaceutical sector.

(a)   *An amendment is not the most expeditious or workable solution*

Looking back at the history of the General Agreement on Tariffs and Trade (GATT), formal amendment of a multilateral trade agreement has always been a cumbersome and time-consuming procedure. Indeed, the creation of the WTO itself is in part due to the difficulties involved in amending the GATT.

In the present case, it could be years before the proposed amendment is accepted by two-thirds of the WTO Members. Moreover, any country that did not positively accept the amendment would continue to operate under the current provisions of Article 31 and would not be bound by the amended text.

Furthermore, the proposal for amendment does not specify whether this amendment would be part of a broader set of changes to the TRIPs Agreement yet to be agreed. Indeed, trade negotiations consist in a balance of concessions. All WTO Members agreed to the current text of the TRIPs Agreement at the Uruguay Round; any amendment that would alter the rights and obligations of the Members would be negotiated with a view to preserving reciprocity. However, some Members might not be ready to make more concessions in other intellectual property areas so as to compensate for the amendment of Article 31. The solution of the Paragraph 6 problem would then be contingent on agreement on other issues, and probably further delayed.

The history of the Paris Convention, with the attempt by the "Group of 77" to amend the Convention with a view to authorizing the exclusive use of compulsory licences, should counsel caution. This initiative resulted in a North–South conflict and in the creation of a deadlock within the WIPO. From the beginning of the 1980s, no progress could be made in the international protection of intellectual property until the TRIPs Agreement was adopted. One can understand that some Members are reluctant to open a Pandora's box and authorize an amendment to TRIPs that could further weaken the Agreement.

Even the proponents of this solution recognize that an amendment could be time-consuming. At the June 2002 TRIPs Council, the delegation of Kenya asked for an assurance that all procedures for amendment would be completed by June 2003 and be binding on all Members.[46] This is not realistic, however, because Members cannot foresee the results of trade negotiations, and an amendment would not necessarily be binding on all Members.[47] Finally, the European Communities consider that an amendment would fully conform to the mandate contained in Paragraph 6, but agree on the need for a temporary arrangement, such as a waiver or a moratorium on disputes, pending the entry into force of the additional paragraph to Article 31.[48] *De facto*, the European Communities thus recognize that a waiver is a more expeditious and workable solution.

(b)   *An amendment is not the most transparent or legally secure solution*

An amendment to Article 31 could provide legal certainty regarding the standard to be applied to all WTO Members, depending on the precision of its drafting. However, it would not provide legal or practical certainty for the private parties that would produce and export pharmaceutical products, or the Members in which those parties reside, unless the TRIPs Council were to establish additional procedures. Instead, parties and Members would only achieve certainty that their actions were consistent with the terms of the agreed-upon solution and the amended TRIPs Agreement standard after litigation involving that entity, or a dispute resolution proceeding involving that Member.

Also, amending Article 31 would not create a transparent mechanism for use of the solution. Members and right holders would not gain advance notice of recourse by other Members to the solution. Instead, the supplier country would take action unilaterally under the legal authority of the amended TRIPs standard. To achieve any transparency in use of the solution, the TRIPs Council would have to develop additional reporting and notification procedures which could operate to postpone the date when the solution would be in peace.

(c)   *An amendment is not the most sustainable solution*

The amendment approach lacks flexibility. An amendment could prove to be either ineffective or seriously harmful in practise–in which

---

[46] In IP/C/M/36, *supra*, footnote 17, para. 6.

[47] See above, text at footnotes 43 and 44; Article X:3 of the WTO Agreement.

[48] *Supra*, footnote 42, IP/C/W/352, para. 7; in IP/C/M/36, *supra*, footnote 17, para. 129.

case another amendment would be needed to correct this situation, and the effective solution to the problem would be further delayed.

C.   A dispute settlement moratorium

A third approach would consist of a dispute settlement moratorium with regard to the non-respect of the restriction under Article 31(f). Such a moratorium would foreclose any WTO dispute against a Member that issues a compulsory licence predominantly for export of a needed pharmaceutical product, consistent with the terms of the agreed-upon solution. WTO Members would agree to refrain in those circumstances from enforcing rights they otherwise would have under Article 31(f).

1.   *Positions of Stakeholders*

In its proposal, the African Group asked for a:

"… comprehensive moratorium on disputes against any Member that takes measures to address the international health crisis in countries with insufficient or no manufacturing capacity".[49]

This moratorium is envisaged to:

"… operate for as long as it would take the international community to effectively combat the diseases, and such a determination could be entrusted to the World Health Organization, mandating it to certify that given diseases in relation to which the moratorium was in force (for instance HIV/AIDS, malaria, tuberculosis) have been successfully contained, particularly in developing and least-developed countries".[50]

However, a moratorium is not envisaged as a solution *per se*, but rather as a supplement to either an amendment to Article 31 or an authoritative interpretation of Article 30.

In their contribution, the European Communities do not see the moratorium as a supplement to the Article 31 option, but rather as a

---

[49] *Supra*, footnote 18, IP/C/W/351, para. 6(g).
[50] Id.

temporary arrangement pending the entry into force of an amendment. They also consider that a moratorium would be a more expeditious temporary arrangement than a waiver.[51]

The Communication from Brazil and the group of developing countries does not consider a moratorium as a "sustainable" or "legally predictable" solution.[52]

To the contrary, the United States considers that a moratorium would be, just as would a waiver, the most appropriate solution to Paragraph 6.[53]

2. *An Unsatisfactory Solution*

(a) *A moratorium is not the most expeditious and workable solution*

If a moratorium were conceived as a voluntary restriction on disputes, it would be the fastest way to implement a solution. Each government would immediately make a policy decision to refrain from enforcing its rights in the circumstances defined in the solution. These individual decisions could eventually be backed by a formal decision of the TRIPs Council, but it would not imply any change of the substantive TRIPs obligations.

However, there is no legal basis for explicitly not applying the dispute settlement mechanism:

> "Whereas the due restraint suggested by developing countries could still be considered as a gentleman's agreement not requiring a specific legal basis, a moratorium on dispute settlement goes beyond such a gentleman's agreement and would *de facto* require an amendment of the TRIPs Agreement, in the absence of the appropriate legal basis".[54]

Other experts have also stressed that it was unclear what procedures should be applied to adopt a moratorium, and whether formal changes to the TRIPs Agreement would be necessary.[55] Article 64.2 of the

---

[51] *Supra*, footnote 42, IP/C/W/352, para. 7.
[52] *Supra*, footnote 21, IP/C/W/355, para. 15.
[53] *Supra*, footnote 22, IP/C/W/358, para. 39.
[54] Roger Kampf, *Patents versus Patients?* 40 Archiv des Völkerrechts 90, 2002, at 125.

TRIPs Agreement is a good illustration of a moratorium on disputes—here limited to non-violation complaints—as an inbuilt provision.

The question is, then, whether a formal decision of the TRIPs Council could be an appropriate legal basis for a moratorium, and whether it could provide substantial security for supplying Members wishing to take actions inconsistent with Article 31(f) under the conditions specified in the solution. Depending on the answers, the process could become less expeditious and workable (e.g. if a formal amendment is required to ensure legal certainty).

(b)   *A moratorium is not the most transparent or legally secure solution*

A moratorium would not provide parties seeking to act under the terms of the solution with certainty that their actions will not give rise to a legal liability. This is because compliance with the terms of the solution could be evaluated only after parties had taken action. For instance, the scope of the moratorium could be contested. Such an approach provides little or no transparency as to when and how Members would act under the terms of the solution. In short, additional procedures would have to be devised to provide transparency in use and operation of the solution.

A major inconvenience of the moratorium option is that the Member would still be in breach of its WTO obligations. At the June 2002 TRIPs Council, the representative of Hungary:

> "… questioned what would happen at the level of the national legal system and whether the moratorium would affect the ability of companies to start legal proceedings at the national level to protect their patents. If that were the case, he questioned whether WTO Members could ensure that such a moratorium was respected by companies and whether… Members should change their patent laws for the period while the solution under Article 31 was being considered to make sure that they were legally correct."[56]

The representative of Brazil also expressed the same concern and stated that:

> "… the moratorium approach offered an expeditious response to the problem posed by Paragraph 6, but not a solution since it would

---

[55] Carlos M. Correa, *Implications of the Doha Declaration on the TRIPs Agreement and Public Health*, WHO, 2002, at 29.
[56] In IP/C/M/36, *supra*, footnote 17, para. 68.

not be straightforward enough either to influence those potential exporting countries to change their legislation, or to permit protection for export, or to induce generic manufacturers to invest in creating or increasing export capacity. "[57]

(c)   A moratorium is not the most sustainable solution

A moratorium, absent any formal and substantive change of the Members' rights and obligations, is based on a policy decision. As such, it is subject to the fluctuation of policy objectives and cannot be considered as a sustainable solution in the long run.

IV.   WAIVER AS A PREFERRED OPTION

None of the first three options–authoritative interpretation of Article 30, amendment of Article 31, moratorium on disputes–meet cumulatively and satisfactorily the criteria of expeditiousness, workability, transparency, sustainability and legal certainty. Therefore, we examine a fourth option: the waiver approach.

The only "TRIPs barrier" to providing a solution under Paragraph 6 is Article 31(f). A waiver would allow a Member to grant a compulsory licence to a producer within its territory to produce and export a patented pharmaceutical to another Member facing public health problems but lacking sufficient manufacturing capacity in the pharmaceutical sector.

Waivers are an existing mechanism built into the GATT/WTO regime to allow Members an exemption from legal obligations under existing WTO rules in "exceptional circumstances" such as those singled out in Paragraph 6 of the Declaration.[58] Waivers have been used in virtually all of the WTO Agreements and have a long history in GATT practise. In particular, waivers of the most-favoured-nation obligation of the GATT have played a major role in addressing the specific needs of developing countries and establishing a special and differential treatment in their favour. For example, waivers were granted to developed countries in order to allow the establishment of general systems of preferences (GSPs), which conceded lower tariffs to developing countries participating in the system.[59]

---

[57] *Ibid.*, para. 158.
[58] An explicit reference to "exceptional circumstances" is found in Article IX:4 of the WTO Agreement.
[59] The "enabling clause" of the GATT is found in Article XXV.

The use of a waiver to solve the developing countries' problem of access to medicines is therefore logical.

A.   Positions of stakeholders

Several Members, including the United States, Canada, Australia, Korea, New Zealand and, most recently, Lesotho,[60] have argued in favour of a waiver approach. They consider this option as being the one best suited for dealing expeditiously with exceptional circumstances. In particular, the representative of the Kingdom of Lesotho emphasized the need to deploy a waiver solution"enabling developing Members to address public health problems" without creating new obligations in addition to those already contained in the Agreement.[61]

The European Communities are in favour of either a moratorium or a waiver, but as a temporary arrangement only.[62] They fear that the waiver option may fall short of providing the type of sustainable and legally secure solution that the European Communities are aiming for and that an amendment would provide.

Other Members, however, do not consider a waiver as a solution. Depending upon the conditions attached to it, some Members have even qualified this solution as "unacceptable".[63]

B   A preferred option

1.   *Waiver is the Most Expeditious and Workable Solution*

In contrast to most other solutions, and in particular to an amendment, a waiver procedure could be defined and adopted by the end of 2002. Only a moratorium on disputes could be adopted and take effect in a similar time-frame.

Some have expressed concern that requiring Members to seek waivers on a case-by-case basis would impose undesirable procedural burdens on Members in situations that demand rapid action. However,

---

[60] *Paragraph 6 of Doha Ministerial Declaration on TRIPs and Public Health: Statement by the Delegation of the Kingdom of Lesotho,* September 2002 TRIPs Council.
[61] *Id.*
[62] At the June 2002 TRIPs Council, Norway also proposed the adoption of a waiver as an interim arrangement.
[63] See, *e.g.* the intervention of the Venezuelan delegate at the June 2002 TRIPs Council, in IP/C/M/36, *supra,* footnote 17, para. 165.

these concerns can be addressed by establishing an efficient and transparent procedure for handling such waivers in the TRIPs Council.

Waivers can be granted in a very short time-frame. In the case of the solution under consideration, Members will have already decided on the circumstances for which a waiver can be granted. This will enable the TRIPS Council to establish an expedited procedure for granting waivers to qualifying Members (i.e. the Members that will be supplying pharmaceutical products to the country in need). Requirements for a waiver can be defined in advance, which will make the "process" in the TRIPS Council a simple review of compliance with those requirements. Since the procedure would ensure that the waiver would be granted if the conditions are met, a decision could be approved in a single TRIPs Council Meeting, and with a formal approval by the General Council in its ordinary course of business.[64] Generally, the adoption by the General Council of a waiver that has already been approved by a subsidiary body happens rapidly. Waivers under such a procedure could thus be processed and granted within a few months of being requested. This time-frame would be entirely compatible with the situation being addressed in the solution, and with the time-frame in which a producer would operate (i.e. to prepare for and begin production).[65]

The recent decision by the WTO Members to extend until 2016 the transition period for least-developed countries to provide patent protection for pharmaceuticals is the best illustration of the use of a waiver as an expeditious and workable solution to tackle serious public health problems.[66] On 27 June 2002, the TRIPs Council adopted a recommendation to grant a waiver to least-developed countries pursuant to the instructions contained in Paragraph 7 of the Declaration and, on 8 July 2002, the General Council approved the decision. Once the Members had agreed on the terms and conditions of the waiver, only about one month was needed to grant the waiver. No other solution could have been so expeditious.

---

[64] According to Article IX:3 of the WTO Agreement, a waiver concerning the TRIPs Agreement shall be submitted initially to the TRIPs Council for consideration during a time period which shall not exceed ninety days. Then, on the basis of the report of the TRIPs Council, the Ministerial Conference, or the acting General Council, shall consider the request within ninety days.

[65] Of course a waiver would only be necessary in instances where the product to be exported is patented in the country of export. If the inventor or his assignee has not obtained a patent on his invention, there is no problem with any producer manufacturing and exporting the product.

[66] *Supra*, footnote 4, IP/C/W/359.

Usually, where no consensus can be reached, waivers shall be adopted by a three-fourths majority of the Members.[67] A consensus or a large majority is easier to reach in the context of the adoption of a waiver because it is subject to later review and possible modification or termination. Unlike an amendment or an authoritative interpretation, a waiver does not permanently alter the balance of rights and obligations of the Members.

2. Waiver is the Most Legally Secure Solution

A waiver of the obligations of Article 31(f) provides the most legally secure way to allow a producer in one country to supply products to a country needing them under the solution of Paragraph 6. A waiver offers legal protection for any measure of a Member taken consistent with the terms of the waiver, and forecloses any legal challenge based on the legal provisions that were waived. In other words, a waiver would provide specific advance authorization for a Member and a producer to take actions that would otherwise violate the TRIPs Agreement and patent rights that exist in the Member.

Other options do not provide this degree of legal and practical certainty to the Member and to the private entity that will be producing and exporting pharmaceutical products under the terms of the solution. Certainty under other solutions could only be provided at the end of litigation involving the patent or at the end of the dispute settlement process. For example, an amendment would redefine the standard governing the circumstances when a compulsory licence for exports could be granted. Whether licences granted in any particular circumstances met the conditions of the solution of the new WTO standard could not be known until after a WTO dispute or litigation. Similarly, a moratorium or other less explicit mechanism would not provide advance approval to the parties to the solution. Each of these other options creates significant uncertainty for parties involved in the solution.

Canada also noticed that the waiver approach:

"... provided considerable legal certainty as it was an established mechanism which would clearly delineate some of the provisions that the Council (for TRIPs) needed to consider".[68]

---

[67] Article IX:3 of the WTO Agreement.
[68] Statement of the representative of Canada at the June 2002 TRIPs Council, in IP/C/M/36, *supra*, footnote 17, para. 27.

3.   *Waiver is the Most Sustainable Solution*

The most recurrent criticism directed at the waiver option is that it could not be a "sustainable" solution.

Waivers can last as long as Members deem necessary. Although the decision to grant a waiver must state the date on which the waiver will terminate, the duration of a waiver is not limited.[69] Moreover, Members can decide to extend the initial period for as long as they want. Many examples exist of multi-year waivers that have been recently granted under the various WTO Agreements.[70]

A TRIPs Council procedure for granting waivers in the particular circumstances defined in the solution could be adopted with an indefinite duration.[71] Other procedures adopted by the TRIPs Council have no "expiration" date, such as the procedures governing notifications. The solution would thus remain available to any Member if and when a circumstance justifying its use arose. Once that occurred, the TRIPs Council could expeditiously act to grant a waiver to a qualifying Member. The availability of a waiver under a TRIPs Council procedure would thus be as "sustainable" as an amendment to the Agreement.

Some could argue that both the annual review and the possibility to modify or terminate the waiver are a source of legal uncertainty in the long run. However, these procedures are aimed at verifying that the exceptional circumstances justifying the waiver still exist. Under unchanged circumstances and continued compliance with any terms or conditions, the waiver could be extended indefinitely.

In the long run, a flexible solution is often more sustainable than a rigid one. A waiver system would enable the TRIPs Council to efficiently monitor use and operation of the solution. In light of experience with the new system, conditions attached to a waiver could be adjusted quickly.[72] This adjustment could take place on the basis of the annual review. If,

---

[69] Article IX:4 of the WTO Agreement.
[70] As of January 1995, there had been 115 original waiver decisions under Article XXV:5 of GATT 1947, as well as many other waiver decisions extending or amending a prior waiver decision: *supra*, footnote 45, IP/C/W/363/Add. 1, citing Analytical Index, *Guide to GATT Law and Practice*, WTO, 1995, at 882-906.
[71] The procedure is to be distinguished from the waiver itself.
[72] On the basis of the annual review, Members can modify the waiver: Article IX:4 of the WTO Agreement.

however, a single modification of the conditions attached to the waiver were not sufficient, and if Members decided to turn to another solution, they could always terminate the waiver.

Finally, reviews of waivers must be conducted on an annual basis. These reviews should not be perceived as a "bureaucratic" burden,[73] but rather as a simple way of enhancing the transparency of the waiver process. Some developing countries have raised concerns that the waiver could be terminated. But in reality, the review process is conducted by consensus in respect to obligations, subject to a transition period, and a majority is needed to extend, modify or terminate a multi-year waiver following expiration of the transition period.[74] It would thus be difficult for one country to overturn a waiver once granted, unless a consensus or majority agreed that the terms of the waiver were violated or the need for the waiver had expired. Moreover, these annual reviews ensure that the "exceptional circumstances" justifying the waiver still exist, and that the terms and conditions attached to the waiver have been met.[75]

4.   *Waiver is the Most Transparent Solution*

A waiver would provide the greatest amount of transparency in comparison to the other options under discussion. To begin with, each decision to grant a waiver shall state the exceptional circumstances justifying the decision, the terms and conditions governing the application of the waiver, and the date on which the waiver shall terminate.[76]

The requirements for a waiver would be defined in advance. The only decision for the TRIPs Council would be to determine whether the circumstances defined in the solution exist with respect to the Member seeking the waiver.

In practise, a waiver, by its very nature, involves a specific request made to the WTO by a Member wishing to be relieved of its obligations under Article 31(f) of the TRIPs Agreement. Thus, the process incorporates notice to interested WTO Members.[77] This conforms to the requirements of

---

[73] Correa, *supra*, footnote 55, at 29.
[74] See Article IX.3, footnote 4, of the WTO Agreement.
[75] Article IX:4 of the WTO Agreement.
[76] *Id.*
[77] It may be useful to notify the right-holder as well in order to provide an opportunity to offer better commercial terms in lieu of issuance of a compulsory licence pursuant to the waiver.

Article 31(b), which states that even in situations of national emergency or other circumstances of extreme urgency, the right holder shall be notified as soon as reasonably practicable of the unauthorized use of the patented product.

V. REMAINING ISSUES: TERMS AND CONDITIONS OF THE WAIVER SOLUTION

Whatever approach the Members eventually agree on, much of the success or failure of the solution recommended by the TRIPs Council to the General Council will depend upon the establishment of adequate terms and conditions to accompany such a solution.

A balance should be found, and unrelated conditions should not be attached to the granting of any waiver. A strictly objective and permissive approach, based on clear criteria, such as lack of, or insufficiency of, local manufacturing capacity in the pharmaceutical sector should be used.[78]

The following discussion provides some examples of issues to be addressed so as to secure the effectiveness of the eventual agreed-upon solution.

A. Which members would be allowed to benefit from the waiver?

One of the most debated questions related to the conditions of application of the adopted solution is whether the solution would also apply to developed countries. The question of Members' qualification is actually twofold. First, which Members facing public health crises as described in Paragraph 1 of the Declaration would qualify for importing these products? And, second, which Members would qualify for exporting these products?

Turning first to the question of potential importers, the Communication from Brazil (on behalf of a group of developing countries) clearly states that:

"... *any* WTO Member could face difficulties in making effective use of compulsory licences due to insufficient or no manufacturing

---

[78] Statement of the representative of New Zealand to the June 2002 TRIPs Council, in IP/C/M/36, *supra*, footnote 17, para. 94.

capacities in the pharmaceutical sector. Therefore, the solutions envisaged by the TRIPs Council to the problem recognized in Paragraph 6 should *not* exclude specific categories of countries." (emphasis added).[79]

The Communication from the United Arab Emirates shares the same views.[80] Two arguments are put forward. First, developed countries can have insufficient or no manufacturing capacities in the pharmaceutical sector due to lack of economies of scale or other conditions for viable economic manufacturing (size matters rather than the level of development). Second, developed countries can face public health crises, relating for instance to HIV/AIDS. Most NGOs support this interpretation of the Declaration, in line with the mandate "to promote access to *medicines for all*" (emphasis added),[81] and call for the application of the solution to "both rich and poor countries ... countries with large or small domestic markets, and... countries with different levels of technological development."[82]

On the other hand, the Communication from the European Communities advocates limiting potential importers to those developing and least-developed countries contemplated in Paragraph 1 of the Declaration as a means of addressing public health crises afflicting these countries.[83] Similarly, the Communication from the United States clearly recognizes as potential importers "developing and least-developed countries" afflicted with grave public health problems.[84] These positions were also supported by Canada at the TRIPs Council.[85]

Recognizing that the Declaration was principally directed at the needs of developing and least-developed countries facing public health crises, most Members agree that least-developed countries should qualify automatically as recipient countries without any further examination as to eligibility. Thus, assuming all least-developed countries are eligible, the quickest way forward might be a delineation of those developing countries

---

[79] *Supra,* footnote 21, IP/C/W/355, para. 4.
[80] *Supra,* footnote 20, IP/C/W/354, para. 11.
[81] Paragraph 4 of the Declaration, *supra,* footnote 1.
[82] Letter addressed to the Members of the TRIPs Council in the name of *Médecins sans Frontières,* Consumer Project on Technology, Oxfam, Global Access Project, Third World Network and Essential Action, 28 January 2002.
[83] *Supra,* footnote 42, IP/C/W/352, para. 12.
[84] *Supra,* footnote 22, IP/C/W/358, paras. 10–13.
[85] In IP/C/M/36, *supra,* footnote 17, para. 26.

lacking capacity in the pharmaceutical sector and thus qualifying as importers.

Turning, then, to the question of potential exporters, the Communication from the United States recognizes a unique role for those developing or least-developed countries with production capacity as possible exporters under a compulsory licence. Here, the Communication of the United States looks beyond Paragraph 6 of the Declaration to broader questions of technology transfer. According to the United States, limiting exporter status to developing and least-developed countries presents an opportunity "under the solution for developing and least-developed countries to expand their pharmaceutical production capacity".[86] This approach preserves current supply options and would encourage investment in developing and least-developed countries in order to supply local needs or, in particular, those of least-developed countries. It is also consistent with Paragraph 7 of the Declaration, which reaffirms the commitment of developed countries to promote and encourage technology transfer. Finally, this approach is compatible with developed countries' initiatives to offer drugs at severely discounted prices to address the situation of developing and least-developed countries, and to engage in aid programmes.

The Communication of the European Communities is silent on this point.[87] However, the Communications of Brazil, and Kenya (on behalf of the African Group), stress the need to develop a Paragraph 6 solution that at the same time promotes Paragraph 7 objectives to encourage technology transfer to least-developed country Members pursuant to TRIPs Article 66.2.[88] A Paragraph 6 approach that recognizes and encourages South-South solutions to the problem of insufficient manufacturing capacity would be a remarkable achievement by the TRIPs Council in that it would add a new dimension to the generally North-South focus of technology transfer discussions in that body. The US proposal–which favours developing country pharmaceutical producers and exporters–

---

[86] *Supra*, footnote 22, IP/C/W/358, para. 15.

[87] At least one EU official has confirmed that the Declaration should be read as placing the "needs and interests of developing and least-developed country Members at the heart of the further work programme of the WTO": Paul Vandoren, *Médicaments sans Frontiéres? Clarification of the Relationship between TRIPs and Public Health resulting from the WTO Doha Ministerial Declaration*, 5 J.W.I.P. 1, January 2002, 5, at p. 12. Aligning implementation of paragraph 6 of the Declaration with important policies of technology transfer would certainly be consistent with such a reading.

[88] See Brazil *et al.*, *supra*, footnote 21, IP/C/W/355. 1.3, endnote 1; African Group, *supra*, footnote 18, IP/C/W/351, para. 6(e).

focuses not only on concerns of public health but also on questions of manufacturing capacity and economic development. The view shared by many delegations that Paragraph 6 should not be implemented in a vacuum but must take into account the objectives of technology transfer and developing pharmaceutical manufacturing capacity could readily form the basis for discussion in the context of a "waiver" approach to implementing the Declaration.

A related question concerns the criterion of capacity; this was not defined in Paragraph 6 of the Declaration. The WTO Secretariat has already prepared a Note providing available information on the manufacturing capacity for medicines in different countries.[89] A waiver approach could contribute to avoiding disputes related to the qualification of benefiting Members. Based on a case-by-case analysis, the grant of a waiver is equivalent to the recognition of the benefiting Member's qualification. Nevertheless, in order to be expeditious, the procedure to grant a waiver should include clear criteria of qualification.

Finally, it should be added that all Members agree that the solution envisaged by the TRIPS Council should also apply to countries where no patents exist.

B.   What would be the product scope of the solution?

Whatever the solution, Members will have to clearly spell out its product scope. Controversies over this question are reflected in the vocabulary used by different Members to qualify the products to be covered by the solution; while most Members refer to "pharmaceutical products", the Communication from the group of developing countries (Brazil) extends the scope of the solution to cover all "public health related products".

A layman's definition of pharmaceutical products would include medicines as final products only. A very broad definition of pharmaceutical products would also include active substances necessary for the manufacturing of the medicines, processes, surgical, therapeutic and diagnostic methods, diagnostic kits and medical equipment. At present, there is no agreement amongst the WTO Members as to a reasonable definition of pharmaceutical products. While the United States suggested that the TRIPs Council should not try, at this stage, to precisely define the

---

[89] *Supra,* footnote 23, IP/C/W/345.

meaning of pharmaceutical products, Brazil declared that there should be, at the very least, "constructive ambiguity" on this issue.[90] In any event, the issue can be resolved on a case-by-case basis in the context of individual waiver applications.

Another related question is whether the reference to some specific epidemics in the Declaration implies that the scope of the solution to Paragraph 6 should be limited to pharmaceutical products targeted at these epidemics. Most Members agree that the product coverage is not limited to the listed epidemics. Indeed, the reference to "other epidemics" in the Declaration suggests that this list was meant to be illustrative only. Furthermore, such a list does not pre-judge each Member's right to determine what constitutes a national emergency.[91]

Nevertheless, several Members, including the European Communities and the United States in their respective contributions, have confined the product scope to pharmaceutical products needed to deal with public health problems afflicting developing and least-developed countries.[92] In other words, the product scope would not include pharmaceuticals needed to deal with public health problems afflicting essentially developed countries. Others have argued that the Declaration covered:

> "... *any* 'public health problem', including those that may be derived from diseases that affect the population in developing *as well as developed countries*, such as asthma or cancer" (emphasis added).[93]

This interpretation of the product coverage would probably go beyond the intended scope of the Declaration. These differing views reveal, however, that the question of product coverage is closely related to the previous question of country qualification. WTO Members will need to bridge these differences and draw a common-sense line around those products to be governed by Paragraph 6, particularly in light of its express concern for developing and least-developed countries.

---

[90] See the statement of the US representative at the June 2002 TRIPs Council, in IP/C/M/36, *supra*, footnote 17, para. 130; and the statement of the representative from Brazil, *ibid.*, para. 155.
[91] Kampf, *supra*, footnote 54, at 106.
[92] *Supra*, footnote 42, IP/C/W/352, para. 11; *supra*, footnote 22, IP/C/W/358, para. 10.
[93] Correa, *supra*, footnote 55, at 5.

C.   How would trade diversion and abuse be prevented?

A major concern of most Members is avoiding trade diversion. The objective is to ensure that the medicines produced in a Member's territory are not diverted from the market for which they were intended, either by being diverted to other markets or by leaking onto the domestic market of the exporting Member. The prevention of trade diversion is in the interests of all, and not least of the importing country, because such abuses dry up the supply of pharmaceutical products at strongly reduced prices to those in need.

In line with the proposal of the European Communities, a waiver, or any other solution, would have to specify that:

(i)   the products manufactured on the basis of the authorization should not be put into circulation on the market of the country of production, but should, in their entirety, be exported to the Member(s) designated by the solution (and not to any other country);

(ii) the products will be offered for sale, sold or distributed solely in the Member(s) designated by the solution and not be re-exported from that (those) Member(s);

(iii) the Member granting the licence for export has taken all necessary regulatory and administrative measures to ensure that condition (i) is effectively respected; and

(iv) the importing Member has taken all reasonable and necessary regulatory and/or administrative measures to ensure that condition (ii) is effectively respected.[94]

A waiver is perfectly adapted to these constraints because the exporting country alone would have its obligations under Article 31(f) waived. The importing country would still be subject to the discipline of Article 31(f), and would be subject to litigation or WTO dispute settlement if it re-exported products imported and used on its territory under a compulsory licence. If the waiver solution were adopted, the above provisions (ii) and (iv) would become obsolete, except in the case where the product is not patented in the importing country.

---

[94] *Supra,* footnote 42, IP/C/W/352, para. 14.

D. How would the right holder be involved and adequate compensation determined?

Paragraph 5(c) of the Doha Declaration on TRIPs and Public Health states that:

> "Each Member has the right to determine what constitutes a national emergency or other circumstances of extreme urgency, it being understood that public health crises, including those relating to HIV/AIDS, tuberculosis, malaria and other epidemics, can represent a national emergency or other circumstances of extreme urgency."

In other words, Members referred to in Paragraph 6 will be able to exempt themselves from the obligation to make efforts, within a reasonable period of time, to obtain authorization of use from the patent holder on reasonable commercial terms and conditions. In such exceptional circumstances, WTO Members remain obligated to notify, as soon as reasonably practicable, the unauthorized use of the product to the right holder.[95] In addition, the WTO Member is obligated to provide compensation to the right holder.[96]

As mentioned earlier, a waiver approach is perfectly compatible with this notification requirement. Notwithstanding this, several Members suggested that patent holders be more involved in the solution to the problem of access to medicines for Members with insufficient or no manufacturing capacities. For example, according to the Communication of the European Communities:

> "… it will be crucial to enable the patent holder to make a proposal to rapidly solve the issue by making sustainable voluntary licensing and strongly reduced pricing offers, though without unduly delaying the procedure leading to the possible granting of a licence".[97]

---

[95] Article 31(b) of the TRIPs Agreement.

[96] Article 31(h) provides that: "…the right holder shall be paid adequate remuneration in the circumstances of each case, taking into account the economic value of the authorization". It may be necessary for donors to provide this renumeration in the case of least-developed or developing countries facing public health crises.

[97] *Supra,* footnote 42, IP/C/W/352, para. 16.

Greater involvement of the patent holder would be facilitated by the waiver approach. The short period of time between the notification to the TRIPs Council of a request for a waiver and the adoption of the waiver by the General Council could be used by the right holder to make an offer to supply the relevant products at reduced prices. It would then be up to the Member without manufacturing capacity to decide whether the offer by the original manufacturer is sufficient to meet its needs, or whether the country with a pending waiver offers better conditions. This competitive process would be transparent, and increase the chances of the importing country getting a better deal.

VI.   CONCLUSION

In this article, four options put forward by WTO Members in the TRIPs Council to address the problem raised in Paragraph 6 of the Declaration have been reviewed. In the light of criteria selected by the Members to ensure an effective solution to the problem, a waiver with regard to Article 31(f) is the only available legal mechanism which will provide, simultaneously, guarantees of expeditiousness, workability, transparency, sustainability and legal certainty.

The importance of the terms and conditions attached to such a waiver have also been stressed, concluding that a waiver would be the most suitable legal framework for a clear presentation of these attached terms and conditions.

A waiver is not only expeditious, but also a sustainable long-term solution. It is, however, without prejudice to the right of WTO Members to eventually agree on an amendment, if they deem it useful, and if they reach a consensus on the terms of such an amendment.

The main point at this stage of the discussion, with regard to the short deadline for the submission of a solution, is to be realistic. Multilateral trade negotiations are not the exclusive prerogative of lawyers, and the WTO is still an instrument of diplomacy. Both the Article 30 authoritative interpretation and the moratorium on disputes are strictly rejected by key major players of the multilateral trading system. Also, if a procedure to amend the TRIPs Agreement were initiated, no one could anticipate the consequences of the re-opening of a Pandora's box, and the time such negotiations would take. Thus, a waiver is not only the best solution from a legal perspective, but also from an economic and political standpoint.

Finally, it is important to recall that a waiver, or any other solution eventually agreed upon, is not intended to be a miracle cure for all public health problems. It is only a response to the challenge identified in Paragraph 6, namely, how to exercise a compulsory licence in those developing and least-developed countries with insufficient or no manufacturing capacities in the pharmaceutical sector. Meeting the mandate of Paragraph 6 of the Doha Declaration on the TRIPs Agreement and Public Health should not slow down other initiatives aimed at pharmaceutical innovation, investment and technology transfer in developing countries–or, for that matter, broader public health and development priorities. Political will and massive efforts such as the Global Fund for AIDS, Tuberculosis and Malaria go to the roots of the problem: adequate financing of the health systems and the development of stable health infrastructures. The TRIPs Agreement is not the problem, but part of the solution.

6. DIRECT TAXATION AND THE WTO:
IN OR OUT?

One of the issues addressed in this contribution was whether a direct taxation measure could be caught by WTO rules on subsidies. It concluded that GATT rules on export subsidies cover direct taxation measures taking the form of tax benefits relating to income from international trade transactions. This issue was subsequently faced in the WTO dispute on the US so-called Foreign Sales Corporation. In its report, the WTO Appellate Body upheld a WTO panel's finding that the US FSC measure constituted a prohibited subsidy under the WTO Agreement on Subsidies and Countervailing Measures (WTO/DS108/ AB/R of 24 February 2000).

I. INTRODUCTION

Even more than the previous round of multilateral trade negotiations, the Uruguay Round has made policy-makers aware of the fact that, as classical barriers to trade are brought down, other governmental measures that were only potential barriers to trade become effective ones. For instance, when a high tariff or a quota which impeded imports is removed, importers are still faced with technical regulations in the importing country. International economists call this the "reef theory": the level of traditional barriers to trade is compared to the sea level, and other barriers to trade as reefs; reefs that did not impede navigation at a given sea level become obstacles as the sea level is lowered.

Negotiations about trade necessarily shifted from trade to trade-related matters. This concern explains the conclusion in the earlier Tokyo Round of an agreement on subsidies, replaced by the Uruguay Round Agreement on Subsidies and Countervailing Measures (hereinafter the WTO Subsidies Code). It also explains the conclusion in the Uruguay Round of a series of agreements extending the disciplines of the General Agreement on Tariffs and Trade (hereinafter the GATT) to measures other than the classic trade measures such as trade aspects of investment measures; i.e., the Agreement on Trade-related Investment Measures (the TRIMs), and of intellectual property rights, i.e. the Agreement on Trade-related Aspects of Intellectual Property Rights (the TRIPs). It likewise led to the qualified extension of the GATT disciplines to trade in services, i.e.

the General Agreement on Trade in Services (the GATS).[1] There was however no TIFFs (Trade Impeding Fiscal Features) Agreement!

The link between indirect taxation and trade in goods has long been recognized and addressed in the GATT. All taxes in connection with importation or exportation of goods are subject to the most-favored-nation treatment (Art. I). Article II provides that products with respect to which a contracting party has bound its custom duties "shall also be exempted from all other duties or charges imposed on or in connection with the importation in excess of those imposed on the date of this Agreement". Article III (2) requires that imported products not be "subject, directly or indirectly, to internal taxes or internal charges of any kind in excess of those applied, directly or indirectly, to like domestic products"; no contracting party may "otherwise apply internal taxes or other internal charges to imported or domestic products" so as to afford protection to domestic production.

The GATT contains in Article XVI a number of obligations with respect to subsidies: an obligation to notify all subsidies which operate to increase exports or to reduce imports (paragraph 1); an obligation not to use an export subsidy on a primary product which results in the "contracting party having more than an equitable share of the world export trade in that product" (paragraph 3); the obligation not to grant an export subsidy on any product other than a primary product which results in an export price lower than the comparable price for a like product on the domestic market of the exporting country (paragraph 4).

The Tokyo Round of Multilateral Trade Negotiations led to the Agreement on Interpretation and Application of Articles VI, XVI and XXIII of the General Agreement on Tariffs and Trade (hereinafter: the GATT Round Subsidies Code).[2] This Agreement does not define what is meant by "subsidy". However, the annexed Illustrative List of export subsidies mentions exemptions or remissions of indirect taxes on exports (items g) and h)) in amounts in excess of those borne by the like product when destined for domestic consumption. These indirect taxes are defined as "sales, excise, turnover, value added, franchise, stamp, transfer, inventory and equipment taxes, border taxes and all taxes other than direct taxes and import charges".

---

[1] The Marrakesh Agreement of 15th April 1994 establishing the World Trade Organization and the agreements and associated legal agreements included in its annexes, and i.a. the GATS, the TRIPs and the GATT in its 1994 version, are published in The World Trade Organization, *The Results of the Uruguay Round of Multilateral Trade Negotiations The Legal Texts* (Geneva, 1995). These agreements are also published in the Official Journal of the European Communities as attachments to the decision of the Council of the European Union concluding the agreements reached in the Uruguay Round (OJ 1994 L 336/1).
[2] GATT, BISD 26S/56.

The new agreement on subsidies resulting from the Uruguay Round and which replaces the GATT Subsidies Code, the WTO Agreement on Subsidies and Countervailing Measures,[3] refers in its Annex I to exemptions, remissions and indirect taxes, using the same language as the GATT Subsidies Code.

These various GATT rules on *indirect* taxation are fairly well developed and have been analyzed in GATT reports,[4] in dispute settlement proceedings[5] and in the literature.[6] Although they raise interesting issues and leave certain questions open they are left aside here.

Provisions dealing with *direct* taxation appear much more infrequently. Yet, the phenomenon identified as the "reef theory" also occurs in the area of direct taxation. The increase in the general level of the abolition of non-tax barriers increases the potency of taxation as a distorting feature of international trade and conversely its susceptibility of international trade.[7] The paucity of references to direct taxation may be explained by the wish of the GATT Contracting Parties, subsequently the WTO Members, to protect their fiscal sovereignty, which means discretion to raise revenue and to use taxation as a policy instrument.

Be that as it may, the tension between direct taxation measures of WTO Members and the reciprocal obligations entered into under the various WTO agreements is bound to be increasingly felt and to give rise to legal arguments. This contribution examines whether these agreements address direct taxation and some of the issues to which they may give rise.

II.   DIRECT TAXATION IN THE GATT AND RELATED AGREEMENTS

A.   GATT clauses

The GATT contains no express reference to direct taxes. Article III, which lays down the national treatment obligation, is generally

---

[3] *Op. cit. supra* n. 1 at 264.

[4] *For example, Working Party Report on Border Tax Adjustments, GATT, BISD 18S/97.*

[5] References to various GATT panel reports can be found in WTO, *GATT Analytical Index, Guide to GATT Law and Practice*_2 Vol. (Geneva, 1995).

[6] A good overview with many references to cases and literature appears in P. Demaret and R. Stewardson "Border Tax Adjustments under GATT and EC Law and General Implications for Environmental Taxes" 28 *JWT* 5 (1994).

[7] A.M. Qureshi, "Trade-Related Aspects of International Taxation. A New WTO Code of Conduct?" 30 *JWT* 161 (1996) with references to literature.

interpreted by the literature to cover only indirect taxes.[8] Although individual contracting parties have claimed that direct taxes having discriminatory effects on the sale of their products were contrary to Article III,[9] there has never been a definitive and authoritative interpretation on this point by the GATT as an international organization.

It was, however, recognized fairly early on that the GATT clauses mentioned above on subsidies (Art. XVI) could cover direct taxation measures. In 1960, a number of contracting parties accepted a "Declaration Giving Effect to the Provisions of Article XVI:4"[10] on the basis of a report of a working party which was adopted by the Contracting Parties.[11] This report listed practices generally to be considered as subsidies within the meaning of Article XVI:4 of the GATT. This list included: "the remission, calculated in relation to exports, of direct taxes or social welfare charges on industrial or commercial enterprises" (item (c)) and "the exemption, in respect of exported goods, of charges or taxes, other than charges in connection with importation or indirect taxes levied at one or several stages on the same goods if sold for internal consumption …" (item (d)).

The issue of GATT compatibility of direct taxes of several contracting parties arose in relation to the prohibition of export subsidies in Article XVI:4.

B.   The DISC and related cases

In 1973, the EC initiated dispute settlement proceedings in the GATT against the US claiming that the US Domestic International Sales Corporation (hereinafter, the DISC) legislation violated Article XVI:4 of the GATT, in that it granted relief from direct taxes by favorable treatment of the export earnings of companies qualifying as DISCs (effectively domestic subsidiary companies involved in export sales activities).[12] The US counterattacked by initiating dispute settlement proceedings against Belgium, France and the Netherlands, claiming that their income tax laws resulted in at least the same tax subsidy to their exporters.[13] These laws

---

[8] K.W. Dam, *The GATT: Law and International Organization* 124–125 (U. Chicago Press, Chicago, 1970); J.H. Jackson, *World Trade and the Law of GATT* 302 (Bobbs Merill, Indranapolis, 1969); E. McGovern, *International Trade Regulation. The GATT, the United States and the European Community* 248 (Globefield Press, Exeter, 1986).
[9] See the cases mentioned by Qureshi *supra* n. 7 at 171
[10] GATT, BISD 9S/32.
[11] GATT, BISD 9S/185
[12] For a description of the DISC legislation, see the Report of the Panel, GATT, BISD 23S/98.
[13] For a description of the Belgian, French, and Dutch legislation, see the Panel Reports, GATT BISD 23S/135 (Belgium), BISD 23S/125 (France) and BISD 23S/145 (the Netherlands).

follow the "territoriality principle" according to which the taxing of residents is limited to income from activities within the State.

The findings of the panel in these four cases have been well analyzed in the literature.[14] They only need to be summarized here.

With respect to DISC, the panel found that "in some cases" it had effects which were not in accordance with the obligations of the US under Article XVI :4 of the GATT, i.e. the deferral of tax in that it did not attract the interest component of the tax normally levied for late or deferred payment, the deduction of certain shipping and air transport costs and the provision allowing 10% of export promotion expenses to be assigned as a deductible expense to DISC.

With respect to the Belgian tax legislation, the panel noted that the particular application of the territoriality principle allowed some part of the export activities, belonging to an economic process originating in Belgium, to be outside of the scope of Belgian taxes, such as partial exemption from direct taxes where different tax treatment in different countries resulted in a smaller tax bill in aggregate being paid on exports than on sales in the home market and flexible application of the arms-length pricing rules. It considered these to be export subsidies prohibited by Article XVI:4 of the GATT.

With respect to the French tax legislation, the panel took the same position on the application of the territoriality principle as in the case of the Belgian taxes. It noted the following features: non-application of French income taxes on export sales income of foreign branches or foreign sales subsidiaries of French companies; treatment of repatriated dividends; flexible application of the arms-length pricing rule; deduction of expenses for certain costs involved in export operations. The panel considered the features to be export subsidies prohibited by Article XVI:4 of the GATT.

With respect to the Dutch tax legislation, the panel noted that the particular application of the worldwide principle in conjunction with the qualified exemption in respect of foreign income allowed some part of export activities, belonging to an economic process originating in the country, to be outside of the Netherlands's taxes. In those cases where in foreign countries income and corporation taxes were significantly more

[14] See *for example,* J. Jackson, "The DISC Case in GATT", 72 *Am. J. Int'l.L.* 747 (1978); J. Fischer-Zernin, "DISC and FISC. The Troublesome Relationship between US Tax Law and GATT"(1986) *Intertax* 40; R. Hudec, *Enforcing International Trade Law. The Evolution of the Modern GATT Legal System,* 59-100 (Butterworth, Salem N.H., 1993); Qureshi, *supra* n. 7 at 184–187.

liberal, this amounted to revenue foregone and created a possibility of pecuniary benefits to exports. Moreover, according to the panel, the "sound business practice" rule according to which profits were allocated between companies and their foreign operations might not always coincide with arms-length pricing. The panel considered these features of the Dutch legislation as export subsidies prohibited by Article XVI:4 of the GATT.

However, panel reports have to be adopted by the GATT Council in order to become binding on the parties to the dispute. Although the four panel reports were issued in November 1976, the GATT Council only approved them in December 1981. But it did so subject to the following understanding:

> "*The Council adopts those reports on the understanding that with respect to these cases, and in general, economic processes (involving transactions involving exported goods) located outside of the territorial limits of the exporting country need not be subject to taxation by the exporting country and should not be regarded as export activities in terms of Article XVI:4 of the General Agreement. It is further understood that Article XVI:4 requires that arm's length pricing be observed... Furthermore, Article XVI:4 does not prohibit the adoption of measures to avoid double taxation of foreign source income .*"[15]

This understanding effectively overruled the panel's findings considering tax benefits inherent in tax systems based on the territoriality principle as prohibited export subsidies.

This was, however, not the end of the story. The US took the position that the understanding also meant that Article XVI: 4 did not require a contracting party to tax any more income from exports than would be taxed under a tax system based on the territoriality principle. The EC and Canada disagreed. In October 1982, while maintaining its position that DISC was not a prohibited subsidy, the US finally announced that its legislation would be amended. In 1984, DISC was replaced by Foreign Sales Corporation legislation (FSC).[16] In November 1997 the

---

[15] GATT, BISD 28S/114.
[16] For a description, see US Department of the Treasury, *The Operation and Effect of the Foreign Sales Corporation Legislation* (January 1993).

European Commission announced that it was requesting formal consultations in the WTO in order to put an end to what it considers export subsidies granted under FSC.[17]

The question of export subsidy effects resulting from the application of the territoriality principle may have been put to rest, provided that the exemption from taxation under that principle concerns "economic processes" outside of the exporting country. However, the application of international tax law concepts to this requirement is likely to lead, as a result of different approaches to the taxation of export earnings, to different results.[18] This does not mean that subsidy effects of direct taxation measures in general escape WTO rules.

The DISC saga illustrates the inherent tension between tax legislation and practice and the GATT rules on subsidies. On the one hand, Belgium, France and the Netherlands had a point when they argued that there was not the slightest evidence that any signatory of the GATT had contemplated that the Article XVI:4 of the GATT required Contracting Parties to abandon the general and long-standing acceptance of the territoriality principle. On the other hand, accepting the consequences of the territoriality principle meant leaving a large loophole in the prohibition of export subsidies and accepting the territoriality principle defense, while considering DISC as a prohibited export subsidy made hardly sense from an economic policy point of view.[19] It remains to be seen how direct taxes have been dealt within subsequent GATT and WTO agreements on subsidies.

C.   The Tokyo Round Subsidies Code

As already indicated, the Tokyo Round Subsidies Code[20] did not define what was meant by "subsidy". However, among examples of possible forms of subsidies other than export subsidies it mentions fiscal incentives (Art. 11:2) and, in the Illustrative List of export subsidies annexed to this Code includes "the full or partial exemption, remission, or deferral specifically related to exports of direct taxes … paid or payable by industrial or commercial enterprises" (item (e)), direct taxes being defined as "taxes on wages, profits, interests, rents, royalties and all other

[17] European Commission IP/97/998.
[18] See T. Fischer-Zernin, "GATT versus tax treaties? The basic conflicts between international taxation methods and the rules and concepts of GATT"(1989) *Intertax* 236 and 310.
[19] Hudec *supra* n. 14 at 84.
[20] *Supra* n. 2 at p. 56.

forms of income, and taxes on the ownership of real property"; "the allowance of special deductions directly related to exports or export performance, over and above those granted in respect of production for domestic consumption, in the calculation of the base on which direct taxes are charged" (item (f)).

These provisions call for three comments. The first comment concerns the different treatment of direct and indirect taxes. As is made clear in a footnote which repeats an interpretative note to Article XVI § 4 of the GATT, the exemption of an export product from *indirect* taxes borne by the like product when destined for domestic consumption, or the remission of such indirect taxes in amounts not in excess of those which have been accrued is *not* a subsidy.

The distinction made in this regard between indirect taxes and direct taxes is usually justified as follows. Indirect taxes are generally passed on to the purchaser of the product (shifted forward) and the product would be double-taxed, i.e. in the importing country and in the exporting country, if not exempted in the exporting country. By contrast, direct taxes are generally borne by the supplier of capital investment (shifted backward). This difference of approach has often been criticized, in particular by countries which depend more on direct taxation than on indirect taxation for their revenues. The counter-argument is that much depends on the product market. If the market situation does not permit a shift in the burden of the indirect tax forward, it will effectively be shifted backward in the form of a lower return to the supplier of capital investment. If the market situation allows it, the burden of the direct tax will be shifted forward in the form of a higher price to the purchaser of the product.

The second comment relates to the impact of the DISC and related disputes on the Tokyo Round Subsidies Code, which was negotiated pending these disputes. In a footnote to the Illustrative List of export subsidies annexed to this code, "[t]he signatories further recognize that nothing in this text prejudices the disposition by the CONTRACTING PARTIES of the specific issues raised in GATT document L/4422", i.e. the DISC and related disputes. Yet, certain provisions of this code confirmed some of the panel's findings.

First, Article XVI :4 GATT prohibits an export subsidy when it "results in the sale of such product for export at a price lower than the comparable price charged for the like product to buyers in the domestic market". It thus requires proof of what is called "bi-level pricing". This meant for the DISC and related disputes that in order to consider the various direct taxation measures as a prohibited subsidy the panel had to find that they resulted in "bi-level pricing". On this point the panel report is rather weak. The Tokyo Round Code abolished this "bi-level pricing" requirement which no longer appeared in the definition of prohibited export subsidies (Art. 9:1).[21] Second, the inclusion in the Illustrative List of export subsidies of "deferral specifically related to export of direct taxes", and the accompanying note making clear that this means deferral without appropriate interest charges, confirmed the panel's findings that the interest free deferral of taxes was an export subsidy.

A third comment concerns some of the controversies which arose after the panel issued its reports in the DISC and related cases. First, note 2 of the Illustrative List of export subsidies reaffirms the arms-length pricing requirement.[22] Second, the same note states that item (e) (exemption, remission, deferral specifically related to exports, of direct taxes) "is not intended to limit a signatory from taking measures to avoid the double taxation of foreign source income earned by its enterprises or the enterprises of another signatory". Quite obviously if this is meant to exempt generally measures to avoid double taxation – be they unilateral or bilateral – this is a major derogation from the GATT rules on export subsidies[23]. It is, however, doubtful that this note is intended to be an unqualified general exemption from the GATT subsidy rules for all conceivable methods of preventing double taxation. Several authors have put forward interpretations that tend to limit the scope of this derogation either by arguing that only "accepted practices" are contemplated[24], or by interpreting the terms "foreign source income".[25]

D.   The WTO Agreement on Subsidies and Countervailing Measures

The WTO SCM Agreement Code[26] does define "subsidy" and specifically states that a subsidy is deemed to exist if "a government

---

[21] From an economic point of view, this "bi-level pricing" requirement did not make much sense. An export subsidy has distortive effects not only when it results in lower export prices but also when it leads to larger quantities exported.

[22] *Supra* n. 2 at p. 82. This is reaffirmed in the understanding of 1981 when the panel reports in DISC and related cases were adopted.

[23] As has been demonstrated by Fischer-Zernin, *supra* n. 18 at 311–312.

[24] T. Kwako "Tax Incentives for Exports Permissible and Proscribed: An Analysis of Corporate Income Tax Implications of the MTA Subsidies Code", 12 *L&P in Int'l Bus.* 677 at 700 (1980).

[25] Fischer-Zernin *supra* n. 18 at 311, 312.

[26] *Supra* n. 1 at 325

revenue that is otherwise due is forgone or not collected (e.g., fiscal incentives such as tax credits" (Art. I 1.1. (a) (ii)). With respect to direct taxes, the Illustrative List of export subsidies in Annex I of the WTO SCM Agreement takes over the wording of the corresponding Annex to the Tokyo Round Subsidies Code. It calls for the following brief comments.

A first comment concerns the distinction between prohibited subsidies and actionable subsidies. Prohibited subsidies include export subsidies, i.e. "subsidies contingent in law or in fact... upon export performance", and "subsidies contingent ... upon the use of domestic over imported goods" (Art. 3.1). This prohibition of import-protecting subsidies is an important strengthening of the GATT rules. To the extent a Member would grant an exemption from direct taxes to manufacturing industries on the conditions that domestic inputs are used, this direct taxation measure would constitute a prohibited subsidy.

Other subsidies are "actionable", i.e. they are not prohibited outright but a Member, whose domestic industry is injured by such subsidy, or whose benefits accruing under GATT 1994 are nullified or impaired, or whose interests are seriously prejudiced, is entitled to begin dispute settlement proceedings. Such proceedings may result in the obligation for the Member to remove the adverse effects of the "actionable" subsidy or the remove this subsidy itself (Art. 5).

A second comment concerns the "specificity" requirement for actionable subsidies. Subsidies other than prohibited subsidies are "actionable" only if they are "specific to an enterprise or industry or group of enterprises or industries" (Art. 1.2 and 2). The underlying assumption is that subsidies which are generally granted are to be assimilated to macro-economic measures which subsidy rules are not meant to regulate.[27] This means that a general reduction of the income tax rate applying to the manufacturing industry of a Member would not be an "actionable subsidy". Within the EC the rules on State Aids (Art. 92) are interpreted in a similar fashion by requiring "selectivity". Experience there tends to show that the underlying economic assumption, according to which the distortive effects on intra-EC trade of general, as opposed to selective, subsidies are compensated by the macro effects of such general subsidies on the economy of the State that uses such measures, may not always hold true.

---

[27] On the concept of "specificity", see J.D. Greewald "US Law and Practice" in J. Bourgeois (ed.), *Subsidies and International Trade. A European Lawyer's Perspective*, 33 at 37; for a critique, see E. Grabitz, "Comment" *ibid.*, 43 at 45; E. Vermulst "Comment" *ibid.*, 49 at 50.

A third comment concerns arms-length pricing and double taxation in connection with export subsidies. A note in Annex I of the WTO SCM Agreement takes over the substance of the corresponding note in the Tokyo Round Subsidies Code. The questions to which the latter note gave rise in relation to measures designed to avoid double taxation remains on the table. Interestingly no similar note qualifies the scope of the rules on import-protecting subsidies and on "actionable subsidies" in relation to measures designed to avoid double taxation.

E.   GATT rules on direct taxations and the WTO dispute settlement system

The dispute settlement system applying to GATT 1994 has been remarkably strengthened. The Dispute Settlement Understanding (hereinafter, the DSU),[28] which is integral part of the Marrakesh Agreement establishing the World Trade Organization contains two important features which distinguish it from the earlier system.[29] First, final rulings and recommendations of panel, or the Standing Appellate Body, are binding in the parties when adopted by the Dispute Settlement Body (DSB) – which is the WTO General Council, composed of representatives of all the Members, with another hat and they are adopted unless there is a *consensus* to *reject* them. Second, the process of "judicialization" of the dispute settlement system is furthered by the possibility for parties to seek review of panel reports by the Standing Appellate Body on matters of law. This strengthened dispute settlement system contains an undeniable law-creating potential, notwithstanding certain "garde-fous" that were included in the DSU: recommendations and rulings of the DSB cannot add to or diminish the rights and obligations provided in the covered agreements (Art. 3:2) and the provisions of the DSU are without prejudice to the rights of Members to seek authoritative interpretations of a covered agreement through decision-making under the WTO Agreement (Art. 3:9). One can only speculate what the outcome of DISC and related disputes on direct taxation measures would have been under this new dispute settlement system.

---

[28] *Supra* n. 1 at 404
[29] For a description, see, i.a. P.J. Kuijper, "The New WTO Dispute Settlement System: the Impact on the Community" in Bourgeois, Berrod, Gippini – Fournier (eds), *The Uruguay Round Results. A European Lawyers' Perspective* 87 (EUP, Bruxelles, 1995); E.U. Petersmann "An Introduction", in E.U. Petersmann (ed), *International Trade Law and the GATT/WTO Dispute Settlement* System 3 (Kluwer, London, Boston, the Hague, 1997).

III.   DIRECT TAXATION IN THE GATS

The General Agreement on Trade and Services (GATS)[30] applies to measures of Members "affecting trade in services" (Art. I:1). Trade in services within the meaning of the GATS involves not only cross-border supply of services without movement of persons but also supply of services whereby either the supplier or the consumer of services crosses borders or "commercial presence" of the service supplier of a Member or "presence of natural persons" of a Member in the territory of another Member (Art. I:(2)). The GATS covers thus not only trade in services but also suppliers and consumers of services.

It should, however, be pointed out that the GATS is a framework agreement rather than an instrument containing substantive obligations. All services are covered (except those supplied in the exercise of governmental authority) but except for the most-favored-nation clause (Art. II), the obligations it lays down on market access and national treatment take the form of commitments already accepted or to be negotiated by mode of supply and apply only to service sectors listed in each Member's schedule of commitments subject to conditions, limitations and qualifications.

A.   The most-favored-nation treatment

With respect to any measure covered by the GATS, each Member is bound to accord immediately and unconditionally to services and service suppliers of any other Member treatment no less favorable than that it accords to like services and service suppliers of any other country (Art. II). There are certain derogations to this MFN obligation and, mostly sectoral, exemptions listed in Annex II of the GATS.[31]

This MFN clause applies also to taxation measures affecting trade in services, at least in principle taking account of the "General Exceptions" clause which exempts, i.a. double taxation agreements from the scope of this MFN clause (see infra). It applies not only to indirect taxes, as the GATT MFN clause, but also to direct taxes,

i.a. because the GATS MFN clause refers not only to "like services" but also to "like service suppliers"[32], resulting from the general scope of

---

[30] *Supra* n. 1 at 325
[31] For an analysis, see Yi Wang "Most-Favored-Nation Treatment under the General Agreement on Trade in Services –And Its Application to Financial Services" 30 JWT 91 (1996).
[32] Qureshi, *supra* n. 7 at 168.

the GATS ("measures by Members affecting trade in services" Art. I:1). This may also be deduced from the provision on "General Exceptions" which refers to qualified taxation measures. If taxation measures were not in principle covered by the GATS, it would not make much sense to address qualified taxation measures in the "General Exceptions".

B.   National Treatment

In the sectors where a Member has undertaken specific liberalization commitments, national treatment is provided for in respect of "all measures affecting the supply of services" (Art. XVII:1). It is noteworthy that this national treatment clause prohibits expressly not only formal discrimination but also substantive discrimination (Art. XVII:2 and 3).

The question arises whether, when a Member undertakes specific liberalization commitments, taxation measures come within the definition of "all measures affecting the supply of services". One could argue that taxation measures are not covered as they are not listed among the measures that a Member may not maintain in sectors where market-access commitments are undertaken (Art. XVI). This provision, however, concerns only access to the market, which is to be distinguished from the national treatment concerning discrimination on the market.

It would thus appear that the national treatment clause covers in principle taxation measures for the same reasons as those put forward with respect to the MFN clause.

C.   The "General Exceptions"

The clause in Article XIV on the "General Exceptions" both from the most-favored-nation clause and from the national treatment clause appears to cover a number of situations where, save for the exceptions, MFN and national treatment would require Members to depart from fairly generally accepted principles of international tax law.

Members may adopt or enforce measures inconsistent with the MFN clause or with the national treatment clause "provided that the difference in treatment is aimed at ensuring the equitable or effective imposition or collection of direct taxes in respect of services or service suppliers of other Members" (Art. XIV (d)). A footnote states that such measures "include measures taken by a Member under its taxation system which:

(i) apply to non-resident service suppliers in recognition of the fact that the tax obligation of non-residents is determined with respect to taxable items sourced or located in the Member's territory; or

(ii) apply to non-residents in order to ensure the imposition or collection of taxes in the Member's territory; or

(iii) apply to non-residents or residents in order to prevent the avoidance or evasion of taxes, including compliance measures; or

(iv) apply to consumers of services supplied in or from the territory of another Member in order to ensure the imposition or collection of taxes on such consumers derived from sources in the Member's territory; or

(v) distinguish service suppliers subject to tax on worldwide taxable items from other service suppliers, in recognition of the difference in the nature of the tax base between them; or

(vi) determine, allocate or apportion income, profit, gain, loss, deduction or credit of resident persons or branches, or between related persons or branches of the same person, in order to safeguard the Member's tax base.

Moreover, a Member may depart from the MFN clause, if the difference in treatment is the result of a double taxation agreement (Art. XIV item (e)).

It is debatable whether these provisions are to be regarded as a genuine "tax carve out".[33] They cover only certain albeit important, taxation measures. There may be other taxation measures which are conceivably in conflict with MFN or national treatment. Moreover, recourse to the tax exception is subject to the general provision of Article XIV: measures taken may not be applied in a manner which would constitute a means of arbitrary or unjustifiable discrimination between countries where like conditions prevail or a disguised restriction on trade in services. Thus even taxation measures which fall within the scope of the "General Exceptions" clause could come under WTO scrutiny.

---

[33] Term used by I. Wilkinson, "The Uruguay Round and Financial Services", in Bourgeois, Berrod, Gippini-Fournier *op. cit., supra* n. 29 405 at 411.

D.   Taxation measures as subsidies

By contrast to the GATT, the GATS does not provide for binding rules on subsidies. While recognizing that subsidies may have distortive effects on trade in services, Members undertook only to enter into negotiations about "the necessary multilateral disciplines" (Art. XV: 1). In the event that a Member is adversely affected by a subsidy of another Member, it may request consultations which is to be "accorded sympathetic consideration" (Art. XV:2).

E.   Dispute Settlement

It is quite unlikely that, as in the case of the GATT, in any Member's legal system the provisions of the GATS will be given "direct effect", allowing private parties to rely on these provisions in court, let alone taking precedence over inconsistent national law. As far as the EC is concerned, the Council of the European Union ruled this out by a statement in the preamble of its decision on the results of the Uruguay Round.[34]

The binding force of the GATS depends thus to a large extent on its being capable of enforcement through a dispute settlement system. The availability of such dispute settlement system was precisely one of the main reasons for negotiating world wide rules on trade in services in the GATT context.[35]

The GATS dispute settlement system provides for two "causes of action". One may be called a "violation complaint":

> "[i]f any Member should consider that any other Member fails to carry out its obligations or specific commitments under this Agreement, it may with a view to reaching a mutually satisfactory resolution of the matter have recourse to the DSU (Art. XXIII: 1)".

DSU stands for the Dispute Settlement understanding which is annexed to the Agreement establishing the WTO.

The other one may be called a "non-violation complaint":

---

[34] See O.J. cited *supra* n. 1.
[35] E.U. Petersmann "An Introduction", in Petersmann *op. cit., supra* n. 29 at 25.

"[i]f any Member considers that any benefit it could reasonably have expected to accrue to it under a specific commitment under Part III of this Agreement is being nullified or impaired as a result of the application of any measure which does not conflict with the provisions of this Agreement, it may have recourse to the DSU" (Art. XXIII:3).

For the remainder, the WTO DSU applies. A cursory look at the modalities of the dispute settlement provisions specific for taxation measures shows that the negotiators were ambivalent and were probably wary of the law creating potential of the dispute settlement system.

1. MFN Treatment

As already indicated, a different treatment resulting from a double taxation agreement is one of the "General Exceptions" (Art. XIV) to the MFN clause of the GATS (Art. II). Yet disputes about such differences of treatment are conceivable on questions such as whether this exception applies and whether differences of treatment resulting from the double taxation agreement are a means of arbitrary or unjustifiable discrimination or a disguised restriction of trade. Within these limits violation complaints relating to a breach of the MFN clause are not excluded by the GATS provisions on dispute settlement. In other words, the MFN obligation excluded by Article XIV item (e) re-enters through the back door, albeit that the discrimination must be arbitrary or unjustifiable or a disguised restriction of trade. Non-violation complaints relating to double taxation agreements are excluded, as the dispute settlement provisions on non-violation complaints are limited to specific commitments under Part III of the GATS (Art. XXII 2:3).

2. National treatment

It may be recalled that pursuant to the "General Exceptions" clause differences of treatment between foreign and domestic services or service suppliers aimed at ensuring the equitable or effective imposition or collection of direct taxes are exempted from the national treatment clause. As in the case of breaches of the MFN clause, differences in treatment contemplated by the relevant exception may give rise to dispute settlement proceedings within the same limits. In addition, there may also be non-violation complaints when certain conditions are met (Art. XXIII:3).

Interestingly, dispute settlement proceedings are excluded when the dispute is about a tax measure, which is in breach of the national treatment clause but falls within the scope of a bilateral double-taxation agreement. In the event of a disagreement between Members on the question whether the measure falls within the scope of such double taxation agreement between them, GATS provides for arbitration (Art. XXIII:3).

The implicit rationale for excluding double-taxation agreements from the GATS dispute settlement system probably is to avoid the contamination of the network of bilateral double taxation agreements by consideration of trade policy which GATS dispute settlement proceeding would involve. One may wonder, however, why the same solution was not adopted where bilateral double taxation agreements breach the MFN clause which, while benefiting from the "General Exceptions" clause may nonetheless, albeit within limits, be the subject of dispute settlement proceedings. Bilateral double taxation agreements conflict with the MFN treatment as much as, if not more than, with national treatment.[36]

3. Taxation measures as subsidies

As already indicated, a Member who is adversely affected by a subsidy granted by another Member on a service or a service supplier may request consultations. One author is of the view that such consultation is to be regarded as a first step of a dispute settlement proceeding. He argues that similar GATT provisions have been interpreted that way.[37] It is doubtful, however, that the clause on subsidies contains the required "obligations or specific commitments under this Agreement" whose non-performance would entitle a Member to file a violation-complaint. Its very wording, which refers to multilateral disciplines still to be negotiated, appears to exclude this.

There does not appear to be scope for a non-violation complaint either. It may well be that a benefit which a Member could reasonably have expected to accrue to it under the clause on subsidies is being nullified. However, the GATS dispute settlement only applies in case of

---

[36] See, for example, E. Kemmeren, "The termination of the 'most favoured clause' dispute in tax treaty law and the necessity of a Euro Model Tax Convention", (1997) *EC Tax Review* 146, with numerous references to the literature.

[37] P.K, Morrison, "WTO Dispute Settlement in Services: Procedural and Substantive Aspects", in Petersmann *op. cit., supra* n. 29, 377 at 380.

nullification of specific commitments under Part III of the GATS and the clause on subsidies appears in Part II.

IV.   CONCLUSION

1.   This contribution has focused on the question whether direct taxation measures come within the scope of the relevant WTO agreements, i.e. the GATT 1994, and the WTO Subsidies Code, one of its implementing agreements, and the GATS. This is only a preliminary, albeit important, question. To the extent that the reply is positive, it opens the way to a series of other questions, which some of the authors referred to in this contribution have anticipated.

2.   GATT law on direct taxation affecting international trade in goods is piecemeal. Its rules on export subsidies cover direct taxation measures taking the form of tax benefits relating to income from international trade transactions. However, by prohibiting domestic subsidies contingent on use of domestic products over imported products and by making other subsidies "actionable", the WTO SCM Agreement now covers direct taxes as barriers to imports and more generally where they have qualified "adverse effects".

Such GATT law regulates the trade distortive effects of certain international tax practices, such as measures against double taxation, imperfectly. The application of such GATT law embodying its own concepts, which are meant to apply generally to all WTO Members, is bound to conflict with differing international tax practices of WTO Members. Disputes on direct taxation measures under the GATT are neither excluded from the scope of the DSU nor subjected to certain qualifications.

3.   Direct taxation measures are likely to have a larger negative impact on the achievement of the objective of expansion of trade in services "under conditions of transparency and progressive liberalization", assigned to the GATS which deals with services and service suppliers, than on the achievement of the objectives of the GATT which deals with trade in goods.

Yet, GATS law on direct taxation is even more piecemeal than GATT law. It does not contain substantive rules on subsidies. Its MFN and national treatment clauses apply in principle to direct taxation measures but their application is subject to a number of important qualifications.

The national treatment clause applies only to specific sectoral liberalization commitments undertaken or to be entered into by each Member. There are important exceptions to both the MFN and the national treatment clause with respect to a number of taxation measures, which turns GATS law into a mosaic with many blank pieces, some of which concern Members' measures designed to avoid double taxation. By contrast to the situation under the GATT, some of these pieces of the GATS mosaic will remain blank as the possibilities to color them in dispute settlement proceedings have been restricted but not entirely excluded.

7. THE EUROPEAN COURT OF JUSTICE AND THE WTO: PROBLEMS AND CHALLENGES

In this contribution a number of questions are broached. The jurisdiction of the Court of Justice of the EC to interpret WTO rules that fall within the powers of EC Member States rather than of those of the EC itself is one of them. In the meantime that Court has clarified its position. Another permanent theme is that of the effect of WTO rules in the EC legal system. In Portugal v. Council, the ECJ concluded that "the WTO agreements are not in principle among the rules in the light of which the Court is to review the legality of measures adopted by the Community institutions" (1999 ECR I-4973, para 47). It confirmed its ruling in subsequent cases (e.g. with respect to the TBT Agreement Omega Air, 2002 ECR I-2569, paras 89-96). This stance continues to fuel debates in the legal literature. One view refreshing as it looks at it from a WTO perspective, is that of Claus-Dieter Ehlermann, a former member of the WTO Appellate Body. He considers that recognition of direct effect to WTO law would harm, instead of help, the WTO ("Six Years on the Bench of the 'World Trade Court'. Some Personal Experiences as a Member of the Appellate Body of the World Trade Organisation" in F. Ortino and E.U. Petersmann (eds), the WTO Dispute Settlement System 1995–2003 (Kluwer, 2004) 499 at 528).

I. INTRODUCTION

The topic chosen for this chapter prompts the question why the World Trade Organization, as an international organization, and the various Agreements that form an integral part of the Agreement establishing the World Trade Organization (hereinafter for brevity's sake: WTO law) raise problems and are challenges for the Court of Justice of the European Communities (hereinafter, the ECJ) that are specific enough to merit an analysis. In other words this topic begs the question whether the issues of the status of WTO law in the EC legal system and of the judicial enforcement of WTO law in that system, have aspects that set them apart from the same issues as they raise or rather do not raise in other jurisdictions.

Generally speaking the EC-specific challenges and problems for the ECJ are related on the one hand to the status of the EC in the WTO and on the other to the ECJ's jurisdiction as it is organized by the EC Treaty. These two items are dealt with in sections I and II. Section III addresses the status of international agreements in the EC legal system and section IV deals with the status of the WTO in the EC legal system.

II.   THE STATUS OF THE EC IN THE WTO

The EC was not a contracting party to the General Agreement on Tariffs and Trade 1947 (hereinafter the GATT); the EC Member States were. However, the EC had over the years acquired the status to all intents and purposes of a contracting party. All trade agreements and accession protocols negotiated in the GATT framework provided in their final provisions that the agreements were open for acceptance "by contracting parties to the GATT and by the EEC" (or "EC"). Moreover, notwithstanding this formal distinction in such final provisions between GATT contracting parties and the EC the substantive and procedural provisions of these Agreements treat the EC like a GATT contracting party. In addition, since 1970, most agreements negotiated in the GATT framework were accepted by the EC alone, i.e. without "acceptance" by EC Member States as such.[1]

The EC exercised practically all rights and fulfilled practically all obligations under GATT law in its own name like a GATT contracting party. Since about 1960 all GATT contracting parties had accepted such exercise of rights and such fulfilment of obligations by the EC and had asserted their own GATT rights, even in dispute settlement proceedings relating to measures of individual EC Member States, almost always against the EC.[2] Although this cannot be described as a case of State succession, the EC had effectively replaced, with the consent of the other GATT contracting parties, its Member States as bearers of rights and obligations under the GATT.

At the outset of the Uruguay Round of Multilateral Trade negotiations, the EC was faced with the issue of the scope of its authority under the EC Treaty in the field of international economic relations, in particular with respect to trade in services and trade related aspects of intellectual property rights, which were a first in GATT history. The issue was put on the back-burner and the negotiations were conducted according to the procedures normally followed for GATT negotiations, albeit that the European Commission (hereinafter: the Commission) negotiated for both the EC and the EC Member States.[3]

---

[1] With the exception at the end of the Tokyo Round of multilateral trade negotiations of two agreements and the part of the Tariff Protocol relating to ECSC products. See for a comment, J. H. J, Bourgeois, "The Tokyo Round Agreements, on Technical Barriers and on Government Procurement", 19 *CML Rev.* (1982) 5 at 22,

[2] See E. U. Petersmann, "The EEC as a GATT Member—Legal Conflicts between GATT Law and European Community Law" in M. Hilf, F. G. Jacobs, E. U. Petersmann, *The European Community and GATT*, (Kluwer, Deventer, 1986), 23 at 37–8.

[3] See the description by P. van den Bossche, "The European Community and the Uruguay Round Agreements" in John H. Jackson and Alan A. Sykes (eds.), *Implementing the Uruguay Round* (Clarendon Press, Oxford, 1997), 23 at 56–7

The creation of the World Trade Organization (hereinafter: the WTO) offered the opportunity to draw the formal international law consequences of these developments in two respects: first, by stipulating that the EC would be a *WTO* Member and, second, by making clear that the EC replaced the EC Member States. When this matter arose two political constraints led the Commission not to stand up for the second consequence. First, the matter was discussed in a meeting of the Council of the European Union (hereinafter: the Council) in November 1993, that is after the Maastricht Treaty on the European Union had entered into effect with some difficulty and it was thought wise not to push this issue at that stage. Second, around this time the last hurdles facing the approval by the Council of the results of the Uruguay Round had to be cleared and Sir Leon Brittan, followed by the Commission, thought it preferable not to table yet another contentious issue and not to upset an apple cart that was already in danger of being out of balance. The end-result was Article XI of the Marrakesh Agreement establishing the World Trade Organization stating that the contracting parties to GATT 1947 (including thus all the EC Member States) and the European Communities shall become original Members of the WTO.[4]

From the perspective of the EC and its Member States, this rather anomalous dual membership may in the end prove to be a bad solution. Under GATT 1947 the other contracting parties had accepted pragmatically the EC as a single entity on the grounds that one should not open the Pandora's box of a review of the GATT in order to formally substitute the EC for its Member States. The solution of Article XI of the WTO Agreement carries with it the risk that all these efforts will come to naught. There are indications that other WTO Members may not continue to show the same forbearance and are tempted to exploit the dual membership of the EC and EC Member States. What was in the GATT a patient acceptance of a passing eccentricity may turn in the WTO into a lingering handicap for both the EC and its Member States.

The very fact that EC Member States are WTO Members alongside the EC is in itself bound to raise issues in relation to the position of the ECJ on WTO law. As far as GATT 1947 was concerned, the ECJ could take the view that as a result of the substitution of the EC for the Member States in relation to commitments under GATT, it had the final word on the interpretation of GATT provisions, even in relation to the compatibility of Member States legislation with GATT.[5] This argument is no longer

---

[4] WTO, *The Uruguay Round Results. The Legal Texts* (Geneva, 1995), 6.
[5] *Amministrazione delta Finanze dello Stato v. Società Petrolifera Italiana (SPI) and SpA Michelin Italiana (SAMI)* [1983] ECR 801, paras 15 and 17.

possible. In line with Article XI of the Agreement establishing the WTO, both the EC and the Member States signed the Final Act.

It is true that the ECJ has stated that the division of powers between the EC and the Member States is a domestic question in which third parties have no need to intervene.[6] The Commission probably relied on this when it had recorded in the minutes of Council meeting 7/8 March 1994 its view that: "the Final Act... and the Agreements thereto fall exclusively within the competence of the European Community".[7] However, that does not allow the *a-contrario* inference that the fact that the Member States and the EC are formally WTO Members is irrelevant for the division of powers within the EC legal system.

At any rate the Agreement establishing the WTO and the agreements that form part of it were approved by the Council on behalf of the EC expressly "as regards matters within its competence".[8] The need to accord an *"effet utile"* to the joint WTO membership of the EC and the Member States is inescapable. It must mean something about the division of powers within the EC and this in turn raises issues in relation to the ECJ's jurisdiction. As will be seen such issues have arisen in relation to other agreements concluded jointly by the EC and the Member States and in relation to the TRIPS Agreement, one of the agreements annexed to the Agreement establishing the WTO.

III.   JURISDICTION OF THE COURT OF JUSTICE OF THE EUROPEAN COMMUNITIES

Only those aspects of the jurisdiction of the ECJ that are particularly relevant for the subject of this chapter are assessed. The analysis is necessarily selective.

A.   An Overview

1.   *The Principle of Limited Jurisdiction*

The ECJ has no inherent jurisdiction; it has jurisdiction only in so far as the EC Treaty and similar instruments have conferred jurisdiction upon it, as results from Article 4 (new Art. 7), paragraph 1 EC Treaty. Such jurisdiction may be implied. The implied jurisdiction exists where there is a prevailing need for it in order to fill a lacuna in the system of

---

[6] Ruling 1/78 (1978) ECR 2151, para. 35.
[7] Cited in ECJ Opinion 1/94 [1994] ECR 1-5267, para. 5.
[8] Council Decision of 22 December 1998 (OJ 1994 L 336/1).

remedies expressly provided for, such as where the complete absence of any other form of legal redress creates a serious injustice and is inconsistent with the rule of law in the EC.[9]

Although the concept of "a Community based on the rule of law" appears nowhere in the EC Treaty, the ECJ relied on this concept to develop a more general theory on which it based such implied jurisdiction. In *Les Verts* the ECJ stated that:

> [T]he European Economic Community is a Community based on the rule of law, inasmuch as neither its Member States nor its institutions can avoid a review of the question whether the measures adopted by them are in conformity with the basic constitutional charter, the Treaty ...

and that:

> the Treaty established a complete system of legal remedies and procedures designed to permit the Court of Justice to review the legality of measures adopted by the institutions.[10]

In a subsequent case, the ECJ was of the view that in order to perform its task under Article 164 (new Art. 220) EC it had to be able to guarantee the maintenance of the institutional balance and the respect for the European Parliaments prerogatives. Although Article 173 (new Art. 230) EC did not provide for an application for annulment by the European Parliament, the ECJ concluded that it had jurisdiction in an annulment proceeding brought by the European Parliament to the extent that the purpose of the proceeding was to protect the European Parliaments prerogatives.[11] This freedom of the ECJ to intervene in the absence of express authority to do so allows the correction of defects in the system of remedies created by the Treaties.[12] In this, the implicit jurisdiction of the ECJ finds its justification and its limits.

[9] Cf. K. P. E. Lasok, *The European Court of Justice. Practice and Procedure*, 2nd edn. (Butterworths, London 1994), 9.

[10] CJEC, Judgment of 23 April 1986, *Les Verts v. European Parliament*, [1986] ECR 1339 (consideration 23).

[11] The "Chernobyl case" *European Parliament v. Council [1990]* ECR 1-2041: contrast this to the so-called "Comitology case" *European Parliament v. Council* [1988] ECR 5615. For a comment on the latter case J. Weiler, "Pride and Prejudice–Parliament c. Council", 14 EL Rev. (1989)334.

[12] A. Arnull, "Does the Court of Justice have inherent jurisdiction?" 27 *CML Rev.* (1990), 683 at 701.

2.   Acts Susceptible to Judicial Review by the ECJ

Article 173 (new Art. 230) EC Treaty provides for an action of annulment against acts adopted jointly by the European Parliament and the Council, acts of the Council, of the Commission and the European Central Bank, other than recommendations or opinions, and of acts of the European Parliament intended to produce legal effects vis-à-vis third parties.[13]

In the area of external relations two developments in the case law are noteworthy in this respect.

(a)   A decision of the Council to Leave it to EC Member States to Negotiate an International Agreement

In the *ERTA* case the Commission had recommended to the Council that it be authorized to re-negotiate on behalf of the EC the European Road Transport Agreement to be entered into with third countries in the framework of the United Nations. The Council resolved that the (then) six EC Member States should negotiate on their own behalf and become individual parties to ERTA. The Commission challenged the Council proceedings in the ECJ, which considered that the Commission application was admissible. Referring to the wording of Article 173 (new Art. 230) EC Treaty the ECJ reasoned that:

Since the only matter excluded from the scope of the action for annulment... are "recommendations or opinions"–which by the final paragraph of Article 189 [EC Treaty] are declared to have no binding force–Article 173 treats as acts open to review by the Court all measures adopted by the institutions which are intended to have legal force.[14]

The ECJ went on to analyze the content and purpose of the Council proceedings and was of the view:

It thus seems that in so far as they concerned the objective of the negotiations as defined by the Council, the proceedings of 20 March 1970 could not have been simply the expression or the recognition of a voluntary co-ordination, but were designed to lay down a course of action binding

---

[13] Note that the *ius standi of* a private applicant is limited to:
- decisions addressed to that applicant
- decisions addressed to others which is of direct and individual concern to the applicant
- decisions taken in the form of a regulation which is of direct and individual concern to the applicant. (An. 173, new An. 230 para. 4, EC).

[14] *Commission v. Council* [1971] ECR 263, para. 39.

on both the institutions and the Member States, and destined ultimately to be reflected in the term of the (EC) regulation (that would have to be amended following the conclusion of ERTA].

In the part of its conclusion relating to the negotiating procedure, the Council adopted provisions which were capable of derogating in certain circumstances from the procedure laid down by the (EC) Treaty regarding negotiations with third countries and the conclusion of agreements.[15]

The ECJ concluded that:

> ... the proceedings of 20 March 1970 [i.e. the position taken by the Council] had definitive legal effects both in relations between the Community and the Member States and in the relationship between the institutions.[16]

In the same vein, in *Commission v. Council (FAO)* the ECJ considered that a Council decision according to which the EC Member States rather than the EC should vote in the FAO for the adoption of an agreement on fisheries conservation measures had legal effects. The ECJ consequently held that the Commission application for annulment of that decision was admissible.[17]

(b) International Agreements

Once the text of an agreement has been initiated or authenticated in some form by the Commission, the Council "concludes" the agreement, following either a simplified procedure or a more complicated procedure involving two or three stages. In doing so, the Council approves the agreement and decides on such steps as are required to express the Community's consent to be bound by the agreement by whatever means are applicable.

In EC practice, "conclusion", within the meaning of the relevant EC Treaty provisions (Articles 114, 228, and 238 (Art. 114 now repealed, new Arts 300 and 310)), thus covers simultaneously two different measures: the measure whereby the *internal* procedure to conclude an agreement is completed and the measure whereby the EC binds itself *internationally*. This final act of the Council takes the form of a decision or a regulation. The decision or regulation, to which the international

---

[15] [1971] ECR 263, para. 53.
[16] [1971] ECR 263, para. 55.
[17] [1996] ECR 11469.

agreement is appended, is published in the *Official Journal* of the EC. A notice announcing the agreements international entry into effect may appear subsequently in the *Official Journal.*

Beyond a certain analogy to legal systems providing for legislative approval of international agreements, these EC Treaty provisions do not offer much guidance on the status and effects of international agreements in the EC legal system, except that under Article 228 (new Art. 300), paragraph 7 EC agreements "concluded" under these conditions are "binding on the institutions of the Community and on Member States".

The institutional provisions are silent on the question of whether and how an international agreement binding on the EC becomes part of EC law. They do not contain any indication of the Treaty framers' views on what, for convenience, are called the "monist" and the "dualist" approaches. The practice followed by the EC institutions does not offer much guidance either. In some cases the practice seems to reflect a 'dualist' attitude; in other cases it reflects a "monist" one. The choice of a regulation (by definition "directly applicable") rather than a decision for the purpose of approving an international agreement normally implies that a regulation was in that case necessary to ensure direct efficacy to an agreement which was itself considered "self-executing". It can thus be seen as the expression of a "dualist" attitude. However, that choice may also be influenced by other considerations, such as the need to adopt simultaneously complementary provisions requiring the use of a regulation. For its part, the ECJ has demonstrated that it does not attach much weight to the type of legal act used for the purpose of deciding whether an agreement has become part of Community law and is directly enforceable.[18]

On the other hand, in EC practice, legislation implementing an international agreement, i.e. transforming it into EC legislation, is considered necessary only where the agreement both entails precise legal obligations and requires changes of, or additions to, rules in force internally, or where the provisions of the agreement, in order to be implemented in a clear and effective manner, call for special measures of internal law.

The question thus arises whether an international agreement concluded by the EC is an act of an EC institution within the meaning of Article 173 (new Art. 230) EC Treaty open to challenge or whether only

---

[18] For example, in *Bresciani* [1976] ECR 129, the ECJ allowed the applicant in the main case to rely on the Yaounde agreement although this international agreement had been approved by a decision and not by a regulation.

the decision to conclude an international agreement can be the subject of a review of legality by the ECJ.

France v. Commission[19] related to the 1991 Agreement entered into by the Commission and the US government regarding the application of their competition laws. France brought an action under Article 173 (new Art. 230) EC for a declaration that this agreement was void, i.e. on the ground that the Commission was not competent to conclude such an agreement.

On the admissibility of the action the ECJ took the following position:

In its defence, the Commission raises the question whether the French Government should have challenged the decision whereby it authorized its vice-president to sign the agreement with the United States on its behalf, rather than challenging the agreement itself.

Suffice it to note that, in order for an action to be admissible under the first paragraph of Article 173 of the EEC Treaty, the contested act must be an act of an institution which produces legal effects (see Case 22/70 *Commission v. Council* [1971] ECR 263 (the 'ERTA' case)).

The Court finds that, as is apparent from its actual wording, the agreement is intended to produce legal effects. Consequently, the act whereby the Commission sought to conclude the agreement must be susceptible to an action for annulment.

Exercise of the powers delegated to the Community institutions in international matters cannot escape judicial review, under Article 173 of the Treaty, of the legality of the acts adopted.

The French Republic's action must be understood as being directed against the act whereby the Commission sought to conclude the Agreement. Consequently, the action is admissible.[20]

This rather short reasoning of the ECJ may be clarified by the following excerpt of the opinion of Tesauro AG (footnotes omitted).

---

[19] [1994] ECR 13641.
[20] [1994] ECR 1-3641, paras 13–17.

Nevertheless, the Commission has argued that under Article 173 the Court may review only acts of the institutions, which clearly cannot encompass an agreement which, being an act that has come into being with the participation of a non-member country, is not – nor can it be considered – a unilateral act of a Community institution. The case-law in which the Court affirms that it has jurisdiction to interpret agreements as well by way of a preliminary ruling confirms, in the Commission's view, that only the decision to conclude an agreement and not the agreement itself can be the subject of a review of legality.

In that regard, it should be noted first of all that the relevant case-law of the Court does not by any means rule out the possibility of challenging an agreement directly. In fact, quite the opposite is true, as suggested by the weight of evidence.

Let us remember that in justifying its jurisdiction to interpret by way of a preliminary ruling agreements concluded by the Community with non-members countries, the Court has equated such agreements with acts of the institutions. Thus, in its judgment in *Haegeman*, the Court expressly stated that an agreement concluded under Article 228 of the Treaty constitutes "so far as concerns the Community, an act of one of the institutions of the Community within the meaning of subparagraph (b) of the first paragraph of Article 177" and that "the provisions of the Agreement, from the coming into force thereof, form an integral part of Community law".

Since in the same judgment the Court referred to the Council decision relating to the conclusion of the Agreement in question, the aforesaid statement has been interpreted as meaning that the Court's jurisdiction to interpret provisions of international agreements can be exercised only because of the existence of an executive act. The fact remains, however, that, even in subsequent judgments, the Court reiterated, for purposes of interpretation, that agreements, so far as concerns the Community, are to be treated as acts of the institutions.

Still more important for the purposes of this case is the fact that the Court's jurisdiction to carry out an *a posteriori* review of legality in relation to international agreements concluded by the Communities has already been affirmed by the Court unequivocally, albeit in an *obiter dictum*, in Opinion 1/75. In that Opinion, the Court stated that 'the question whether the conclusion of a given agreement is within the power of the Community and whether, in a given case, such power has been exercised in conformity with the provisions of the Treaty is, in principle, a question which may be submitted to the Court of Justice, either directly, under Article 169 or Article 173 of the Treaty, or in accordance with the preliminary procedure'.

It is clear, therefore, first of all that the possibility of review under Article 173 (as well) arises from the exercise of the Community's external powers being subject to compliance with the procedural and substantive rules laid down by the Treaty, and secondly that the possibility of direct review of the agreements concluded by the Community is by no means excluded since the Court has expressly stated that it can review, in proceedings under Article 173, whether the power to conclude an agreement has been exercised in accordance with the provisions of the Treaty.

Admittedly, the Court has not so far had occasion to exercise that power *of a posteriori* review in a specific case, although it has already ruled on the legality of a Community act relating to the conclusion of an agreement. The question remains, therefore, for the purposes of this case, whether such review is permissible only indirectly, that is to say where it is carried out as a result of an action challenging the regulation or decision relating to the conclusion of the agreement, or also where the agreement is challenged directly.

It seems to me that the question is merely one of form. In my view, under the Community legal system which makes provision for judicial review, without exception, of all the acts and practices of the institutions, of individuals and of the Member States, which affect the system itself, it is not reasonably possible to exclude review of the legality of the procedure for concluding an agreement with a non-member country. The possibility of doing so on the basis of a complaint expressly directed at the agreement as such or at the act connected therewith, or else at an implied act, strikes me as a secondary and wholly irrelevant matter.[21]

The ECJ, however, adhered to the more formalistic approach. It did not annul the agreement. It declared void the act whereby the Commission sought to conclude the agreement with the US.

Some might consider that in so doing the ECJ followed a dualist approach in that it distinguished between the agreement which France sought to have declared void and the Commission decision on the

---

[21] [1994] ECR 1-3641, Opinion of Tesauro AG, paras 8–11.

conclusion of this agreement. This is doubtful. Under the monist approach the domestic effect of an international agreement depends normally on the approval of the conclusion of the agreement by the proper national authorities. The ECJ limited itself to reviewing the legality of such approval.

(c)   Acts Susceptible to Interpretation by the ECJ

Quite obviously, where the ECJ has jurisdiction to annul or declare void an act of an EC institution, it also may interpret such act. One of the interesting features of the EC system of judicial review is the preliminary ruling. Pursuant to Article 177 (new Art. 234) EC, an EC Member State court may, or as the case may be, must submit to the ECJ a question of interpretation of the EC Treaty or of secondary EC law or a question of legality of secondary EC law– more precisely "on the validity and interpretation of acts of the Institutions of the Community".

i.   Agreements entered into by the EC

In *Haegeman*,[22] a Belgian company importing Greek wines sought repayment of countervailing charges exacted from it by Belgium. It argued before a Belgian court that the imposition of those charges was unlawful having regard to the (then) Association Agreement between the EEC and Greece. The Belgian court submitted a number of questions of interpretation of the Association Agreement to the ECJ.

The ECJ examined *in limine its* jurisdiction. It referred to Article 177 (new Art. 234) EC Treaty and went on to state:

The Athens Agreement was concluded by the Council under Articles 228 and 238 of the Treaty as appears from the terms of the decision [of the Council approving the conclusion of the Agreement] of 25 September 1961.

The Agreement is therefore in so far as concerns the Community, an act of one of the institutions of the Community within the meaning of subparagraph (b) of the first paragraph of Article 177.

The provisions of the Agreement, from the coming into force thereof, form integral part of Community law.

---

[22](1974) ECR 449.

Within the framework of this law, the Court accordingly has jurisdiction to give preliminary rulings concerning the interpretation of this Agreement.[23]

In this case the provision whose interpretation was sought by the Belgian court was not the decision approving the Association Agreement, but a provision of this agreement itself, which, as such, is not listed in Article 177 (new Art. 234) EC among the acts covered by the ECJ's jurisdiction. The ECJ assimilated the Association Agreement to "an act of an institution of the Community", and considered that its provisions form an integral part of Community law, having found that this agreement had been approved by a Council Decision. It has been argued that the ECJ's argument would be justified only if the EC adopts a strictly dualist approach to international agreements.[24] However under the monist approach, an international agreement must be properly concluded under national constitutional law to have domestic effect.

The ECJ has taken the same view in subsequent judgments,[25]

ii.   "Mixed Agreements"

The EC and its Member States have recourse to the "mixed agreements" formula "when it appears that the subject-matter of an agreement or contract falls in part within the competence of the Community and in part within that of the Member States".[26] This formula has been analysed in the literature to which we refer for further reading.[27] The advantage of the formula is that it allows fudging the issue of the exact demarcation of EC competence. If that issue had to be definitively resolved every time an international agreement was concluded, the process would be even more fraught than it usually is.[28]

---

[23] [1974] ECR 449, paras 3–6.
[24] T. C. Hartley, "International Agreements and the Community Legal System: Some Recent Developments", 8 *ELR* (1983), 383 at 390.
[25] *Polydor* [1989] ECR 329; *Kupferberg* [1982] ECR 3641; *Demirel* [1987] ECR 3719; *Greece v. Commission* [1989] ECR 3711.
[26] Opinion 2/91 (ILO Convention concerning the Safety in the Use of Chemicals at Work), [1993] ECR 1-1061. para. 36.
[27] O'Keefee and Schermers (eds)., *Mixed Agreements* (Kluwer, December 1983); Bourgeois, Dewost, Gaiffe (eds.), *La Communauté européenne et les accords mixtes. Quelles perspectives?* (P.I.E.. Bruxelles, 1997).
[28] A. Dashwood, "Why continue to have Mixed Agreements at all?" in Bourgeois, Dewost, Gaiffe (eds), n. 27 above, at 94.

The question addressed here is the extent of the ECJ's jurisdiction with respect to mixed agreements. In the literature various views have been put forward. According to some the ECJ may interpret such agreements in their entirety;[29] others take the view that the ECJ's jurisdiction is limited to clauses of a mixed agreement that do not extend beyond the EC's field of operation.[30]

Leaving aside earlier cases the ECJ faced this issue in *Demirel*[31] The request for a preliminary ruling by the ECJ was made by a German court in which Mrs Demirel, a Turkish national, challenged her expulsion which was ordered on the grounds that her visa, which was only valid for a visit, had expired. Mrs Demirel wanted to remain in Germany with her husband who resided in Germany. Mrs Demirel relied on certain provisions of the Association Agreement between the EEC and Turkey. Two Member States intervened in the proceedings in the ECJ and called the jurisdiction of the ECJ into question.

The ECJ ruled as follows:

However, the German Government and the United Kingdom take the view that, in the case of 'mixed' agreement such as the Agreement and the Protocol at issue here, the Court's interpretative jurisdiction does not extend to provisions whereby Member States have entered into commitments with regard to Turkey in the exercise of their own powers which is the case of the provisions on freedom of movement for workers.

In that connection it is sufficient to state that that is precisely not the case in this instance. Since the agreement in question is an association Agreement creating special, privileged links with a non-member country which must, at least to a certain extent, take part in the Community system, Article 238 must necessarily empower the Community to guarantee commitments towards non-member countries in all the fields covered by the Treaty. Since freedom of movement for workers is, by virtue of Article 48 *et seq.* of the EEC Treaty, one of the fields covered by that Treaty, it follows that commitments regarding freedom of movement fall within

---

[29] For example, A. Bleckmann, "*Der Gemischte Vertrag im Europarecht*", (1976) *Europarecht* 301; H. Krück Ad Art. 177 in Groeben, Thiesing, Ehlerman (eds), *Kommentar zum EU-/EG-Vertrag*, 5th ed., Vol. 4 (Nomos, Baden-Baden. 1997), at 615.

[30] For example, Schermers and Waelbroeck, *Judicial Protection in the European Communities*, 5th edn., (Kluwer, Deventer, Boston, 1992), at 430; T. Hartley, *The Foundations of European Community Law: an Introduction to the Constitutional and Administrative Law of the European Community (Oxford* University Press, 1994), 186, 273.

[31] *Meryem Demirel v. Stadt Swäbisch Gmünd* [1987] ECR 3719.

the powers conferred on the Community by Article 238. Thus the question whether the Court has jurisdiction to rule on the interpretation of a provision in a mixed agreement containing a commitment which only the Member States could enter into in the sphere of their own powers does not arise.

Furthermore, the jurisdiction of the Court cannot be called in question by virtue of the fact that in the field of freedom of movement for workers, as Community law now stands, it is for the Member States to lay down the rules which are necessary to give effect in their territory to the provisions of the agreements or the decisions to be adopted by the Association Council.

As the Court held in its judgment of 26 October 1982 in Case 104/81 *Hauptzollamt Mainz v. Kupferberg* [1982] (ECR 3641), in ensuring respect for commitments arising from an agreement concluded by the Community institutions the Member States fulfil, within the Community system, an obligation in relation to the Community, which has assumed responsibility for the due performance of the agreement.

Consequently, the Court does have jurisdiction to interpret the provisions on freedom of movement for workers contained in the Agreement and the Protocol.[32]

It should be noted that whatever may have been the reasons why Member States wanted to conclude this agreement alongside the EC, it could probably have been concluded by the EC alone. Moreover, the clauses of the agreement for whose interpretation the ECJ considered that it had jurisdiction came within the competence of the EC under Article 238 EC. The situation is arguably different with respect to the interpretation of those clauses of mixed agreements that come squarely within the competence of EC Member States

B.   The ECJ's Jurisdiction in Relation to WTO Law

1.   *The ECJ's Jurisdiction in Relation to the GATT*

There have been a series of cases involving the GATT. The point addressed here is whether the ECJ has jurisdiction under Article 177 (new Art. 234) EC to give preliminary rulings on the interpretation of the GATT.

---

[32] [1987] ECR 3719, paras 8–12.

This question was submitted to the ECJ by the Corte Suprema di Cassazione in SPI[33] in a dispute between several importers and the Italian Treasury about duties for administrative services levied on imports from GATT contracting parties. Under Italian law the provisions of the GATT were held to create subjective rights for private parties. As it was aware of previous case law of the ECJ interpreting EC law in light of the GATT, the Corte Suprema di Cassazione apparently wanted to avoid a conflict between its own interpretation and that of the ECJ. By the same token it wanted to clarify whether pursuant to Article 177 (new Art. 234) EC the ECJ considered that it had the final say on the interpretation of GATT provisions also where EC Member State courts were asked to rule on the compatibility of EC Member State measures with the GATT.

The Corte Suprema di Cassazione put the question squarely before the ECJ:

As a preliminary point: Since the Community has been substituted for the Member States with regard to the fulfilment of the obligations laid down in GATT and since it negotiated the concessions and bindings made within the framework thereof before 1 July 1968, do the provisions of GATT and the schedules thus negotiated fall (and if so, since when and subject to what limitations) within the measures on the interpretation of which the Court of Justice has jurisdiction to give a preliminary ruling under Article 177 of the Treaty, even where the national court is requested to apply them or to interpret them with reference to relations between parties for purposes other than that of determining whether or not a Community measure is valid?[34]

The ECJ replied as follows:

As the Court had occasion to stress in the judgments cited, it is important that the provisions of GATT should, like the provisions of all other agreements binding the Community, receive uniform application throughout the Community. Any difference in the interpretation and application of provisions binding the Community as regards non-member countries would not only jeopardize the unity of the commercial policy, which according to Article 113 of the Treaty must be based on uniform principles, but also create distortions in trade within the Community, as a result of differences in the manner in which the agreements in force

---

[33] *Amministrazione delle Finanze dello Stato v. Società Petrolifera Italians (SPI) and SpA Michelin Italiana (SAMI)* [1983] ECR 801.
[34] [1983] ECR 801, para. 11.

between the Community and non-member countries were applied in the various Member States.

It follows that the jurisdiction conferred upon the Court in order to ensure the uniform interpretation of Community law must include a determination of the scope and effect of the rules of GATT within the Community and also of the effect of the tariff protocols concluded in the framework of GATT. In that regard it does not matter whether the national court is required to assess the validity of Community measures or the compatibility of national legislative provisions with the commitments binding the Community ...

The answer to be given to the question submitted is therefore that, since as regards the fulfilment of the commitments laid down in GATT the Community has been substituted for the Member States with effect from 1 July 1968, the date on which the Common Customs Tariff was brought into force, the provisions of GATT have since that date been amongst those which the Court of Justice has jurisdiction, by virtue of Article 177 of the EEC Treaty, to interpret by way of a preliminary ruling, regardless of the purpose of such interpretation ... [35]

It should be noted that the ECJ did not say that the GATT was "an act of one of the Institutions of the Community" within the meaning of Article 177 (new Art. 234) EC. It relied on the purpose of this provision and on the substitution of the EC for its Member States in relation to commitments under GATT. This ruling has been approved in the literature;[36] it has also been criticized.[37] It would seem that, once the ECJ had ruled that the EC had replaced the EC Member States concerning the compliance with the obligations of the GATT, the ECJ could hardly have come to another conclusion in *SPI*.

2. The ECJ's Jurisdiction in Relation to the WTO

In view of the 'joint competence' of the EC and its Member States, a specific issue on the ECJ's jurisdiction arises in relation to the General Agreement on Trade in Services (GATS) and the Agreement on Trade-Related Aspects of Intellectual Property Rights (TRIPS).

---

[35] [1983] ECR 801, paras 14-19.
[36] For example, A. Giardina, 'International Agreements of the Member States and their Construction by the Court of Justice' in Capotorti, Ehlermann, Frowein, Jacobs, Joliet, Koopmans, Kovar (eds), *Du droit international au droit de l'intégration. Liber Amicorum PierrePescatore* (Nomos, Baden-Baden, 1987), 263 at 270.
[37] For example, T. C. Hartley, n. 24 above

The issue of the ECJ's jurisdiction has been put to the ECJ by a request for a preliminary ruling in *Hermès International on* Article 50, paragraph 6 of the TRIPS Agreement dealing with procedural rules applying to judicial remedies contemplated by the TRIPS Agreement.

It should be recalled that in its *Opinion 1/94 on* the EC competence to conclude the GATS and the TRIPS Agreements the ECJ rejected the European Commission view that the EC had exclusive competence to conclude these agreements. The ECJ also rejected the view of Member States that a number of clauses of the TRIPS Agreement (i.e. those relating to judicial remedies) fall within the exclusive competence of Member States. The ECJ was of the opinion that the EC and its Member States "are jointly competent to conclude the TRIPS Agreement".[38]

In his opinion of 13 November 1997 in *Hermès International Tesauro* AG concluded that the ECJ had jurisdiction to interpret Article 50 of the TRIPS Agreement. He relied on the fundamental requirement of a uniform interpretation and application of all provisions of mixed agreements, on the EC's international responsibility (the EC is a party to the TRIPS Agreement alongside its Member States, and this Agreement is, pursuant to Article 228 (new Art. 300) EC Treaty, binding on the EC and its Member States), the duty of the EC and its Member States to co-operate implying the duty to endeavour to adopt a common position, and the EC legal system that seeks to function and to represent itself to the outside world as a unified system.[39]

In its judgment of 16 June 1998[40] the ECJ pointed out the following. The WTO Agreement was concluded by the EC and its Member States "without any allocation between them of their respective obligations towards the other contracting parties". When the WTO was signed the EC Regulation on the Community trade mark, which contains provisions on safeguarding the Community trade mark by the adoption of provisional measures, had been in force for one month. The EC is a party to the TRIPS Agreement, which applies to the Community trade mark. EC Member State courts are required, when applying the remedies of the EC Regulation on the Community trade mark, "to do so, as far as possible, in the light of the wording and purpose of Article 50 of the TRIPs Agreement". The ECJ concluded from this that it had jurisdiction to interpret Article 50 of the TRIPS Agreement.

[38] *Opinion 1/94*, [1994] ECR 1-5267, para. 105.
[39] [1998] ECR 1-3603, 3606, at paras 20–1.
[40] [1998] ECR 1-3603.

In *Hermès*, the ECJ thus managed to avoid the issue of its jurisdiction. It is however bound to face sooner or later the issue of its jurisdiction with respect to clauses of mixed agreements that cannot be regarded as coming within the EC's powers. The consequences that would result from the absence of a uniform interpretation throughout the EC of GATS and TRIPS Agreement provisions are undoubtedly "undesirable, artificial and perhaps unworkable".[41] One might add that if the EC, and in particular, in the absence of a determination by the EC political bodies, the ECJ fails to rule on whether and how GATS and TRIPS provisions are to be interpreted uniformly within the EC, a WTO panel or the WTO Appellate Body could very well be called upon to do so.

The challenge for the ECJ is to devise a theory to justify its jurisdiction to interpret the whole of WTO law and not just those provisions that can be regarded as coming within the ECs powers. It seems fairly obvious that such clauses can hardly be assimilated to an "act of an institution of the Community" within the meaning of Article 177 (new Art. 234) EC.

In *Hermès*, Tesauro AG noted that the EC is a party to the TRIPS Agreement vis-à-vis the other WTO Members and that an international agreement concluded by the EC is, pursuant to Article 228 (new Art. 300) EC Treaty, binding on *both* the EC Member States and the EC institutions. From this, Tesauro AG concluded that the EC is responsible for each part of the agreement in question. He inferred from that the ECJ's jurisdiction to give a preliminary ruling in order to ensure the uniform interpretation, and thus application, of the international provisions in question within the EC and to protect the EC interest not to be liable for breaches by one or several EC Member States.

In the relations with third countries that probably makes sense. The EC is a rather anomalous phenomenon in international law, i.e. an actor without the entirety of external powers other actors, i.e. states, usually enjoy. Except where, upon the conclusion of a mixed agreement third parties have insisted on, and the EC has accepted to make, some declaration making clear which parts of the agreement are concluded by the EC, third parties will be in a position to call the EC rather than one or several EC Member States to account. Being in part responsible for the uncertainty on who had the power to bind itself for which parts of a mixed

---

[41] P. Eeckhout, "The Domestic Legal Status of the WTO Agreement: Interconnecting Legal Systems", 34 *CML Rev.* (1997) 11 at 20; the point is illustrated by telling examples.

agreement, in line with Article 46 of the Vienna Convention on the Law of Treaties the EC would probably be estopped from claiming that under its 'constitution' Member States rather than itself are bound by a given clause of a mixed agreement.

In the relations between the EC and its Member States the ECJ's jurisdiction over clauses of mixed agreements that are not coming within the EC's powers is more difficult to justify.

In *Hermès*, the Commission argued that there is no perfect and necessary parallelism between the EC's powers to enter into international agreements and the ECJ's jurisdiction to interpret such agreements. This is right but is subject to limitations. While recourse to Article 164 (new Art. 220) EC may justify the ECJ's jurisdiction to interpret an international agreement that is not binding on the EC,[42] this jurisdiction is incidental; it depends on a question of interpretation or validity of EC law for which the interpretation of such international agreement is relevant.[43] Such jurisdiction is not incidental where a Member State court requests a preliminary ruling by the ECJ on a clause of a mixed agreement that is squarely outside the scope of the EC's external powers in a case in which no EC rule or measure is at stake.

Eeckhout argues that the extension of the ECJ's jurisdiction to such cases could not affect the division of competence between the EC and the Member States.[44] This may very well be, but raises the question of the legal basis of the ECJ's jurisdiction in such cases.

Rosas distinguishes between different types of mixed agreements. He differentiates between "parallel" and "shared" competences of the EC and Member States. "Parallel competence" refers to cases where the EC may adhere to an international agreement with full rights and obligations as any other contracting party, alongside Member States. Rosas cites as an example the Agreement establishing the European Bank of

---

[42] As in *Burgoa* [1980] ECR 2787; or in *Poulsen and Diva Navigation* [1992] ECR 1-6019.
[43] According to Warner AG in *Haegeman v. Belgium* [1974] ECR 449 at 473, the ECJ has jurisdiction to interpret an international Agreement only "where its interpretation is relevant to the question of the validity of an act of a Community institution or to the question of the interpretation to be given to such an act"; in *Opinion 1/91* (First EEA Opinion) [1991] ECR 6079, para. 39, the ECJ limits its interpretation "insofar as that Agreement is integral part of Community law". See, also, the reasoning of the ECJ rejecting the challenge to its jurisdiction to interpret the Eurocontrol Agreement in *SAT v. Eurocontrol* [1994] ECR 1-43, para. 9.
[44] N. 41 above, at 23–4.

Reconstruction and Development open to states and the EC alike and obliging each contracting party to provide financial assistance to a third state or an international fund. "Shared" competence refers to some division, between the EC and its Member States, of rights and obligations contained in an international agreement. Rosas cites as an example of this category an agreement containing one chapter on trade in goods and another on military defence. One can further distinguish between mixed agreements with "coexistent" competence–i.e. containing clauses that fall under the exclusive competence of Member States–and mixed agreements with "concurrent" competence–i.e. the agreement as a whole cannot be separated into parts covered by EC competence and parts covered by Member States' competence.[45] According to Rosas, the ECJ would be competent to interpret the whole agreement where mixing is of a "parallel" nature and of a "concurrent" nature.[46]

Using Rosas's terminology the difficult cases are likely to arise in relation to mixed agreements of a 'concurrent' nature. Two types of cases should be distinguished. A first case arises where neither the Council nor an international document related to the mixed agreement identify those parts of the mixed agreement that are covered by EC competence. A second case arises where Member States insist on the identification of those parts of the agreement that are covered by EC competence or, alternatively, where the EC accepts requests of third countries to that effect.

In the first type of cases the absence of identification of the parts of the mixed agreement that are covered by EC competence and thus of Member States' competence may indicate that Member States' participation is more symbolic than real. In that event there does not seem to be any serious objection to the ECJ's jurisdiction. Alternatively it may indicate that the Council could not agree on where to draw the line between EC and Member States' competences. Arguably, that means that ultimately it is incumbent on the ECJ to resolve this issue and by the same token to define whether it has jurisdiction.

In the second type of cases, i.e. where the parts of the agreement covered by EC or Member States' competences are clearly identified, the ECJ could conceivably justify its jurisdiction to interpret the parts of the

---

[45] A. Rosas, "Mixed Union–Mixed Agreements" in M. Koskenniemi (ed.), *International Law Aspects of the European Union* (Kluwer Law International, The Hague, London, Boston, 1998), 125 at 129–31.
[46] Ibid., at 141.

agreement covered by Member States via the EC Member States Community loyalty duty laid down in Article 5 (new Art. 10) EC. It does not appear inconceivable to infer from Article 5 EC the duty for Member States to apply clauses of mixed agreements uniformly in view of the consequences which would result from disparate interpretations by Member States and thus the ECJ's jurisdiction to ensure such uniform interpretation. This may appear as a second-best remedy[47] but it would be a remedy for difficulties created by the recourse to mixed agreements, which is itself a second-best formula.

C. The Mandate of Article 164 EC Treaty

Article 164 (new Art. 220) EC provides that:

[t]he Court of Justice shall ensure that in the interpretation and application of this Treaty the law is observed.

Article 173 (new Art. 230) EC mentions among the grounds of illegality governing applications for annulment of EC acts: "infringement of any rule of law relating to the application of the Treaty". It is generally accepted that these grounds of illegality apply for the other methods of challenging EC acts.[48]

In *International Fruit*,[49] the first case in which it was faced with an alleged conflict between an EC measure and the GATT, the ECJ had to examine whether the 'validity' of the EC measure also referred, within the meaning of Article 177 (new Art. 234) EC, to its validity under international law. The ECJ held that this jurisdiction "extends to all grounds capable of invalidating those measures" and that:

the Court is obliged to examine whether their validity may be affected by reason of the fact that they are contrary to a rule of international law… provided that the EC is bound by that rule of international law.[50]

The ECJ did not refer to Article 164 (new Art. 220) EC, although Mayras AG had done so in his opinion.

---

[47] Which S. Prechal called "a magic box; the amalgam of all sorts of obligations which can be pulled out of a hat as one pleases", note in 29 *CML Rev.* (1992), 374 at 375.
[48] For example, Schermers and Waelbroeck, n. 30 above, at 193; with respect to validity, see G. H. Krück in Groeben, Thiesing, Ehlermann, n. 29 above; see, also, M. J. Hahn and G. Schuster, "*Le droit des Etats Membres de se prèvaloir en justice d'un accord liant la Communauté*" (1995) RGDIP 367 at 369.
[49] [1972] ECR 1219.
[50] Ibid., paras 6 and 7.

The question arises whether in reviewing EC measures as against an international law rule the ECJ is interpreting and applying EC law. Kapteyn, a member of the ECJ, argues that this is the case and that it must be: there is an implicit premise in the ECJ's reasoning i.e. the international law rule is part of EC law and may thus be interpreted and applied by the ECJ.[51]

Another interpretation is however possible in light of Article 164 (new Art. 220) EC. When interpreting and applying EC law, the ECJ is called upon to review it by reference to "the law". This "law" may be the EC Treaty itself or general principles common to the laws of the EC Member States which are considered by the ECJ as part of EC law. As results from Article 164 (new Art. 220) "the law" to be observed does not necessarily coincide with "this Treaty".[52] Members of the ECJ have argued by reference to Article 164 EC that, in seeking to resolve disputes by judicial process the ECJ may take into consideration every relevant legal factor, whatever its nature and sources.[53] Arguably, Article 164 EC does not require that the "law" to which it refers be part of EC law in order to be relied upon by the ECJ when interpreting and applying EC law. If one takes the monist view defended by Kapteyn that international law binding on the EC is incorporated in EC law,[54] the issue becomes moot.

It is interesting to note that in certain judgments the ECJ interpreted EC law by reference to international law or reviewed EC measures against international law as a matter of course without examining whether such international law was incorporated in EC law. In the *Radio Tubes* case,[55] for the purpose of interpreting Article 234 (new Art. 307) EC, the ECJ referred to a principle of international law that has since then been codified in Article 30 of the Vienna Convention on the Law of Treaties. In the *Woodpulp* case, the ECJ relied on "the territoriality principle as universally recognized in public international law" to control the EC's jurisdiction to apply its competition rules.[56] In *Opel Austria*, the

---

[51] *"Quelques réflexions sur les effets des accords internationaux liant la Communauté dans l'ordre juridique communautaire"*, in *Hacia un nuevo or Jen international y europeo. Estudios en homenaje al Profesor Don Manuel Diez de Velasco* (Technos, Madrid, 1993), 1007 and 1009.
[52] G. H. Krück in Groeben, Thiesing. Ehlermann, n. 29 above, at 374.
[53] Pescatore, A. Donner, R. Monaco, H. Kutscher, "Aspects of the Court of Justice of the European Communities of interest from the point of view of international law" 32 *ZaöRV* (1972)239–46.
[54] Kapteyn. n. 51 above, at 1010.
[55] [1962] ECR 10.
[56] *Ahlström e.a. v. Commission*, [1988] ECR 5243.

Court of First Instance of the EC considered that "the principle of good faith, a rule of customary international law, is binding on the Community" and may be relied upon by private parties.[57] It remains to be seen whether the same applies to international agreements binding on the EC.

IV.   THE STATUS OF INTERNATIONAL AGREEMENTS IN EC LAW

The question of the status of international agreements in EC law has two aspects which are not always properly distinguished: on the one hand, the relationship between international law and EC law; on the other, the effect of international law in the EC legal system.

A.   The Relationship between International Law and EC Law

1.   *The Problem*

As is well known, traditionally one distinguishes two approaches to the relationship between international law and national law: the "monist" and the "dualist" theories. Basically they relate to the question whether ("monism") or not ("dualism") an international agreement applies as such in the national legal system.

There are intermediate forms; for example, among the EC Member States[58] there are three different approaches. In a first category (e.g. Belgium, France, the Netherlands), an international agreement entered into by the state that has been duly approved by the state and has entered into force in the international plane automatically becomes part of the law of the state, without any separate act of "incorporation" or "transformation" being required. In a second category (e.g. Germany and Italy), an international agreement has, of itself, no effect in the internal legal system and requires a legislative act in order to produce that effect. Once such act is passed the international agreement is applicable as such. In a third category (e.g. Denmark and the UK), the effect of an international agreement is dependent upon a process of transformation: an international agreement, as such, has no effect, and the effect is produced only by national rules which purport to incorporate the international agreement.

---

[57] [1997] ECR 11-39, paras 90 and 93.
[58] See F. G. Jacobs, "Introduction" in F. G. Jacobs and S. Roberts (eds), *The Effects of Treaties in Domestic Law* (Sweet & Maxwell, London, 1987), XXIII. This analysis referred to the then EC Member States.

The dualist approach very often results from theories defended[59] and options taken in a given historical setting and at a time where international agreements dealt mainly with inter-state matters. However, the fact that nowadays international agreements deal increasingly with intra-state matters may precisely be used as an argument to justify a dualist approach. Such international agreements touch on matters regulated by national law; yet, parliaments are not involved in the treaty-making process. Parliaments may wish to adapt the international agreement to tailor it to national circumstances. They may want to impose their interpretation of the international agreement for the purposes of national law.[60]

There are thus two categories of arguments put forward in favour of a dualist approach: those that are derived from democratic principles and those that relate to the desire of a state to modulate as it sees fit the effect of an international agreement in its national legal system. The arguments of the first category are not entirely convincing. It is possible to involve parliaments at national level in the negotiating process. Moreover, constitutions that do not require specific legislation to incorporate an international agreement in the national legal system provide that certain categories of international agreements are not binding on the state or have no effect in the national legal system in the absence of some form of parliamentary approval. The arguments of the second category are somewhat dubious in that they appear to reserve the possibility of departing from international obligations. If that is the purpose, the right approach is to negotiate a proper clause or to enter reservations to that effect rather than to do so by the back door.

In the EC, the situation is at the same time more simple and more complicated. The EC Treaty does not pronounce on the effects of an international agreement in the EC legal system. Under the decision-making process set forth by the EC Treaty, EC Member States have a built-in guarantee that their interests will be duly taken into account,[61] since international negotiations are concluded by the Council consisting of representatives of Member States.

---

[59] Ch. Sasse recalls the theories put forward by Triepel, Anzilotti, and Kelsen in "The Common Market: Between International and Municipal Law" 75 *Yale L. J.* (1966), 695 at 712–13.
[60] See J. H. Jackson, "Status of Treaties in Domestic Legal Systems: A Policy Analysis" 86 *Am. J. Int. L.* (1992), 310 at 323–5.
[61] See, *e.g.* J. H. J. Bourgeois, "Trade Policy-making Institutions and Procedures in the European Community" in M. Hilf and E. U. Petersmann (eds), *National Constitutions and International Economic Law* (Kluwer, Deventer, 1993) 175 at 191; see, also, D. McGoldrick, *International Relations Law of the European Union* (Longman, London and New York, 1997), 89–92.

One may object that the instances in which international agreements are concluded by the Council acting by qualified majority increase and parliamentary control of the Member States in the minority will not prevent the international agreement from having effect in those Member States. This however is "compensated" by increased involvement of the European Parliament. The EC Treaty now provides that the European Parliament must be consulted before the conclusion of international agreements (Art. 228(2) (new Art. 300)) (except for international agreements based on Article 113(3) (new Art. 133)) (Art. 228(3)–in practice the European Parliament is usually consulted even on these agreements). Moreover certain types of international agreements now require the assent of the European Parliament (association agreements; agreements establishing a specific institutional framework by organizing co-operation procedures; agreements having important budgetary implications for the EC; agreements entailing amendments of an act adopted under the co-decision procedure) (Art. 228(3)).

It has been said that the European Parliament does not offer an effective substitute as a result of its limited powers, inadequate representativeness, the absence of a European political party system, and the insufficient democratic accountability of its members.[62] One begs to disagree. With respect to international agreements as indicated one can no longer argue that the European Parliaments powers are 'limited' and at any rate that they would be more limited than those of national parliaments. One fails to see in what sense its representativeness is inadequate. As to a European political party system, one wonders whether this is a necessary element: is there really in the USA a political party system similar to those in the EC Member States? Quite obviously the MEPs' democratic accountability could be improved. The question, however, is whether members of national parliaments are more accountable to their constituencies than to their party. Petersmann recognizes this as he pleads for a foreign policy constitution that does not replicate the constitutional failures of nation states.[63]

This having been said, an international agreement that has entered into force and that has been properly "concluded" by the EC is as such part of EC law according to the case law of the ECJ, from

---

[62] E. U. Petersmann, "Proposals for a New Constitution for the European Union: Building Blocks for a Constitutional Theory and Constitutional Law of the EU" 32 *CML Rev.* (1995), 1123 at 1126.
[63] Ibid., at 1140.

Haegeman[64] to *Racke*.[65] This approach of the ECJ has been generally approved in the legal literature.[66]

There is a debate in the literature on whether the ECJ is following a dualist or a monist approach. According to Pescatore, the case law analysed by him can only be explained within a pragmatic monistic theory.[67] Other writers consider that the ECJ is tending towards a dualist approach.[68] Still others take the view that it is not possible to provide a general answer to the question of the relationship between EC law and public international law[69] or that recourse to dualist and monist theories is unproductive.[70]

It would seem that the debate rests on a certain view of what monism and dualism mean. In our view, under the monist approach an international agreement is as such part of the EC legal system once the EC's "constitutional" procedures required for the EC to be bound internationally have been complied with; in other words in order to have effect in the EC legal system the international agreement does not need to be transformed in a regulation or a directive.[71] In that sense, it would

---

[64] 1974] ECR 449: "the [Association] Agreement [with Greece] was concluded by the Council under Articles 228 and 238 of the Treaty... The Agreement is therefore, in so far as concerns the Community, an act of one of the institutions of the Community...The provision of the Agreement, from the coming into force thereof, form an integral part of Community law."

[65] [1998] ECR 1-3655: "An agreement with a third country concluded by the Council in conformity with the provisions of the EC Treaty, is, as far as concerns the Community, an act of Community institutions and the provisions of such Agreement form an integral part of Community law" (para. 41).

[66] See Ch. Tomuschat ad Article 228 in Groeben, Thiesing, Ehlermann, n. 29 above, Vol. 4 at 502 and literature cited; *contra* T. Hartley n. 24 above, at 383.

[67] P. Pescatore, '*Die Rechtsprechung des Europäischen Gerichtshofs zur innergemeinschaftlichen Wirkung Völkerrechtlicher Abkommen*' in *Völkerrecht als Rechtsordnung, Internationale Gerichtsbarkeit, Menschenrechte–Festschrift Mosler* (Springer, Berlin, 1986); 661-89; this view is shared by E. U. Petersmann, 'Constitutional Principles Governing the "EEC's Commercial Policy" in M. Maresceau (ed.), *The European Community's Commercial Policy after 1992: the Legal Dimension* (Martinus Nijhoff, Dordrecht, 1992) 21 at 36; K. J. Kuilwijk, *The European Court of Justice and the GATT Dilemma* (Nexed Editions Academic Publishers, Beunougen, 1996), 84.

[68] For example, T. Hartley, n. 24 above; A. Th. S. Leenen, *Gemeenschapsrecht en Volkenrecht* (T. M. C. Asser Instituut, den Haag, 1994), 74–5 and literature cited.

[69] For example, K. Meessen, 'The Application of Rules of Public International Law within Community Law' 13 *CML Rev.* (1976) 485 at 500–1; P. Verloren van Themaat, "The Impact of the Case Law of the Court of Justice of the European Communities on the World Economic Order", *Festschrift Eric Stein* 82 *Mich. L Rev.* (1984), 1423 at 1435.

[70] U. Everling, "The Law of the External Economic Relations of the European Community" in M. Hilf, F. Jacobs and E. U. Petersmann, *The European Community and the GATT* (Kluwer, Deventer, 1986), 85 at 95.

[71] See Chapter 3 above.

seem that the ECJ has followed a monist approach from *Haegeman* to *Racke*. As will be seen, this does not mean that EC international agreements are assimilated without further ado to EC law.

However, the ECJ has never explained why an international agreement forms an integral part of EC law as a result of the fact that such agreement is concluded by the EC. Pescatore refers to Article 228 (new Art. 300) (E)EC and states: "[a]s a consequence these agreements have to be considered as being an integral part of the law applicable inside the Community".[72] But Article 228 EC only provides that international agreements are binding on the EC and EC Member States.[73] Article 228 EC is in fact stating the obvious as far as the EC institutions are concerned and it is an application of the Community loyalty clause as far as Member States are concerned.[74] Quite clearly, the act whereby the Council approves the conclusion is not considered by the ECJ as a "normative act". In *Bresciani*,[75] it held that a private party could rely on the Convention of Yaounde even though its conclusion had been approved by way of a "decision" rather than by way of a regulation which is by definition "directly applicable". Against the background of *Bresciani* the Council has maintained its non-consistent practice of approving the conclusion of international agreements by way of "decisions" or regulations making at least clear that it considers the type of the legal act as irrelevant for the status of international agreements in the EC legal system.

2. *What Does "Integral Part" of EC Law Mean?*

Having seen that according to the ECJ international agreements form an integral part of the EC legal system, the question then arises what "integral part" means, and what the ECJ has said and not (yet) said about this.

Forming an integral part of the EC legal system may mean becoming EC law. Whether this is the case has divided legal writers.[76]

---

[72] "Treaty-making by the European Communities", in F. G. Jacobs and Sh. Roberts, n. 58 above, 171 at 179.

[73] For the same assumption see O. Jacot-Guillarmod, *Droit communautaire et droit international public* (Georg, Librairie de l'University, Genève 1979), 92, who elsewhere refers to *"la forte connotation moniste"* of Article 164 EC. But isn't the question precisely whether the "law" referred to in Article 164 (new Art, 220) EC includes international law?

[74] Ch. Tomuschat ad Art. 228 in Groeben, Thiesing, Ehlermann, n. 29 above, at 501; R. Kovar, *"Les accords liant les Communautés européennes et l'ordre juridique communautaire: à propos d'une jurisprudence de la Cour de Justice"* (1974) RMC 345.

[75] [1976] ECR 129.

[76] See literature cited by Jacot-Guillarmod, n. 73 above, at 104–5.

This is not just of academic interest: it has implications for the interpretation of international agreements (EC law methods or international law methods?) and for their hierarchical status in the EC legal system (does the *lex posterior priori derogat* principle apply when an EC legal act of a later date conflicts with the international agreement?). The extent to which an international agreement forms an integral part of EC law depends also on how far it is assimilated to EC law.

(a)   Interpretation

Some of the implications of international agreements "forming integral part of Community law" became apparent in *Polydor?*[77] RSO Records Inc. and Polydor Ltd, respectively the UK owner and the executive UK licensee of the copyright of a sound recording entitled 'Spirits Having Flown' and featuring The Bee Gees, had brought an action in the UK courts against Harlequin Record Shops Ltd, a retailer. The retailer sold in the UK records reproducing the same song by the same group; these records had been produced and marketed in Portugal–before Portugal's accession to the EC–by two Portuguese licensees of RSO, the UK copyright owner.

As was established during the proceedings, Simons and Harlequin, respectively the importer-wholesaler and the retailer of the Portuguese records, had by their acts infringed section 16(2) of the UK Copyright Act of 1956. That provision, which implements the territoriality principle of the protection of copyrights, provides that a copyright is infringed by any person who, without the licence of the owner of the copyright, imports an article into the UK, if to his knowledge the making of that article constituted an infringement of that copyright, or would have constituted such an infringement if the article had been made in the place into which it was so imported. Harlequin and Simons claimed, however, that under EC law Polydor was not entitled to enforce the rights conferred upon it by section 16(2) of the Copyright Act. To that purpose they relied on the 1972 Free-Trade Agreement between the EEC and Portugal and in particular on two provisions thereof–Articles 14(2) and 23–on elimination of restrictions on trade between the two parties. These provisions are expressed in terms similar to those of the EC Treaty on the abolition of restrictions on trade within the Community (Articles 30 and 36 (new Arts. 28 and 30)). There is no doubt that if the records had as in this case been lawfully produced and marketed by a licensee in one of the

---

[77] *Polydor v. Harlequin Record Shops Ltd* [1982] ECR 329.

EC Member States instead of Portugal, the EC Treaty provisions as interpreted by the ECJ would have prevented the enforcement by RSO Records and Polydor of their UK copyrights.[78]

The ECJ first stressed the structural differences between the EEC Treaty and the Agreement. Referring to its case law interpreting the EEC Treaty provisions, the ECJ emphasized that its scope "must indeed be determined in the light of the Community's objectives and activities" and recalled that "the Treaty, by establishing a common market and progressively approximating the economic policies of the Member States, seeks to unite national markets into a single market having the characteristics of a domestic market".[79] In contrast, the Portugal Agreement, "although it makes provision for the unconditional abolition of certain restrictions… and measures having equivalent effect", does not have the same purpose as the EEC Treaty.[80] Second, there is also, according to the ECJ, an institutional difference. A distinction as to interpretation between EEC Treaty provisions and similarly worded provisions of the Portugal Agreement "is all the more necessary inasmuch as the instruments which the Community has at its disposal in order to achieve the uniform application of Community law and the progressive abolition of legislative disparities within the common market have no equivalent in the context of the relations between the Community and Portugal".[81]

This led to the conclusion that, unlike Articles 30 and 36 (new Arts 28 and 30) of the EEC Treaty, concerning intra-Community trade, the similarly worded provisions of the Portugal Agreement do not exclude a prohibition, based on the protection of copyright, on the importation into the EC of a product originating in Portugal.

---

[78] In a series of decisions involving industrial and commercial property rights, the ECJ developed the doctrine of "exhaustion of rights". Article 36 (new An, 30) of the EC Treaty, which permits restrictions in intra-Community trade where such restrictions are justified to protect industrial and commercial property rights, does not cover the right under national law to prevent importation from another Member State of products protected by an industrial or commercial property right in the importing Member State, if these products have been lawfully made and sold in the exporting Member State by the holder of the right or with his permission. See, with respect to copyrights, *Dansk Supermarked A/S v. A/S Imerco* [1981] ECR 181; *Musik-Vertrieb Membran GmbH v GEMA* [1981] ECR 147; *Deutsche Grammophon Gesellschafi mbH v. Metro-SB-Grossmärkte & Co.* [1971] ECR 487.

[79] [1982] ECR 329, para 16.

[80] Ibid., para. 18.

[81] Ibid., para. 20. Such an approach finds support in international law. See Schermers, 'The Direct Application of Treaties with Third States: Note Concerning the Polydor and *Pabst Cases*" 19 *CML Rev.* (1982), 563 at 568.

From the absence of transposition of the case law on EC law provisions, the following general indications may reasonably be inferred. Existing interpretations relating to similarly worded EC law provisions are useful only to the extent that they do not relate to the purpose of the EC Treaty, which seeks to create a single market reproducing as closely as possible the conditions of a domestic market. This is particularly relevant for provisions of international agreements relating to charges on imports other than customs duties, to measures applying specifically to imported products other than import bans or import quotas, to discrimination in taxation and in domestic legislation on manufacturing, marketing, and so on, to competition, and to state aid. To be compatible with an international agreement, it will be sufficient that a measure having a restrictive effect on trade be either justified by an exception or a derogation or pursue an aim which is legitimate under the agreement. Neither the restrictive effect[82] nor the aim[83] of such a measure will be weighed against the broader objectives of the agreement. This kind of assessment, in which considerations of expediency have a large part to play, is left to the contracting parties.

In *Polydor*, the ECJ thus made it clear that clauses of international agreements mirroring provisions of the EC Treaty, while "forming integral part of Community law", were not, for that reason, to be interpreted in the same fashion. In other words, they remain international law for the purpose of their interpretation: they are interpreted by using the customary rules of interpretation of public international law as codified in Articles 31 and 32 of the Vienna Convention on the Law of Treaties. This leads the ECJ in particular to distinguish the EC context from the context of the international agreement entered into by the EC.

Obviously, this does not mean that clauses of international agreements mirroring provisions of the Treaty will never be interpreted in the same fashion.[84]

---

[82] See the distinction between intra-Community trade and trade with third countries made in *International Fruit*, [1971] ECR 1107. See, also, *EMI* [1976] ECR 811.

[83] In *Polydor* [1982] ECR 329, the injunction restraining the sale and distribution of the imported records was tantamount to an import ban. The aim which the restrictive measure pursued, i.e. the protection of the copyright, was accepted; the ECJ did not examine whether this aim and the restrictive effect of the measures outweighed the objectives of the Agreement.

[84] In fact, judgments interpreting such clauses in the same fashion as EC provisions are more numerous from *Bresciani* [1976] ECR 129 to *Opel Austria* [1997] ECR II-39.

(b) Hierarchical Ranking of International Agreements

It is now well established that in the event of a conflict between an international agreement and the EC Treaty itself, the international agreement does not take precedence. This has been made clear by the ECJ in *Opinion 1/91* on the Agreement establishing the European Economic Area (EEA) between the EC and EFTA countries. The ECJ found that the jurisdiction conferred on the EEA Court was incompatible with EC law. It was likely to adversely affect the allocation of responsibilities defined, *inter alia,* by the European Communities Treaties and, hence, the autonomy of the EC legal order and the Agreement had "the effect of introducing into the EC legal order a large body of legal rules which is juxtaposed to a corpus of identically-worded Community rules".[85] In other words, before the EEA Agreement could lawfully be entered into, the European Communities Treaties had to be amended. The implication is that the Treaties are the "constitution" of the EC and that international agreements which conflict with the Treaties cannot take precedence over these Treaties. The Maastricht Treaty amended Article 228 (new Art. 300), whose paragraph 6 is to be seen as drawing the formal consequence from *Opinion 1/91.*[86]

There are some early *obiter dicta* to the effect that according to the ECJ in case of conflict between an international agreement and EC secondary law the former takes precedence over the latter.[87] As other courts usually do, the ECJ makes every effort to interpret EC law so as to avoid a conflict between an EC measure and international obligations.[88] So far, subject to the cases referred to in the next section, the ECJ has not found a conflict between an EC measure and an international agreement. The prevailing view in the literature is that, in the event of conflict, international rules binding on the EC take precedence over inconsistent EC secondary law.[89] To the extent that one supports a monist approach, the precedence of international rules over inconsistent EC secondary law is a logical consequence. Much depends, however, on the effect recognized

---

[85] [1991] ECR 1-60791, paras 35, 36, and 42; for a comment see M. A. Gaudissart. *'La porté des avis 1/91 et 1/92 de la Cour de Justice des Communautés européennes relatifs à la creation de l'Espace Economique Européen'*, (1992) *Rev. M.U. Eur* 121 (No. 2).

[86] Tomuschat, n. 66 above, at 511.

[87] From *International Fruit* [1972] ECR 1219, para. 7 to *Germany v. Council* [1994] ECR 1-5039, para. 111.

[88] From *Carciati* [1980] ECR 2773, para. 2 to *Poulsen and Diva Navigation* [1992] ECR 1-6019, para. 16.

[89] *E.g.* O. Jacot-Guillarmod. n. 73 above, at 120; J. Krück, n. 29 above, at 386; P. Pescatore, n. 72 above, at 182; H. Schermers in Commission of the EC (ed.), *Thirty Years of Community Law* (OOPEC, Luxembourg, 1981), 241 at 253; Schermers and Waelbroeck, n. 30 above, at 217; C. Tomuschat, n. 66 above, at 512.

to international rules, and more particularly international agreements, in the EC legal system.

B.   The Effect of International Agreements in the EC Legal System

This question is about the various functions which international agreements may have as legal rules under which courts–EC Member State courts and EC courts–review measures of the EC and of its Member States. The effect of international law in the EC legal system, and in any national legal system for that matter, has many aspects which cannot be limited to the sole question whether international law gives rise to individual rights that may be enforced in national courts.[90] The issue addressed here is probably the most important one: once an international agreement forms integral part of EC law, can it be relied upon as such in court or does it have to meet certain requirements in order to be successfully relied upon to challenge the legality of an EC act?

1.   Reliance on an EC International Agreement in an EC Member State Court

Quite obviously, there are legal rules that are not as such capable of being applied by courts either on account of their preparatory nature or because their general nature needs further legislation. In order to be relied upon in an EC Member court, an EC law provision must meet certain requirements. In particular, in order to be capable of regulating the legal position of private parties before an EC Member States court, to create rights which a private party may enforce in an EC Member States court, an EC law provision must have "direct effect", i.e. it must meet certain technical requirements:

- the provision contains a clear obligation on the Member State

- its content must be such that it can be applied by a court

- no further acts either by the EC or by Member States are required

- the provision is unconditional

---

[90]   See *for example*, with respect to WTO rules Eeckhout, n. 41 above, at 13; see also P. Pescatore, who argues that the reality cannot be summarized by the insufficiently qualified questions of whether international agreements are "applicable" within the EC and whether they are "directly enforceable", n. 67 above, at 663.

- the Member State has no discretion in the implementation of the obligation.

In its landmark judgments *Van Gend en Loos and Costa v. Enel*, the ECJ determined that where EC law provisions meet such technical requirements, they are as such enforceable in EC Member States courts because the EC "constitutes a new legal order of international law...the subject of which comprise not only Member States but also their nationals"[91] and because "the EEC has created its own legal system, which, on the entry into force of the Treaty, became an integral part of the legal system of the Member States … ".[92]

When the question arose as to the right of a private party to rely in a Member State court on an international agreement entered into by the EC, the ECJ used quite naturally the concept of "direct effect". In *Bresciani*, the ECJ held that the prohibition in Article 2(1) of the Yaounde Convention on the abolition of charges having equivalent effect to customs duties was "capable of conferring on those subject to Community law the right to rely on it before the courts" on the ground that "this obligation is specific and not subject to any implied or express reservation on the part of the Community".[93] It came to that conclusion having found that Article 2(1) of the Yaounde Convention met the technical requirements making it capable of being applied by a court. Following a similar reasoning as in *Van Genden Loos and* in *Costa/Enel*, it did not consider that such technical requirements were enough: it also relied on 'the spirit, the general scheme and the wording of the Convention".[94]

In *International Fruit*,[95] where a private party relied in court on the GATT against an EC measure, the ECJ required that a provision of international law be not only binding on the EC but also "capable of conferring rights on citizens of the Community which they can invoke before the courts". What this exactly meant is unclear. According to Kapteyn, this was equivalent to the term "self-executing".[96] Schermers criticized the ECJ for introducing an additional and unwarranted condition for the application of international law in EC law.[97]

---

[91] [1963] ECR 1 at 12.
[92] [1964] ECR 585 at 593; in *Opinion 1/91* the ECJ refers to the EEC Treaty as "the constitutional charter of a Community based on the rule of law" ([1991] ECR 1-6079, para. 21).
[93] [1976] ECR 129, para. 25.
[94] [1976] ECR 129, para. 16.
[95] [1972] ECR 1219, para. 8.
[96] "The Domestic Law Effect of Rules of International Law within the European Community System of Law and the Question of the Self-Executing Character of GATT Rules" 8 *The International Lawyer* (1974), 74 at 76.
[97] "Community Law and International Law" 12 *CML R* ev.(1975), 77 at 80.

As has been further clarified in subsequent judgments, when defining the relationship between international law (or at least international agreements) and EC law and, through EC law, EC Member State law, the ECJ does not use the same "direct effect" concept which it developed to define the relationship between EC law and EC Member State law.

In *Kupferberg*,[98] the ECJ analysed Article 21 of the FTA with Portugal on which Kupferberg relied and found that it:

> imposes on the Contracting Parties an unconditional rule against discrimination in matters of taxation, which is dependent only on a finding that the products affected by a particular system of taxation are of like nature, and the limits of which are the direct consequence of the purpose of the Agreement. As such this provision may be applied by a court and thus produce direct effects throughout the Community.[99]

However, before examining whether this provision of the Agreement was as such capable of being applied by a court, the ECJ verified whether "the nature" or "the structure" of the Agreement "may prevent a trader from relying on the provisions of the said Agreement before a court in the Community".[100]

In *Demirel*,[101] the ECJ stated this as follows:

> A provision of an agreement concluded by the Community with non-member countries must be regarded as being directly applicable when, regard being had to its wording and *the purpose and nature of the agreement* itself, the provision contains a clear and precise obligation which is not subject, in its implementation or effects, to the adoption of any subsequent measure [emphasis added].

The possibility for a private parry to rely on an international agreement depends thus not only on whether the provision relied upon is technically capable of being applied by a court but also on the nature

98 [1982] ECR 3641.
99 Ibid
100 Ibid., paras 10-22.
101 [1987] ECR 3747, para. 14.

and the structure of the international agreement of which it is part. This approach has been criticized by some writers[102] and approved by others.[103]

Whether there is a real doctrinal difference between the ECJ's concept of "direct effect" applied to EC law and the concept of "direct application" or the "self-executing" character applied to international agreements used by the International Court of Justice and national courts is left aside here.[104] The practical consequences may be important; when relying on EC law provision a private party needs to demonstrate only that that provision meets the technical criteria of "direct effect". When relying on a clause of an EC international agreement, a private party must also demonstrate that the context of this clause, i.e. the agreement, its wording, nature, and purpose, is such as to justify "direct effect".

That clauses of an international agreement are as a result denied direct effect while similarly worded EC provisions are granted direct effect is not inconsistent with a monist approach, bearing in mind the different contexts in which they originate. An EC legal provision is given direct effect, regard being had to the EC context. The concept of direct effect of EC law was developed in relation to the inner workings of the EC legal order, both as a legal system of its own right and as a creation of its "constitution" or its institutions as a "primary instrument of integration".[105] The specific purposes of developing this doctrine of direct effect may neither be easily nor appropriately transferred to a creation outside the EC legal system.[106] However, this does not mean, as several ECJ judgments show, that EC international agreements never have "direct effect", i.e. never give rise to rights that are legally enforceable in EC Member State courts. Except for the GATT and the WTO, the contrary appears to be the rule.

---

[102] For example, P. Pescatore n. 72 above, at 187.

[103] For example, C. Tomuschat n. 66 above, at 506–10.

[104] No difference: e.g. B. de Witte, *"Retour à Costa. La primauté du droit communautaire au service du droit international"* (E.U.I. Working Paper No. 49, 1983) and with qualifications H. N. Tagaras, *"L'effet direct des accords internationaux de la Communauté"*, 20 CDE (1984) 15 at 24–5; difference: *e.g.* C. Tomuschat, *"Zur Rechtswirkung der von der Europäischen Gemeinschaft abgeschlossenen Verträge in der Gemeinschaftsordnung"* in *Gedächtnisschrift LJ. Constantinesco* (Carl Heymanns, Köln, 1983), 801 at 803.

[105] G. Bebr, "Agreements concluded by the Community and Their Possible Direct Effect", 20 *CML Rev.* (1983), 35 at 66.

[106] I. Cheyne, "International Agreements and the European Community Legal System", 18 ELR (1994), 582 at 594.

2.   *Reliance on an EC International Agreement in the EC Courts*

When an applicant relies in a direct action in the ECJ or the Court of First Instance of the EC on an EC rule, he need not demonstrate that such rule has "direct effect". There is, at any rate, no judgment that states such requirements. This is not surprising. The "direct effect" concept was developed to define the relationship between the EC legal system and the legal systems of the EC Member States. It has arguably no place within the EC legal system: if, as the ECJ has repeatedly stated, private parties are subjects of that legal system, they are entitled to rely on any provision of that legal system, provided this provision is technically capable of being applied by a court.

The question then arises whether the ECJ would require that, in order to be relied upon in a direct appeal before it, a clause of an EC international agreement meet the same sort of "direct effect" test as it requires where such clause is relied upon in a national court. Subject to situations in which there has been some form of legislative implementation by the EC (see below), it would seem that the same "direct effect" test would apply: that is, the enforceability of a clause of an EC international agreement in the ECJ and in the CIF would depend not only on the technical requirements of the clause but also on its context–i.e. the international agreement (wording, nature, structure) of which it is part.[107] Here again this does not mean that no EC international agreement would ever pass the test. A case in point is *Opel Austria*,[108] in which the applicant challenged in the Court of First Instance a duty imposed on gearboxes manufactured by Opel Austria to counteract subsidies granted by Austria to Opel Austria. The applicant claimed, *inter alia*, that such duty infringed several clauses of the Agreement on the European Economic Area. The CFI applied only the technical test to Article 10 of the EEA Agreement to find that it had "direct effect".[109] It apparently took for granted that the EEA Agreement itself, its wording, nature, and purpose justified the direct effect of that Article.

---

[107] This seems to result clearly from one of the *Bananas* cases. Gulman AG took the view that it is not because a provision does not have direct effect in a Member State court that it may not be relied upon in a direct appeal in the ECJ ([1994] ECR 1-4980, para. 135). The ECJ, however, rejected his view and applied the same test in this direct appeal as the test it applied in preliminary rulings for the purposes of application by EC Member State courts ([1994] ECR 1-4973, para. 105).

[108] [1997] ECR 39.

[109] Ibid., para. 102.

3.   EC Implementing Measures

The cases described so far are to be distinguished from cases where there is some form of legislative implementation by the EC. In *Fediol III*,[110] the applicant claimed that the Commission had misinterpreted a number of GATT provisions when it rejected the applicants complaint lodged under the EC's so-called New Commercial Policy Instrument. The ECJ held that the applicant could rely on those provisions on the grounds that the New Commercial Policy Instrument defined "illicit practices" against which private parties may complain, *inter alia*, by reference to the GATT. In his opinion, Van Gerven AG took the view that an international law provision which does not have direct effect *per se* may none the less be transformed within a particular legal order, by a rule of that legal order, into a rule having direct effect.[111]

In a later case, the ECJ has taken a further step. In *Nakajima*, the applicant was questioning in an incidental manner under Article 184 (new Art. 241) EC the applicability of the EC basic anti-dumping regulation by claiming that it was incompatible with Article VI of the GATT and certain clauses of the GATT Anti-dumping Code. The ECJ considered that the applicant could rely on these GATT provisions on the ground that the basic anti-dumping regulation had according to its preamble been "adopted in order to comply with the international obligations of the Community".[112] In one of the *Bananas* cases, the ECJ made clear that it will review the legality of an EC act under the GATT "only if the Community intended to implement a particular obligation entered into within the framework of GATT, or if the Community act expressly refers to specific provision of GATT".[113]

Thus, where a provision of an international agreement does not as such have "direct effect", it may none the less acquire it where it is incorporated, even by reference, into EC law or where the EC makes clear when enacting legislation that it intended to implement the international agreement. It has been argued[114] that the latter exception is not logical: if an international agreement does not as such have "direct effect" as a result of an objective test, why and how could it acquire such direct effect as a

---

[110] [1989] ECR 1781.

[111] Ibid., at 1806, fn. 8.

[112] [1991] ECR I-2069, para. 31.

[113] *Germany v. Council* [1994] ECR I-4973. para. 111.

[114] Ph. Manin, "*A propos de l'accord instituant l'Organisation mondiale du commerce et de l'accord sur les marches publics: la question de l'invocabilité des accords internationaux conclus par la Communauté européenne*" (1997) RTDE 399 at 409.

result of some statement of the Council of the European Union in an EC legal act that this act is designed to implement that agreement? The counter-argument is that where under the objective test an international agreement has no "direct effect", this means that contracting parties have no international duty to allow its enforcement by national courts. This does not mean that a contracting party may not do so.

V.   THE STATUS OF THE GATT AND THE WTO AGREEMENT IN EC LAW

The purpose of this section is to examine in light of the findings of the previous section the status of the GATT and the WTO Agreement in EC Law.

A.   The Relationship between the GATT, and the WTO Agreement, and EC Law

It may be recalled that the ECJ has avoided stating, unlike it did for other international agreements, that the GATT "forms integral part of Community law". This may be due to the fact that the EC was not a contracting party to GATT 1947. The ECJ has, however, avoided this qualification also in relation to WTO Agreements.

1.   Interpretation

In view of the ECJ's stance on the effect of GATT and WTO law in the EC legal system, there is little to say about the question how GATT and WTO law are interpreted by the ECJ and about their hierarchical rank in the EC legal system.

In *Fediol II*,[115] the ECJ examined the Commission's interpretation of the term "subsidy" in light of the GATT and the Tokyo Round Subsidies Code. It held that "the Commission was not wrong or arbitrary in concluding that the concept of subsidy... presupposes the grant of an economic advantage through a charge on the public account". In *Nakajima*, in which it accepted that the Tokyo Round Anti-dumping Code could be relied upon in a plea of illegality under Article 184 (new Art. 241) EC, the ECJ compared the EC Anti-dumping Regulation and the relevant international provision. It concluded that the EC Anti-dumping Regulation was in conformity with the international law provision

---

[115] [1988] ECR 4155, para. 12.

"inasmuch as, without going against the spirit of the latter provision, it confines itself to setting out, for the various situations which might arise in practice, reasonable methods of calculating the constructed normal value".[116] In the *International Dairy Agreement* case the Commission brought proceedings against Germany for the latter's breach of obligations under the EC Treaty resulting from its failure to comply, *inter alia*, with the International Dairy Agreement (hereinafter the IDA), one of the agreements concluded in the framework of the Tokyo Round. Germany contended that the IDA did not cover goods imported and exported under inward processing arrangements. The ECJ rejected Germany's interpretation of the IDA on one point on the basis of the text[117] and on another point on the basis of the context of the relevant provision and of "the general rule of international law requiring the parties to any agreement to show good faith in its performance",[118] together with the purpose of the IDA.[119] It should be noted that Germany did not argue, even in the alternative, that the IDA did not form an integral part of EC law or that it could not otherwise be relied upon by the Commission.

From this limited evidence, it seems to follow that when *interpreting GATT* provisions the ECJ follows the same approach as in the case of other international agreements.

2. Hierarchical Ranking

Although so far the ECJ has not held a provision of secondary EC law illegal for breach of a GATT or a WTO obligation, it has accepted that possibility in Fediol II and *Nakajima*. That possibility is, however, very limited in view of the ECJ's stance on the effect of the GATT in the EC legal system. It would very probably take the same stance as regards other WTO agreements.

B. The Effect of WTO Agreements in the EC Legal System

1. Reliance on WTO Agreements in EC Member States Courts

As already indicated, since *International Fruit* the ECJ has held that GATT and GATT agreements cannot be relied upon by private parties in EC Member State courts in order to challenge EC or national measures.

---

[116] (1991) ECR 1-2069. para. 37.
[117] [1996] ECR 1-3989.
[118] Ibid., para. 30.
[119] Ibid., paras 31-7.

After *Nakajima,* in which the ECJ set the door to reliance on a GATT agreement ajar, one could have wondered whether the ECJ would display a similar, more open attitude with respect to enforcement of GATT and GATT agreements by Member State courts. Certainly the ECJ no longer needed to be concerned about the risk for the uniform application of EC law if Member State courts were to enforce the GATT and GATT agreements. In *Foto-Frost,* the ECJ had held that a Member State court faced with a plea of illegality of an EC measure could only disapply such measures following a preliminary ruling by the ECJ to that effect.[120] The ECJ could thus ensure the uniform application of EC law in light of GATT obligations.

However, subsequent judgments, in particular the main *Bananas* judgment,[121] revealed that uniform application of EC law by Member State courts was not the ECJ's main concern. At any rate, as already indicated, the ECJ's concern about uniform application of EC law by Member State courts and beyond that the integrity of EC law in the face of international obligations acquired a new dimension in the wider WTO context. The EC and the Member States being jointly competent for concluding the GATS and the TRIPS Agreement, it is likely, as the *Hermes* case shows, that some Member State courts, will consider that provisions of these agreements may be relied upon before them and enforced by them. Less than ten days after the ECJ rendered judgment in *Hermes,* another Dutch court in another case specifically submitted to the ECJ a request for preliminary ruling on the direct effect of the same TRIPS provisions.[122] Even if an EC measure is not directly at issue, disparate enforcement by Member State courts of an international agreement, such as the TRIPS, may well have an impact on the movement of goods across Member State lines within the EC.[123]

2. *Reliance on WTO Agreements in the EC Courts*

As already indicated, when an applicant relies in a direct action in the ECJ or the Court of First Instance on an EC rule, he need not demonstrate that such rule has "direct effect": this is not the case with

---

[120] [1987] ECR 4199.

[121] [1994] ECR 1-4973.

[122] The Hague District Court on 25 June 1998 in *Parfums Christian Dior v .Tuk Consultancy,* cited by M. C. E. J. Bronckers, "The Exhaustion of Patent Rights under *WTO* Law", 32 *JWT* (No. 5, 1988), 137 at 141; see, also, the Dutch Supreme Court on 30 October 1998 in *Assco Holland Steigers Plettac v. Wilhelm Lagher GmbH* (OJ 1999 C1/6).

[123] This is one of the reasons why the ECJ interpreted the First EC Directive on Trademarks as excluding the exhaustion theory in relation to goods put on the market by the trademark holder or with his consent outside the EC in *Silhouette* [1998] ECR 1-4799.

international agreements. As has been mentioned, in the main *Bananas* case, the ECJ subjected the possibility to rely on the GATT in a direct appeal to practically the same 'direct effect' test as the test to be used by EC Member State courts for the purposes of applying international agreements.

In this case the ECJ defined the issue as "assessing the scope of GATT in the Community legal system". It applied the test based on "the spirit, the general scheme and the terms of the GATT".[124] It then stated:

> 106   It is settled law that GATT which according to its preamble is based on the principle of negotiations undertaken on the basis of 'reciprocal and mutually advantageous arrangements', is characterized by the great flexibility of its provisions, in particular those conferring the possibility of derogation, the measures to be taken when confronted with exceptional difficulties and the settlement of conflicts between the contracting parties.

> 107   The Court has recognized that those measures include, for the settlement of conflicts, depending on the case, written recommendations or proposals which are to be 'given sympathetic consideration', investigations possibly followed by recommendations, consultations between or decisions of the *contracting parties,* including that of authorizing certain contracting parties to suspend the application to any other of any obligations or concessions under GATT and, finally, in the event of such suspension, the power of the party concerned to withdraw from that agreement.

> 108   It has noted that where, by reason of an obligation assumed under GATT or of a concession relating to a preference, some producers suffer or are threatened with serious damage, Article XIX gives a contracting party power unilaterally to suspend the obligation and to withdraw or modify the concession, either after consulting the contracting parties jointly and failing agreement between the contracting parties concerned, or even, if the matter is urgent and on a temporary basis, without prior consultation (see Joined cases 21 to 24/72 *International Fruit Company v. Produktschap voor Groenten en Fruit* [1972] ECR 1219, paragraphs 21, 25 and 26; Case 9/73 *Schlüter v. Hauptzollampt Lörrach* [1973]

---

[124] [1994] ECR I-4973, para. 105.

ECR 1135, paragraph 29; Case 266/81 *SIOT v. Ministero delle Finanze* [1983] ECR 731, papragraph 28; and Joined Cases 267 to 269/91 *Amministrazione delle Finanze dello Stato v. SPI and SAMI* [1983] ECR 801, paragraph 23).

It concluded that:

110   The special features noted above show that the GATT rules are not unconditional and that an obligation to recognize them as rules of international law which are directly applicable in the domestic legal system of the contracting parties cannot be based on the spirit, general scheme or terms of GATT.

The end-result is that the GATT cannot be relied upon in the EC courts to challenge the lawfulness of EC measures, be it by private parties or by Member States. The ECJ added that:

it is only if the Community intended to implement a particular obligation entered into within the framework of GATT, or if the Community act expressly refers to specific provisions of GATT, that the Court can review the lawfulness of the Community act in question from the point of view of the GATT rules.[125]

C.   Some Comments

The ECJ's case law on the GATT has been abundantly commented on in the literature. The judgment in the main *Bananas* case has likewise prompted many to put forward their views.[126] Some points should be noted in particular at this stage.

From an EC law perspective the ECJ's approach has an obvious dualist flavour: the GATT may only be relied upon against EC measures if the EC political bodies have so decided. This results from the statement

---

[125] [1994] ECR. 1-4973, para. 111.

[126] For example, G. Berrisch, *"Zum Bananen-Urteil des EuGH vom 5.10.1994"*, (1994) *EWR* 461; M. Dony. *"L'affaire des Bananes"*, 31 *CDE* (1995) 461; F. Castillo de la Torre, "The Status of GATT in EC Law, Revisited", 29 *JWT* (No. 1,1995) 53; P. Eeckhout and S. Coppieters, *"Hoe krom zijn de bananen nu nog?"*, 46 *SEW* (1998) 402; U. Everling, "Will Europe slip on Bananas? The Bananas Judgment of the Court of Justice and National Courts", 33 *CML Rev.* (1996) 401; M. J. Hahn and G. Schuster, n. 48 above; Ph. Lee and B. Kennedy, "The Potential Direct Effect of GATT 1994 in European Community Law", 30 *JWT* (No. 1, 1996) 67; Ph. Manin, n. 114 above; C. Schmid, *"Immer Wieder Bananen; der Status des GATT/WTO-Systems im Gemeinschaftsrecht"*, (1998) NJW 189 (No. 4).

in the main *Bananas* case reported earlier.[127] This stands in contrast to *Kupferberg*[128] where the ECJ considered that it was up to the courts to decide on the effect of an international agreement in the internal legal order, where contracting parties to such agreement have not agreed on this effect. By leaving it to the EC political bodies to decide on the effect in the EC legal system of the GATT, the ECJ has effectively introduced some sort of 'sovereignty shield'"[129] in the hands of these political bodies against the GATT. The ECJ appears to have bowed in advance to the statement in the preamble of the Council Decision approving the WTO Agreements according to which "the Agreement establishing the World Trade Organization, including the Annexes thereto, is not susceptible to being directly invoked in Community or Member State courts".[130] Interestingly, Advocates General have different views on whether this statement is binding on the ECJ.[131]

From an international law perspective, the different outcomes of the "direct effect" test as applied by the ECJ to the GATT and as applied to other EC international agreements remain puzzling. The distinctions made in the past[132] do at any rate no longer apply since the entry into force of the WTO Agreement.

From a WTO perspective the ECJ did not draw any consequences from the considerable change brought about by the Understanding on Rules and Procedures Governing the Settlement of Disputes (hereinafter the DSU): the settlement of disputes is compulsory and panel and Appellate Body reports are adopted by the Dispute Settlement Body, representing the WTO Members, unless there is a consensus against the adoption. As part of the WTO Agreement the DSU entered into force on 1 January 1995, that is, after the main *Bananas* judgment. However, in *Chiquita Italia* the ECJ gave its preliminary ruling on 12 December 1995 and it repeated its stance in the main *Bananas* case without even mentioning the DSU.[133] If the ECJ is to maintain its doctrine that the GATT

---

[127] [1994] ECR 1-4973, para. 111.

[128] [1982] ECR 3641, para. 18.

[129] Term used in the EP's *Report on the Relationship between International Law, Community Law and Constitutional Law of the Member States* (PE 220.225/fin).

[130] OJ 1994 L 336/1.

[131] No: Tesauro AG in *Hermès*, n. 39 above; not without relevance; Cosmas AG in *Affish* ([1997] ECR 1-4315, opinion para. 127); quoted by Elmer AG in support of denying 'direct effect' of GATT in T-Port ([1998] ECR 1-1023, opinion para. 28).

[132] In *Kziber* van Gerven AG contrasted the GATT and the Co-operation Agreement with Morocco (much more restricted possibilities for adopting safeguard measures and compulsory settlement of disputes) [1991] ECR 1-199.

[133] [1995] ECR 1-4533. para. 26

does not meet the "direct effect" test and extends it to other WTO agreements, it will need to devise standards, other than the standards it used up to now to deny "direct effect" to the GATT and WTO agreements.

1. Tentative Assessment

Irrespective of the merits or disadvantages of the ECJ case law on the GATT 1947 and the GATT 1994 from other perspectives, its internal logic cannot be disputed. As other international agreements, the GATT is binding on the EC as an international instrument. Its effect in the EC legal system, or as the ECJ calls it, its "scope" (*"portée" "Bedeutung"*), is to be determined according to rules of interpretation of public international law. In order to be relied upon to challenge the legality of EC acts that are in conflict with the GATT, its provisions must meet the requirements of "direct effect"; that is, the provisions must be clear and unconditional, and the agreement of which they form part must be such as to justify "direct effect" in light of its wording, nature, and purpose.

This having been said, as already indicated it is remarkable that the outcomes of the same test as applied to a series of EC international agreements and as applied to the GATT 1947 and even more so to the GATT 1994 are fundamentally different. The fairly widespread criticism which the ECJ's approach to the GATT 1947 and to the GATT 1994 met in legal literature prompts the question why, from a legal and a legal policy point of view, the ECJ is bound to, or, as the case may be, ought to accord the GATT 1994 and other WTO agreements the effect in the EC of a rule of law that may be relied upon to review the lawfulness of EC measures; and this, irrespective of whether the EC political bodies have decided to give it such effect.

(a) The Legal Point of View

Regard should be had to the GATT and to the EC Treaty in order to verify whether they contain any principle or rule requiring the ECJ to recognize 'direct effect' to GATT rules.

> i. Is the Denial of "Direct Effect" of GATT Rules Inconsistent with the EC's International Obligations?

It has been argued that in denying the possibility of relying on GATT rules to challenge inconsistent EC acts, the ECJ is disregarding, even breaching, international law. One of the most outspoken advocates of this theory is Petersmann.[134] However gallant, Petersmann's efforts are not persuasive *de lege lata*. It is obvious that a number of GATT rules are perfectly capable of being applied by a court of law, as they are applied by WTO panels and the WTO Appellate Body. But this is not the point. Save for a few scattered provisions, the WTO Agreement leaves it clearly to each individual Member to decide how to comply with its obligations or, to coin the phrase used by the ECJ, to determine on its own the "scope" *("portée", "Bedeutung")* of the various agreements that form part of the WTO Agreement in its internal legal system. The only requirement on each Member is to "ensure the conformity of its laws, regulations and administrative procedures with its obligations"[135] as provided in the WTO Agreement.

There certainly was no consensus within the WTO membership on the advisability of a clause providing how Members should incorporate WTO rules and even less so on any clause providing for domestic remedies to ensure that their laws, regulations, and administrative procedures comply with WTO obligations. A Swiss proposal made during the Uruguay Round and designed to ensure that the resulting agreements would be capable of having direct effect or some equivalent status in the national law of all participants was rejected by most big players in the negotiations and dropped.[136] Roessler's remark, made in 1990, that the citizen had so far not been seriously considered by the trade negotiators in the GATT as a candidate to enforce GATT rules[137] is still valid.

The negotiations on the dispute settlement system illustrate this. At the end of the dispute settlement process, there *can* no longer be any doubt about the precise substantive scope of a Member's obligation. Yet, no agreement could be found on a provision entitling the Dispute Settlement Body to recommend to a Member how it should comply in bringing its measures into conformity with WTO rules: a panel or the

---

[134] See, *inter alia*, *"Darf die EC das Völkerrecht ignorieren?"* 8 EuZW (No. 11, 1997) 325; for a reply J. Sack, *"Von der Geschlossenheit und den Spannungsfeldern in einer Weltordnung des Rechts"*, 8 EuZW (No. 21, 1997) 650; for a rejoinder E. U. Petersmann, *"GATT/WTO—Recht: Duplik"*, 8 EuZW (No. 21, 1997) 651; for a second reply J. Sack. *"Noch einmal: GATT/ WTO und europäisches Rechtschutzsystem"*, 8 EuZW (No. 22, 1997) 688.
[135] Marrakesh Agreement establishing the World Trade Organization An. XVI:4 published in WTO, *The Results of the Uruguay Round of Multilateral Trade Negotiations, The Legal Texts* (Geneva, 1995), at 6.
[136] P. J. Kuijper, "The New WTO Dispute Settlement System: the Impact on the Community" in Bourgeois, Berrod, Gippini-Fournier (eds), *The Uruguay Round Results. A European Lawyers' Perspective (EIP*, Brussels, 1995), 87 at 106.
[137] F. Roessler, "The Constitutional Function of the Multilateral Trade Order" in Hilf and Petersmann, n. 61 above, 53 at 62.

Appellate Body may only "suggest" ways to do so.[138] There is thus no GATT/WTO obligation that would require the ECJ to grant 'direct effect' to GATT/WTO rules.

ii.   Denial of "Direct Effect" and EC Legal Principles

One should distinguish between the position of private parties on the one hand, and that of EC Member States (and conceivably that of EC Institutions) on the other.

As far as *private panics* are concerned, Petersmann has for many years brilliantly and with unceasing determination defended the theory of the "domestic policy functions of GATT law".[139] He has argued, *inter alia*, that the EC's GATT obligations on the use of transparent, non-discriminatory and proportionate policy instruments must be taken into account in the interpretation of the foreign trade law of the EC.[140]

Certain constitutional law principles have been laid down in the EC Treaty such as proportionality (Art. 3(b) (new Art. 5), para. 3) and non-discrimination (Art. 6 (new Art. 12)). Are these principles to be construed as requiring the ECJ to enforce, and thus to recognize 'direct effect' to any GATT/WTO obligation? Article 6 EC which lays down the non-discrimination principle does not expressly limit its scope to citizens of EC Member States or to situations within the EC. Yet, so far, the ECJ has held that there exists in the EC Treaty no general principle obliging the EC, in its external relations, to accord to non-member countries equal treatment in all respects.[141] Similarly the ECJ has effectively held that the EC Treaty does not require according national (EC) treatment to non-EC goods.[142] This appears to be right as far as Article 6 (new Art. 12) EC as such is concerned. Relying on this provision as a mandate for the ECJ to interpret it in light of EC international obligations on non-discriminatory

---

[138] Understanding on Rules and Procedures Governing the Settlement of Disputes, Art. 19:1 published in WTO, *The Results of the Uruguay Round of Multilateral Trade Negotiations* (Geneva, 1995), 404.

[139] For example, in "The EEC as a GATT Member–Legal Conflicts Between GATT Law and European Community Law" in Hilf, Jacobs, Petersmann, n. 70 above, 25 at 28.

[140] "National Constitutions and International Economic Law" in Hilf and Petersmann, n. 61 above, at 20.

[141] *Faust v. Commission* [1982] ECR 3745; recently *United Kingdom v. Council*, judgment of 19 November 1998 (not yet reported).

[142] For example, *EMI Records v. CBS U.K.*[1976] ECR 811 where the ECJ stated that 'the provisions of the Treaty on commercial policy do not, in Article 110 *et seq.*, lay down any obligation on the part of the Member States to extend to trade with third countries the binding principles governing the free movement of goods between Member States... " (para. 17).

treatment is a circular reasoning. It presupposes that the international obligation is to be interpreted as creating individual rights which are enforceable in a court of law.

The proportionality principle could possibly come into play in connection with Article 110 (new Art. 131) EC, according to which the aims of the EC's commercial policy are to contribute to the harmonious development of world trade, the progressive abolition of restrictions on international trade, and the lowering of customs barriers. Reliance on the proportionality principle to require the ECJ to enforce compliance with GATT obligations faces several hurdles. First, it implies that GATT obligations are to be subsumed in the aims set forth in Article 110 (new Art. 131) EC as a benchmark to test the proportionality of an EC trade policy measure or, more precisely, the direct objective pursued by that measure. This is far from obvious. Article 110 has been inserted in the EEC Treaty to quieten fears that had been raised in some third countries as a result of the proposal leading to the creation of the EEC.[143] This can, however, hardly be construed as a condition to which the Member States have subjected the transfer of trade policy powers to the then EEC. Second, the possible review of the lawfulness of an EC trade policy measure in light of the aims of Article 110 EC, incorporating compliance with GATT obligations, would involve assessing the proportionality of the balance struck by political bodies weighing conflicting policy objectives. The ECJ has not ruled out such weighing as being non-justiciable.[144] However, the ECJ carries out at best a marginal review. It considers that the lawfulness of a measure can be affected only if the measure is manifestly inappropriate having regard to the objective pursued.[145] The ECJ even lets such decisions stand when challenged as disproportionate in light of certain fundamental rights.[146] When fundamental rights are at stake the ECJ errs probably on

---

[143] A. Sciolla-Lagrange, P. Herzog and Article 110 in Smit and Herzog (eds) *The Law of the European Economic Community. A Commentary* (Matthew Bender, New York, NY, 1976); cf. U. Everling in Wohlfarth, Everling, Glaesner, Sprang (eds), *Die Europäische Wirtschafisgemeinschaft* (Berlin-Frankfurt a.M., 1960); J. Mégret in J. Mégret, J. V. Louis. D. Vignes, M. Waelbroeck (eds.) *Le droit de la Communauté économique européenne*, Vol. 6. (Ed. ULB, 1976), t.1, 393.
[144] For example, in ADBHU ([1985] ECR 531) the ECJ reviewed rules of a Directive on the collection of waste oils in light of the principle of freedom of trade and held that their restrictive effect on that freedom did not 'go beyond the inevitable restrictions which are justified by the pursuit of the objective of environmental protection, which is in the general interest'.
[145] E.g. most recently with respect to quantitative restrictions on imports of toys from China, *United Kingdom v Council*, judgment of 19 November 1998 (not yet reported).
[146] The result in the main *Bananas* case, in which Germany relied, *inter alia*, on fundamental rights, amounts, according to Everling (n. 126 above, at 419), to granting *carte blanche* to the EC political bodies.

the side of caution when applying the proportionality test. It let decisions stand which were arrived at by the EC political bodies with difficulty and after much debate. However, the aims of the EC's trade policy set forth in Article 110 (new An. 131) EC can hardly be assimilated to fundamental rights against which trade policy measures are to be reviewed via the proportionality test.

As far as *Member States* are concerned, the ECJ's ruling that the scope of GATT is such that Member States also cannot rely on its provisions to challenge the legality of an EC act has been criticized in the literature. It has been argued that the ECJ is preventing Member States from protecting themselves against their international liability for breaches of GATT/WTO law[147] It is, to say the least, debatable that another WTO Member could call EC Member States to account for breaches of WTO rules by the EC in matters for which the EC is the proper WTO Member. In *T-Port*, another *Bananas* case, a *Finanzgericht* thought that as a result of Article 234 (new Art. 307) EC, Germany should have the power to fulfil its obligations under GATT law which takes precedence over the EC common organization of the banana market of a later date. The ECJ considered the question as irrelevant, as Ecuador, the country from which the bananas were imported, was not a party to the GATT 1947. In its opinion Elmer AG was quite rightly of the view that claims arising from GATT 1994 can only be addressed to the EC and not to the various Member States.[148] According to some writers EC Member States are acting in an *"amicus curiae"* capacity; they may be defending their own interests but they may also do so to seek to ensure that the law is observed by the EC.[149] To the extent that the ECJ would in the main *Bananas* case have assimilated Germany's *ius standi* to that of a private party, Everling's criticism would be justified. Denying a Member State the right to challenge an EC measure on account of its inconsistency with WTO law, as the ECJ did in the main *Bananas case*, while allowing the European Commission to challenge a Member State measure on account of its inconsistency with GATT law, as the ECJ did in the *IDA* case, is on balance not satisfactory, if one considers that the two situations are comparable.[150] It is true that both cases involved a breach of GATT obligations of the EC. In EC law terms both cases

[147] Everling, n. 126 above, at 423; Hahn and Schuster, n. 48 above, at 374; M. Hilf, 'The Role of National Courts in International Trade Relations' in Hilf, Petersmann, n. 61 above, 559 at 575.
[148] [1998] ECR 1-1023, opinion, para. 16.
[149] Everling, n. 126 above, at 422; Hahn and Schuster, n. 48 above, at 375. Schmid, n. 126 above, at 193; doubtful: P. Manin, n. 114 above, at 409, fn. 31.
[150] See, *inter alia*, C. Schmid, n. 126 above, at 192; in the *IDA case* Tesauro AG expressed his 'misgivings' as to this approach ([1996] ECR 1-3992, para. 23).

involved a breach of Article 228 (new Art. 300), paragraph 7 EC. They can however be distinguished. The main *Bananas* case was about the enforcement of an obligation of the EC *vis-à-vis* the GATT while the *IDA* case was about enforcement of a Member State obligation primarily vis-à-vis the EC. The rationale of *IDA* seems to be that it cannot be left to a Member State to appreciate autonomously whether or not to respect an obligation under the GATT. In the main *Bananas* case the rationale appears to be that the decision whether or not to respect an obligation under the GATT should be reserved for the EC.[151] Alternatively, in both cases the ECJ upholds EC law rather than international law. In *Bananas* it denies a Member State the right to challenge an EC measure as being inconsistent with an international obligation of the EC. In *IDA*, it accepts the right of the Commission to challenge a Member State measure as being inconsistent with the EC decision to comply with an international obligation of the EC.

As an aside it would seem that the ECJ's stance with respect to review of trade policy decisions in general, of which its stance with respect to the exclusion of the GATT as grounds for reviewing EC trade policy measures could be one example, is not in effect out of line with the position of the judiciary in at least some of the Member States that follow a monist approach. In France the application of the *"actes de gouvernement"* doctrine[152] could very well lead to the same result. In Germany courts tend to interfere only where an individual may be affected directly by an individual executive act rather than by an international treaty, and in the field of foreign trade law courts do recognize that their own expertise in the evaluation of notions like "public interest", "general welfare", and others is not better than that of the Parliament or the executive.[153]

2.   *The Legal Policy Point of View*

As far as the position of private parties is concerned, the arguments found in the literature in favour of permitting private parties to rely on GATT, now WTO, rules to challenge EC measures are attractive. One may leave aside the economic and political economy justifications;[154]

---

[151] Sec C. Timmermans, "The Implementation of the Uruguay Round by the EC" in Bourgeois, Berrod, Gipppini-Fournier, n. 133 above, 501 at 507.
[152] For a short description see E. Zoller, "EEC Foreign Trade Law and French Foreign Trade Law" in Hilf, Petersmann, n. 61 above, 265 at 268.
[153] M. Hilf, "Treaty-making and Application of Treaties in Germany", in Hilf, Petersmann, n. 61 above, 211 at 230.
[154] As some of the arguments put forward by C. J. Kuilwijk, n. 67 above, at 263-333 and by F. L. Abbott, 'Regional Integration Mechanisms in the Law of the United States: Starting Over' I *Ind. J. Global Leg. Stud.* (1993), 155.

they are a matter of political choice beyond the remit of the ECJ. There is however a legal policy argument. GATT and WTO law is made by states for states, but it is also made for private parties. Notwithstanding respectable arguments to the contrary,[155] at the end of the day there is something wrong with a system that on the one hand generates rules designed to regulate international trade, even it if is to regulate what states are supposed to do or not to do in matters of trade, but, on the other, denies people, affected by what states do or do not do in matters of trade, the possibility of relying on these rules to protect their interests.

The opposing legal policy consideration has to do with the position of EC governments. Clearly, many Member States would not welcome a review by the ECJ of EC measures against GATT/WTO rules at least at the request of private parties. In *Kupferberg* several Member States intervened in the proceeding to urge the ECJ to reply in the negative to the *Bundesfinanzhof's* question on the direct effect of the EEC–Portugal Free Trade Agreement.[156] Interestingly, in that case the German government referred to its observations in *Polydor,* in which, alongside the Danish, French, Netherlands, and UK governments, it had supported Polydor's argument against direct effect of the EEC–Portugal Free Trade Agreement. The German government added that the structure of the Agreement and the intentions of its authors were such that infringements of a provision of the Agreement were to give rise to consultations between the two contracting parties; in view of that, it would, according to the German government, be contrary to the general scheme of the Agreement to confer direct effect on provisions of this type.[157] The message conveyed to the ECJ by the EC Member States intervening in *Kupferberg* was clear: this was a matter for governments not for courts. While in the main *Bananas* case two Member States intervened to support Germany's application, other Member States intervened in support of the Council's defence that the GATT could not be relied upon by Germany to challenge the lawfulness of the import rules for bananas. It may be recalled that when approving the conclusion of the WTO Agreement, the Council, and thus (at least a qualified majority of) Member States, stated that this agreement and the agreements forming part of it are not susceptible to being directly invoked in EC or Member States' courts. This reflects the view traditionally held by most governments of EC Member States that trade policy, as part

[155] For example, J. H. Jackson, n. 60 above.
[156] As aptly recalled by P. Mengozzi, "The Marrakesh DSU and its Implications on the International and European Level" in Bourgeois, Berrod, Gippini-Fournier (eds), n. 133 above, 115 at 126.
[157] [1982] ECR 329 at 340.

of foreign relations, is the preserve of governments and that interference by courts is to be avoided in order to pursue fully the possibilities of resolving disputes by negotiation.

With respect to the GATT and more generally the WTO, the main policy argument why it is thought preferable not to have "direct effect" and thus keep the EC's hands free is well known. As long as other Members do not allow private parties to rely on WTO rules in their courts, their political bodies keep their hands free. Should courts in the EC enforce GATT/WTO rules for the benefit of private parties – or Member States– the EC political bodies would have their hands tied behind their backs. This argument has, however, become significantly less persuasive. The much-vaunted flexibility of the GATT is no more. The new WTO dispute settlement system, while leaving room for negotiated settlements before the Dispute Settlement Body adopts a panel report–which it does absent a consensus against adoption–is for all practical purposes adjudication. Once a panel report–or, as the case may be, an Appellate Body report– has been adopted, discussion about who is legally right or wrong is no longer possible. The only flexibility left is about remedies; that is, comply or pay with new trade concessions.

Another policy argument put forward against "direct effect" of GATT and more generally WTO rules is that in none of the other main *WTO* Members can these rules be directly enforced in national courts. This is the case, *inter alia,* in the USA and in Japan. In the USA, the "political question" doctrine[158] could be relied upon to exclude review of US laws or measures against WTO rules, if this were not excluded *de plano* by Congress. In Japan there is a general negative attitude of the courts towards arguments relying directly upon treaties and alleging conflicts between Japanese law and treaties.[159] "Direct effect" of these rules in the EC would, it is argued, upset the balance of rights and obligations within the WTO.[160] Whether as a result the EC would necessarily be worse off from a general economic point of view is questionable. The fact is that from a political point of view a stricter enforcement of GATT/WTO rules by the EC is perceived as detrimental to the EC's interests.

---

[158] F. L. Morrison and R. E. Hudec, 'Judicial Protection of Individual Rights under the Foreign Trade Laws of the United States', in Hilf, Petersmann, n. 61 above, at 112-14.
[159] Yuji Iwasawa, 'Implementation of International Trade Agreements in Japan', in Hilf, Petersmann, n. 61 above, 299 at 344.
[160] See *inter alia* P. Kuijper in Bourgeois, Berrod, Gippini-Fournier, n. 133 above, 87 at 105 and Ph. Lee and B. Kennedy, n. 126 above.

From an EC Member State perspective, there is conceivably an additional policy reason why Member States should not be permitted to challenge EC trade policy measures on the grounds that they are inconsistent with the GATT and more generally the WTO. To the extent that such policy measures are decided by the Council of the European Union by qualified majority voting, EC Member States may want to avoid giving outvoted Member States a second bite at the cherry, i.e. the possibility of overturning a qualified majority decision by a judicial challenge based on the GATT or more generally the WTO, which would make compliance by the EC with its international obligations into a device protecting Member States against qualified majority decisions prejudicial to their interests. Yet, as the example of Germany's legal challenge in the main *Bananas* case shows, this is not (or no longer) a unanimous view. Germany was supported by Belgium and the Netherlands. That challenge has been followed by a challenge by the Netherlands of an EC Directive on the Legal Protection of Biotechnological Inventions on the grounds, *inter alia*, that a provision of this Directive is in breach of the TRIPS Agreement and of the WTO Agreement on Technical Barriers to Trade.[161] Whatever may be the underlying reasons, attitudes of governments of at least some EC Member States are changing. They are obviously concerned about the possibility for them (as opposed to private parties) to rely on GATT and more generally on WTO rules in the ECJ. Yet once it is accepted that WTO obligations of the EC are relevant for the lawfulness of EC measures within the EC legal system, it is difficult to see how they would be relevant only where they would be relied upon by Member States.

3.   *The WTO Perspective*

From a WTO perspective, as already indicated, it appears safe to assume that governments of most WTO Members are not ready to enter into commitments on enforcement of WTO rules by national courts. Yet, there is increasing pressure for more direct involvement of private parties in WTO dispute settlement proceedings. Although the WTO Dispute Settlement Understanding does not provide it, the Appellate Body considered in *Shrimp*[162] that panels could accept and consider submissions of non-governmental organizations. Moreover, in the literature there now are calls for granting private parties access to WTO dispute settlement proceedings.[163]

---

[161] Case C 377/98 (OJ 1998 C 378/13).

[162] WT/DS58/AB/R of 12 October 1998. para. 106.

[163] 'Is the WTO Dispute Settlement Mechanism Responsive to the Needs of Traders? Would a System of Private Action by Private Parties Yield Better Results?' Panel discussion, 32 JWT (No. 2, 1998), 147.

Leaving other considerations aside, it would seem more appropriate to grant private parties the possibility of invoking WTO rules in national proceedings than to allow private parties access to a WTO dispute settlement system that is already now overburdened. It would also be more sensible to leave it to national courts, where possible, to handle disputes about the application of WTO rules: they are better equipped to deal with the facts and are the natural forum for citizens.[164]

There is in the wider WTO context a case to be made for a change in the ECJ's approach. The main WTO Members have manoeuvred themselves into a deadlock. Everybody expects someone else to make a move with the result that nobody moves. Many years ago the ECJ faced the issue of the *ius standi* of third country exporters in direct appeals against regulations imposing antidumping measures. The European Commission pleaded in favour of a broad interpretation by referring to the fact that EC exporters could challenge US anti-dumping measures in the Federal Court of International Trade. The ECJ held that third country exporters had standing, even though Article 173 (new Art. 230) EC does not provide for such appeals by private parties.[165] It would obviously be naïve to think that, likewise, should the ECJ recognize "direct effect" to WTO rules, courts in other WTO Members would as a result start allowing private parties to rely on WTO rules. However, such a decision of the ECJ would reverberate beyond the EC borders. It would have repercussions in those WTO Members where pressure for change exists. It would break the deadlock.

D. Elements of a Possible New Approach

The main legal policy considerations that obviously led the ECJ to continue denying "direct effect" to GATT provisions and would normally lead it to do so for the provisions of WTO agreements in general, weighty as they are, are counterbalanced by other legal policy considerations in favour of recognizing such effect to those provisions where they are, as such, capable of being enforced judicially.

The *Nakajima* doctrine is a step in this direction. Even though it may be characterized as an "indirect effect",[166] it opens the door to judicial enforcement with respect to EC legislative measures intended to bring

---

[164] *Contra:* Eeckhout, n. 41 above, at 50; Tagaras, n 104 above, at 50.
[165] *Allied Corporation* [1984] ECR 1005.
[166] Eeckhout, n. 41 above, at 45–6.

EC law in line with WTO agreements and, conceivably, to EC legislative measures in areas covered by WTO agreements, except where EC political bodies have explicitly excluded judicial enforcement.

Reassessing the general issue of the status and effect of WTO agreements in the EC legal system can at any rate not be avoided by the ECJ even if it were to maintain the stance it took in the main *Bananas* case. As illustrated by the request of a preliminary ruling by the Netherlands Supreme Court on the TRIPS Agreement[167] and the application for annulment of provisions of the EC Directive on protection of biological inventions filed by the Netherlands on the grounds, *inter alia*, of inconsistency with the same TRIPS Agreement and the WTO Agreement on Technical Barriers to Trade,[168] it is difficult to see how the ECJ could escape the dilemma it is facing. It could not even escape it where WTO agreements provisions are concerned with respect to which it held in *Opinion* 1/94 that the EC and its Member States were jointly competent: it cannot simply declare that it has no jurisdiction, if it wants, as it should, to prevent the interference with the functioning of the internal market that would result in the event that these provisions are enforced judicially in certain Member States and not in others.

There is also some truth in the point made by Cottier that the dual membership of the EC and the Member States is perhaps the most important policy argument in favour of reassessing judicial policies in the EC: the costs of denying direct effect to GATT provisions amount to a real risk of turmoil within the EC legal order.[169] Cottier referred to the bananas debate in Germany. In other Member States not only courts but also policy makers are of the view that judicial enforceability of WTO agreements cannot be rejected across the board. On the other hand recognizing direct effect to WTO agreements would probably also cause turmoil in other EC Member States.

Two further aspects of the issue of the status and effect of WTO agreements on the EC legal system deserve some comments: reciprocity and the relationship between EC judicial enforcement and WTO dispute settlement.

---

[167] OJ 1999 C1/6.
[168] OJ 1998 C378/13.
[169] *The Relationship of WTO Law, National and Regional Law*, discussion paper, ILA International Trade Law Committee (June 1997).

1. Reciprocity

The ECJ has dealt in the past with the reciprocity argument in connection with 'direct effect' of international agreements. In *Kupferberg* it considered that the fact that the courts of one party to an agreement do not recognize direct application, whereas the courts of the other party do so, is not in itself such as to constitute a lack of reciprocity in the implementation of the agreement.[170] The ECJ left the door ajar by using the term 'in itself'. It has been argued that national courts do not normally take reciprocity into account when interpreting international agreements or when considering the effect of international agreements in their legal system,[171] and that where they do so, as in France, they enter into almost inextricable difficulties.[172] Yet it does not seem out of order for a court to take into account possible manifest and substantial non-performance by the other party that would upset the balance of an agreement. As Mengozzi argued, in examining the *bonafide* performance of an agreement by another State, a court must not only have regard to the lack of direct effect but also more broadly to the overall behaviour of that State.[173]

There are, however, considerable practical difficulties in applying a non-reciprocity doctrine to a multilateral agreement such as the GATT or another WTO agreement. Some conclude from this that non-reciprocity should not stand in the way of enforceability by the ECJ.[174] Considering that a substantive non-performance by a contracting party to a multilateral treaty may not always permit the suspension of the EC's obligations, others are of the view that the ECJ may be much more reticent on the issue of accepting that multilateral treaties may have direct effect.[175] Montana I Mora proposed applying the 'equilibrium principle'. This would entail a more analytical test; that is, whether or not the granting of 'direct effect' to a precise and unconditional provision of such an agreement would substantially impair the balance of rights and obligations of the EC.[176]

---

[170] [1982] ECR 3641, para. 19.

[171] Decaux, *La réciprocité en droit international* (C. Rousseau, Paris, 1980), *passim*.

[172] J. Groux *"L'invocabilité en justice des accords internationaux des Communautés européennes"* RTDE (1983), 203 and 212.

[173] N. 156 above, at 131.

[174] E. U. Petersmann, "Application of GATT by the Court of Justice of the European Communities", 20 *CML Rev.* (1983), 397 at 433.

[175] N. Neuwahl, "Individuals and the GATT: Direct Effect and Indirect Effects of the General Agreement on Tariffs and Trade in Community Law" in Emiliou and O'Keeffe (eds), *The European Union and World Trade Law* (J. Wiley & Sons, Chichester, 1996), 313 at 320.

[176] "Equilibrium: A Rediscovered Basis for the Court of the European Communities to Refuse Direct Effect to the Uruguay Round Agreements?", 30 *JWT* (No. 5, 1996), 43 at 53–4.

Such a test would obviously not be easy to apply, as it would involve assessing whether the legislation and the practice of other Members are in compliance with their WTO obligations. However, much would depend on how this test would be carried out. First, it does not seem necessary to apply the test on an individual WTO Member basis in order to verify whether, with respect to goods imported from a given WTO Member, that particular WTO Member complies with its WTO obligations. Denying enforceability of a WTO rule selectively *vis-à-vis* single WTO Members would hardly be consistent with the MFN treatment provided by the great majority of the WTO agreements. The test would rather be designed to verify whether enforcing a WTO rule would on the whole upset the balance of the EC's rights and obligations. This could be done by limiting the exercise to the EC's major trading partners. The Council of the European Union took a similar position by stating in the preamble of the Anti-dumping Regulation and the Anti-subsidy Regulation that 'in applying the rules it is essential, in order to maintain the balance of rights and obligations which the GATT Agreement establishes, that the Community take account of how they are interpreted by the Community's major trading partners'.[177]

Second, the exercise should be limited to the WTO agreement in question. This is not only to make the test more workable. It is also more appropriate: the issue is whether a provision of a given WTO agreement should be judicially enforced in light of the question whether this would upset the balance of the EC's rights and obligations. In this regard rights and obligations under other WTO agreements are hardly relevant.

In view of this a "reciprocity" assessment should not face the ECJ with insuperable difficulties, in particular if it were requesting the defendant Council or Commission, or, as the case may be, the Commission intervening in Article 177 (new Art. 234) EC proceedings, to state why granting 'direct effect' to a provision of a given WTO agreement would upset the balance of the EC's rights and obligations under that agreement.

2. Relationship between EC Judicial Enforcement and WTO Dispute Settlement

What Eeckhout called "connecting the judicial operators"[178] raises certain issues. He illustrates this by referring to the *Bananas* case with its

---

[177] Regulation (EC) 384/96 (OJ 1996 L 56/1); Regulation (EC) 3284/94 (OJ 1994 L 349/22) contains comparable language.
[178] N. 41 above, at 48.

various developments under the (old) GATT and subsequently under the WTO[179] and wonders whether and when it was up to the ECJ to intervene and to state that Germany could rely on the GATT to challenge the EC import rules on bananas and, one might add, to state that private parties could also do so.

One should make several distinctions: first, between panel and Appellate Body reports adopted by the Dispute Settlement Body in general and such reports where they find that the EC breached WTO rules and, second, between pending WTO dispute settlement proceedings on alleged breaches by the EC of WTO rules and the subsequent, adopted panel or Appellate Body reports.

(a) Panel and Appellate Body Reports in General

Adopted panel and Appellate Body reports in general interpret WTO rules. It is still debated whether such interpretations are part of the WTO *"acquis"* and are binding on Members other than the parties to the dispute. In practice, however, a Member will take such interpretations into account if it wants to avoid a dispute settlement proceeding in which a panel or the Appellate Body will rely on such interpretations.

In its *Opinion 2/91* on the EEA Agreement, the ECJ accepted that the EC could enter into an international agreement establishing a court with jurisdiction to settle disputes between the parties to that agreement and that such decisions of such a court would be binding on the EC, including the ECJ.[180] One could argue that where the ECJ held that GATT does nor have "direct effect", interpretations of the GAIT under the dispute settlement system cannot have "direct effect" either. This is probably correct as far as these interpretations would be relied upon to challenge the lawfulness of EC measures.[181]

(b) WTO Disputes on EC Measures

The issue of enforceability of a WTO rule in the EC legal system against an EC measure may arise at different stages: absent, pending, or after a WTO dispute settlement proceeding on such an EC measure.

---

[179] N. 4 J above, at 31–2 and 53.
[180] [1991] ECR 1-6079.
[181] Acc. Eeckhout, n. 41 above, at 52.

In the absence of a dispute settlement proceeding, the ECJ could maintain its stance on the non-enforceability of the WTO rule on which a private parry or a Member State relies to challenge an EC measure allegedly in breach of that WTO rule, arguably by using the reasons it gave in the main *Bananas* case. At that stage, in the face of another Members allegations of a breach of a WTO rule, the EC has a number of avenues open to it: it can seek a negotiated solution with that Member; under the GATT it can request a waiver; it can 'unbind' customs duties; it can, if the conditions are fulfilled, take a safeguard measure under one of the escape clauses, etc. A good argument could be made that it would be premature for the ECJ to recognize enforceability of the WTO rule in the EC legal system with the normal consequence that it would declare the EC measure unlawful.

When a dispute settlement proceeding is initiated, as the respondent Member the EC still has many avenues open to it to find a solution to avert the subsequent adoption by the Dispute Settlement Body of an adverse panel or Appellate Body report. There is a possible additional argument against the ECJ enforcing at this stage the WTO rule against the EC measure: the need to avoid conflicting decisions of two adjudicating bodies where both are seized by cases in which the lawfulness of the same measure is called into question. This argument is less persuasive. It would not seem impossible for the ECJ to stay the proceedings pending the outcome of the WTO dispute.[182]

Once a panel or an Appellate Body report finding that an EC measure is in breach of a WTO rule is adopted by the Dispute Settlement Body, there still are arguments *pro* and *contra* enforceability of the relevant WTO rule within the EC legal system. One of the arguments is derived from EC law: a declaration by the ECJ that an EC measure is unlawful operates as a rule *ex tunc*. However, compliance with WTO law does not require this. The Member, whose measure is found to be inconsistent with a WTO agreement, is bound to bring the measure into conformity with the agreement:[183] decisions of the Dispute Settlement Body are prospective. The ECJ could rely on Article 174(2) (new Art. 231) EC and decide likewise.

Even assuming that the "pay" option is not a measure of last resort, once a breach of a WTO rule is established by the Dispute Settlement

---

[182] See for some cases K. P. E. Lasok, The European Court of Justice, Practice and Procedure, 2nd edn. (Butterworth, London, 1994), at 72.
[183] Understanding on Rules and Procedures Governing the Settlement of Disputes, Art. 19(1) in WTO, The Uruguay Round Results. The Legal Texts (Geneva, 1995), 404.

Body that option can no longer justify denying enforceability of the WTO rule in the EC legal system. If that were the case, hardly any international agreements, would be enforceable in the EC legal system. Moreover, in the event that the ECJ wanted to take the option into account, it could probably do so by ruling pursuant to Article 174(1) (new Art. 231) EC that the effects of the EC measure are maintained pending the exercise by the EC of that option.

VI.   SOME CONCLUSIONS

The ECJ faces a series of challenges with respect to GATT and WTO agreements in general.

The first challenge is about the jurisdiction. As a result of both the mixed WTO membership of the EC and its Member States and the "joint competence" of the EC and the Member States for most of the matters covered by the General Agreement on Trade in Services (GATS) and the Agreement on Trade-Related Aspects of Intellectual Property Rights (TRIPS), the ECJ will face squarely–without being able to avoid it as in *Hermès*–the issue of its jurisdiction over matters which justified, or even required, according to conventional views, Member States' participation in so-called mixed agreements and with respect to which EC rules have been enacted. There are two options for the ECJ.

The first option is to take a narrow approach: the ECJ could declare it has no jurisdiction whatsoever over GATS and TRIPS provisions coming within the scope of Member States' powers and leave it to the Member States and the EC political bodies to sort out the rather messy situation both within the EC and vis-à-vis other WTO Members. The ECJ could conceivably make a distinction between situations that are purely internal to a Member State and those that are not, and not exercise jurisdiction in the former type of situations. The result would be that provisions of GATS and TRIPS would be interpreted differently depending on the situation. Apart from the fact that this would be hardly conducive to legal certainty, one may wonder how a different meaning to one and the same provision of the GATS or the TRIPS could work where implementation within the EC context and in a purely national context may be inextricably linked. An additional drawback of this option is that it would be up to the ECJ to draw the line dividing EC and Member States' external powers. This would be a difficult but more importantly a politically controversial exercise. The EC political bodies and Member States find the mixed agreements formula convenient. It is a solution of creative ambiguity that avoids talmudic discussions and difficult decisions. It also allows escape from casting in stone the division of external powers which needs to be flexible enough to cater for evolving policy requirements.

The second option is for the ECJ to take jurisdiction without, however, on the one hand, calling into question its *Opinion 1/94 on* the results of the Uruguay Round and, on the other, pre-empting a decision of the EC political bodies, under paragraph 5 of Article 113 (new Art. 133) on trade in services and on intellectual property rights (once this amendment to Article 113 EC inserted by the Amsterdam Treaty to that effect enters into force). This would mean exercising jurisdiction over Member States' legislation and their international obligations in cases where the ECJ is not able to link Member State legislation to EC legislation or to rely on a substitution of Member States by the EC. Although it would be skating on thin legal ice, the ECJ could exercise jurisdiction via a broad interpretation of Article 5 (new Art. 10) EC laying down the Community loyalty principle. Without referring expressly to Article 5 EC, in *Opinion 1/94* the ECJ identified a duty of "close cooperation" which extends to "the fulfilment of the commitments entered into". Such close co-operation could also apply to Member States' courts and imply for them a duty to seek preliminary rulings under Article 177 (new Art. 234) EC.

The second challenge which GATT 1994 and more generally the WTO agreements present to the ECJ is that of their enforceability in the EC legal system. Quite obviously the rationale for denying 'direct effect' of GATT 1947 can no longer be sustained. If the ECJ is to maintain its stance, it will need to have recourse to another rationale. The fundamental aspect of this challenge, however, is whether or not to recognize a degree of enforceability to GATT 1994 and more generally to WTO agreements where they contain provisions that are as such capable of being enforced judicially. Within the EC there no longer seems to be a consensus among Member State governments against judicial enforceability of GATT 1994 and other WTO agreements as a matter of principle; alternatively there no longer is passive acceptance by some of a majority view. The ECJ will not be able to avoid a decision and whatever its decision it will test the acceptability by some EC Member States, as it will touch on traditionally held views on the effect of international agreements and on their perceived interests in a globalizing world economy. Steps could and ought to be taken in this direction. *"A vivre sans péril, on triomphe sans gloire."*

8. INTERNATIONAL JURISPRUDENCE AND DOMESTIC LAW: SOME COMMENTS FROM A EUROPEAN COMMUNITY PERSPECTIVE

Several of the issues addressed in this short article destined for an audience of US trade lawyers have in the meantime been dealt with by the EC courts. One of them is the effect, if any, in the EC legal system of decisions of international adjudicative-type bodies. This is particularly relevant for reports of WTO panels and the WTO Appellate Body. Recently in Biret *(judgment of 30 September 2003, not yet reported in the European Court Reports) involving the EC rules on imports of hormone-treated beef, the Court of Justice of the EC on appeal from a judgment of the Court of First Instance of the EC seems to have left the door ajar to private parties wanting to rely on the WTO panel and Appellate Body Reports (paras 64 and 67 of the judgment).*

I.   INTRODUCTION

1.   Before addressing two specific topics, it may be appropriate to make a few preliminary and general remarks about the European Community's (hereinafter: EC) legal system and the effect of international agreements in that legal system.

A.   The Judicial System In The European Community

1.   *Applying EC law*

2.   Following the 1963 landmark opinion of the Court of Justice of the European Communities (hereinafter: CJEC) in *Van Gend & Loos*,[1] confirmed and elaborated upon in later judgments, EC law - i.e. what one could call the "constitution", represented by the treaties establishing the European Coal and Steel Community, the European Atomic Energy Community and the European Economic Community and their subsequent amendments, and the law generated by the EC institutions – is part of the law applying in the EC Member States. In the words of the CJEC

> "Independently of the legislation of Member States, Community law […] not only imposes obligations on individuals but is also intended to confer upon them rights which become part of their legal heritage."[2]

---

[1] 1963 ECR 1.
[2] 1963 ECR 1 at 12.

EC law is as such to be applied and enforced by the courts of the EC Member States. Whether it can be relied upon by private parties does not depend on EC Member State legislation : it only depends on whether the EC law provision to be relied upon has "direct effect".

3.   Following a fairly long line of opinions from *Costa*[3] to *Francovich*[4], an EC law provision has "direct effect"

  −   where the obligation imposed on Member State is *clear* and *unconditional* and,

  −   where, if implementing measures are called for, the EC institutions or (the Member States are *not* allowed any *margin of discretion*.[5]

Uniform interpretation

4.   Uniform interpretation of EC law is pursued through the system of "preliminary rulings" by the CJEC (Art. 177 EEC Treaty). Under this system, when an EC Member State court is faced with a question of interpretation of EC law in a case pending before it and considers that a decision on that question is necessary to enable it to give judgment, such court may, and where a court against whose decisions there is no judicial remedy under national law is concerned must, refer the question to the CJEC.

2.   Challenging EC legal acts

(a)   In the CJEC −Standing of private parties.

5.   Apart from the fact that some types of acts are not capable of judicial review (recommendations, opinions, preparatory measures[6] and more generally measures which are not intended to have legal effects[7]), private parties may only challenge directly in the CJEC[8] the legality of:

---

[3] 1964 ECR 585.
[4] Judgment of 19 November 1991, not yet reported, in which the CJEC denied the "direct effect" of a Directive on the protection of employees against the employer's insolvency but in which it held that Mr Francovich derived from the EC legal system a right to compensation by the Italian State for the damage caused to him by Italy's failure to implement that Directive.
[5] Comp. *Hurd* v. *Jones* 1986 ECR 29, and *Francovich* cited *supra* n. 4.
[6] See *e.g. IBM v. Commission* 1981 ECR 2639. in which the CJEC held that the initiation of (administrative) antitrust proceedings and the notification to IBM of the EC Commission's "statement of Objections" were not open to judicial review.

- decisions addressed to them or

- decisions which, although in the form of a regulation or decision addressed to another person, are of direct and individual concern to the applicant (Art. 173 (2) EEC Treaty).

6.   The CJEC has kept fairly well within these limitations set by the EEC Treaty. It considers that in order to be open to direct challenge a regulation must be in substance a decision which concerns the applicant directly and individually, The CJEC does not always make clear whether there are three distinct requirements, i.e. the regulation must in substance be a decision, it must affect the applicant directly and it must affect the applicant individually and whether the first requirement and the second and third one are cumulative.[9]

Notwithstanding these constraints, the CJEC sometimes manages to interpret liberally the standing requirements. Three examples relating to anti-dumping deserve to be mentioned.

Since *the Allied Corporation* cases,[10] measures imposing antidumping duties may be directly challenged in the CJEC by foreign producers and exporters where they can establish that they were identified in the measures adopted or were concerned by the investigation.

In *Fediol I*,[11] the complainant federation of EC oil processors was held to have a right to review by the CJEC "appropriate to the nature of the powers reserved to the Community institutions".

---

[7] See, *e.g. Brother Industries v. Commission* 1987 ECR 3757 in which the CJEC held that a memorandum sent by the EC Commission to Member States customs authorities drawing their attention to the fact that it had found in the course of an anti-dumping investigation that Brother's electronic typewriters shipped from Taiwan did not "originate" in Taiwan and would thus be subject to existing anti-dumping duties on electronic typewriters originating in Japan "does not constitute in act which may adversely affect the legal position of the producer / *exporter* concerned". Note that under the EC system origin is normally determined by Member State customs authorities applying EC law. See, also, Sunzet *(Europe)* B. V. and Sunzet *(Netherlands) B. V. v. Commission*, order of 13 June 1991 (not yet reported).
[8] Since November 1989, in certain fields, i.a. antitrust, the newly established Court of First Instance is *competent*.
[9] For more details, see, *e.g.* L. Collins, *European Community Law in the United Kingdom*, 236-256 (4th ed. Butterworths, London 1990); H.G. Schermers & D. Waclbroeck, *Judicial Protection in the European Communities*, par. 267–285 (4th ed, Kluwer, Deventer, 1987).
[10] 1984 ECR 1005 and 1985 ECR 1622. For the position of related importers see *Canon Inc. v. Council* Judgment of 10 March 1992 (not yet reported).
[11] 1983 ECR 2913; See, also, *Timex* 1985 ECR 849.

Independent importers cannot directly challenge antidumping measures in the CJEC, [12] However, in *Extramet*,[13] the CJEC recognized the applicant's standing considering that:

> "It is the most important importer of the product found to have been dumped and at the same time the ultimate user of this product Moreover the applicant's business depends to a large extent on the imports and is seriously affected by the antidumping measures, account being taken of the limited number of producers of the product in question and of the fact that the applicant was meeting difficulties in obtaining supplies from the only EC producer, who, moreover, is his main competitor for the processed product" (own translation).

(b) In EC Member State courts.

7.   As the CJEC has made clear in several cases

> "... there is nothing in Community law to prevent an action from being brought before a national [i.e. an EC Member State] court against a measure implementing a decision adopted by a Community institutions where the conditions laid down by national law are satisfied. When such an action is brought, if the outcome of the dispute depends on the validity of that decision the national court may submit questions to the Court of Justice by way of reference for a preliminary ruling, without there being any need to ascertain whether or not the plaintiff in the main proceeding has the possibility of challenging the decision directly before the Court."[14]

Private parties may thus challenge EC law in EC Member State courts by challenging the EC Member State measure which applies such EC law to them. In many cases, especially where regulations are concerned, this is the only way, in view of the restrictions on standing for direct appeals to the CJEC.

8.   For a long time, it has been a matter for debate whether an EC Member State court could refuse to apply an EC law provision

---

[12] For example, *Alusuisse v. Council and Commission* 1982 ECR 3463; *Electroimpex e.o. v. Council*, 1990 ECR I-3021.
[13] Judgment of 16 May 1991 (not yet reported).
[14] *Rau v. BALM* 1987 ECR 2289 at 2338.

which it considers as being illegal. While the EEC Treaty (Art. 177) entitles the CJEC to have the last word on interpretation of EC law and legality ("validity") of EC secondary law, the wording of Article 177 suggests that only the courts "against whose decisions there is no judicial remedy under national law" have a duty to refer. However, in Foto-Frost,[15] the CJEC held in substance that, faced with a plea of illegality of an EC law provision, a Member State court can either dismiss the plea and apply the EC law provision or refer the question of legality of that EC law provision to the CJEC. *Tertium non datur.* In other words variations in the interpretation of EC law by all but the highest EC Member State courts are accepted, non-application of EC law by any court is acceptable only where the CJEC has ruled that the EC law provision in question is illegal.

B. Effect Of International Agreements In The Ec Legal System

1. *The position of international agreements*

9. The position may be summarized as follows:[16]

Pursuant to article 228(1) of the EEC Treaty, international agreements are negotiated by the Commission of the European Communities (hereinafter; the Commission) and concluded, as a rule, by the Council of Ministers of the European Communities (hereinafter: the Council). With respect to tariff and trade agreements, Article 113 lays down a procedure consisting of a recommendation by the Commission to the Council. followed by an authorization by the Council to the Commission to open and conduct negotiations within the framework of negotiation directives issued by the Council and in consultation with a special committee appointed by the Council to assist the Commission. In practice, this procedure has been extended to other agreements.

Once the text of the agreement has been initiated or authenticated in some other form by the Commission, the Council "concludes" the agreement, following either a simplified procedure or a more complicated procedure involving two or three stages.[17] In doing so, the Council

---

[15] 1987 ECR 4199.

[16] J.II.J. Bourgeois, *Effects of International Agreements in European Community Law: Are The Dice Cast?*, 82 MICH.L. REV. 1250 at 1256-1257 (1984); for further reading, see P. Pescatore "Treaty-making by the European Communities", in F. G. Jacobs and S. Roberts (eds), *United Kingdom National Committee of Comparative Law, The Effects of Treaties in Domestic Law* 171 (1987).

[17] For a detailed description, see Louis & Brucckner, Relations *Extericures* in 12 *Le Droi't de la Communaute Economique Europenne* 35–45 (J. Megret, M. Waelbroeck. J. Louis. D. Vignes and J. Dewost (eds) 1980).

approves the agreement and decides on such steps as are required to express the EC's consent to be bound by the agreement by whatever means are applicable, [18] In EC practice, "conclusion" within the meaning of the relevant EEC Treaty provisions (Articles 114, 228 and 238), thus normally covers simultaneously two different measures; the measure whereby the internal procedure to conclude an agreement is completed and the measure whereby the EC binds itself internationally. Theoretically, it is possible that the authorization to express the EC's consent by signature or by deposit of the act of acceptance is not made use of, just as in a State the executive may decide not to ratify, even after having obtained parliamentary approval. This final act of the Council takes the form of a decision or regulation. The decision or regulation, to which the international agreement is appended, is published in the Official Journal of the European Communities. A notice announcing the agreement's international entry into effect may appear subsequently in the Official Journal.

Beyond a certain analogy to legal systems providing for approval of international agreements by the legislative branch, these EEC Treaty provisions do not offer much guidance on the status and effects of international agreements in the EC legal system, except that under Article 228(2) agreements "concluded" under these conditions are "binding on the institutions of the Community and on Member States".

The institutional provisions are silent on the question of whether and how an international agreement binding on the EC becomes part of EC law. They do not contain any indication of the EEC Treaty framers' views on what, for convenience, are called the "monist" and "dualist" approaches. The practice followed by the EC institutions does not offer much guidance either. In some cases it seems to reflect a "dualist" attitude; in other cases it reflects a "monist" one. The choice of a regulation (by definition "directly applicable") rather than a decision for the purpose of approving an international agreement normally implies that a regulation was in that case necessary to ensure direct efficacy to an agreement which was itself considered "self-executing". It can thus be seen as the expression of a "dualist" attitude. However, that choice may also be influenced by other considerations, such as the need to adopt simultaneously complementary provisions requiring the use of a regulation. After *Kupferberg I*, [19] a decision has become the standard method, precisely in order not to prejudge the question of direct effect. For its part, the CJEC has demonstrated that it does not attach much weight to the type of legal

---

[18] See Vienna Convention on the Law of Treaties, May 23, 1969, art. 11, UN Doc. A/CONF. 39/27, reprinted in 63 *Am. J. Int. L.* 875 (1969).
[19] 1982 ECR 3641.

act used for the purpose of deciding whether an agreement has become part of EC law and is directly enforceable. [20]

On the other hand, in EC practice, legislation implementing an international agreement, i.e. transforming it into EC legislation, is considered necessary only where the agreement both entails precise legal obligations and requires changes of or additions to rules in force Internally, or where the provisions of the agreement, in order to be implemented in a clear and effective manner, call for special measures of internal law.[21]

One should add that an international agreement does not necessarily need to have been concluded by the EC in order to be relevant to the interpretation and application of EC law.

10.   The position of the GATT is particularly interesting in this respect, From the point of view of *international law* the EC is as such not a Contracting Party, but other Contracting Parties are dealing with the EC as the entity that has taken over the rights and obligations under the GATT of its Member States and the EC conducts itself as having these rights and as being bound by these obligations.[22] In addition, it may be argued that as a result of consistent practice of the GATT its institutional law has changed, as the ICJ accepted in its *Namibia* opinion.

From the point of view of EC law, whatever may be the theory on which this may be based, it is well established that the EC is bound by GATT, following a series of opinions from the CJEC from *International Fruit* [23] to *Nakajima*.[24]

---

[20] In *Conceria Daniele Bresciani* v. *Amministrazione Italicua delle Finanze*, 1976 ECR 129, 144, 155, the CJEC allowed the plaintiff in the main case to rely on the Yaoundé Agreement although it had been approved by a Decision and not by a Regulation.

[21] On the way in which some of the results of GATT multilateral trade negotiations were implemented, sec J.H.J. Bourgeois. *The Tokyo Round Agreements on Technical Barriers and on Government Procurement in international and EEC Perspective*, 19 C.M.L. Rev. 5, 26-31 (1982).

[22] There is too much literature on the subject to be cited here. Many interesting contributions and references appear in M. Hilf, P.G. Jacobs and E.U. Petersmann (eds), *The European Community and Gau* (Kluwer, Deventer 1986). *for* an interesting description *of* a recent challenge of the EC's position by one of its own Member States and the confirmation of the EC's position by other Contracting Parties see Y. Devuyst, GATT *Customs Union Provisions and the Uruguay Round: the European Community Experience*. 26 JWT 15 (1992).

[23] 1972 ECR 1219.

[24] Judgment of 7 May 1991 (not yet reported).

2.   The effect of international agreements

11.   Most of this debate has been centred around the "direct effect" of international agreements and what a ruling of the CJEC recognizing or denying such "direct effect" implied.

12.   At least since *Kupferberg I*, [25] it is established law that international agreements concluded by the EC may have "direct effect", depending on whether the provision relied upon is "unconditional and sufficiently precise", a question which is to be examined "in the light of both the object and purpose of the agreement and of its context"[26] Applying these standards to a provision of the free trade agreement with Portugal (before Portugal's accession to the EC) against fiscal discrimination of imported products, the CJEC held that the provision in question had "direct effect". The importer could thus rely on it against German law provisions.

13.   As far as the GATT and GATT-implementing agreements are concerned, the CJEC applying on the face of it the same standards has held repeatedly that the provisions of these agreements relied upon in the case at hand did not have direct effect.[27]

The terms "direct effect" are borrowed from the CJEC's case law on the relationship EC-Member State law and mean that EC law provisions having such effect confer on private individuals rights that are to be enforced by Member State courts. For quite some time, it has been a matter of debate whether by denying "direct effect" the CJEC not only meant that private parties could not rely on GATT in Member State courts but also intended to rule that GATT could not be invoked at all as a source of legality. [28]

To add to the confusion, the denial of "direct effect" does not mean that the CJEC completely disregards GATT rules : as probably most courts tend to do, it attempts in many cases when faced with an alleged conflict between these rules and EC law to interpret the latter so as to avoid the conflict. [29]

---

[25] 1982 ECR 3611.

[26] *Kupferbers 1982* ECR 3665.

[27] From *International fruit*, cited *supra* n. 22, on.

[28] F. Castillo de la Torre, *The Status of GATT in EEC law —Some New Developments*, 26 JWT 35 at 36 (1992) with numerous references.

[29] See examples in P. Pescatore, *Die Rechtsprechung des Europäischen Gerichtshofs zur imergemeinschafuicluen Wirkung völkerrechtlicher Abkommen* in *Festschrift Fuer II. Mosler*

Continues

14.   Strictly speaking, the denial of "direct effect" means that a private party cannot claim in an EC Member State court the benefit of a GATT rule. One of the remaining questions was whether this also implied that, in those cases where a private party has standing to challenge on EC act directly in the CJEC, that private applicant could not rely on a GATT rule.

In *Nakajima,*[30] applicant brought a direct appeal against a regulation imposing antidumping duties. Applicant claimed that these duties were illegal, i.a. on the ground that Nakajima's normal value had been based on constructed value following a method as prescribed by the EC Antidumping laws, but that on this point these laws violated the 1979 GATT Antidumping Code. Nakajima claimed that, pursuant to Article 184 EEC Treaty, the CJEC should declare the EC Antidumping laws inapplicable. Rejecting the defendant's argument to that effect, the CJEC found that the applicant did not invoke the direct effect of the 1979 GATT Antidumping Code but questioned the applicability of the EEC antidumping Regulation and pleaded one of the grounds for judicial review stated in Article 173 EEC Treaty, i.e. infringement of the EEC Treaty or of any rule of law relating to its application. Referring to the preamble of the EEC Antidumping Regulation which states that this Regulation is adopted in accordance with existing international obligations in particular those arising from Article VI of the GATT and from the 1979 GATT Antidumping Code, the CJEC reviewed the legality of the EEC Regulation under the 1979 GATT Antidumping Code. While the CJEC rejected the applicant's argument as unfounded, the very fact that it was willing to verify the "Gattability" of the EEC Regulation is an important development.

15.   One may wonder whether *Nakajima* opens the door for a recognition of "direct effect" to GATT rules whenever such rules are unconditional and sufficiently precise. One of the concerns which in the past prompted the CJEC to deny "direct effect" to GATT and GATT implementing agreements was that some EC Member States courts would, in cases of conflict between EC law and GATT provisions, give precedence to the latter, while others would not. In *SPI*, the CJEC considered that

> "any difference in the interpretation and the application
> of provisions binding the Community as regards non-

...661 (Springer, Berlin 1983): see also the cases cited by M. Maresceau, *The GATT in the case law of the European Court of Justice* in Hilf, Jarnbs and Petersmann 107 cited *supra* n. 21.
[30] Cited *supra* n. 23.

member countries would not only jeopardize the unity of the commercial policy which according to Article 113 of the [*EEC*] Treaty must be based on uniform principles, but also create distortions in trade within the Community, as a result of differences in the manner in which the Agreement in force between the Community and non-Member countries were applied in the various [EC] Member States".[31]

However, this risk is now excluded, as since *Foto-Frost*, [32] EC Member Member State courts may no longer set EC law aside without reference to the CJEC for a preliminary ruling.

II.   THE INTERPLAY OF INTERNATIONAL JURISPRUDENCE AND DOMESTIC LAW –THE LAW AS STANDS

16.   Except where an international agreement contains precise obligations to that effect, it would seem that the interplay of international jurisprudence and domestic law depends essentially on, or is conditioned by, the status and effect of international law in a given domestic law system, "International jurisprudence" in the sense used here does not refer to various forms of subsequent practice which may have a law-creating force, such as the development of Customary law in derogation to an international treaty, informal treaty amendment through silent consent, estoppel etc... [33]. It refers either to recommendations and decisions of international bodies administering treaties or to decisions of adjudicative-type bodies.

A.   The EC System

17.   As far as the EC is concerned, the brief foregoing analysis of the status and effect of international law in the EC legal system throws up the following questions:

–   where an international agreement has "direct effect" or when it can be relied upon in direct appeals to the CJEC, what are the status and effects of "international jurisprudence" relating to such agreement?

---

[31] For example, *Amministrazione delle Finanze v. SPI and SAMI* 1983 ECR 801 at 828.
[32] Cited *supra* n. 16.
[33] For further developments with respect to GATT, see G.M. Berrisch, The *Establishment of New Law through Subsequent Practice in GATT*, 16 N. Carol, J. Int'l L. 497 (1991).

–   is a distinction made or should one be made between recommendations and decisions of international bodies administering an international agreement on the one hand, and decisions of adjudicative-type bodies on the other ?

1.   Recommendations and decisions of international bodies

18.   Certain international treaties entered into by the EC provide for an institutional machinery (e.g. "Association Council", "Joint Committee", international "Fisheries Commission" etc...) in the framework of which Contracting Parties agree on implementing measures or to which certain powers are given to issue recommendations or to adopt decisions, This gives rise to two issues: first, to what extent are such recommendations and decisions not only binding on the EC in the international law sphere bat also in the EC legal system ? Second to what extent are they directly enforceable by private parties?

(a)   EC status of recommendations and decisions of international bodies

19.   The practice followed by the Council consists normally in adopting EC law measures for the implementation of recommendations and decisions of such international bodies only where such measures are necessary, i.e. where the internal effect in EC law is not inherent in such recommendations and decisions themselves or is not achieved by other means. To put it simply the EC practice follows the "monist" theory.

This practice has been upheld by the CJEC. In *Greece* v. *Commission* [34], the Greek government argued that decisions of the Association Council, consisting of representatives of the EC and its Member States, on the one hand, and of Turkey, on the other, could only be implemented following proper EC law measures. The CJEC rejected the argument by stating.

> "... by providing for cooperation with regard to the implementation of the aid ... made available, to Turkey, the Association Council placed that aid within the institutional framework of the Association [between the EC and Turkey]. Since it is directly connected with the

---

[34] 1989 ECR 3711.

Association Agreement, Decision N$ 2/80 forms, from its entry into force, an integral part of the Community legal system."[35]

(b)   Enforceability of recommendations of international bodies by private parties

20.   At the origin of *Sevince* [36] was a dispute before Dutch courts between a Turkish national and the Dutch authorities concerning the latter one's refusal to grant him a residence permit Mr Sevince relied i.a. on a decision of the Association Council, referred to earlier, according to which a Turkish worker who has been in legal employment for five years in an EC Member State is to enjoy free access in that Member State to any paid employment of his choice. The CJEC held that the provisions of the decision on which Mr Sevince relied had "direct effect" – he could consequently ask the Dutch court to apply them to his case – To reach that conclusion the CJEC applied substantially the same tests as it did in earlier opinions on the effect of international agreements, i.a.:

> "Article 2 (1) (b) of Decision N$ 2/76 and the third indent of Article 6 (1) of Decision N$ 1/80 uphold, in clear, precise and unconditional terms, the right of a Turkish worker, after a number of years' legal employment in a Member State, to enjoy free access to any paid employment of his choice."[37]

The CJEC added that this finding:

> "is confirmed by the purpose and the nature of the decisions of which those provisions form part and of the Agreement to which they relate."[38]

2.   Decisions of adjudicative-type bodies

It should be noted that the EC's initial reluctance to agree on dispute settlement clauses has given way to a more open approach, as illustrated by the conclusion of fisheries agreements providing for interna-

---

[35] 1988 ECR 3711 at 3737–3738.
[36] 1990 ECR 1-3461.
[37] 1990 ECR 1-3461 at 1-3502.
[38] 1990 ECR 1-3461 at 1-3502

tional arbitration and of multilateral agreements such as the 1974 Paris Convention for the Prevention of Marine Pollution from Land-based Sources (Annex B)[39] and by the creation of an international court as contemplated by the 1990 draft Treaty on an European Economic Area.

The CJEC has confirmed that the EC may enter into an international agreement whereby a jurisdictional body is set up, provided the structure[40] and the jurisdiction of such body are compatible with the EEC Treaty.[41] There are, however, so far no instances in which the EC was a party to an international dispute settlement proceeding other than consultation and conciliation, except in the GATT where it has been involved in an increasing number of proceedings.[42] The EC cannot be a party to proceedings in the International Court of Justice. Status and effect in the EC legal system are thus for the time being largely theoretical questions.

In its first opinion on the Draft Treaty on a European Economic Area[43] the CJEC was of the view that the European Economic Area Court, whose creation was then contemplated, conflicted with the EEC Treaty. One should, however, probably not draw the conclusion that the CJEC intended to reject any effect in the EC legal system of decisions of international adjudicative bodies. The CJEC's reasoning does not support such a conclusion. The main reason was that the Treaty on a European Economic Area takes over an essential part of fundamental provisions of the Community legal order and introduces thus in the Community legal order a large body of legal rules which is juxtaposed to a corpus of identically–worded Community rules. By conferring to the European Economic Area Court jurisdiction to interpret such rules, the Draft Treaty was likely adversely to affect the autonomy of the Community legal order and the exclusive jurisdiction of the CJEC for the interpretation and application of EC law.

22. As far as GATT dispute settlement proceedings are concerned, more particularly the findings of GATT panels adopted by the Contracting Parties or the relevant Committees, whether the CJEC

---

[39] OJ 1974 L 194/75.
[40] Opinion 1/76 *Draft Agreement establishing a European Laying-up Fund for Inland Waterway Vessels* 20 CMLR 2, 279 at 300–301 (1977).
[41] Opinion 1/91 *Draft Treaty on a European Economic Area*, 63 *CML Rev.* 5,245 at 271 (1992).
[42] For further reading see, i.a. J.H.J. Bourgeois, "*Les relations extércures de in Communauté européenne, et la règle de droit: quelques réflexions* in *Du Droit International an Droit de l'Integration. Liber Amicorum Pierre Pescatore* 59 at 67–74 (Nomos, Baden-Baden 1987).
[43] *Supra n.* 38.

would recognize their "direct effect" depends on the effect of the GATT and its implementing and side-agreements themselves (see *supra* paras 13–15).

In *Dürbeck* relating to protective measures against imports of table apples from Chile, the CJEC held that

> "... the argument advanced by the plaintiff in the main action that the protective measures in issue are contrary to the commitments entered into by the Community under GATT is not capable in this case of putting the validity of these measures into question".

The CJEC added –it is not clear whether it did so *ad abundantiam* or to support that finding –

"According to the uncontested information on this matter supplied by the Commission during the oral procedure the special GATT group charged with examining the conformity of the Community measures with the General Agreement found that in adopting the protective measures in issue the Commission did not infringe either Article I or Article II of that agreement".[44]

B.   The Us System

1.   *Status and effect of international agreements*

23.   Able writers are dealing in this publication with US law as it stands with respect to international agreements and in particular with respect to the GATT and its implementing and side-agreements. The few remarks that follow rely mainly on some writers.[45]

---

[44] 1981 ECR 1095 at 1120. "Special GATT group" is an translation error; the CJEC obviously meant "GATT panel". It appears that the CJEC had been misinformed: according to the GATT Panel there had been an infringement of Article XIX GATT.
[45] On international law in general: i.a. L. Henkin, *International Law as Law in the United States*, 82 *Mich. L. Rev.* 1555 (1984); *Restatement (Third) of the Foreign Relations Law of the united States*, Ch.2 (1987). On international trade law and GATT, i.a. R.E. Hudec and F.L. Morrison. *Judicial Protection of Individual Rights under Foreign Trade Law of the United State*, in M. Hilf and F.U. Petersmann (eds), *National Constitutions and International Economic Law* (forthcoming).

For the purposes of dealing with the topic to be addressed, the position may be summarized as follows.

24. It would seem that under US jurisprudence - assuming a treaty is valid and binding under international law and valid under the US constitution both as to substance and as to procedure - the first question is whether the treaty is "self-executing" in which case it will be directly applied. "Self-execution" depends on a series of factors, but (it seems) primarily on the intent of the drafters, including intent implied or expressed in the treaty itself. When that language is sufficiently precise and indicates that no further government action is needed to apply treaty norms, a US court will be willing to conclude that a treaty is self-executing.[46]

From an international law point of view, doubts are permitted about the practice of the US Congress when approving international agreements, such as those resulting from the Tokyo Round Multilateral Trade Negotiations, to decide that they are not self-executing. Although this point has been debated in the literature,[47] it would seem that this question is primarily an international law question and at least that for determining whether an international agreement is self-executing the views of a single Contracting Party cannot be decisive. This question is to be distinguished from another one viz. whether a treaty is to be executed by incorporating it in domestic law or not. It would seem that how a treaty is executed is a matter of domestic law, provided that it is effectively executed.

25. The second question is then whether there is no later federal law which is inconsistent with the treaty, in which case federal law will prevail over the treaty.[48] As the CJEC, US courts are normally inclined to interpret, where possible, domestic law in a manner consistent with international obligations.

---

[46] J.H. Jackson, *Status of Treaties in Domestic Legal Systems: a Policy Analysis, 86 AJIL* 310 at 320 (April 1992).
[47] A. Bleckmann, *Begriff and Kriterien Der Innerstuarlichen Anwendbarkeit Völkerrechtliche Vertrage,* 138, 213 (1970) (arguments rooted in the domestic legal system ought to have the most weight); J. Verhoeven, La *notion d'"applicabilité directe" du droit international.* 15 *Rev. B. Dr. Intl.* 243, 258 (1980) (this is an international question); S. Riesenfeld. *The doctrine Self-Executing Treaties and US v. Postal: Win at Any Price ? 74 Am. J. Int'l. L,* 892, 900 (1980) : the self-executing character of a treaty is a product of international and domestic law rules.
[48] Jackson in Jacobs *and* Roberts, *supra* n 16, at 141.

With respect to GATT and implementing agreements and GATT-side agreements it would seem that one can divide the cases in which a conflict was alleged between US law and these international instruments into three categories: those that stress the primacy of US law over the GATT, those that interpret US law in light of the GATT and those where the court merely declares that US law is consistent with the GATT, without stating a position on the interrelationship between them.

2. Status and effect of "international jurisprudence"

26. For an analysis of the law as it stands with respect to the status and the effect, in the US legal system, of recommendations and decisions of bodies administering international agreements and of decisions of adjudicative-like bodies, reference is made to what other more able writers have to say in this publication.

III. THE INTERPLAY OF INTERNATIONAL JURISPRUDENCE AND DOMESTIC LAW. THE POLICY ISSUES

27. In the final analysis the question whether and to what extent "international jurisprudence" should be part of the "law of the land" and if so whether it should even trump domestic law is a policy question. It is a policy question for legislative bodies if and when they care to address it.

It is a policy question also for the judiciary. For the judiciary it is obviously a difficult and complex one. Not only does it require the judiciary to deal with policy issues and with international policy issues, but in certain jurisdictions it may also involve a departure from traditional theories on status and effect of international law in general and international treaties in particular; moreover, the judiciary may be faced with the question whether it should give precedence to "international jurisprudence" over inconsistent national law of a later date. Finally, sociologically it may be difficult for domestic courts to accept the authority of bodies that generate "international jurisprudence".

28. The policy arguments, the pro's as well as the con's, on direct application of treaties and on the status vis-à-vis domestic legislation, i.e. whether treaties trump domestic legislation, have been clearly and comprehensively set out by Prof. Jackson in a recent article [49]. Prof. Jackson

---

[49] J.H. Jackson, *supra* n. 43.

concludes his study by raising the question whether it would not be better to devote efforts and attention to making treaty norms more effective, by devising processes for dispute settlement and for ensuring the democratic participation of each party's citizens in accepting treaty norms, than to rely too heavily on the notions of direct applicability and higher status[50]. This calls for some remarks.

First, Prof. Jackson is not alone. Similar views have been expressed also on the other side of the Atlantic. When the issue of "direct effect" of international agreements was before the CJEC, EC Member States argued in their briefs as intervening parties against "direct effect"; underlying their formal arguments was the traditional view that enforcement of international agreements was not the judiciary's business, and that the judiciary's intervention would only complicate things and interfere with the more competent administration of international agreements by governments.[51]

Second, the "democratic deficit" argument used against direct applicability of international treaties and their supremacy over inconsistent domestic law is a very important one. The question, however, is whether an act of transformation is a better check on the treaty-making process than other procedural devices such as parliamentary approval preceded by consultations of parliaments during the negotiations. The argument about the need to keep the options open at a later stage to escape from the rigidity that compliance with international agreements entails in the domestic sphere is in the final analysis a call for less international law or for less ambitious international law. One may wonder if this is not at odds with the increasing interdependence and globalization of economies.

Third, if one of the alternatives to direct applicability is better processes for international dispute settlement, does not the improvement of these processes entail the domestic enforceability of the results of the dispute settlement? Or must one consider that these processes have only a diplomatic function and have no role to play in interpreting the law and in contributing to its enforcement?

---

[50] Jackson, *supra* n.43 at 340.

[51] For example, in *Polydor* five governments argued against "direct effect" of the EC free trade agreement with Portugal on the ground that the structure of the Agreement and the intention of the negotiators were such that infringements of an Agreement are to give rise to consultations between the contracting parties of possibly to the adoption of Safeguard measures, and that this precludes giving direct effect on provisions of this type. 1982 ECR 329 at 340

Surely, for a State that accepts direct application of international treaties it is consistent and logical to recognize the same effect to recommendations or decisions of bodies administering such treaties and to decisions of adjudicative-type bodies interpreting them, For some States this entails further steps on reinforcing the binding character of international law and in accepting that their room for manouvre vis-à-vis matters regulated at the international level is being reduced. But isn't this a price worth paying to have a workable international regulatory framework that does not unravel at the stage where arguably it matters most, i.e. where parties that are engaged in international transactions need to rely on it?

Some will argue that this will result in asymmetries, in that some States, in particular those that do not recognize direct application of international treaties, would probably keep their options open, This is a fact. But some States have to show the way and as we live in an interdependent world with instant communication the chance is greater than ever that the example set by some will ultimately be followed by others.[52]

---

[52] It is well known that agencies charged with applying antidumping laws often borrow interpretations and techniques from each other. Why shouldn't the judiciary do so where possible? In *Allied, supra* n. 10, which recognized fully the standing of foreign exporters to challenge EC antidumping measures, the EC Commission in an unusual move argued in favour of recognizing such standing, i.a. by referring to the example of other parties to the 1979 GATT Antidumping Code.

9. TRADE POLICY-MAKING INSTITUTIONS AND PROCEDURES IN THE EUROPEAN COMMUNITY

This paper deals with three apparently unconnected issues in the field of external trade: EC constitutional law principles, institutional and procedural checks and balances in the political decision-making process and legislative delegation of foreign trade policy powers. The paper was designed to provide some of the ground for a discussion. The analysis of the law as it stands raises questions rather than offering answers. Does the political decision-making process allow for a proper balance of all interests involved? Would replacing the center-periphery dialogue between EC Institutions and Member States by a dialogue between an EC Executive and the European Parliament lead to a better balance? Does the (limited) delegation in the EC system create problems from that perspective? Is the Court of Justice's judicial restraint in the field of external trade producing results that are about right in the sense that they reflect mainstream societal values within the EC? Is the Court of Justice right in not rocking the boat once in a while?

I.   EC CONSTITUTIONAL LAW PRINCIPLES RECOGNIZED TO BE APPLICABLE TO FOREIGN TRADE LEGISLATION

A.   Some General Observations

The absence in the EEC Treaty of express rules, with the exception of the non-discrimination (Art. 7 EEC) and the solidarity (Art. 5 EEC) principles, containing constitutional law-type principles does not mean that, assuming that they have substantive jurisdiction under the EEC Treaty or under secondary legislation, the Community "legislator", "regulator" and "administrator" are not bound by any such principles. Over the years the Court of Justice of the European Communities (hereinafter: the Court) has developed a series of general principles of law such as good faith, legal certainty, due diligence, equality, legitimate expectations and proportionality.[1] In addition, it is established that at least the principles on which the European Convention on Human Rights is based must be taken into consideration in Community law.[2] Finally, the Court has on its own made constitutional law in the well-known *Stauder* type cases.

---

[1] There is a considerable amount of legal literature on this subject. See *inter alia* Schermers and Waelbroeck, *Judicial Protection In The European Communities*, 25-83 (4th ed., December 1987); see, also, FIDE, *Reports to the 12th Conference*, Vol. I (Paris, 1986) and especially the Community Report by Pescatore 17–54.
[2] *Johnston*, 1986 ECR 1651 para. 18.

225

There is no need to deal here with the question of the source of such general principles nor to enter into a theoretical debate relating to the status of such principles. It is perhaps more interesting to try to distinguish between several types of general principles and to analyze their proper function.[3]

There are several types of general principles. A *first category* includes general concepts relating to the institutional, economic or social foundations of the Community. It includes the principle of solidarity, expressed, *inter alia*, in Art. 5 EEC, the principle of Community preference expressed in Art. 41 EEC and the "common market" principle, meaning that conditions must be achieved which are as close as possible to those of a domestic market. These principles are mainly used in interpreting the scope/extent of obligations imposed on Member States and the provisions conferring powers on the Community.

A *second category* includes concepts relating to the Community as a community of law. They are used essentially to review the exercise by the Community institutions of their discretionary powers.[4] They can be grouped in three subcategories: general principles concerning the respect for fundamental rights and freedoms; principles of sound and proper administration; and principles relating to the notion of legal certainty.

It should be pointed out that these general principles seem to come into play normally only with respect to the exercise of genuine discretionary powers. This should be distinguished from power of appraisal which refers to situations where the exercise of a given power is made conditional on certain economic facts, the assessment of which itself implies discretion.[5] In the latter situation, judicial review focuses on the question whether the alleged facts have actually been established and whether the legal significance attributed to them by the authorities corresponds to the significance attributed to them by the legal provision in question.[6]

---

[3] I relied on Mertens de Wilmars, "The Case-law of the Court of Justice in Relation to the Review of the Legality of Economic Policy in Mixed-Economy Systems," (1982) *LIEE* 1-16.
[4] But also sometimes to review Member State action under Community Law.
[5] According to Mertens de Wilmars, *supra* note 3 at 4, "in the case of a power of appraisal there is, in fact, to a considerable degree, a limited delegation of powers (compétence liée) in the sense that the authority has no freedom of action unless the conditions have been satisfied and when the conditions exist it is bound to act in a specific way, while discretionary power is intended to allow the authority to choose one of a number of possible courses of action [...]".
[6] Mertens de Wilmars, *supra* note 3 at 7.

Where the appraisal concerns complex economic situations, the Court's review is "marginal" in that it is only prepared to declare the measure illegal when it finds a 'manifest error of judgment'.[7] This point is sometimes missed by authors criticizing the Court's limited review of the facts in anti-dumping cases.[8]

The application of these principles will be examined with respect to legal acts relating to foreign trade only where the subject matter, i.e. foreign trade, was specifically considered by the Court as a relevant element for its judgment. In other words, no reference will be made to cases in which the subject matter is incidental and in which it may be assumed that the outcome would have been the same if the legal act had related to another subject matter.[9]

Whether this assumption always holds true is far from certain. It is altogether another question whether and to what extent the rationale of certain judgments dealing with *intra-Community* trade applying some of these general principles could/should be extrapolated to similar factual situations *in foreign trade.* The question arises because certain of these principles are given a concrete content in relation to other principles or rules.

Two examples illustrate this point. First, the principle of proportionality may lead the Court to declare a penalty for a false declaration of origin illegal under Community law when applied in intra-Community trade and legal when applied in foreign trade, in view of the different regimes applying to intra-Community and foreign trade.[10]

Second, in *ADBHU* the Court stated that "the principle of free movement of goods and freedom of competition, together *with freedom of trade as a fundamental right,* are general principles of law of which the Court ensures observance"[11] (emphasis added). It also stated that "the

---

[7] *Remia,* 1985 ECR 2545.
[8] As was correctly noted by P.J. Kuyper, "Judicial Protection and Judicial Review", in J. Jackson and E. Vermulst (eds), *Anti-dumping Law and Practice,* 374 at 382 (Harvester Wheatsheaf, New York, 1990).
[9] See for example, the series of cases involving the forfeiture of securities as a form of penalty in which the Court referred to the principle of proportionality.
[10] This may be inferred from *Rivoira,* 1979 ECR 1147 para. 20; this was the practical result in the underlying criminal cases under national law in *Bouhelier I,* 1977 ECR 197 and *Bouhelier II,* 1979 ECR 3151.
[11] 985 ECR 531, para. 9.

principle of freedom of trade [...] is subject to certain limits justified by the objectives of general interest pursued by the Community provided that the rights in question are not substantively impaired".[12] Reviewing in the light of these principles certain rules laid down in a Community Directive on the collection of waste oils, the Court held that the restrictive effect thereof on the freedom of trade did not "go beyond the inevitable restrictions which are justified by the pursuit of the objective of environmental protection, which is in the general interest".[13]

Does the principle also apply in foreign trade, and if not, should it? If it should, should it carry the same weight as in intra-Community trade when put in balance with the restrictions deemed necessary, e.g. to protect the European Community industry?[14]

B.   Proportionality

Apart from some cases involving anti-dumping measures in which it was argued but dismissed as not established or was not addressed by the Court,[15] the principle of proportionality has been applied so far by the Court in three foreign trade cases.[16] In *Dürbeck*, the Court held that "when the Commission believes that the conditions requisite for the application of [protective] measures are fulfilled, it must observe the principle of proportionality underlying the Community legal order".[17] It did, however, not find a violation of this principle, but considered it as providing some justification for the unsuccessful attempts made by the Commission to secure a VER of the exporting country.

In *Edeka*, the Court rejected the claim that the almost total ban of imports from Taiwan and South-Korea contravened the principle of proportionality; it held that by imposing the ban on countries that did

---

[12] Para. 12.
[13] Para. 15.
[14] *See infra.*
[15] *Nachi-Fujikoshi Corp.*, 1987 ECR 1861; *Minebea*, 1987 ECR 1975; *NTN Toyo*, 1987 ECR 1809; *Nashua*, 1990 ECR 1-719.
[16] The so-called Art. 115 EEC cases, *inter alia Bock* (1971 ECR 897) and *Kaufhof* (1976 ECR 431) concern intra-Community trade, albeit in goods of foreign origin. *Schäfer Shop* (1989 ECR 2937) related to intra-German trade. In *National Dried Fruit Trade Association* (1988 ECR 757, para. 32), a countervailing tax was held invalid because the Commission had not established that the system applying "even where the difference between the import price and the minimum price is very small" was necessary for attaining the aim of the underlying regulation. See *also* parallel case *Central-Import Münster*, 1988 ECR 3679.
[17] 1981 ECR 1095 para. 40.

not agree to a VER and, in so doing, giving an advantage to imports from China which had accepted a VER, the Commission had not exceeded the limits of its discretionary power.[18]

In the parent *Faust* case, the Court held that "[i]n view of the fact that the Commission sought by means of the contested measure to achieve two equally legitimate objectives, namely stabilization of the market and implementation of a Community policy relating to external trade, the measures adopted cannot be considered to be disproportionate to the objectives pursued".[19]

Interestingly enough the principle of proportionality is relied upon – or at least such reliance can be derived from the system – by the Community "legislator" (the Council) when it delegates powers to the Community "regulator" and "administrator" (the Commission). Several Council regulations in the area of foreign trade direct the Commission to take the *necessary* protective measures, which are a derogation from the general prohibition of restrictions on imports laid down in these regulations.[20]

C.   Legal Certainty

The principle of legal certainty is not well defined and, when it is applied not to regulate legislative action (e.g. application of norms *ratione temporis*) but to interpret and apply substantive law to individual cases, it overlaps to a certain extent with "legitimate expectations" and "vested rights". One might add that the departure from "legal certainty" is permitted provided "legitimate expectations" are protected: in circumstances where the purpose to be achieved so demands, Community measures may apply retrospectively, provided the legitimate expectations of those concerned are duly respected.[21]

The principle of 'legal certainty' finds expression in Community legislation relating to foreign trade. This is the case for the regulation on the import regime applying to imports from all countries except State-trading countries,[22] and the import regime applying to imports from State-

---

[18] 1982 ECR 2745 para. 23.
[19] 982 ECR 3745 para. 23.
[20] As is pointed out *inter alia* by Tesauro A-G in *Sofrimport*, judgment of 26 June 1990 (1990 ECR 1-2477).
[21] For example, *Racke*, 1979 ECR 69.
[22] Council Regulation (EEC) No. 288/82, of 5 February 1982 (OJ L 35/82), Art. 15(3).

trading countries[23] which contain certain rules with respect to the application of safeguard measures on existing contracts or to goods already dispatched to the EC. Similar rules appear in regulations on the import regime applying to particular sectors.[24]

Moreover, one of these regulations contains a provision directing the Commission, when setting import quotas, to take account *inter alia* of "the volume of goods exported under contracts concluded on normal terms and conditions before the entry into force of a protective measure, [...] ".[25]

The regulation against dumping and subsidization provides that anti-dumping and countervailing duties can be imposed retrospectively but not more than 90 days prior to the application of provisional duties, i.e. at any rate in practice after the initiation of anti-dumping or countervailing proceedings.[26] The conditions to be fulfilled are, however, such that this provision has not been applied so far.[27]

D. Vested Rights

The principle that "vested rights" must be respected does not seem to play an important role in EC law. The purpose which this principle seeks to achieve under the laws of the EC Member States seems to be pursued under EC law by the principle of legal certainty and that of the protection of legitimate expectations.[28]

In the field of foreign trade, this principle has been relied upon by a party in *Balkan-Import-Export*; the Court held that "the importer has no vested right to have that advantage maintained and, without prejudice to undertakings which may have been entered into with regard to third countries, the Community must always reserve its freedom to determine the conditions of importation for agricultural products originating in third countries, having regard to the common organization of the agricultural markets and the needs of its commercial policy'.[29]

---

[23] Council Regulation (EEC) No. 1766/82, of 30 June 1982 (OJ L 195/82), Art. 11(3).
[24] Council Regulation (EEC) No. 4136/86, of 30 June 1982 (textiles) (OJ L 387/86), Art. 11(12); also, in a series of regulations on agricultural products; one of them is referred in the *Sofrimport* case *supra* note 20.
[25] Regulation 288/82, Art. 15(2).
[26] Council Regulation (EEC) No. 2423/88, of 11 July 1988 (OJ L 209/88).
[27] The conditions were presumably met in one case, but duties were not applied retrospectively in view of the fact that the imports during the 90 days preceding the imposition of provisional duties were negligible. *Mercury from the USSR*, OJ L 346/87.
[28] See Pescatore, *supra* note 1 at 42.
[29] 1977 ECR 2031 para. 17.

E. Protection of Legitimate Expectations

The principle of "protection of legitimate expectations", which is borrowed from German law ("Vertrauensschutz") plays an important function in the Court's case law. There is no need to analyze it here:[30] it suffices to refer to cases relating to foreign trade in which it has been referred to.

In *IFG-Intercontinentale Fleischhandelsgesellschaft*, the Court rejected the claim, based on this principle, that the Commission should have adopted transitional measures when it extended the scope of a safeguard measure. The Court stated that:

> [The] import system at issue required no previous authorization or any firm commitment on the part of the person concerned with respect to the authorities responsible for the management of the organization of the markets in question and the Commission conveyed nothing to importers which could have justified the expectation that, regardless of the development of the conditions of the market, the previous rules would be maintained without alteration during the time when prior contracts were to be performed.[31]

In *Dürbeck*, the Court rejected the argument against the validity of a regulation imposing safeguard measures that was also based on this principle. It held that:

> [I]n view of the needs which temporary suspension of imports met, transitional measures which exempted contracts already entered into from the suspension of imports would have robbed the protective measures of all practical effect by opening the Community market in dessert apples to a volume of imports likely to jeopardize that market.[32]

---

[30] For a short but good overview see Pescatore, *supra* note 1 at pp. 35–41.

[31] 1978 ECR 353 para. 8.

[32] 1981 ECR 1095 para. 50.

In *Edeka,* the Court repeated its view that there is no legitimate expectation 'that an existing situation which is capable of being altered by decisions taken by [the Community] institutions within the limits of their discretionary power will be maintained'. The Court added that in the case at hand the conclusion of a trade agreement with China "was of such a nature as to alert traders to an imminent change of direction in the Community's commercial policy".[33]

In *Sofrimport,*[34] involving once again safeguard measures against imports of apples, the Commission had not adopted transitional provisions with respect to apples originating in Chile which were in transit at the time the measures were taken. Referring to a Council Regulation directing the Commission to "take account of the special position of products in transit to the Community", the Court annulled the measures in so far as they concerned goods in transit, as the Commission had not "demonstrated the existence of any overriding public interest justifying the application of suspensory measures [i.e. the safeguard measures] with regard to goods in transit". The Court further held that this constituted a sufficiently serious breach of a superior rule of law justifying the award of damages under Art. 215 EEC.

Interestingly, the principle of protection of legitimate expectations has also been invoked in connection with protective measures on exports.

In *Luehrs,* involving a tax levied on exports of potatoes in the face of a situation of shortage on the EC market resulting from a poor harvest in 1975, the Court rejected an argument against the validity of the tax based on that principle. It first referred to an overriding public interest pursuant to which the tax was introduced. It then found that the trader in question could not plead legitimate expectations: the situation was abnormal, traders had been warned by earlier Commission measures, and transitional measures had been adopted for contracts concluded before a given date for supplies to certain countries with which there were well-established customary economic relations.[35]

From this perusal of the Court's case law one may conclude that, in the field of foreign trade, the existence of legitimate expectations is not easily admitted. Originally, the principle was based on the idea that when

---

[33] 1982 ECR 2745 para. 27; same holding in *Faust,* 1982 ECR 3745 para. 27.
[34] *Supra* note 20.
[35] 1978 ECR 169 paras 6–9

public authorities make known to persons under their administration their willingness to take a decision coinciding with the wishes of those persons, subject to some condition or other, they should respect the legitimate hopes aroused by the assurances given, unless there are compelling reasons for not doing so.[36] Although the Court has extended this to legislative measures, basically the underlying idea remains that there is some 'basis of trust' with individuals protecting their situation against the application of the general rule.[37]

F.   Non-Discrimination

The principle of non-discrimination is written into Art. 7 EEC. The terms are worth recalling:

> Within the scope of application of this Treaty, and without prejudice to any special provision contained therein, any discrimination on grounds of nationality shall be prohibited.

The Court has seen in this article and in other articles of the EEC Treaty the expression of the general principle of equality, which is one of the fundamental principles of EC law.[38] The scope of this principle, the extent and the content thereof, would deserve many comments. However, only the case law relating to foreign trade will be examined and comments will be limited to specific foreign trade aspects.

Two general remarks seem appropriate.

– First, the principle of equality implies in its positive form that identical situations should be treated in the same way, and in its negative form that different situations, as the case may be, should not be treated identically. However, a difference of treatment may be objectively justified *inter alia* in the light of the particular provisions of EC law concerned.[39]

---

[36] Following the description given by Mertens de Wilmars, *supra* note 3 at 14.
[37] Pescatore *supra* note 1 at 35.
[38] *Hochstrass*, 1980 ECR 3005 para. 7; with reference to Art. 40 EEC, see Edeka *supra* note 18 para. 11 referring to earlier judgments.
[39] For example, *Sermide*, 1984 ECR 4209 para. 28. Nationality cannot offer such objective justification, in view of the wording of Art. 7 EEC *(Walt Wilhelm*, 1969 ECR 1 para. 13).

– Second, third country nationals are not in the same position as Community nationals, although views expressed in the literature may differ in this regard.[40] With respect to intra-Community relations, the debate can, however, be narrowed down to situations for which the EEC Treaty does not contain express provisions such as Articles 9, 48, 52, 59, and 67(1) which either contemplate transactions or use a residency criterion. With respect to foreign relations the EEC Treaty does not contain substantive rules save those on customs duties and those on trade policy. This led some to conclude that the principle of non-discrimination as laid down in Art. 7 EEC does not apply.[41]

The question whether EC law contains a principle of equal treatment of third countries arose in *Balkan-Import-Export*. The case involved the levying of so-called monetary compensatory amounts on imports of goat cheese from Bulgaria. In one of the questions concerning the legality of these levies submitted to the Court, the national court referred to the exemption from payment of such levies for certain Italian and Swiss varieties of cheese and asked whether, in refusing the same treatment to goat cheese from Bulgaria, the Commission did not violate the principle of equality of treatment. The Court began by stating that "[i]n the Treaty there exists no general principle obliging the Community, in its external relations, to accord to third countries equal treatment in all respects" adding that "in any event traders do not have the right to rely on the existence of such a general principle".[42] It nonetheless went on to review the reasons given by the Commission: vis-à-vis Italian cheese, it found that "the general principle of Community preference justifies a different assessment of the possibilities of disturbance" which monetary compensatory

---

[40] For example, with respect to Art. 7 EEC, discrimination is also prohibited between Community nationals and third country nationals (Bleckmann in *Kommentar Groeben Boeckh*, 3d ed.; Ad Art. 7 para. 3); the prohibition applies only to discrimination of other EC Member State's nationals in favour of the Member State's own nationals (I. Bode, *Die Diskriminierungs-verbote im Vertrag ueber die EWG*, at 302) (Göttingen, 1968). According to the Court, Art. 7 EEC docs not prevent "reverse-discrimination" (see analysis of the case law by K. Mortelmans, *"La discrimination à rebours et le droit communautaire,"* 1980, *Diritto Comunitario* 1).

[41] Bleckmann, *supra* note 400 para. 4. For another view, see E.-U. Petersmann, "Application of GATT by the Court of Justice of the European Communities," 20 *CML Rev.* 397 (1983) who claims that there are "constitutionally guaranteed individual freedoms against any restrictions imposed by the executive of the Community in contravention of GATT obligations" (at 417).

[42] 1976 ECR 19, para. 14.

amounts were designed to avoid;[43] vis-à-vis Swiss cheese, the Court noted, without disapproving it, the Commission's argument that "because of their high free-at-frontier offer price [...] the importation of Swiss cheeses causes less danger of disturbance than that of the Bulgarian cheese [...]".[44]

This question arose also in the *mushroom* cases, *Edeka* and *Faust*.[45] In *Edeka*, quoting *Balkan-Import-Export*, the Court affirmed that "the Treaty contains no general principle which may be relied upon by traders, compelling the Community in its external relations to accord equal treatment in all respects to non-member countries. Therefore the fact that the Commission's regulations give rise to a deflection in the flow of imports from Taiwan and South Korea towards the People's Republic of China does not provide any ground for criticism".[46] In *Faust* the Court restated that there is no general principle obliging the Community, in its external relations, to accord to non-member countries equal treatment in all respects.[47]

In both cases, however, one of the importer's arguments added a new twist. The importing undertaking claimed that *it* had been discriminated against as an established importer of Taiwanese mushrooms and that EC law protected long-standing commercial relationships entered into by the importer with Taiwan. In his opinion in *Faust*, Slynn A-G accepted that the importer could rely on Art. 40(3) EEC. Assuming that it would be sufficient to constitute a breach of this provision that the unequal treatment of operators based inside the EC results directly from unequal treatment of third countries, Slynn A-G considered that any different treatment could only constitute wrongful discrimination if the position of the countries in question were the same or comparable. In his view it was objectively justifiable to impose restrictions on imports from countries which had not accepted a VER but not on countries which had accepted a VER because only imports from the former continue to constitute a threat to the market.[48]

---

[43] *But see Providence Agricole*, 1980 ECR 2823 which rejected the application of the Community preference principle on the ground that monetary compensatory amounts must be strictly compared to neutralizing variations in exchange rates in both extra- and intra-Community trade.

[44] Para. 15.

[45] *Supra* note 19.

[46] *Edeka*, para. 19.

[47] *Faust*, para. 25.

[48] 1982 ECR 3745 at 3772-3773.

In *Faust*, the Court gave this argument short shrift by stating that:

> [I]f different treatment of non-member countries is compatible with Community law, different treatment accorded to traders within the Community must also be regarded as compatible with Community law, when that different treatment is merely an automatic consequence of the different treatment accorded to non-member countries with which such traders have entered into commercial relations.[49]

It should be remembered, however, that the Court had already addressed this issue in *Edeka*. As a result of the importer's argument reflected in the national court's request for preliminary ruling, in *Edeka* the Court did in effect review the Commission's regulations under the principle of equality of some sorts, while denying in the end its existence (para. 19). Under the Court's case-law "equal treatment" does not exclude differences in treatment that are objectively justified.[50] This is precisely what the Court examined in *Edeka*, since it was willing to consider whether the policy which resulted in the differences of treatment appearing in the challenged regulation was "arbitrary" in nature. After reviewing the facts the Court concluded that the regulation in question:

> [...] answered the needs of the Community market [...] and thus the different treatment which it accords to the supplier countries in question and consequently to the traders importing from these countries must be considered as objectively justified so that the submission relating to an infringement of the second subparagraph of Article 40(3) of our [sic] Treaty must be rejected.[51]

Finally, it is interesting to note that in *Dürbeck*, the Court also dealt with the merits of the claim that safeguard measures violated the principle of non-discrimination. This was, as in *Edeka* and *Faust*, a claim about discrimination between importers rather than between exporting countries, albeit that the Court did not treat it explicitly so. The argument was about the treatment of apples not yet in transit which differed between exports from Chile and those from other supplying countries which had accepted a VER. The Court held that:

---

[49] Para. 25.
[50] *Supra* para. 14.
[51] Para. 20.

[...] the extension of those arrangements to imports, limited as they were, from a country which had not accepted the voluntary export restraint clause proposed by the Commission would have been discriminatory in regard to the other countries in the southern hemisphere which had accepted such a clause and would have endangered the observance of the commitments assumed by those countries.[52]

From this brief review of the case-law one may tentatively draw the following conclusions:

— First, while there is no recognition of a principle of equal treatment under EC law of third countries as such, this principle applies to EC importers. Where the different treatment of importers is the consequence of the different treatment of the exporting countries, the Court is willing to review the legality of foreign trade measures under the principle of equality.

— Second, in such cases the equality at issue is that between exporting countries, not the equality between an exporting country and a Member State, assuming that a Community measure singles out a Member State. *Balkan-Import-Export* rested this on the principle of Community preference. Arguably, the legitimacy of treating Member States differently from third countries could also be rested on the very existence of a "common market" along the lines of the case-law interpreting clauses of international agreements differently from similarly worded EEC Treaty provisions dealing with intra-Community trade.[53]

G.   The Search for Other Principles

Attempts have been made in the literature to find other principles that (ought to) apply to EC foreign trade legislation.[54] The duty to comply with international law, about which the last word has not been

---

[52] 1981 ECR 1095, para. 55.

[53] For example, *Polydor*, 1982 ECR 329; for a brief comment on this point, J. Bourgeois, "Effects on International Agreements in European Community Law : Arc the Dice Cast?," 82 *Mich. L R.* 1250 at 1268–1270(1984)

[54] See *inter alia* Petersmann in several of his writings, among which the article cited *supra* note 41.

said,[55] is left aside since it is dealt with by others. The following remarks are limited to the aims of the trade policy as set out in the EEC Treaty and to the freedom to trade and the freedom to compete.

1. Article 110 EEC

Leaving aside some interpretative problems of Art. 110 EEC, the essential question which this provision raises is whether it is to be regarded as a legally binding one, in the sense that it lays down a duty for the EC to materialize its liberal guidance in the measures the EC takes and in the international agreements which the EC enters into.

In the literature contrasting views are defended. According to some, Art. 110 EEC is not a normative provision; it merely expresses a political commitment entered into by the Member States.[56] According to others, Art. 110 EEC lays down a genuine legal obligation for the EC and its Member States.[57]

In practice, the problem boils down to the question whether Art. 110 EEC is a provision against which the legality of a trade policy measure can be reviewed. The Court seems to hesitate. In one case the Court limited itself to pointing out that "the provisions of the Treaty on commercial policy do not, in Art. 110 *et seq.*, lay down any obligation on the part of the Member States to extend to trade with third countries the binding principles governing the free movement of goods between Member States".[58] In another case, it has rejected a claim that certain trade policy measures contravened Art. 110 "since it has not been established [...] that by adopting such measures the Council overstepped the boundaries of the wide powers of assessment conferred on it by this provision in matters of commercial policy".[59]

---

[55] It is interesting to see how much as a matter-of-course the Court entertained international law arguments in *Wood Pulp*, 1988 ECR 5193.

[56] Mégret in Mégret, Louis, Vignes and Waelbroeck, *Le Droit de la Communauté Economique Européenne*, Vol. 6, at 367 (Bruxelles, 1976); Pescatore in Ganshof van der Meersch, *Droit des Communautés Européennes*, n° 2298 (Bruxelles, 1969); Pipkorn in Beutler, Bieber, Pipkorn and Streil, *Die Europäische Gemeinschaftsrechtsordnung und Polilik*, 3. Auflage at 526 (Baden-Baden, 1987).

[57] Quadri, Monaco and Trabucchi, *Trattato Istitutivo della Comunita Economica Europea*, Art. 110, nr. 3 (Milano, 1965); Vedder in Grabitz (Hg.), *Kommentar zum EWG-Vertrag*, Art. 110. nr. 1 (München, 1986).

[58] The EMI/CBS judgments, *inter alia* 1976 ECR 811 para. 17.

[59] *Balkan-Import-Export*, 1973 ECR 1091 para. 27.

In another case, it held that Art. 110 "cannot be interpreted as prohibiting the Community from enacting, upon pain of committing an infringement of the Treaty, any measure liable to affect trade with non-member countries even where the adoption of such a measure is required, as in this case, by the risk of a serious disturbance which might endanger the objectives set out in Article 39 of the Treaty and where the measure is legally justified by the provisions of Community law" .[60] This language is interesting in the light of the views expressed by several Advocates-General who considered effectively that Art. 110 cannot be relied upon to review the legality of trade policy measures.[61]

The Court has yet to declare a trade policy measure illegal for contravening Art. 110. It refrained, however, from dismissing as inadmissible or irrelevant claims based on Art. 110 and rejected them albeit summarily on the merits. This seems to indicate that, possibly via the principle of proportionality, Art. 110 could yield some criteria to test the "constitutionality" of legislative, regulatory or administrative acts in the field of foreign trade.

2.   *Freedom of Competition*[62]

Trade policy measures affect the flow or patterns of trade. Taken at the import side they raise directly or indirectly the price at which imported products compete with domestic products and/or limit directly the quantity of imported goods supplied on the domestic market. Thus some of the competition that would otherwise exist for like or competing products on the domestic market is restricted or (partially or wholly) eliminated.

The question thus arises whether the Community's mandate to ensure "that competition in the common market is not distorted" (Art. 3(f) EEC) would yield a constitutional-type principle, rule or standard applying to foreign trade legislation.

---

[60] *Dürbeck*, 1981 ECR 1095 para. 44.

[61] Capotorti A-G in *Dürbeck*, 1981 ECR 1095 at 1138; Capotorti A-G in *Internationale Fleischhandelsgesellschaft*, 1978 ECR 353 at 378; Mayras A-G in *Stimming*, 1978 ECR 995 at 1016; but Roemer A-G did express a view on whether Art. 110 had been properly applied in *Balkan-Import-Export*, 1973 ECR 1091 at 1128.

[62] I have dealt to some extent with this topic in a paper on "Trade Measures, Competition Policy and the Consumers - EC Perspective," in Bourgeois, Demaret and Van Bael (eds.), *Trade Laws of the European Community and the United States in a Comparative Perspective*, 227 (Brussels, 1992). See *also* J. Temple-Lang, "Reconciling European Community Antitrust and Antidumping, Transport and Trade Safeguard Policies –Practical Problems", in B. Hawk (ed.), 1988 *Fordham Corporate Law Institute* 7-1 –7-90 (New York, 1989).

It should be borne in mind that under the EEC Treaty, competition policy and competition rules are part and parcel of an array of policies and rules designed to achieve the general aims of the EEC Treaty.

The balancing of the sometimes contradictory requirements resulting from the need to ensure that competition is not distorted and the conduct of other policies is an eminently political task. Yet, in several cases where the Court has been called upon to pass judgment on this political assessment, it has not rejected it out-of-hand as a non-justiciable issue and has marked the perimeter of the discretion of the EC's political institutions.[63]

As mentioned *supra, in ADBHU* the Court was faced with an EC Directive regulating the disposal of waste oils with a view to protecting the environment. The system established for collecting waste-oils had restrictive effects on competition. The Court developed a standard – the measures may neither be discriminatory nor go beyond the inevitable restrictions which are justified by the pursuit of the objective of environmental protection, which is in the general interest – and, applying this standard to the measures in question, held that there were no grounds for considering them illegal.[64]

It would seem that so far the Court has not been called upon to deal with the issue of whether the political institutions have struck a legitimate balance between the requirements of competition rules (or the principle of the freedom of competition) and the restrictions inherent in trade policy measures.[65] The interesting aspect of such a case would be that the interests involved are more obviously intra-Community interests than in "normal" trade policy litigation (e.g. about anti-dumping measures).

3. Freedom of Trade

As was pointed out *supra, ADBHU* recognized the existence of the fundamental right of freedom of trade.[66] For the reasons mentioned (*supra* p. 178), this is a fundamental right of EC citizens and maybe of

---

[63] *Valsabbia*, 1980 ECR 903; *Maïzena*, 1980 ECR 3393.
[64] 1985 ECR 538 para. 15.
[65] With the exception maybe of *International Fruit* (1971 ECR 411); in *Extramet* (judgment of 16 May 1991, not yet reported) the issue arose but was sidestepped by the Court.
[66] The constitutions of a large number of Member States do not contain such a guarantee. See Prechal and Heukels, Dutch Report in FIDE Conference papers, *supra* note 1 at 272

third country citizens residing in the EC. It was referred to by the Court in connection with intra-Community relations. The unanswered question is whether this fundamental right of EC citizens (and maybe third country citizens residing in the EC) extends to foreign trade.

II.   INSTITUTIONAL AND PROCEDURAL CHECKS AND BALANCES –THE DECISION-MAKING PROCESS

A.   Introduction

Observers of the US scene will agree that Henkin's qualification of competition between Congress and the Administration still holds: "the dominant, least-tractable constitutional issue of American foreign relations".[67]

The trade policy power struggle at US federal level between Congress and the Executive has no counterpart in the EC. The dispute between Commission and Council on the scope and nature of the EC's external relations powers is, in fact, more with several Member States than with the Council proper and is part of the "center-periphery" tensions.

In the EC checks and balances work at different *levels:* "center-periphery", i.e. EC Member States; at the "center" itself, i.e. Council, Commission and European Parliament. They also differ in *nature:* political or judicial. They may also concern different *matters,* i.e. the balance of power between EC and Member States, between institutions, but also judicial protection of private parties' interests against government.

So far as a result of the felt *political* need to reach consensus among Member States in the Council, the checks and balances at the "center-periphery" level have been mainly operated by the political process rather than by a judicial process.

In practically all cases in which the Court has been called upon to adjudicate a dispute on the existence or scope of the EC's external powers, it has come down in favor of EC powers. This is hardly a sufficient counterweight for the political process that has tended to favor the most restrictive interpretation.

---

[67] *Foreign Affairs and the Constitution* (New York, 1972), at 90.

Things are, however, changing. The Council nowadays takes more decisions by qualified majority. It is not surprising that, while in the past litigation on external powers involved private parties or Commission and Council, there has been a recent case in which a Member State challenged a Council Regulation based on the EEC's trade policy powers as being outside the scope of such powers.[68]

The increasing reliance on qualified majority voting may well mean that checks and balances will have to be provided in the future more by the judicial process than by the political one. In this connection the so-called "subsidiarity" principle, whose enforcement will ultimately lie with the Court, could be an important element.

A proper analysis of the EC's political decision-making process, as it stands, in the field of foreign trade implies that one should distinguish between autonomous action and international agreements, between "legislating", "regulating" and "administering".

B.   International Agreements

The procedure followed to negotiate and to conclude most international agreements on foreign trade is characterized by three elements.

–   For the *opening* of negotiations, while acting on a mandate conferred by the EEC Treaty itself (Art. 113(3), Art. 228(1)), the Commission opens negotiations only after having been authorized by the Council, which may address to the Commission negotiating directives. This stage is practically always preceded by so-called "exploratory talks"; although the Commission does not need to be authorized, it will often raise the matter in the Council before engaging in such "exploratory talks".

–   The *conduct* of negotiations is also the Commission's task. The Commission is assisted by a committee of Member States' officials, the so-called 113-Committee. This Committee of "mothers-in-law" performs several functions: it monitors the Commission; it "clarifies" the Council's negotiating directives as the negotiations develop; and it acts as a litmus paper on which the Commission measures the acceptability of the results that emerge from negotiations.

---

[68] *Greece v. Council,* judgment of 29 March 1990, 1990 ECR 1-1527.

–   Negotiations are *concluded* by the Council. Technically, this con-
    clusion covers two different measures: the measure whereby the
    internal procedure to conclude the agreement is completed and
    the measure whereby the EC decides to bind itself *internationally*.

Apart from the advantages it implies for third countries negotiating with the EC, this system offers Member States a built-in guarantee
that their interests will be duly taken into account. The Council "directives"
do not legally bind the Commission, and the "mothers-in-law" committee cannot by a negative vote block Commission initiatives in the negotiation. It should, however, be obvious that the Commission will not lightly
put its reputation the EC negotiator at stake by running great risks that
the results of the negotiations would be rejected by the Council refusing
to conclude the agreement.

The European Parliament's involvement in this process is limited.
Save where the conclusion of an agreement rests on an EEC Treaty Article
requiring consultation of, cooperation with or the assent of the European
Parliament, there is at present in the EEC Treaty no provision requiring
Commission or Council to involve the European Parliament in this process
or entitling the European Parliament to be involved in it. There are,
however, a certain number of "soft-law" type arrangements. Under the
"Luns-procedure", accepted by the Council in 1964, a debate may take
place before the opening of negotiations for "association" with the EC;
during the negotiations the Commission communicates with the relevant
EP committees, and at the end of the negotiations information is provided
to these committees on a confidential and informal basis about the
substance of the agreement. A similar procedure was accepted in 1973 for
trade agreements, with the addition that the EP is informed of the content
of the agreements before their conclusion (the so-called "Westerterp-
procedure").[69] Moreover, the Declaration on the European Union of 1983
provides that the informing of the EP on a confidential and informal basis
is extended to all international agreements of significant importance and
that the opinion of the EP will be sought on such agreements before they
are concluded.[70]

---

[69] See Bull. EC 5-1982 para. 2.4.2 *et seq.*
[70] Bull. EC 6-1983 para. 2.3.7.

C.   Autonomous Action

The general EC decision-making system applies in the foreign
trade area, subject to certain qualifications.[71] For the purpose of analysis,
a distinction is to be made between "legislative", "regulatory" and
"administrative" action, albeit that in the EC system these three categories
overlap to some extent. Before looking at each one of these categories,
one observation is called for with respect to the "openness" of the
"legislative" and "regulatory" processes in the EC in the foreign trade
area.

These processes are more removed from public debate in the EC
than, e.g. in the USA or Canada. They frequently depart from the practices
followed by the EC in other areas.

-   First, legislation proper is usually adopted under Art. 113 EEC
    for which consultation of the European Parliament is not required
    as a matter of law. When submitting proposals to the Council,
    the Commission, however, recommends the so-called non-
    obligatory consultation of the European Parliament except where
    the matter is urgent, of minor importance or confidential.[72] What
    is of minor importance is not always clear. Thus the European
    Parliament was not consulted on the latest amendments to the
    EEC Antidumping Regulation.[73] When the Commission does not
    recommend the non-obligatory consultation of the European
    Parliament, the proposed legislation is usually not published in
    the *Official Journal* Part C.

-   Second, as to "regulatory" action exercised by the Commission,
    apart from consultation of Member States in one form or another
    (see infra), there is practically never consultation of interested
    parties, and, if there is any at all, it does not take the form of
    public hearings.[74] This practice contrasts with the practice

---

[71] For a recent description, see Stein, "Towards a European Foreign Policy? The European
Foreign Affairs Systems from the Perspective of the United States Constitution", in *Integration
Through Law, Europe and the American Federal Experience* (Cappelletti, Seccomhe and
Weiler, (eds) (Berlin 1986).
[72] Commission Communication to the European Parliament of May 30, 1973. Text in R. Bieber,
Die Organe der erweiterte Gemeinschaft: Das Parlement, at 185 (Baden-Baden, 1974).
[73] This failure to consult the EP was criticized in the literature: see *inter alia* C. Norall, "The
New Amendments to the EC's Basic Anti-dumping Regulation," 26 *CML Rev.* 83 at 84 (1989).
[74] In an unusual step, before issuing "guidelines" on refunds of anti-dumping duties (OJ C
266/86), the Commission consulted UNICE, the EC-wide representative organization of
industry, and an EC-wide representative organization of importers.

followed in other areas, where the Commission publishes or otherwise makes available drafts of regulations it intends to adopt and invites comments from interested parties.

1. *"Lgislative Action"*

Apart from the earlier observation with respect to "openness", there are no important points to be made that would be specific for the foreign trade area, except the following one.

The Commission jealously guards its prerogative to initiate legislation. It has successfully resisted attempts made by the Council to insert in legislation provisions requiring the Commission to consult with Member States before submitting proposals for fresh legislation to the Council. It is not unusual, however, for the Commission to ask for the views of national experts before it adopts such proposals. In the foreign trade area, the Commission services will often air their ideas in the so-called 113-Committee of the Council. However useful it might be for the Commission to test the acceptability in the Council of an intended proposal, this practice is at odds with the Commission's independent role under the EEC Treaty as an initiator of legislation.

2. *"Regulatory Action"*

"Regulatory action" means in practice delegated implementing legislation. One of the factors that was seen to contribute to the slowness of the political decision-making process before the adoption of the Single European Act was the Council's reluctance to delegate to the Commission the power to adopt implementing legislation. Pursuant to Article 145 EEC as amended by the Single European Act, the Council adopted a general decision on the Commission's implementing powers.[75] It is interesting to note that as far as "administrative action" is concerned, this decision left foreign trade matters untouched. As far as "regulatory action" is concerned, much depends on the willingness of the Council to delegate "regulatory action", i.e. implementing legislation, to the Commission and on the Commission's resolve to test that willingness. So far matters have remained as they were with the Council reserving to itself the bulk of "regulatory action".

---

[75] OJ L 197/87. For a comment: C.D. Ehlermann, *"Compétences d'exécution conférées à la Commission - La nouvelle décision-cadre du Conseil,"* (1988) *in Revue Du Marché Commun* 232–239 (April 1988).

3. "Administrative Action"

"Administrative action" means the application of preexisting rules to specific circumstances when a given set of economic conditions obtains.

In the foreign trade field this refers mainly to safeguard measures under the import and export regimes, to antidumping and countervailing action and to action against illicit commercial practices of third countries and importation of counterfeit goods.[76]

By and large "administrative action" is delegated to the Commission subject to certain procedural safeguards *(see infra)*.

The interesting feature to note here is the existence of various procedural rights for 'interested parties'. The following procedural rights can be distinguished:

–   the right to make written submissions,[77]

–   the right to inspect the information made available to the Commission,[78]

–   the right to an oral hearing,[79] and

–   the right to disclosure.[80]

It should be noted, however, that according to the relevant regulations not all "interested parties" benefit from all these rights.[81]

D.   The 'Day-to-Day Business'

The system - provided it deserves that name – for handling "day-to-day business" in the field of foreign trade is murky. This has two aspects:

---

[76] For a description, see Prof. Völker's paper in this book.
[77] Regulation 2423/88, Art. 7(l)(a); Regulation 288/82, Art. 6(l)(a); Regulation 2641/84, Art. 6(l)(a).
[78] Regulation 2423/88, Art. 7(4)(a); Regulation 2641, Art. 6(4)(a).
[79] Regulation 288/82, Art. 6(4); Regulation 2641/84, Art. 6(5); Regulation 2423/88, Art. 7(5).
[80] Regulation 2641/84, Art. 6(5); Regulation 2423/88, Art. 7(4)(b); Regulation 2641/84, Art. 6(4)(b).
[81] The European Bureau of Consumers' Unions challenged the Commission's refusal to allow it to inspect the Commission's non-confidential files in an anti-dumping proceeding, but the Court rejected the application *(BEUC v. Commission,* judgment of 28 November 1991, not yet reported).

– First, at present, save for certain areas, the practical application of EC law is in the hands of Member States. This practical application may involve a whole range of measures, from issuing documents to businesses to adopting certain legislative provisions to enforce EC law. There is work left for the national ministerial departments in charge of foreign trade. The dividing line between application of EC foreign trade legislation and autonomous activities of Member States in the area of foreign trade cannot be traced with any great certainty.

– Second, at EC level, although the day-to-day business of conducting foreign trade policy is the Commission's business under the EEC Treaty, the Commission seeks in fact some sort of political coverage by airing this day-to-day business in the so-called 113-Committee of the Council. While this pragmatic *modus operandi* avoids turf battles between the two institutions, it tends to blur the distinction between the Commission's and the Council's responsibilities.

III.   LEGISLATIVE DELEGATION OF FOREIGN TRADE POLICY POWERS AND THE CONSTITUTIONAL REQUIREMENT OF LIMITED DELEGATION OF POWERS

A.   Introduction

Under the EC system this issue arises in two contexts: the division of powers between the EC and its Member States on the one hand, and the relation between the Council as "legislative body" and the Commission as "executive body" on the other hand.

As to the EC's powers in the field of foreign trade (and the nature of these powers), it suffices to refer to the literature and the Court's case law analyzed by that literature.[82] Apart from the observation made *supra* (II.A) there is nothing to add from an EC law perspective.

---

[82] For example, Ehlermann, "The Scope of Article 113 of the EEC Treaty", in *Mélanges Offerts à P.H. Teitgen* (Paris, 1984); P. Gilsdorf, 'Die Grenzen der Gemeinsamen Handelspolitik,' in *Europa Institut der Universität des Saarlandes* (n° 125) (1988); P. Demaret, "*La politique commerciale: Perspectives d'évolution et faiblesses présentes,*" in Schwarze and Schermers, *Structure And Dimensions Of European Community Policy, 69* (Baden-Baden, 1988).

B.   Delegation of Powers to the Commission

There is no delegation of genuine legislative powers by the Council to the Commission. In the foreign trade field there is no delegation of regulatory powers either, save for agricultural products under the common organization of the market; since the issues that such delegation raises are not specific to foreign trade, they are left aside.

The area for which power has been delegated by the Council to the Commission is that of "administrative action", in the sense mentioned earlier of applying preexisting rules to specific circumstances when a given set of economic conditions obtain. The theoretical question may be whether this is really a case of "delegation" in view of the proper functions of the Commission under the EEC Treaty.

Where such powers are delegated to the Commission, various procedural devices are used through which either the Council or the Member States exercise a form of supervision or control over the Commission's activities. For example, provisional anti-dumping and countervailing measures are applied by the Commission, but the Council may, acting by qualified majority, "act differently";[83] the Commission may terminate an anti-dumping or a counter vailing investigation without measures or by accepting an undertaking offered by the exporters, but if a Member State objects, the matter is referred to the Council who may, within one month, decide differently by qualified majority.[84] Safeguard measures are taken by the Commission, but a Member State may refer the measure to the Council; if within three months the Council has not acted, the Commission measure lapses.[85]

The Commission may adopt rules on the administration of export or import quotas, but it has to follow a management committee procedure.[86]

The Commission may, under the so-called 'new commercial policy instrument', decide to initiate international consultations or international dispute settlement proceedings, but its decision may be referred to the

---

[83] Regulation 2423/88, Art. 11(4).
[84] Regulation 2423/88, Articles 9(1) and 10(1).
[85] For example, Regulation 288/82, Art. 15(5) and (6).
[86] Regulation 1023/70 (OJ L 124/70).

Council who may, by qualified majority, take a different decision within 30 days.[87]

In the light of these procedural devices and of the limited use made by the Council to delegate powers to the Commission, it does not appear that there is any danger that the constitutional requirement of limited delegation – under EC "constitutional law" the institutional balance as it now stands under the EEC Treaty – would be contravened.

Under the Court's case law, while it is clear that 'implementation' by the Commission of rules laid down by the Council within the meaning of Art. 155 EEC is not restricted to non-regulatory powers,[88] the Council must decide on the essential elements of the matter which has to be regulated.

C.   Delegation of Powers to Other Bodies

Under the ECSC Treaty it has been established that delegation of broad discretionary powers is not permitted where it concerns institutions different from those set up by the Treaty, as this would amount to a breach of a basic guarantee which is afforded by the Treaty to the subjects of the EC and which is implied in the balance of powers which is characteristic of the institutional structure of the EC.[89] The same rationale has been followed by the Court under the EEC Treaty. For example, according to the Court it follows from Art. 155 EEC and from the judicial system created by the EEC Treaty - in particular Articles 173 and 177 – that a body such as the Administrative Commission on Social Security for Migrant Workers could not be empowered by the Council to adopt acts having the force of law.[90]

In certain areas things are moving. One might expect some important changes as a result of the impending revision of the EEC Treaty. Some of the problems resulting from the creation of the European Monetary Fund have already been dealt with in the literature.[91] It appears,

---

[87] Regulation 2641/84, Art. 11(2) (a).
[88] *Chemifarma*, 1970 ECR 661 at 688.
[89] *Meroni*, 1957/1958 ECR 157 at 173.
[90] *Romano*, 1981 ECR 1241 at 1256.
[91] Louis, "*Le Fonds européen de coopération monétaire*," 1973 CDE 255; with respect to other bodies see M. Hilf, "*Die Abhängige juristische Person des Europäischen Gemeinschaftsrechts*," (1976) ZaöRV 1551; Lawaars, "Auxiliary Organs and Agencies in the EEC", 16 *CML Rev.* 365 (1979).

however, highly unlikely that foreign trade matters would be affected by these changes.

IV.   THE FEDERAL STRUCTURE AND THE CONDUCT OF FOREIGN POLICY

A.   Introduction

The way in which the "federal" structure affects the conduct of foreign policy in the EC can be viewed under three different headings: the division of powers; the effects of the "federal" structure on the exercise of EC powers; and the effects on the implementation of foreign policy decisions.

B.   The division of powers

It should be recalled that there is no general grant of foreign affairs powers to the EC under the EEC Treaty (nor for that matter under the ECSC Treaty or the EAEC Treaty). There are only specific attributions of external relations powers; the main ones relate to trade policy and to the extension to relations with third countries of common internal policies under the so-called ERTA doctrine of the Court.[92]

Foreign policy proper is a Member State matter. Member States coordinate their foreign policy action within the framework of European Political Cooperation (EPC). Provisions on EPC have been included in the Single European Act, but the negotiators were very careful to keep EPC separate from the European Community.[93]

Quite obviously, the EC trade policy cannot be explained merely by the search for an economic optimum while attempting to strike a balance between conflicting interests. Foreign policy concerns of Member States are bound to be taken on board. From a Member State's perspective, EC trade policy will sometimes be seen as a purely foreign policy instrument, especially when the EC imposes trade sanctions.[94]

---

[92] *Commission v. Council*, 1971 ECR 263. For a recent analysis of this doctrine, see J. Temple-Lang, "The ERTA-judgment and the Court's case law on competence and conflict," 6 *YBK-Eur. L* 183 (1987).

[93] See J. De Ruyt, *L'acte Unique Européen*, at 228 (Bruxelles, 1987); *also* Pescatore, "Some Critical Remarks on the 'Single European Act'", 24 *CML Rev.* 9 (1987).

[94] For example, the embargo on Iraq and Kuwait; see Regulation (EEC) 2340/90, of 8 August 1990 (OJ L 213/90).

The more general question of whether the EPC has a positive or negative impact on the conduct of EC trade policy gets mixed replies.[95] At least EPC eases the path towards adoption of trade sanctions where necessary.

One of the least explored areas is the possible impact on foreign trade policy of another aspect of the "federal" structure of the EC: the absence of an EC-wide general economic policy and the corresponding absence of a series of economic policy instruments which could be used to bring about the necessary trade-offs between "winners" and "losers" in the foreign trade game.[96] Some economists claim that, e.g. the absence of EC "adjustment assistance" results in EC trade policy measures tailored to the needs of the Member States whose economy is the weakest.[97]

This would, however, require further investigation, e.g. in light of a comparison with the US scene.

Another aspect relates to the domestic enforcement in federal systems of international obligations. The circumstance that the subject matter being dealt with in international negotiations comes in the domestic sphere within the scope not of the powers of the federation but of those of the constituent state could be relied upon, and has been relied upon, by federal negotiating parties, rightly or wrongly, to refuse to accept international obligations. This position has been taken *inter alia* by the US in the previous GATT round of multilateral trade negotiations on certain specific matters.[98]

It is interesting to note that, so far, the EC has not been faced with this sort of problem save in a few marginal cases, where the issue had

---

[95] Nuttall, "Interaction Between European Political Cooperation and the European Community," 6 *YBK Eur. L.* 211 (1987): "Examples of [positive impact] arc few and far between"; Lak, "Interaction Between European Political Cooperation and the European Community," 26 CMLRev. 281 (1989): "[a]t present there is insufficient evidence of negative impact". Schoutheete is more positive and gives examples *(La Cooperation Politique Enropéenne* at 60–61) (Bruxelles, 1986).

[96] D. Lorens, *"Liberale Handelspolitik versus Protektionismus - Das Schutzargument im Lichte neuer Entwicklungen der Aussenhandelstheorie,"* in *Arbeitskreis europäische Integration, neuer Protektionismus in der Weltwirtschaft und EG-Handelspolitik* 9 (Baden-Baden, 1985).

[97] G.N. Yannopoulos, "The European Community's Common External Commercial Policy. Internal Contradictions and Institutional Weaknesses," 19 *JWTL* 451 (1985).

[98] See J. Bourgeois, *"Les engagements internationaux de la Communauté et leurs implications sur le plan interne,"* in P. Demaret (ed.), *Relations exterieures de la Communauté européenne et Marché Interieur: Aspects juridiques et fonctionnels* at 171–172 (Bruxelles, 1987).

more to do with the scope of external relations powers of the EC than with the fact that in the internal EC sphere the matter came within the scope of Member States powers.[99]

C.   The Effects of the "Federal" Structure on the Exercise of Powers

There is a substantial amount of literature on the alleged deficiencies of the EC's decision-making process. Interestingly, the views put forward by some academic writers[100] are less negative than those put forward by some practitioners.[101] As is evidenced by the relative speed with which legislation is adopted in the EC nowadays, the political climate is an important factor.

In the foreign trade area, the decision-making system as set out *supra* has a number of drawbacks. First, when decisions have to be taken by the Council, the EC often needs an inordinate amount of time to "agree with itself". In view of the economic weight the EC carries in world trade, its inability to come to a position in a reasonably short period of time has been seen as a negative factor for the operation of the world trading system.[102] It would, however, seem that other actors in the world trading system have similar difficulties, but they are less conspicuous or less well reported. Moreover, if one were to make some cost-benefit analysis, the result could well be less negative for the operation of the world trading system. An experienced practitioner has noted that when the EC reaches a position, this position is often broadly the compromise solution also for the widely divergent views of other developed GATT Contracting Parties.[103]

Second, at least in multilateral negotiations, the EC is reactive rather than active. It does not often take the lead but waits for others to make proposals. This does not seem to correspond to some inbred wait-and-see attitude, but is probably to be attributed to the decision-making

---

[99] Ibid at 174-175.

[100] For example, Bieber, Jacqué and Weiler in their introduction to *An Ever Closer Union* at 8 (Commission of the EC, Luxembourg, 1985).

[101] For example, Ambassador Dondelinger in his farewell speech to the Committee of Permanent Representatives ("Agence Europe," 22 May 1984, n° 1310 *Europe Documents*),

[102] Patterson, "The European Community as a Threat to the System," in Cline (ed.), *Trade Policy in the 80's*, at 223–224 (Washington, 1983).

[103] P. Luyten, "Trade Agenda for the Eighties," in T. Peeters (ed.), *United States –European Community Trade Relations: The Search for Common Ground*, 18 (Leuven, 1985).

system. If it is to be a successful EC negotiator, as it wants to be, the Commission needs to build consensus more in reaction than in action. This avoids major difficulties between Commission and Council during negotiations and at the conclusion stage. It has a price. Where it does not determine the draft of multilateral negotiations by failing to lead, the EC finds itself in a position of having initially to try to change the current or to go against it.

D. The Effects of the "Federal Structure" on the Implementation of Foreign Policy Decisions

Federations may be faced with the problem that, while for a given subject matter the power to accept international obligations is theirs, in their domestic sphere the same subject matter comes within the scope of the powers of the constituent states. They rely on varying devices to solve this problem.[104]

Within the EC, in legal terms, the problem is resolved by Articles 5 and 228 EEC. It is moreover well established that an international agreement which has been properly concluded by the EC is an integral part of EC law.[105] *Kupferberg I* has allowed the Court to add some clarifications:

– such agreements are binding on the Community institutions *and* on the Member States;

– it is incumbent upon these institutions, *as well* as upon the Member States, to ensure compliance with the obligations arising from such agreements;

– the measures needed to implement the provisions of an agreement concluded by the Community are to be adopted, according to the state of Community law for the time being in the areas affected by the provisions of the agreement, *either* by the Community institutions *or* by the Member States.[106]

---

[104] See *"Les Etats fédéraux dans les relations Internationales,"* XVII *Rev. B. Dr. Int.* (1983): for Australia: Prott at 31 and Shearer at 37; for Canada: Jacomy-Millette at 75–76; for the US: Stein at 96–97; for Switzerland: Wildhaber at 121 and 128.
[105] *Haegeman,* 1974 ECR 459.
[106] *Kupferberg I,*1982 ECR 3641 para. 11-12.

In practice, there do not seem to have been major problems which in the end could not be resolved by applying the principles and rules set out in the Court's case law. The need has not been felt so far by the EC to rely on the sort of solution advocated in the literature whereby the EC would take the necessary implementing measures which it is normally incumbent on a Member State to take, instead of a Member State who failed to do so.[107]

---

[107] Louis and Steenbergen, *loc. cit.* note 91 at 363.

10. THE EC IN THE WTO AND ADVISORY OPINION 1/94: AN ECHTERNACH PROCESSION

I.   INTRODUCTION

Rather than for its charming surroundings and attractive character, the Luxembourg town of Echternach is known for its peculiar annual procession: for each three steps forward participants take two steps backward. This procession comes to mind when reflecting on what happened to the EC on its way to the World Trade Organization (hereinafter: the "WTO") and when reading Opinion 1/94.

On 22 December 1994, the Council of the European Union (hereinafter: the "Council") formally approved the conclusion of the Agreement establishing the WTO and the agreements and associated legal instruments included in the annexes to the WTO Agreement. According to its Article XIV the WTO Agreement is open for acceptance *inter alia* by "contracting parties to GATT 1947 and the European Communities, which are eligible to become original Members of the WTO". Throughout the whole Uruguay Round negotiation, the European Community (hereinafter: the "EC") had acted as an entity with the European Commission negotiating, assisted by the usual committee of representatives of Member States, called "the mothers-in-law", and reporting from time to time to the Council to obtain fresh negotiation directives. However, partly as a result of the dispute between the Commission and several Member States on the question whether all matters negotiated in the Uruguay Round come within the EC's exclusive powers under Article 113 EC, the EC insisted itself that not only the EC but also its Member States be considered as members of the WTO.

This was admittedly the case in the GATT. There was, however, a rational explanation for that: the EC Member States were contracting parties to the GATT before the creation of the EC. As the EC progressively took trade policy over from its Member States, this substitution of the Member States by the EC came to be recognized both within the EC[1] and within the GATT.[2] For all practical purposes the EC had become a GATT contracting party in the place of its Member States. The pragmatic

---

[1] For example, Joined cases 267-269/81, SPI and *SAMI*, [1983] ECR 801 para 17.
[2] See Petersmann, "The EEC as a GATT Member – Legal conflicts between GATT law and European Community law" in Hilf, Jacobs and Petersmann (eds), *The European Community and the* GATT (Kluwer, Deventer 1986), pp. 23 at 37–39.

acceptance by the other GATT contracting parties of the EC as a single entity replacing its Member States had been obtained without amending the GATT *inter alia* on the basis of the argument that one should not amend the GATT solely for the purposes of formally substituting the EC for its Member States; this could wait until the GATT was amended for other reasons. The creation of the WTO and the review of the GATT offered such opportunity. The EC missed it. This is the first reason for referring to the Echternach procession.

The second reason is Advisory Opinion 1/94 of the Court of Justice of the European Communities (hereinafter: the Court).

On 15 November 1994, the Court rendered the advisory opinion which the Commission had requested on 6 April 1994 pursuant to Article 228(6) EC. The Commission sought to ascertain whether or not the EC has exclusive competence to conclude the Multilateral Agreements on Trade in Goods, in so far as those Agreements concern products coming under the ECSC and Euratom Treaties, and whether the EC has exclusive competence – under Article 113 EC, alternatively under other EC Treaty provisions – to conclude the General Agreement on Trade in Services (hereinafter: "the GATS")[3] and the Agreement on Trade-related Aspects of Intellectual Property Rights (hereinafter: "TRIPs Agreement").[4]

The issues thus brought before the Court were important.

First, the GATS, and the TRIPs Agreement are important agreements. The GATS subjects the supply of services to international rules which draw their inspiration from GATT rules which have regulated trade in goods since 1947. GATS is mainly a framework agreement: it lays down essentially a series of general obligations and disciplines, such as the most favoured nation treatment and certain more specific obligations; it will progressively include other specific obligations following further negotiations. GATS covers trade in all services in all sectors, except "services supplied in the exercise of governmental authority" (Article I(3)). Trade in services within the meaning of GATS may take various forms: "cross-border supply", "consumption abroad", "commercial presence" and "movement of persons". It thus regulates not only the activity of supplying services but also establishment in view of the supply of services.

---

[3] The GATS will be dealt with in more detail in a forthcoming article by Weiss.
[4] See Bronckers, "The impact of 'TRIPS': Intellectual property protection in developing countries", 31 *CML Rev.*, 1245–1281.

The TRIPs Agreement covers a wide range of intellectual property rights, copyright and related rights (including those protecting computer programmes), trademarks, rights protecting geographical indications and industrial designs, patents, rights of protection of topographies of integrated circuits and of "undisclosed information", to which a section is added on "control of anti-competitive practices in contractual licences". The TRIPs Agreement contains specific rules relating to the existence, the scope and the exercise of intellectual property rights (Part II) and to the enforcement of such rights (Part III). It also sets out obligations with respect to national procedures for acquisition and maintenance of such rights (Part IV).

Second, the debate brought before the Court dealt with the division of powers between the EC and the Member States which has implications for their respective roles in the functioning of the WTO, the dispute settlement mechanism[5] and the recourse to "cross retaliation", i.e. the possibility, in the event of a violation by a WTO Member of its obligations under a given agreement (e.g. GATS), to suspend one's obligations *vis-à-vis* that WTO Member under another agreement (e.g. one's protocol on tariff concessions).

Third, and more importantly, the debate had obvious internal EC aspects of a constitutional and institutional nature. Article 113 EC, on which the Commission sought to rely, provides for qualified majority voting by the Council and does not provide for the European Parliament's participation in the decision making. Moreover, under the Court's case law, the EC powers under that Article are exclusive. Other possible EC Treaty articles under which the EC could act to conclude the agreements in question, may provide for unanimous voting by the Council and, at any rate, provide for the EP's participation in the decision making: either the EP must be consulted (Article 63 on the supply of services) or the "co-decision procedure" (Article 189B, to which refer Article 54 on the right of establishment and Article 100 on approximation of laws) or the "cooperation procedure" (Article 189C, to which Article 75 on transport policy refers) apply. Moreover, one could defend the view that under such provisions, the EC's powers are not exclusive but shared with Member States and, at any rate, unlike for commercial policy under Article 113, there is no transfer "en bloc" of powers from the Member States to the EC.

---

[5] See extensively on this Petersmann, "The dispute settlement system of the World Trade Organization and the evolution of the GATT dispute settlement system since 1948", 31 *CML Rev.*, 1157-1244.

The importance of the issues is illustrated by the fact that observations were submitted by the Council, by the EP and by no less than eight Member States (Denmark, Germany, Greece, France, the Netherlands, Portugal, Spain and the UK).

The Commission took the position that Article 113 EC was the proper legal basis for entering into all agreements, including the GATS and the TRIPs Agreement, alternatively that the GATS and TRIPs Agreement could be entered into by the EC under other EC Treaty provisions following the *ERTA* doctrine[6] or Opinion 1/76 of the Court.[7]

Not only the Council and the Member States defended views radically opposed to the views of the Commission. The EP also did, notwithstanding the fact that the Commission had proposed that the Council decision on the approval of the agreements resulting from the Uruguay Round be taken following the procedure laid down in Article 228(3), second subpara of the EC Treaty, which provides for the EP's assent. This did not persuade the EP to side with the Commission.

II.   THE COURT'S REPLIES

The Court replied to the Commission's questions as follows:

–   the EC has exclusive competence, pursuant to Article 113 EC, to conclude the Multilateral Agreements on Trade in Goods (para 34), including the Agreement on Agriculture (para. 29); this competence also extends to goods subject to the Euratom Treaty (para 24) or to the ECSC Treaty (para. 27);

–   cross-frontier supplies of services are covered by Article 113 EC and international agreements in the field of transport are excluded from it (para. 53);

–   apart from those of its provisions which concern the prohibition of the release into free circulation of counterfeit goods, the TRIPs Agreement does not fall within the scope of the Common Commercial Policy (para. 71);

---

[6] Case 22/70, *Commission v. Council*, [1971] ECR 263.
[7] Opinion 1/76, of 26 April 1977, [1977] ECR 741.

- the competence to conclude GATS is shared between the EC and the Member States (para. 98);

- the EC and its Member States are jointly competent to conclude the TRIPs Agreement (para. 105).

III.   THE COURT'S REASONING

A.   On the scope of Article 113 EC

The differences of view between Member States and the Commission and between the Council and the Commission on the proper scope of the "Common Commercial Policy" within the meaning of Article 113 EC, both as to the measures which the EC may take and as to the economic activities which the EC may regulate in the framework of that policy, are too well known to be described here.[8]

1.   *Euratom and ECSC products – agricultural products*

The reply to the question whether agreements concluded pursuant to Article 113 EC may extend to trade in Euratom products was fairly easy. Neither the Council nor Member States had made observations on that question. The Court could limit itself to referring to Article 232(2) EC.

The question whether the same applies to trade in ECSC products was disputed: the Commission considered that Article 113 EC also covers ECSC products, the Council and most Member States which submitted observations pointed to Article 71 ECSC and argued that Member States were competent. It is one of the recurrent topics for discussion of EC external relations law. Past practice was no guide whatsoever as it is rather untidy.[9]

---

[8] For a good overview of case law, practice and literature see Eeckhout, *The European Internal Market and International Trade: A Legal Analysis* (Clarendon Press, Oxford, 1994) pp. 20-34; as to intellectual property, see Govaere "Intellectual Property Protection and Commercial Policy" in Maresceau (ed), *The European Community's Commercial Policy after 1992: The Legal Dimension* (Martinus Nijhoff, Dordrecht, 1993), pp. 197 et seq.; as to services in particular see Mengozzi, "Trade in Services and Commercial Policy", ibid., at p. 223.

[9] See for example, the description by Ehlermann, "The Scope of Article 113 of the EEC Treaty", in *Melanges P.-H. Teitgen*, (Pedone, Paris, 1984) pp. 163–166.

The Court considers that Article 71 ECSC could only have reserved competence for the Member States as regard agreements relating specifically to ECSC products, which is not the case for the Multilateral Agreements on Trade in Goods. Referring to its Opinion 1/75 it holds that the EC's exclusive competence under Article 113 EC "cannot be impugned on the ground that [these Agreements] also apply to ECSC goods" (para. 27).

Another recurrent topic for discussion of EC external relations law is whether international agreements on trade in agricultural goods within the meaning of Article 38(3) EC may be entered into pursuant to Article 113 EC or whether Article 43 EC is the only appropriate legal basis. The Council contended that Article 43 EC was the proper basis for concluding the Agreement on Agriculture, since this agreement concerns not only commercial measures applicable to international trade in agricultural products but also internal rules on the organization of agricultural markets. The UK took the position that the commitments to reduce domestic support and export refunds fall outside the framework of Article 113 EC, since they will affect the common organizations of the markets and concern EC products rather than imported products.

The Court rejects these arguments. It refers to the objective of the Agreement on Agriculture, i.e. establishing on a world-wide basis "a fair and market-oriented agricultural trading system" and considers that:

> "the fact that commitments entered into the Agreement require internal measures to be adopted on the basis of Article 43 of the Treaty does not prevent the international commitments themselves from being entered into pursuant to Article 113 alone" (para. 29).

2. The Agreement on Sanitary and Phytosanitary Measures – The Agreement on Technical Barriers to Trade

The Council contended that the Agreement on Sanitary and Phytosanitary measures should be entered into on the basis of Article 43 EC on the ground that it would affect the internal rules on the organization of the agricultural markets.

The Court refers to the preamble of this agreement which confines it to "the establishment of a multilateral framework of rules and disciplines to guide the development, adoption and enforcement of sanitary measures in order to minimize their negative effects on trade". It concludes that such an agreement can be concluded on the basis of Article 113 EC alone (para. 31).

The Netherlands Government recalled that the Tokyo Round Agreement on Technical Barriers to Trade had been concluded by the EEC and the Member States jointly.[10] It referred to the own competence of Member States in this respect, to the optional nature of certain EC directives and to the incomplete harmonization within the EC. The Court here again refers to the objective of the Agreement on Technical Barriers to Trade to conclude that it falls within the ambit of the Common Commercial Policy (para. 33).

3. Supply of services

Whether supply of services comes within the scope of the "Common Commercial Policy" within the meaning of Article 113 EC is a subject on which the Court had so far not had the opportunity to pronounce.

After referring to the Commission submission which argued that services had become the dominant sector in the economy of developed countries and recalling its Advisory Opinions 1/75 and 1/78 the Court states:

> "Having regard to this trend in international trade, it follows from the open nature of the Common Commercial Policy, within the meaning of the Treaty, that trade in services cannot immediately, and as a matter of principle, be excluded from the scope of Article 113, as some of the governments which have submitted observations contend" (para. 41).

The Court, however, subjects this principle to the condition that the definition of trade in services given in GATS must fit in the overall scheme of the EC Treaty (para. 42).

---

[10] Arguably more for political reasons than for reasons related to the substance of this agreement. See Bourgeois, "The Tokyo Round Agreements on Technical Barriers and on Government Procurement", 19 *CML Rev.* 5 at 22.

In cross-frontier supplies of services, where the suppliers are established in one country and the consumer in another, a situation obtains which is not unlike that of trade in goods. According to the Court, "there is thus no particular reason why such a supply should not fall within the concept of the Common Commercial Policy" (para 44). For the three other modes of supply of services ("consumption abroad", "commercial presence" and "presence of natural persons") there are, according to the Court, particular reasons why they should not fall within the concept of the Common Commercial Policy: i.e. "the existence in the Treaty of specific chapters on the free movement of natural and legal persons ..." (para 46).

4.   *Transport Services*

Transport services are entirely excluded from the scope of commercial policy within the meaning of Article 113 EC.

First, the Court points out that they are the subject of a specific title of the Treaty, distinct from Title VII on the commercial policy.

Second, the Court refers to its *ERTA* judgment noting that "[t]he idea underlying that decision is that international agreements in transport matters are not covered by Article 113" (para 48). The *ERTA* doctrine covers all external aspects of transport policy. The Court rejects the distinction drawn by the Commission between commercial agreements and technical agreements. To do so the Court refers to its Opinion 1/76 concerning an agreement intended to rationalize the economic situation in the inland waterways sector, which was not a technical agreement either (para 50).

Third, the Court refers to the numerous international agreements concluded on the basis of the Transport Title (para 50).

Fourth, the precedents of embargoes based on Article 113 and involving suspension of transport services cited by the Commission are rejected as being not relevant: in those cases suspension of transport services "is to be seen as a necessary adjunct to the principal measure" (para 51). Moreover, "a mere practice of the Council cannot derogate from the rules of the Treaty and create a precedent binding on Community institutions with regard to the correct legal basis" (para 52).

5.   Intellectual property protection

As in the case of supply of services, the Court had so far not had the opportunity to pass judgment on the question whether measures to protect intellectual property in international trade come within the scope of the Common Commercial Policy within the meaning of Article 113 EC.

As in the case of services, the Court distinguishes between rules of the TRIPs Agreement concerning measures to be applied at border crossing points and rules concerning other measures.

As to the former, the Court refers to Regulation 3842/86 laying down measures to prohibit the release for free circulation of counterfeit goods. According to the Court, that regulation was rightly based on Article 113 EEC as "it relates to measures taken by the customs authorities at the external frontiers of the Community" (para. 55).

As to the latter, they do not fall within the scope of the Common Commercial Policy. The Court relies on the following reasons.

First, while recognizing that "there is a connection between intellectual property and trade in goods" the Court considers that this is not enough to bring them within the scope of Article 113:

> "Intellectual property rights do not relate specifically to international trade; they affect internal trade just as much, if not more than, international trade" (para. 57).

Second, as it did with respect to GATS, the Court refers to the EC Treaty scheme relating to internal EC legislation.

> "If the Community were to be recognized as having exclusive competence to enter into agreements with non-member states to harmonize protection of intellectual property and, at the same time, to achieve harmonization at Community level, the Community institutions would be able to escape the internal constraints to which they are subject in relation to procedures and to rules as to voting"(para. 60).

The Commission was aware of this when it proposed that the WTO Agreement be concluded pursuant to Article 228(3), second sub-paragraph EC, which requires the *assent* of the European Parliament.

Third, the precedents cited by the Commission are rejected:

"Institutional practice in relation to autonomous measures or external agreements adopted on the basis of Article 113 cannot alter this conclusion" (para. 61).

At any rate, the taking of commercial policy measures on the basis of Article 113 to protect intellectual property rights

"does not in any way show that the Community has exclusive competence pursuant to Article 113 to conclude an agreement with non-member countries to harmonize the protection of intellectual property world-wide" (para. 65).

The inclusion in certain international agreements, concluded on the basis of Article 113, of clauses relating to the protection of intellectual property rights does not mean that the Community has exclusive competence to conclude an international agreement of the type and scope of the TRIPs Agreement. These are either ancillary provisions for the organization of purely consultative procedures or clauses binding on the other party (para. 68).

The EC–Austria agreement on the reciprocal protection of descriptions of wine concluded on the basis of Article 113 EEC is rejected as a precedent. It is directly linked to measures covered by the Common Agricultural Policy and does not deal with all the other intellectual property rights covered by the TRIPs Agreement (para. 70).

B.   On the EC's implied external powers

As is well known, the Court has in the past held that the EC has powers to act in the international sphere on matters with respect to which the EC has powers to act in the internal EC sphere. It has set out this theory in its *ERTA* judgment and in its Opinion 1/76.[11] As mentioned earlier the Commission relied alternatively on these theories as justification

---

[11] *Supra* notes 6 and 7. For a comment, see Temple Lang, "The ERTA Judgment and the Court's Case-Law on Competence and Conflict", 6 *YEL* (1986), 183; R. Kovar, *"Les compétences implicites: jurisprudence de la Cour et pratique communautaire"* in Demaret (ed.), *Relations Extérieures de la Communauté Européenne et Marché Intérieur, Aspects Juridiques et Fonctionnels* (Story Scientia, Brussels 1988), pp. 15 et seq.

that the EC could enter into the GATS and the TRIPs Agreement. It is worth recalling here two elements. On the one hand, according to the Court, whenever Community law has created for the institutions of the Community powers within its internal system for the purpose of attaining a specific objective, the Community has authority to enter into the international commitments necessary for the attainment of that objective, even in the absence of an express provision in that connection.[12] On the other hand, such external powers are exclusive, inasmuch as, when the EC has adopted provisions laying down common rules, Member States may no longer assume international obligations which might affect those rules or alter their scope.[13]

1. Supply of Services

The Court does not conclude that the EC has exclusive competence to enter into the GATS, be it following Opinion 1/76 or under the *ERTA* theory.

With reference to the Commission's argument based on Opinion 1/76, the Court concludes that there is no need for the EC to conclude the GATS in order to achieve a Community objective, as there are other means to achieve the objectives referred to by the Commission (para. 79).

The Court does not stop here. It interprets its Opinion 1/76 by distinguishing it on the facts from the present case.

> "That is not the situation in the sphere of services: attainment of freedom of establishment and freedom to provide services for nationals of the Member States is not inextricably linked to the treatment to be afforded in the Community to nationals of non-member countries or in non-member countries to nationals of Member States of the Community" (para 86).

The Court does not state clearly its position on the EC's external powers with respect to the GATS following the Opinion 1/76 reasoning. From its statements on the nature of the EC's external competence under the *ERTA* theory it would seem to follow that, according to the Court, such competence exists but results from the existence of common rules

---

[12] Opinion 1/76, para. 3.
[13] *ERTA* judgment, para. 22.

already adopted in the internal sphere, rather than from the need to conclude the GATS in order to achieve an EC objective.

With reference to the Commission's argument based on the ERTA theory, the Court points out that the EC Treaty chapters on the right of establishment and the supply of services

"contain no provisions on the problem of the first establishment of nationals of non-member countries and the rules governing their access to self-employed activivities"

and concludes

"One cannot therefore infer from those chapters that the Community has exclusive competence to conclude an agreement with non-member countries to liberalize first establishment and access to service markets, other than those which are the subject of cross-border supplies within the meaning of GATS, which are covered by Article 113 ..." (para. 81).

The Court, however, states that

"it does not follow that the Community institutions are prohibited from using the powers conferred on them in that field in order to specify the treatment which is to be accorded to nationals of non-member countries" (para. 90)

The Court then reviews a series of EC legislative acts containing provisions on third country nationals' treatment. It concludes that

"[w]henever the Community has included in its internal legislative acts provisions relating to the treatment of nationals of non-member countries or expressly conferred on its institutions powers to negotiate with non-member countries, it acquires exclusive external competence in the speres covered by those acts" (para. 95).

With respect to access to a self-employed activity the Court adds that the *ERTA* theory applies "where the Community has achieved a *complete* harmonization of the rules" (para. 96) (emphasis added).

2. Intellectual property rights

The Court dismisses the Commission's argument based on Opinion 1/76:

> "The relevance of the reference to Opinion 1/76 is just as disputable in the case of TRIPs as in the case of GATS: unification or harmonization of intellectual property rights in the Community context does not necessarily have to be accompanied by agreements with non-member countries in order to be effective" (para. 100).

The Court dismisses the Commission's argument based on the *ERTA* theory by using similar language to that in the case of the GATS.

Member States had argued that a number of clauses of the TRIPs Agreement (i.e. those relating to the effective protection of intellectual property rights, to a fair and just procedure, to the submission of evidence, to the right to be heard, to the giving of reasons for decisions, to the right to appeal, to interim measures and to the award of damages) fall within the competence of Member States. According to the Court, the Community is certainly competent to harmonize Member States' rules on those matters in so far as they "directly affect the establishment or the functioning of the common market" (para. 104).

IV.   SOME COMMENTS

A.   As to Opinion 1/94

The Court was obviously aware of the need to render its opinion within a short time period so that the EC and the Members could approve and ratify the WTO Agreement and the associated agreements by mid-December. The urgency probably explains the inconsistencies of the reasoning in Opinion 1/94.

According to the Court, the existence of Article 43 EC on the Common Agricultural Policy or, – as the Court puts it – the fact that the implementing measures of an international agreement are to be adopted under Article 43 - does not prevent international commitments themselves from being entered into pursuant to Article 113 (para. 29). However, as far as transport policy is concerned, the existence of a specific title of the Treaty and the ERTA theory leads the Court to conclude that international agreements in transport matters are *not* covered by Article 113 (para. 48).

The Court rests its conclusion that the Agreement on Technical Obstacles to Trade falls within the scope of the Common Commercial Policy on the finding that its provisions are designed merely to ensure that no unnecessary obstacles to international trade are created (para. 33). However, the Court derives its conclusion that intellectual property rights do not fall within the scope of the Common Commercial Policy from the fact that intellectual property rights affect internal trade just as much as, if not more than, international trade. But isn't this the case for technical rules as well? Moreover, if this were a relevant criterion to define the scope of the Common Commercial Policy, quite a few other matters, such as the Agreement on Sanitary and Phyto-sanitary Measures and the Agreement on Subsidies and Countervailing Measures, would be excluded from the scope of Article 113.

The Court is selective in its references to the Uruguay Round agreements. It refers to the preamble of the Agreement on Technical Obstacles to Trade to justify the finding that it comes within the scope of Article 113 EC. Yet, where it deals with the same issue in relation to the TRIPs Agreement, it does not refer in this respect to the preamble of this agreement.

The Court is also somewhat confused by preambles. In para 57 the Court states that the primary objective of TRIPs is to strengthen and harmonize the protection of intellectual property on a world-wide scale. But that is not what the preamble of the TRIPs Agreement says: in fact the preamble states that TRIPs Agreement's *objective* is "to reduce distortions and impediments to international trade and *taking into account* the need to promote effective and adequate protection of intellectual property rights" (emphasis added).

The Court considers that past EC measures on transport taken under Article 113 are not relevant precedents, as such measures were a necessary adjunct to the principal measure (para. 51).[14] But isn't the TRIPs Agreement a "necessary adjunct" to the GATT, the "principal measure"?

In several instances, the Court dismisses Commission arguments relying on the practice of the EC institutions. Thus:

---

[14] The Court does not, however, mention measures taken against Libya under Art. 113 EC, which were not an adjunct to a principal measure (O.J. 1992, L 101/92).

"[i]n any event, the Court has consistently held that a mere practice of the Council cannot derogate from the rules laid down in the Treaty and cannot, therefore, create a precedent binding on Community institutions with regard to the correct legal basis ..." (para. 52).

And further on

"Institutional practice in relation to autonomous measures or external agreements adopted on the basis of Article 113 cannot alter this conclusion" (para. 61).

Very well, but the Court refers elsewhere to precedents. One of the reasons given by the Court for excluding transport from the scope of Article 113 is the fact that numerous agreements have been concluded with non-member countries on the basis of the Transport Title (para 50). In addition, in the case at hand, the Commission relied on the practice of the EC institutions as a method of interpretation rather than to justify a failure to act or an interpretation that ran counter to a textual or a contextual interpretation. The Commission did not claim that the Court should derogate from the rules laid down in the Treaty. The whole point was how the rules of the Treaty should be interpreted. Precisely, in this respect, there are several examples in the case law where the practice of the EC institutions is held to be a relevant element for the purpose of interpreting the law.[15]

In support of its conclusion rejecting the relevancy of Opinion 1/76 for the GATS, the Court refers to the fact that the chapters of the Treaty on the right of establishment and on services do not contain provisions expressly extending the powers of the Community to "relationships arising from international law". Yet, further on, the Court accepts that, although the only objective expressly mentioned in those chapters is the attainment of those freedoms for nationals of Member States, the Community institutions may specify the treatment which is to be accorded to nationals of non-member countries (para. 90).

---

[15] For example, the practice of the EC institutions which has made concrete in the GATT the transfer of powers made by the EEC Treaty: Joined cases 21-24/72, *International Fruit*, [1972] ECR 1219.

Opinion 1/94 is helpful on a number of points.

First, by clarifying, in line with Opinion 1/75[16] and *Deutsche Babcock,*[17] that regulating trade in ECSC products with third countries comes within the scope of Article 113 EC, except for agreements relating specifically to ECSC products, it puts an end to uncertainties and byzantine discussions.

Second, by confirming that international agreements on trade in agricultural products are to be entered into on the basis of Article 113 EC – even when they affect the operations of common organizations of agricultural markets, e.g. variable levies, export refunds, internal subsidies – it considers that a common sectoral policy does not constitute a completely separate niche in the EC Treaty. This will hopefully remove the occasion of talmudic disputes.

Third, by stating that the fact that Member States, rather than the EC, will bear some of the expenses of the WTO cannot of itself justify participation of Member States in the conclusion of the WTO Agreement (para. 21), Opinion 1/94 makes clear that participation of Member States to international commodity agreements is justified under Opinion 1/78[18] only where a commodity agreement includes a financial policy instrument.

In light of earlier pronouncements of the Court, Opinion 1/94 is a step back with respect to the definition of the scope of the Common Commercial Policy.

First, in line with Opinion 1/78, the Court recognizes that changes in the international economy – the fact that in certain developed countries the service sector has become a dominant sector of the economy and the structural changes in the global economy – are relevant for the interpretation of the scope of the Common Commercial Policy (paras 40 and 41). This general statement is, however, deprived of any effect as far as services and intellectual property are concerned. They cannot be part of the Common Commercial Policy within the meaning of Article 113 because of the division of powers and decision-making procedures *foro interno.*

---

[16] Opinion 1/75 of 11 Nov. 1975, [1975] ECR 1361.
[17] Case 328/85, *Deutsche Babcock,* [1987] ECR 5119.
[18] Opinion 1/78 of 11 Oct. 1979, [1979] ECR 2909.

Second, other principles and criteria on which the Court had relied in the past to define the scope of the Common Commercial Policy are left aside. According to Opinion 1/75 the concept of commercial policy has "the same content whether it is applied in the context of the international action of a State or to that of the Community". Can one seriously sustain the view that the negotiating with a third country of an agreement on the establishment of subsidiaries of financial institutions, on the exchange of air traffic rights, or on the mutual protection of intellectual property rights, is not part and parcel of a State's commercial policy? According to Opinion 1/78, the list of measures in Article 113 "is conceived as a non-exhaustive enumeration which must not, as such, close the door to the application in a Community context of any other process intended to regulate external trade" (para. 45). Isn't the TRIPs Agreement a series of processes intended to regulate international trade?

Opinion 1/94 is also a step back from the implied external powers as defined in Opinion 1/76.

The Court's view on the question as to when entering into international commitments is "necessary" for the purpose of attaining a specific Community objective – the criterion set out in Opinion 1/76 – is applied very restrictively in Opinion 1/94: attainment of freedom of establishment and freedom to provide services for Member States' nationals must be "inextricably linked" to the treatment to be afforded in the EC to nationals of non-member countries or in non-member countries to nationals of EC Member States (para. 86). Experience shows, however, that effectively ensuring within the EC free supply of services and the right of establishment is difficult to reconcile with leaving to Member States the freedom to do as they please in their relations with third countries: when dealing with third countries in this respect, Member States are not only granting access to their territory, but also to the whole of the EC via Article 58 EC, which pursuant to Article 66 EC also applies to the supply of services.

For this and other reasons a series of Directives contain provisions on relations with third countries.[19] The Court recognizes this but considers that this does not make it "necessary" for the EC to enter into the GATS. According to the Court it is sufficient to arrange concerted action of

---

[19] For example, The Second Banking Directive (89/646/EEC; O.J. 1989, L 386/); and a series of Directives in the insurance and in the securities field mentioned in Opinion 1/94 (para. 94).

Member States or to prescribe the approach to be taken by Member States in their external dealings (para. 79).

The criterion of "necessity" of Opinion 1/76 on which the existence of implied external powers depended is now supplemented by a "proportionality" test, i.e. even if external action by the EC may be necessary, one should assess whether the aim could not be achieved by, e.g. a concerted action of Member States. One should add that experience shows that, when Member States promise to sing together in international negotiations, they more often than not produce a cacophony.

The reading by the Court of its Opinion 1/76 appears surprising in light of Opinion 2/91[20] in which it considered:

> "The Community's tasks and objectives of the Treaty would also be compromised if Member States were able to enter into international commitments containing rules capable of affecting rules already adopted in areas falling outside common policies or of altering their scope" (para. 11).

It would appear that Opinion 1/94 is also a step back from the *ERTA* theory.

First, both in relation to the GATS and the TRIPs Agreement the Court seems to accept the existence of external EC powers only where Member States' international commitments would conflict with existing secondary law EC rules. This would mean a radical departure from *ERTA* in which the Court held that Member States could no longer assume international obligations which might not only affect such EC rules but also alter their scope (para. 22). Some commentators will probably argue that this is what the Court meant, i.e. reducing the *ERTA* doctrine to a device designed to prevent a conflict between an existing EC rule and an international commitment contemplated by Member States. This is not the proper conclusion to be drawn from Opinion 1/94. *ERTA* still applies when the EC achieves complete harmonization of rules governing access to a self-employed activity (para. 96), which does not necessarily imply regulating access to such activity of third country nationals. Opinion 1/76 still applies, and thus presumably *ERTA*, where the internal rules are inextricably linked with the treatment to be afforded to third country nationals (para. 86).

---

[20] Concerning the ILO, [1993] *CML Rev.* 800.

Second, the underlying rationale of *ERTA* (and of Opinion 1/76) appears to have been abandoned. It is fairly obvious that in the area of services and intellectual property, as the Court correctly pointed out with respect to commercial policy in Opinion 1/75, policies are in fact made up by the combination and interaction of internal and external measures, without priority being taken by one over the others; sometimes agreements are concluded in execution of a policy fixed in advance, sometimes that policy is defined by the agreements themselves. How far the Court has moved from *ERTA* and Opinion 1/76 appears from its statement with respect to the TRIPs Agreement:

> "The relevance of the reference of Opinion 1/76 is just as disputable in the case of TRIPs as in the case of GATS: unification or harmonization of intellectual property rights in the Community context does not necessarily have to be accompanied by agreements with non-member countries in order to be effective" (para. 100).

Third, by narrowing down the implicit external EC powers with respect to the matters governed by the GATS and the TRIPs Agreement, Opinion 1/94 leads to a result that is the opposite of *ERTA* and Opinion 1/76: preemption of the field by Member States' action.

One wonders how much there will be left for "unification or harmonization of intellectual property rights in the Community context". It is true that the GATS contains a customs-union exception along the lines of Article XXIV GATT and it can be argued that this GATT Article applies to the TRIPs Agreement which mainly concerns trade in goods. The EC could thus in theory enact rules applying to intra-EC trade that would depart from the GATS and from the TRIPs Agreement. Whether it would be wise and practicable to do so is another matter. As such and as far as the substance of the rules is concerned, it is probably not a bad thing that such unification and harmonization occur in the wide WTO context. What is surprising is that the Court seems to accept lightly that, by entering into the GATS and the TRIPs Agreement, Member States effectively adopt policies and rules that will relate to intra-EC relations and that such rules will operate outside the EC legal system.[21]

---

[21] One of the fundamental reasons on which the Court relied to reject in Opinion 1/92 ([1991] ECR I-6079) the system of judicial review of the EEA Agreement. For a comment, see M.A. Gaudissart, *"La portée des avis 1/91 et 1/92 de la Cour de Justice des Communautés européennes relatifs à la création de l'space Economique Européen"*, (1992) *Revue du Marché Unique Européen*, 121 (No. 2).

B. The "institutional" aspect

The restrictive interpretation of the EC's powers by the Court may be explained by the importance which it obviously attaches to the institutional implications of the issues which the Commission submitted. It refers to such implications only in relation to the TRIPs Agreement, where it states that if the EC were to be recognized as having exclusive competence, "the Community institutions would be able to escape the internal constraints to which they are subject in relation to procedures and to rules as to voting" (para. 60). The Court must have had this also in mind when dealing with the other questions.

This consideration is a weighty one. One should, however, put it in perspective.

The Commission had proposed that the WTO Agreement be concluded pursuant to Article 228(3), second sub-paragraph EC which provides for the EP's assent. The EP could probably have insisted that certain important implementing measures be taken on the basis of other EC Treaty provisions involving the EP in the decision-making process. In Opinion 1/94, the Court refers to such a solution for the Agreement on Agriculture.

In addition, the alternative legal bases in the EC Treaty practically all provide for qualified majority voting as well.

Moreover, the difference as to scope between external powers and internal powers is an issue which other legal systems also face.[22] Such issue is, however, capable of being resolved by other means than interpreting restrictively the external powers.

C. As to the duty of cooperation between the Member States and the Community Institutions

In light of the conclusion of Opinion 1/94 the duty of cooperation between the Member States and the Community institutions is obviously a crucial element.

---

[22] See e.g. Bourgeois, "*Les engagements internationaux de la Communauté et leurs implications sur le plan interne*" in Demaret (ed.), op. cit. *supra* note 11, pp. 165–166 and 172–173.

The Court recognizes this and links that obligation to cooperate to "the requirements of unity in the international representation of the Community" (para 108). It fails, however, to draw conclusions on the ground that the Commission had only put a question in this respect on the assumption that the Court recognized the EC's exclusive competence.

This is to be regretted. How will the cacophony be avoided when, within the WTO, matters under the GATS or under the TRIPs Agreement are discussed? Is there a duty for individual Member States to take positions only following EC coordination and within the framework of what has been agreed?

In addition, in Kramer the Court held that Member States were under a duty to proceed by common action and not to enter into any commitment which could hinder the EC in carrying out its tasks.[23] The situation is arguably not identical. In Opinion 1/94 the Court has, however, recognized that, at least in the area covered by the GATS, the EC has the power to specify the treatment which is to be accorded to nationals of non-member states (para 90). To that extent, the duties referred to in Kramer apply to Member States in the WTO framework at least with respect to matters covered by the GATS.

This having been said, one cannot help feeling a certain sympathy for the Court. Being called upon to rule on a major constitutional and institutional issue, it was faced with the views of the Commission and with opposing views put forward and by the EP, i.e. the branch of the "legislative" power directly representing EC citizens, and by the Council, i.e. the other branch of the "legislative" power, and by eight of the Member States which still exercise the constitutional powers in the EC.

V.   THE PARADOXES OF THE URUGUAY ROUND AFFAIR

The whole affair is rather paradoxical.

First precisely when practically all States have drawn the obvious conclusions from some fundamental changes in the nature and structure of international economic relations and have recognized that services and certain aspects of intellectual property are to be subjected to multilateral rules and brought within the framework of the WTO, the EC

---

[23] Joined cases 3, 4-6/76, *Kramer,* [1976] ECR 1305, paras 44–45.

takes the position that these matters are for its Member States to decide *ut singuli* and are not part of its commercial policy.

Second, within the GATT the EC has managed to be treated as a contracting party. Rather than drawing the proper conclusion from this development on the occasion of the creation of the WTO, the EC has insisted on having its Member States as well as itself recognized as members of the WTO. The argument according to which the EC thus managed to secure twelve, and now fifteen votes, is unworthy of an entity that is the most powerful trading entity in the world.

Third, from the outset the EC had defended the position that the Uruguay Round negotiations were a whole. This position, which was opposed by many other negotiating parties, prevailed and the WTO Agreement together with the other multilateral agreements were in the end qualified as a "single undertaking". Yet at the EC level there is no "single undertaking": there is an EC "undertaking" concerning some parts and a Member States' "undertaking" concerning other parts.

Fourth, it is interesting to note that the media presented the affair as a struggle between the Commission and the Member States, rather than as a case illustrating the tensions between the Community concept and the centrifugal tendencies of Member States. It is maybe less of a paradox that the Commission appeared as the embodiment of the Community and that the Council found itself in the position of a secretariat of an international organization or, at best, in that of a chamber of states.

VI.   SOME TENTATIVE CONCLUSIONS

First, as indicated earlier, the EC missed the opportunity to draw the formal conclusion from the developments within GATT which had allowed it to acquire the status of a de facto contracting party. Pursuant to its Article XIV, Member States are members of the WTO alongside the EC. One wonders whether the other WTO members will continue to show the same forbearance for the EC's idiosyncrasies: what used to be in the GATT a patient acceptance of a passing eccentricity may in the WTO turn into a lingering handicap for the EC.

Second, Opinion 1/94 is likely to have negative effects on the administration on the EC side of the WTO Agreement and its related agreements and on the status of the EC within the WTO. The division of powers with respect to services along the lines set out in Opinion 1/94:

–   cross-border supplies of services coming within the scope of the EC's exclusive trade policy powers and other forms of supply of services not

–   is obviously impracticable. The division of powers between the EC and Member States with respect to the other forms of supply of services and with respect to the matters covered by the TRIPs Agreement is not set out at all. This is likely to lead to endless discussions in the EC framework. However, more importantly, in the WTO framework the EC and the Member States will probably be compelled whenever GATS or TRIPs matters are discussed to explain who is taking positions on what, negotiating about what and entering into further commitments on what. With a bit of negotiating skill, other WTO Members will have a field day in exploiting the situation. *Roma locuta, causa finita*, all this could probably be avoided if, having "scored and converted the try", Member States now have the wisdom to agree on a procedure providing for binding coordination and ensuring that they will speak with one voice through the EC which, wherever necessary, would be given the authority to act in the Member State's name and on their account. At the time of writing no such procedure has been agreed upon.

Third, Opinion 1/94 is an obvious break with previous developments in the Court's case law on external relations. This break can be explained by the combined opposition of the Council, the European Parliament and eight Member States. Beyond this episode, there may be another development which could explain recent judgments of the Court in other matters. About eight years ago – already – Tim Koopmans announced "a Return to Minimalism". He noted that in the future the Court's willingness to construct a solid legal basis on its own initiative may diminish. He compared this to the evolution going from composers like Wagner and Bruckner, who had done everything one could possibly do with an orchestra, to Debussy, from jazz drowned by the sound of the big band to Steve Reich's "minimal music".[24] What is, however, unfortunate is that this break with past developments in the case law on the EC's external relations and this return to minimalism occur precisely in relation to the WTO.

---

[24] "The Role of Law in the Next Stage of European Integration", 35 *ICLQ* (1986), 925 at 931.

11. THE EC'S TRADE POLICY POWERS AFTER NICE: PAINTING ONESELF IN A CORNER?

As evidenced by his writings, Jean-Victor Louis has always dealt very expertly with the institutional aspects of the EC/EU, also in the area of its (or rather their?) external relations [1].

In an early comment on the Nice Treaty, the latest instrument amending the Treaty establishing the European Community, Jean-Victor Louis described, i.a. the amended provisions on the EC trade policy powers, the new paragraph 5 of Article 133 EC, as establishing the extension, subject to the conditions and within the limits set, of the EC treaty making power in trade policy matters to trade in services and to the commercial aspects of intellectual property rights. This new paragraph also provides that it does not affect the right of the Member States to maintain and conclude agreements with third countries or international organizations in so far as such agreements comply with Community law and other relevant international agreements. Jean-Victor Louis noted that such a provision was not new and referred to Article 111 paragraph 5 EC on economic and monetary policy, Article 174 paragraph 4 EC on environment policy and Article 181 paragraph 2 EC on development cooperation, as inserted by the Maastricht Treaty. He drew the attention to a declaration of the Maastricht Intergovernmental Conference according to which these provisions "do not affect the principles resulting from the judgment handed down by the Court of Justice in the *AETR* case" [2]. He argued that the absence of such declaration of the Nice Intergovernmental Conference in relation to the amended Article 133 paragraph 5 EC does not allow to conclude that the *AETR* doctrine does not apply in the case of Article 133 paragraph 5.

In the Editorial of the last 2002 issue of the Cahiers *de droit européen* on the work of the Convention, Jean-Victor Louis noted the tendency *"de mettre l'accent sur les objectifs et les politiques internes, tout en donnant une vision minimaliste des tâches externes, et de projeter ainsi vers l'extérieur, l'image d'une Union repliée sur elle-même et manquant d'ambition dans le monde".*[3]

---

[1] For example, "Les relations extérieures de l'Union européenne: unité ou complémentarité", *RMUE*, 1994/4, pp. 5–10.
[2] J. -V. Louis, *"Le traité de Nice"*, *JTDE*, 2001, 76, pp. 25–33.
[3] *CDE*, 38/3-4, 2002, pp. 235–240.

The present contribution[4] in his honor elaborates the points made by Jean-Victor Louis and puts them in the context of the new Article 133, which raises also other questions.

A brief analysis of the scope of the extended trade policy powers, their nature and the modalities of their exercise is followed by a tentative assessment.

I.   INTRODUCTION

There is no need to deal here with the EC's external powers and the allocation of external powers between the EC and its Member States before Nice.[5]

A cursory glance at the amended Article 133 EC shows a number of things.

First, it brings together in one EC Treaty article trade in services and (trade aspects of) intellectual property rights, alongside trade in goods. Article 133 paragraph 5, as inserted by the Amsterdam Treaty, which provided that the Council could unanimously include international negotiations and agreements on services and intellectual property in the scope of Article 133, is replaced by the new paragraphs added to Article 133. The Intergovernmental Conference has attempted to take account of important changes in the EC's external economic relations and the inclusion of trade in services and the trade-related aspects of intellectual property rights in the WTO system.

Second, this has obviously been achieved by hammering out difficult compromises. Article 133 EC as amended has some of the features of the Christmas tree that grew out of the negotiations of the previous

---

[4] This contribution draws on a draft paper presented by the author on "The Post-Nice Distribution of Powers between the EC and its Member States in the Area of External Economic Policy" at the European Community Studies Association 6/7 September 2002 meeting at the World Trade Institute in Bern on "*Perspektiven der Aussenwirtschaftspolitik in der EU und der WTO*".

[5] This issue has been dealt with by the ECJ in a number of cases, the latest ones being the "*Open Skies*" cases; see the series of judgments of 5 November 2002 (nyr). It has given rise to an abundant literature. The most recent overall exposé on Article 133 EC and its relations to other external EC powers with references to case law and literature is by Ch. Vedder in E. Grabitz, M. Hilf (Hrsg.), *Das Recht der Europäische Union* I, EL 17, München, Beck, 2001. See, also, A. Dashwood, Ch. Hillion (eds.), *The General Law of EC External Relations*, London, Sweet & Maxwell, 2000.

intergovernmental conference and that was finally not planted in the Amsterdam Treaty.

Third, its ambiguity on certain points leads to divergent interpretations which have already appeared in the literature.[6]

Fourth, the Ariadne thread woven through the amendments is the idea that the EC's external powers with respect to trade in services and commercial aspects of intellectual property need to correspond to the division of powers between the EC and its Member States and to the voting procedures in the internal sphere: the so-called "logic of parallelism".[7]

II.   TRADE POLICY WITH RESPECT TO TRADE IN GOODS AND ASSIMILATED MATTERS

The trade policy powers as conferred to the EC in Article 133 ante-Nice and as interpreted by the ECJ in Opinion 1/94, i.e. limited to regulating trade in goods (including entering into the WTO Agreement on the Application of Sanitary and Phytosanitary Measures, in short SPS Agreement, and the WTO Agreement on Technical Barriers to Trade, in short TBT Agreement, and the Agreement on Subsidies and Countervailing Measures) and to cross-border trade in services and to border measures against counterfeit goods, are not put into question by the amended Article 133. The distinction between measures implementing classical instruments of trade policy and measures with trade policy aims proposed in the literature[8] appears to be outdated: e. g. the WTO SPS and TBT agreements can hardly be considered as classical trade policy instruments, yet the ECJ considered in Opinion 1/94 that they came within the scope of Article 133 EC.

---

[6] St. Griller, "*Die gemeinsame Handelspolitik nach Nizza-Ansätze eines neuen Aussen wirtschaftsrechts?* ", in St. Griller, W. Hummer (Hrsg.), *Die EU nach Nizza, Ergebnisse und Perspektiven*, Wien, New York, Springer, 2002, p. 131-189; Ch. Hermann, "*Vom misslungenen Versuch der Neufassung der gemeinsamen Handelspolitik durch den Vertrag von Nizza*", *EuZW* 2001, p. 269-274; H. G. Krenzler, Ch. Pitschas, "*Fortschritt oder Stagnation ? Die gemeinsame Handelspolitik nach Nizza*", *EuR*, 2001, p. 442-461; J. -V. Louis, "*Le traité de Nice*", op. cit., p. 25-34; E. Neframi, "*La politique commerciale commune selon le traité de Nice*", *CDE*, 2001/5-6, p. 605-645; P. van Nuffel, "*Le traité de Nice. Un commentaire*", *RDUE*, 2/2001.
[7] Commission, "The Reform of Article 133 by the Nice Treaty. The Logic of Parallelism", http://europa.eu.int/comm/trade/faqs/133.htm.
[8] E. Neframi, *op. cit.*, p. 621-622.

Paragraph 5 recognizes that agreements in the field of trade in services and the commercial aspects of intellectual property may be covered by paragraphs 1 to 4, which seems to be an implicit *coup de chapeau* to the ECJ, which stated *obiter* in Opinion 1/94 that "it follows from the open nature of the common commercial policy, within the meaning of the Treaty, that trade in services cannot immediately and as a matter of principle, be excluded from the scope of Article [133]...".[9]

The question is, however, whether this is a mere endorsement of Opinion 1/94 [10] or whether the provision on services other than cross-border and the protection against counterfeit goods going beyond border measures is now covered by paragraphs 1 to 4.[11] Alternatively, does it mean that the borderline between paragraphs 1 to 4 and paragraph 5 is a flexible one capable of being moved by the ECJ?

III.   TRADE IN SERVICES AND TRADE ASPECTS OF INTELLECTUAL PROPERTY RIGHTS UNDER PARAGRAPH 5 AND 6

A.   Introductory Remark

The Commission had proposed to include in paragraph 1 of Article 133 EC trade in goods and services, investments and intellectual property rights, so that the ante-Nice Article 133 would extend to these areas. The rejection of that proposal and the insertion of paragraph 5, as it is, result in significant differences with the regime of paragraphs 1 to 4 of Article 133 EC with respect to the scope and the nature of the powers and to the modalities of their exercise.

B.   Scope of the Powers

As to the scope of the new powers under the amended Article 133, the rejection of the Commission proposal means (a) that investments are all together excluded and (b) that only the negotiation and conclusion of international agreements are covered by the amended Article 133. Thus, neither autonomous EC measures nor EC measures designed to implement such agreements are covered by the amended Article 133.[12] Except where such agreements are implemented by the EC, relying on

---

[9] Opinion 1/94, *ECR*, 1994, p. 1-5267, par. 41.
[10] E. Neframi, *op. cit.*, p. 614.
[11] As claimed by H. G. Krenzler, Ch. Pitschas, *op. cit.*, p. 450-451.
[12] Acc. Ch. Hermann, *op. cit.*, p. 271.

EC Treaty articles granting the EC powers in the internal sphere, this opens the door to differences in implementation between Member States with attending consequences for the operation of the internal market and, probably, differences in the rights of private parties, to the extent that the ECJ would rule that, since implementation is left to Member States, the issue of the effect of such agreements is a matter of Member State law.

The question arises when an agreement concerns "commercial aspects" of intellectual property. Interestingly, this terminology differs from the WTO terminology: "trade-related aspects of intellectual property rights". There can probably be no doubt that this includes the Agreement on Trade-Related Aspects of Intellectual Property Rights, in short the TRIPs Agreement. It goes conceivably further. It is certainly not limited to "trade in intellectual property rights", a proposal to that effect having been rejected by the Intergovernmental Conference. Other future agreements are likely to lead to the same old controversy of instruments versus aims for the purpose of finding when such agreements have "commercial aspects".[13]

The grant of powers in paragraph 5, subparagraph 1 is without prejudice to paragraph 6. This provides that an agreement may not be concluded by the Council of it includes provisions which would go beyond the EC's internal powers. This is an example of the so-called "logic of parallelism".

Paragraph 6 also provides that the negotiation and conclusion of international agreements in the field of transport continues to be governed by the provisions of the EC Treaty on transport policy and Article 300. This may appear to be another *coup de chapeau* to the ECJ for its stance in Opinion 1/94. It had probably more to do with some bureaucratic insistence of several Member States to keep transport separate.

C.   Nature of the powers

In contrast with paragraphs 1 to 4, the powers in paragraph 5 and 6 are not exclusive.[14] Subparagraph 4 of paragraph 5 states that this paragraph does not affect the right of the Member States to maintain and

---

[13] *"distinction tellement subtile qu'elle ne paraît pas opportune"*, according to E. Neframi, *op. cit.*, p. 624.

[14] See St. Griller, *op. cit.*, p. 167 who considers this to be a case of "concurrent powers". E. Neframi makes a gallant effort to construe these powers as exclusive and. sees in subparagraph 4 of Article 133(5) a *"habilitation spécifique"*, *op. cit.*, p. 626 and f.

conclude agreements with third countries or international organizations, in so far as such agreements comply with EC law and other relevant international agreements.

This obviously concerns agreements on services and agreements on commercial aspects of intellectual property rights, to the extent that their subject matter is not covered by paragraphs 1 to 4. This is partly in line with Opinion 1/94, but it does not take over the qualification that this is a matter of "shared competence" or for which the EC and the Member States are "jointly competent". Query whether the special duty of cooperation between the EC and its Member States referred to in Opinion 1/94 applies in this case.

The requirement in subparagraph 4 of paragraph 5 that in the exercise of their concurrent power Member States must comply with EC law means that Member States must abstain from entering into agreements in matters for which the EC has enacted intra-EC rules.[15] In the course of the Intergovernmental Conference, a declaration stating that this subparagraph did not affect the principles of the *AETR* doctrine was drafted but not adopted. This does arguably not mean that this doctrine does not apply to paragraph 5. A clear mention to that effect would be required to set aside such a fundamental doctrine.[16] This provision is likely to raise the same difficulties of interpretation as the *AETR* doctrine.

The provision on agreements in the area of trade in cultural and audiovisual services, educational services and social and human health services (Article 133(6)) is drafted in a rather peculiar way. It starts off by stating that an agreement may not be concluded by the Council if it includes provisions which would go beyond the Community's internal powers. Obviously, the Intergovernmental Conference meant to say that the EC alone may not conclude such agreement. This is confirmed by the following subparagraph's lead in: "In this regard" which refers to shared competence of the EC and its Member States. The first subparagraph mentions "in particular by leading to harmonization of laws and regulations of the Member States in an area in which this Treaty rules out such harmonization". Yet, the second subparagraph refers to trade in audiovisual services, an area in which the EC Treaty does not rule out harmonization and in which internal rules have been enacted by the EC. These agreements are falling within the "shared competence" of the EC

---

[15] Ch. Hermann, *op. cit., p.* 272; H. G. Krenzler, Ch. Pitschas, *op. cit.,* p. 455.

[16] J. -V. Louis, op. *cit.,* p. 31.

and its Member States. Subparagraph 2 provides that the negotiation of such agreements requires the common accord of the Member States and that these agreements are concluded jointly by the EC and the Member States. Here, Article 133 paragraph 6 endorses the formula used by the ECJ in its Opinion 1/94 which raises the question of who is competent for what in relation to an international agreement for which the EC and its Member States have shared competence [17]. The reference to Article 300 EC raises the interesting question whether the European Parliament must be consulted. It should be recalled that this provision excepts agreements referred to in Article 133(3) from the mandatory consultation. The agreements in question are not referred to in Article 133(3). This appears to mean that the European Parliament must be consulted.

D.   Modalities of the Exercise of these Powers

In contrast with paragraphs 1 to 4, unanimity in the Council is required when negotiating and concluding an agreement on trade in services or on the commercial aspects of intellectual property in a number of cases.

The *first* case occurs where such agreement includes provisions for which unanimity is required for the adoption of internal EC rules (Article 133(5), 2nd subparagraph). Whether this "logic of parallelism", which can also be found in Opinion 1/94 with respect to intellectual property rights,[18] is logical can be left aside here. Two points need to be mentioned.

First, unanimity appears to be required whether or not such agreement requires amending EC internal rules. Second, "provisions" are referred to, in contrast to Article 300(2) which refers to "a field for which unanimity is required".

As far as trade in services is concerned, there are only few instances in which adoption of internal EC rules requires unanimity, i. e. with respect to certain measures only Articles 47(2) and 57(2), second paragraph. Whether Article 133(5) subparagraph 2 will apply when an agreement on the commercial aspects of intellectual property rights is to be concluded depends on what the proper legal basis is for enacting

---

[17] See, e. g. the analysis of A. G. Tesauro in his opinion in *Hermès International*, 1998, ECR, p. 1-3603.
[18] Opinion 1/94, *supra*, n. 9, par. 40.

internal rules in this field, either Articles 94, possibly 308, or Article 95 EC.

The *second* case arises when the agreement relates to a field in which the EC has not yet exercised its powers to adopt internal rules (Article 133(5), 2nd paragraph). Here, the "logic of parallelism" appears to be abandoned: the EC Treaty does not require unanimity in the Council for adopting internal rules in all of these fields. Moreover, one wonders what the meaning of this provision can be since the EC has already exercised its powers to adopt internal rules in the field of services and intellectual property. It can hardly mean "provisions" which the EC has not yet enacted, which would require unanimity in all cases in which a field has not been completely regulated by the EC. Using in the same subparagraph "field for "provisions" appears rather unlikely.

The *third* case refers to "horizontal agreements" containing provisions of the kind referred to in the two preceding cases (Article 133(5), 3d subpar.). "Horizontal agreements" probably means agreements concerning several fields. On its face, this third case is stating that unanimity is required because it contains provisions requiring unanimity as the two preceding cases. One wonders whether the Intergovernmental Conference wanted to set the case law of the ECJ aside. According to the ECJ, where several EC Treaty provisions provide the power to adopt a given legal act, the Council should rely on the EC Treaty provision corresponding to the main aim of the legal act in question,[19] whether or not one of the "competing" EC Treaty provisions provides for unanimity in the Council. If that were so, the unanimity requirement of Article 133(5), 3rd subparagraph would be a case of the tail wagging the dog.

The *fourth case* concerns the conclusion of agreements relating to trade in cultural and audiovisual services, educational services and social and health services (Article 133(6)). Unanimity in the Council is required in all cases. With respect to audiovisual services, the "logic of parallelism" is abandoned since the adoption of internal rules on such services does not require unanimity (Article 52 EC).

IV.   INTELLECTUAL PROPERTY RIGHTS

Pursuant to paragraph 7, the Council, acting unanimously on a proposal from the Commission and after consulting the European

---

[19] *Parliament v. Council*, 1991, ECR, p. I-4529, par. 17; *Parliament v. Council*, 1994, ECR, p. I-2857, par. 25.

Parliament, may include international negotiations and agreements on intellectual property rights *tout court* in the scope of the common commercial policy, in so far as they are not covered by paragraph 5.

This provision is modeled on paragraph 5 of the version of Article 133 as inserted by the Amsterdam Treaty, which remained a dead letter. According to one commentator of this Amsterdam Treaty amendment, it may be regarded as a face-saving device, putting off any effective amendment of Article 133 until the Greek Calends.[20] The same could probably be said about the amended Article 133 paragraph 7.

V.   A TENTATIVE ASSESSMENT

1.   The inclusion by the Nice Intergovernmental Conference of trade in services and the commercial aspects of intellectual property rights in the scope of the EC's trade policy powers by amplifying Article 133 EC is a half-way house. The Intergovernmental Conference could have drawn all the consequences from the overriding importance of services in the EC economy and the growing share of trade in services in the EC's external trade, from the developments at the WTO level in matters of negotiations and rule-making in the services sector and in trade-related aspects of intellectual property rights, and could have included *sic et simpliciter* these matters within the scope of Article 133 EC as it stood. Instead, the Intergovernmental Conference has opted to an important extent for effectively sharing the external powers with respect to these matters between the EC and its Member States and for subjecting many of the decisions to unanimity in the Council. Moreover, the Intergovernmental Conference has extended the EC trade policy powers with respect to these matters only to the conclusion of international agreements - not to unilateral action by the EC – and not to implementation of such agreements, with the likely attending consequences.

2.   The "logic of parallelism" has been the guiding principle: as a rule, the EC external powers have been extended in so far as internal powers with respect to the same area have already been conferred on the EC and the Council will be required to decide by unanimity when exercising the new external powers, either where the exercise of the parallel internal powers requires unanimity in the Council or where such

[20] A. Dashwood, "EC: External Relations Provision Post-Amsterdam", in A. Dashwood and Ch. Hillion (eds.), *The General Law of EC External Relations*, London, Sweet & Maxwell, 2000, p. 279 at 281.

parallel internal powers have not yet been exercised. While in practice politically weighty decisions are taken by consensus, quite obviously the very possibility of decisions being taken by qualified majority leads Member States to make compromises they would not be prepared to make otherwise. In the same vein are the provisions designed to enable Member States to continue to act on their own in the external sphere.

This "logic of parallelism", which is also inspired by the concerns about the "reverse" *AETR* [21] effect, is considered by some as an obvious requirement.[22].It is not, and certainly not in the *lege ferenda* situation of an intergovernmental conference: in most federal systems, the federal government has external powers with respect to matters that are reserved to the constituent parts of the federation in the internal sphere.[23] One might object that the comparison is not appropriate. The point, however, is that in the operation of its external policies in a context of division of powers the EC faces comparable challenges as federations.

This should be seen against the background of the EC decision-making process which is the opposite of the "them and us" process that one finds in several federal systems in the area of external relations. Member States are in the EC decision-making process: from committees assisting the Commission in the day-to-day administration of trade policy instruments, to the 133 Committee operating under the Council umbrella assisting the Commission in international negotiations, to the Council itself composed of Member States ministers.

---

[21] On that concept, see i.a. F. ZAMPINI, "*Les limites de la compétence externe de la Communauté européenne selon la CJCE et les limites de l'intervention judiciaire*", in J. H. J. Bourgeois, J.-L. Dewost, M. A. Gaiffe (ed.), *La Communauté européenne et les accords mixtes. Quelles perspectives ?*, Bruxelles, PIE, 1997, p. 27 at 42; A. Dashwood, "Why continue to have mixed agreements at all? ", *ibid*, p. 93 at 96.

[22] According to P. van Nuffel "*tout à fait logique dans le système du Traité*" *op. cit.*, p. 369.

[23] For a description of the situation in Australia, Canada, Switzerland and the US, see: "*Les Etats fédéraux dans les relations internationales*", RBDI, 1983, p. 1; in Germany, the Lander can act internationally subject to being authorized by the Bund. Belgium forms an exception, see: J. Steenbergen, "*Les accords mixtes et le système fédéral belge*", in J. H. J. Bourgeois, J. -L. Dewost, M. A. Gaiffe (eds.), *op. cit.* In a judgment of 22 March 1995, the German Constitutional Court rejected an application for a declaratory judgment by the Freistaat Bayern, to the effect that the federal government could not agree to the proposed EC Television without Frontiers Directive on the ground that under the German Constitution the subject matter came within the scope of the powers of the Freistaat Bayern. The Constitutional Court held that in such a case, the Bund is competent as "*Sachverwalter der Länderrechte*", B Verf GE, 92, p. 203.

3.   In the Intergovernmental Conference, the Member States have thus equipped themselves with belts and suspenders. This is obvious even for those matters where under Article 133 post-Nice the Council may decide by qualified majority: by providing that certain matters fall within the "shared competence" of the EC and its Member States (Article 133 par. 6), the Intergovernmental Conference has effectively given to the Member State which did not join the qualified majority in the Council a second bite at the cherry. This may even be the case where Member States maintain and conclude agreements with third countries in the situations referred to in Article 133 paragraph 5, subparagraph 4, if contrary to Jean-Victor Louis' view, the absence of the declaration on the *AETR* case law were to be held as allowing a Member State to conclude on its own in parallel an agreement on the same subject matter.

4.   Scope, nature and modalities of the exercise of the EC trade policy powers are about the defense and the promotion in the wider world of the interests of the EC as a whole. The Intergovernmental Conference has failed to give the EC the position it needs to do so by not fully treating trade in services and commercial aspects of intellectual property rights in the same fashion as trade in goods. The Intergovernmental Conference has been mainly concerned by internal matters. Franklin Dehousse considered the Treaty of Nice as "un *traité trop petit pour une Europe trop grande*".[24] The preservation of national interests within the EC context that explains the sharing of competences and the insistence on unanimity in the Council does not look well for the effectiveness of the EC as it is now and as it will be following the enlargement. The EC has painted itself in a corner.

5.   Jim Cloos considered the Nice Treaty as "*une étape obligée*".[25] This raises the question whether in this area the Convention will succeed in being "*l'étape suivante*".

In its Report on "External Action",[26] the Dehaene Working Group states that it reached "a very large consensus" on the following recommendations:

"– the Treaty should indicate that the Union is competent to conclude agreements dealing with issues falling under its internal competences;

---

[24] Title of his article in 120 *JT*, 2001, p. 13.
[25] Title of his article in *RMCUE*, 444, 2001 p. 5.
[26] CONV 459/02 of 16 December 2002.

- the new provision in the Treaty should also specify that the Council should deliberate on such agreements according to the same voting procedure which would apply to internal legislative deliberations on the same issues (normally QMV) ".

This Working Group adds: "This provision should in no way modify the delimitation of competences between the EU and Member States".[27]

Further on decision-making in commercial policy, it states that:

"[t]here was a high degree of support in favor of the use of QMV in all areas of commercial policy, including services and intellectual property, without prejudice to current restrictions on harmonization in internal policy areas".[28]

The first recommendation could be a step in *"l'étape suivante"*. On its face, it goes beyong the current case law of the ECJ (the *AETR* doctrine and the doctrine set out in Opinion 1/76, as it has been qualified in Opinion 1/94 and in the judgments in the *"Open Skies"* cases). The second recommendation would apparently lead to an amendment of the post-Nice Article 133(5).

The first recommendation remains within the so-called "logic of parallelism": the EC will have in the external sphere no more powers than in the internal sphere. Wouldn't the "logic of parallelism" require to recognize that these powers in the internal sphere may be used not only for international agreements as recommended but also for unilateral action and for the implementation of international agreements?

The qualification that this should not "modify the delimitation of competences between the EU and Member States" is, at first blush, not more than a confirmation of the first recommendation, which is based on the delimitation of competences.

So far, the Convention appears set to only partly lift the EC and its Member States out of the corner in which the Nice Intergovernmental Conference has painted them.

---

[27] *Ibid*, at p. 4.
[28] *Ibid*, at p. 7.

12. EC RULES AGAINST "ILLICIT TRADE PRACTICES"– POLICYCOSMETICS OR INTERNATIONAL LAW ENFORCEMENT?

I.   INTRODUCTION

The few cases in which the European Community's Regulation Against Illicit Trade Practices[1] (the "Regulation") has been applied so far and the comments to which it has given rise,[2] explain the attempt to go over a question of one commentator: whether the EC interpretation of the new rules or the relative inefficiency of the international settlement of dispute machinery will discourage parties from invoking them, or whether the pressure that these rules can help to generate will contribute to a more effective and equitable enforcement of international trade law.[3] This Regulation contains rules dealing with two matters that it treats separately: on the one hand, "responding to any illicit commercial practice with a view to removing the injury resulting therefrom", on the other "ensuring full exercise of the Community's rights with regard to the commercial practices of third countries".[4] Only with respect to the first subject matter does the Regulation grant the EC industry a right to complain. And it is also only with respect to that subject matter that the Regulation brings something new in relation to the EC decision-making process. Contrary to the views of one commentator,[5] the Regulation does not add anything to the EC external relations powers. While the exact scope of the EC's trade policy powers does occasionally give rise to discussions and even

---

[1] Council Regulation No. 2641/84, O.J. L 252/1 (1984), Common Mkt. Rep. (CCH) ¶ 3,845 (on the strengthening of the common commercial policy with regard in particular to protection against illicit commercial practices).

[2] Atwood, *The European Economic Community's New Measures Against Unfair Practices in International Trade: Implications for United States Exporters*, 19 *Int'l Law* 361 (1985); Bourgeois and Laurent, *Le "nouvel instrument de politique commerciale": un pas en avant vers l'élimination des obstacles aux échange internationaux*, 21 Revue Trimestrielle de Droit Européén 41 (1985); Denton, *The New Commercial Policy Instrument and AKZO v. Dupont*, 1 *Eur. L. Rev.* 3 (1988); Hilf and Rolf, *Das "Neue Instrument" der EG. Eine rechtstaatlichle Stärkung der gemeinsamen Handelspolitik?*, RIW 297-311 (1985); Steenbergen, *The New Commercial Policy Instrument*, 22 *Common Mkt L. Rev.* 421 (1985); Zoller, *Remedies for Unfair Trade: European and United States Views*, 18 Cornell Int'l L.J. 227 (1985). Comments also appear in M. Bronckers, *Selective Safeguard Measures in Multilateral Trade Relations* 209-40 (1985); I. Van Bael and J. F. Bellis, *International Trade Law and Practice of the European Community*, Part IV (1985).

[3] Steenbergen *supra* n. 2 at 439.

[4] Council Regulation No. 2641/84, Art. 1, O.J. L 252/2 (1984), *Common Mkt Rep.* (CCH) ¶ 3,845A.

[5] Zoller, *supra* n. 2, at 227.

to disputes,[6] nobody really questions anymore that in the area of trade policy, at least when the use of classical trade policy instruments is called for, the EC has the necessary powers to act under Article 113 EEC.[7] The Regulation is no more and no less than the EC exercising its trade policy powers. Subject to how one interprets a provision inserted in the Regulation stating that it is without prejudice to the measures which may be taken pursuant to Article 113 EEC with respect to "the full exercise of the Community's rights with regard to the commercial practices of third countries", the EC does not acquire new rights by the Regulation; the Regulation is as far as the EC's trading partners are concerned a signal that the EC is prepared to use its existing rights. It appears appropriate to focus on the part of the Regulation dealing with "illicit commercial practices. " This Regulation is not the only piece of EC legislation dealing with international trade practices which are considered as "unfair". The EC applies, as some of its trading partners, antidumping and antisubsidy legislation.[8] Parallel provisions have been adopted in the maritime

---

[6] The latest instance is the Commission's appeal before the Court of Justice of the European Communities against decisions of the Council of Ministers. Action brought on 4 June 1987 by the Commission of the European Communities Against the Council of the European Communities, Case No. 165/87, O.J. C 204/3 (1987); Action brought on 25 September 1987 by the Commission of the European Communities Against the Council of the European Communities, Case No. 288/87, O.J. C 284/11 (1987); Action brought on 16 September 1987 by the Commission of the European Communities Against the Council of the European Communities, Case No. 275/87, O.J. C 285/6 (1987).

[7] The EC's powers with respect to economic sanctions is still questioned by some: see, *e.g.* J. Verhoeven, *Sanctions internationales et Communautés européennes. A propos de l'affaire de Iles Falklands (Malvinas)*, 20 Cahiers de Droit Européen [CDE] 259 (1984); for a reply, see C.D. Ehlermann, *Communautes européennes et sanctions internationales. une résponse à J. Verhoeven, Rev. B. Dr. Int'l* 96 (1984). Those who rely on Article 224 EEC to exclude any EC power cannot expect to find much sympathy from the Court of Justice. In Johnston v Chief Constable of the Royal Ulster Constabulary, 1986 E.C.R. 1651, Common Mkt Rep. (CCH) ¶ 14,304 it stated that because of this limited character Articles 36, 48, 56, 223 and 224 EEC "do not lend themselves to a wide interpretation and it is not possible to infer from them that there is inherent in the Treaty a general proviso covering all measures taken for reasons of public safety." Johnston, 1986 E.C.R. at 1684, ¶ 26, Common Mkt. Rep. (CCH) ¶ 14,304, at 16,888.

[8] Following some amendments, a redraft has been enacted recently. Council Regulation No. 2423/88, O.J. L 209/1 (1988). For comments see J.F. Beseler & A.N. Williams, *Antidumping and Anti-Subsidy Law–The European Communities* (1986); W. Davey, *An Analysis of European Communities Legislation and Practice Relating to Antidumping and Countervailing Duties*, 1983 Fordham Corp.L.Inst, 39 (B. Hawk ed. 1984); J. Bourgeois, *EC Antidumping Enforcement–Selected Second Generation Issues*, 1985 Fordham Corp.L.Inst. (B. Hawk (ed.) 1986): E. Vermulst, *Antidumping Law and Practice in the United States and the European Communities* (1987).

transport sector.[9] In addition, a 1986 Regulation introduced with effect on 1 January 1988 a procedure whereby, on complaint of the EC industry, imports of allegedly counterfeit goods may be suspended by the Member State customs authorities for a period of ten days. After that period they are released if the matter has not been referred to the authority empowered to take substantive measures.[10]

II.   BACKGROUND

As early as 1964, the Commission had discussed with the Council "common principles and a Community procedure concerning abnormal trade practices of third countries",[11] but the Commission had met with so little enthusiasm that it shelved the idea of making a formal proposal. In 1980 the Welsh report to the European Parliament recommended legislation to complement the existing antidumping and antisubsidy rules, so as to cover all aspects of unfair trading practices.[12] In 1982, the French government addressed a memorandum to the Commission and the other Member states, in which it stated that it would be useful to adopt EC provisions having analogous effect to section 301 of the 1979 US Trade Agreements Act.[13] The Commission reacted cautiously. It referred to the existing provisions against unfair trade (antidumping and antisubsidy) but agreed with the French government that there were other forms of unfair trade that were not caught by these provisions. In the Commission's view, dealing effectively with other forms of unfair trade did not depend on granting new powers under the EEC Treaty (Article 113), but on using them efficiently by introducing procedures comparable to those applying for anti-dumping and antisubsidy action and safeguard (i.e. escape clause) action. Some Member States rejected the idea of new provisions that would inevitably, in their view, turn out as new form of protectionism.

In the meantime, however, EC/US relations had one of their periodic crises on agricultural policy. The "business as usual" feeling did not prevail following when the all-out attack launched by the US steel

---

[9] Council Regulation No. 4057/86, O.J. L 378/14 (1986) (on unfair pricing practices in maritime transport). See Bellis, Vermulst and Musquar, *The New EEC Regulation on Unfair Pricing Practices in Maritime Transport: A Forerunner of the Extension of Unfair Trade Concepts to Services?*, 22 Journal of World Trade 47 (1988)

[10] Council Regulation No. 3842/86, O.J. L 357/1 (1986) (laying down measures to prohibit the release for free circulation of counterfeit goods).

[11] EEC Bulletin 1964, Supp. 1

[12] Committee for external economic relations, *Europ*, Carl. *Doc*, 1 422/811.

[13] Memorandum on Strengthening the Instruments of the Common Commercial Policy, E.C. Bull. No. 4 (1982).

industry (using about all the weapons of US trade legislation[14] in a situation where the EC itself was imposing on the EC steel industry an overall crisis programme containing some rather drastic measures)[15] had become an *affaire d'état*. On top of this came the politically rather insensitive decision of the Reagan Administration to extend to EC undertakings and to EC exports measures taken under the Export Administration Act against the Siberian gas pipe-line.[16]

In its June 1982 meeting the European Council (consisting of heads of state and/or heads of the government of the Member States) referred to these events and concluded inter alia that "it was of the highest importance: (b) . . . to make sure that the Community, in managing trade policy, acts with as much speed and efficiency as its trading partners ...",[17] The Commission waited until some of the dust had settled and submitted in March 1983 to the Council a proposal for a new regulation on the strengthening of the common commercial policy.[18] Both the European Parliament[19] and the Economic and Social Committee[20] reacted favourably and issued their opinion in a few months.

---

[14] For a description see F. Benyon and J. Bourgeois, *The European Community -United States Steel Arrangement*, 21 *Common Mkt L. Rev.* 305 (1984); G. Horlick, *American Trade Law and the Steel Pact between Brussels and Washington*, World Economy 361 (1983).

[15] The severity of the measures of this policy, whose architect was Commission Vice President Davignon, is reflected in a joke that circulated at the time all over the EC. It goes as follows. Davignon dies. He presents himself at the gates of Heaven. After all the harm he has done to the EC steel industry, quite naturally he is not admitted but sent straight to Hell where he belongs. A few days later a furious Lucifer, the head devil, bangs on Heaven's door. He demands that Davignon be withdrawn from Hell immediately: the situation in Hell has become intolerable; two days after his arrival there Davignon had already closed down six blast furnaces!

[16] These measures led to diplomatic *démarches* of the Commission and the Member States challenging the extraterritorial application of the US Export Administration Act. See "Notes and Comments" of 12 August 1982 and Memorandum of 13 March 1983, published in A. Lowe, *Extraterritorial Jurisdiction and Annotated Collection of Legal Materials* 197–211 and 215-19 (1983).

[17] European Council in Brussels, E.C. Bull. No. 6 (1982).

[18] Proposal for a Council Regulation on the Strengthening of the Common Commercial Policy with Regard in Particular to Protection Against Unfair Commercial Practices, O.J. C 83/6 (1983).

[19] Regulation on the Strengthening of the Common Commercial Policy (Vote), O.J. C 205/2 (1983).

[20] Opinion on the Proposal for a Council Regulation on the Strengthening of the Common Commercial Policy with Regard in Particular to Protection Against Unfair Commercial Practices, O.J. C 211/24 (1983). The ECS referred to views it had expressed earlier on the need to strengthen the common commercial policy against all attempts at protectionism of which unfair trade practices are one of the forms.

In the Council, however, more time was needed to overcome the opposition of several Member States against the concept as such—some argued that there was no need for it[21]–and against some of the features of the Commission proposal, among others, granting the EC industry a right to complain and the decision-making procedure. Several amendments put forward by the Commission in the course of the discussions in the Council to meet some of the objections led finally to the adoption on 17 September 1984 of the Regulation by a qualified majority, with Germany voting against it and the Netherlands and Denmark voicing substantial objections.[22] Some of the arguments put forward by the opponents will be addressed below when examining specific elements of this Regulation.

III.   ILLICIT PRACTICES

A.   Introduction

Not surprisingly, defining the scope of the Regulation proved to be one of the sticking points of the Commission proposal. On the one hand, in the light of the EC's repeated criticism of the US section 301,[23] in particular the inclusion of any *unreasonable* act, policy or practice, there was a perceived need for a more precise and objective definition. On the other hand, limiting the Regulation to violations of international law did not seem worth the effort. However, granting the EC industry a right of complaint beyond this point and allowing it, via a formal complaint procedure, to trigger action against whatever practice of a foreign country was tantamount to opening up a Pandora's box.

The Regulation as finally adopted reflects a compromise reached among the supporters of a US section 301-type instrument, the institutional development sought by the Commission and those advocating a restrictive attitude to all form of countervailing duties or retaliatory measures as well as towards the more traditional forms of non-tariff barriers.[24]

---

[21] Among others, the Federal Republic of Germany whose views are reflected in its reply to question in the German Parliament (BT - Drs. 10/1700 of 2 July 1984). See *also* the report of the Parliamentary Committee of Economic Affairs (BT - Drs. 10/596 of 10 November 1983).

[22] Denton, *supra* n. 2 at n. 20. For a description of the difficult passage through the Council see *also* Bronckers, supra N. 2, at 217-19.

[23] *E.g.*, Commission Vice-President Haferkamp in EP Annex N° 1-300/243 and Blumenfeld Report, EP Doc. 1-376/83 at 18.

[24] Steenbergen, *supra* n. 2, at 423.

The Regulation defines "illicit practices" as follows: any international trade practices attributable to third countries which are incompatible with international law or with generally accepted rules.[25]

The Commission proposal also used the term "unfair". Both the European Parliament and the Economic and Social Committee disliked this value-laden term. The latter suggested the term "illicit".

The following sections deal with the elements of this definition.

B.   What is "incompatible"?

The practice must be "incompatible" with international law or generally accepted rules. Contrary to what some commentators assert,[26] by the use of the word "incompatible" the Regulation does not achieve the same breadth and subjective content as section 301 (a)(2) of the US legislation ("any act, policy or practice of a foreign country or instrumentality that is *unjustifiable, unreasonable* or *discriminatory,* and burdens or distorts United States commerce"). The Regulation refers to standards contained in "international law or generally accepted rules"; section 301 has no such benchmark, any unreasonable act being any act deemed to be unfair or inequitable.[27]

At any rate, whether or not "incompatible" is a lesser standard than "inconsistent" under European law or under French law, the Commission interprets the Regulation on this point as requiring that the practice complained of be *contrary* to a sufficiently precise rule. *In Soya Meal from Argentina* the Commission received in 1986 a complaint from FEDIOL, an EC-wide association of oil-seed crushers and oil processors, against measures applied by Argentina to the benefit of its oil-seed and oil-processing industry. FEDIOL alleged that Argentina's system of differential export taxes for soya products and export restrictions were incompatible with the GATT. In an unpublished decision of December 1986 the Commission refused to initiate a proceeding on the ground that the complaint did not establish prima facie that the measures complained of were contrary to Articles III and XI of GATT, as these provisions clearly do not prohibit internal taxes discriminating against exports or export taxes; in addition, according to the Commission, neither the preamble of

---

[25] Council Regulation No. 2641/84, Article 2(1), O.J. L 252/2 (1984).
[26] Zoller, *supra* n. 2, at 234–37.
[27] Denton, *supra* n. 2, at 9.

GATT nor Articles XX and XXXV lay down obligations that are sufficiently precise to give rise to "illicit practices" within the meaning of the Regulation.[28]

C. The "International Law" Standard

1. The Regulation does not clarify, neither in its operative part nor in its preamble, what is meant by "international law". The context makes clear that not any international law rule whatsoever is relevant: it must be a rule concerning international trade practices.

Although the concept of "international trade" includes or is capable of including not only trade in goods but also trade in services, it is questionable whether the Regulation applies to trade in services. In its opinion on the Commission proposal, the European Parliament stated that the Regulation should be extended to trade in services.[29] The Commission wanted to avoid discussions in the Council about the controversial issue of the scope of the EC trade policy powers under Article 113 EEC and refrained from proposing an amendment providing expressly that the Regulation would apply to trade in services. In addition, in view of the definition of 'Community industry" referring to producers, consumers or processors of products, it appears doubtful that the Regulation applies to trade other than trade in goods.[30]

The same arguments plead against interpreting "international trade practice" and thus "international law" within the meaning of the Regulation as referring, e.g. to the protection of investments. Consequently under the Regulation as it stands it could probably not be applied against a foreign country's practice regarding investment by EC undertakings.

This does not mean that the Regulation could not be extended to practices affecting the supply of services or foreign investment by EC undertakings. Such a decision depends on the Council's willingness to follow the Commission, where it interprets Article 113 EEC extensively in an attempt to define broadly the Community's scope of action in the trade policy field.[31] In this connection it is noteworthy that in *Unauthorized*

---

[28] This decision is under appeal. O.J. C 96/8 (1987).

[29] O.J. C 205/9 (1983)

[30] Council Regulation No. 2641/84, Art. 2 (4), O.J. L 252/2 (1984).

[31] See P. Gilsdorf, *Die Grenzen der Gemeinsamen Handelspolitik*, Vorträge, Reden und Berichte aus dem Europa Institut/Nr. 125 (Europa-Institut der Universitat des Saarlands, 1988) at 24.

Reproduction of Sound Recordings in Indonesia the Commission initiated proceedings and terminated them under the Regulation in view of certain commitments entered into by Indonesia, without legal objections being raised by Member States against the application of the Regulation even though the action was taken to protect intellectual property rights.[32]

2.   "International law" within the meaning of the Regulation obviously refers to the GATT and to GATT-implementing and GATT side agreements, such as those resulting from the Tokyo Round of multilateral trade negotiations, called codes.[33] Non-compliance with concrete obligations laid down in the GATT and in these Codes can be considered as an "illicit commercial practice". Moreover, it would seem that non-compliance with certain OECD instruments, e.g. on export credits, could also be considered as "illicit practices".[34] Among other international-law rules that could be relied upon are the numerous bilateral and multilateral agreements to which the EC is a party.[35]

3.   In *Certain Aramid Fibres Into the US*[36] acting on a complaint by Enka, filed on behalf of the Akzo group, which had developed but was not yet producing full-scale commercial quantities of aramid fibres in the EC, the Commission initiated an investigation with respect to alleged illicit commercial practices of the US Following a petition by Dupont, the US ITC had issued an order prohibiting the unlicensed importation in the US of aramid fibres manufactured abroad by Akzo, after having determined that, by reason of production overseas by a process covered by Dupont's US patent, Akzo had violated section 337 of the 1930 Tariff Act. According to Akzo's complaint under the Regulation, the exclusion order was not necessary under Article XX(d) of GATT and the US was in breach of Article III (4) of GATT by reason of certain discriminatory

---

[32] See Commission Decision, O.J.L 123/51 (1988).

[33] Hilf and Rolf, *supra* n. 2, at 299-300 mention as examples: export and import restrictions, restrictive administrative practices and generally all violations of the prohibition of discrimination (GATT, Art. 1 (&), non-compliance with the rules of conduct of the 1979 GATT Code on Technical Barriers to Trade and of the 1979 GATT On Government Procurement, export subsidies to third country markets, unjustifiable antidumping duties; Bourgeois and Laurent, *supra* n. 2 also mention non-compliance with other 1979 GATT codes, such as the Customs Valuation Code and Licensing Code.

[34] Acc. Hilf and Rolf *supra* N 2, at 300.

[35] With respect to earlier agreements concluded by Member States in the area of international trade or so-called mixed agreements (i.e. concluded by the EC and its Member States jointly), under EC law the Regulation would apply. However in the external sphere, claims by the EC with respect to such agreements could run into difficulties. See J. Groux and P. Manin, *The European Communities in the International Order* 151–54 (1984).

[36] For a fuller description, see Denton, supra N. 2, at 14–18.

features of the section 337 procedure. Referring to the Community interest clause of the Regulation, the Commission considered that the complaint raised a serious question on the interpretation of GATT, which had considerable economic implications.[37] At the end of its investigation the Commission concluded that section 337 was discriminatory, in that the procedure under that provision in the U.S. ITC is less favourable to the respondents than the procedures in the U.S. courts in respect of goods produced in the US and therefore results in a denial of national treatment which is contrary to Article III of GATT.[38] At the time of writing, a GATT Panel is drafting its report.[39]

In *Unauthorized Reproduction of Sound Recordings in Indonesia* the complaint relied *inter alia* on the Paris Convention for the Protection of Intellectual Property and alleged that the unauthorized reproduction of phonograms as carried out in Indonesia is an act of "unfair competition" within the meaning of Article 10*bis*, para. 2 of the Convention and that Indonesia was not providing "effective protection" or "appropriate legal remedies" to counter such unfair competition, as required by Article 10bis, para. 1 and Article 10*ter* of the Convention. By initiating the proceeding,[40] the Commission considered that the complainant had established prima facie that the alleged practice was contrary to the international rules cited.[41]

As indicated earlier, in *Soya Meal from Argentina* the Commission considered that the complaint did not establish prima facie that the practices complained of were contrary to the GATT provisions cited.[42]

---

[37] Notice of initiation, O.J. C 25/2 (1986).

[38] Commission Decision, of 12 March 1987, on the initiation of an international consultation and dispute settlement procedure concerning a United States measure excluding imports of certain aramid fibres into the United States of America, O.J. L 117/18 (1987). [Ed. note: The GATT panel found that the section 337 action was contrary to the GATT rules.]

[39] On the general question, see Knight, *Section 337 and the GATT: A Necessary Protection or an Unfair Trade Practice*, 18 Ga. J. Int'l & Comp. L. 47 (1988).

[40] Notice of Initiation of an 'Illicit Practice' Procedure Concerning the Unauthorized Reproduction of Sound Recordings in Indonesia, O.J.C 136/3 (1987), [hereinafter, Notice of Initiation],

[41] On this point W. Alexander, *Indonesian Copyright Law as an "Illicit Commercial Practice"*, Bar European News, N° 20, 1 February 1988 states that he is not impressed by references to Articles 10*bis* and 10*ter* of the Paris Convention, inter alia, because he does not remember having heard that copying in Italy of foreign patented pharmaceuticals constituted an act of unfair competition within the meaning of Article 10*bis* of the Paris Convention. This is a nice debating point but hardly an argument.

[42] *Supra* sec. III (B).

D. The "Generally Accepted Rules" Standard

1.   The reference to "generally accepted rules" was included in the definition of "illicit practices" after long discussions.

The Commission proposal referred to "rules regarding commercial policy commonly accepted by the Community's principal partners". This was criticized by the European Parliament and by the Economic and Social Committee. In the Council, the Commission, which was keen on a formula extending the scope of the Regulation beyond the enforcement of international rules mainly because it was seeking to bring about certain institutional developments, somehow prevailed. Its argument that a definition limited to incompatibility with international law would have precluded the application of the Regulation to practices of third countries not bound by GATT carried the day.[43]

While the vagueness of this formula cannot be denied,[44] much of the criticism to which it is giving rise misses the point that, from a strictly legal point of view, the proper definition of "illicit commercial practices" really matters only for the right of complaint of the EC industry and the Commission's competence under the Regulation to initiate and conduct the proceedings. This will be explained below.

2.   As a starting point it seems obvious that, if "generally accepted rules" were to refer to unwritten rules accepted by all trading nations, they would be part of customary international law and this reference would be redundant. It is bound to mean something else.

In this connection, it can be argued that the notion of "generally accepted rules" could include "soft law".[45] It could also include rules of conduct in international trade that are generally accepted; such rules should, however, be distinguished from commonly accepted usage pertaining to international law of commercial transactions. In addition, the use of the term "rules", whose interpretation will have to be clarified on a case-by-case basis, not unlike the notion of "unfair trade practices" used in certain domestic commercial statutes,[46] implies certain legal

---

[43] This argument is also mentioned by Hilf and Rolf, *supra n.* 2, at 301–02; Bronckers, *supra* n. 2, at 218, who considers that this may amount to a violation of the generally accepted rule *pacta tertiis nec nocent, nec prosunt*. This raises another issue, see *infra* sec. III (D)(5).

[44] Similar vague formulas are not unknown elsewhere.

[45] Acc. Hilf and Rolf, *supra* note 2, at 302 with reference to literature.

[46] It is interesting to note how many statutes rely on similar and other general formulas, see *Pinner's World Unfair Competition Law,* Sub N° 77 *Unfair competition* (Sijthoff & Noordhoff, Leiden 1978).

qualities. This, together with the requirement that they are "generally
accepted", sets this formula apart from the much looser and potentially
unilateral "unreasonable" standard of the US legislation.

3. In *Unauthorized Reproduction of Sound Recordings in
Indonesia*[47] the complainant also alleged a breach of generally accepted
rules. According to the complainant, by restricting protection of works
by foreign nationals to those "first published" in Indonesia, while
protecting works by Indonesian nationals irrespective of the place of first
publication, Indonesia failed to comply with the national treatment rule
of the Berne Convention for the Protection of Literary and Artistic Works
and the Universal Copyright Convention. Indonesia not being a party to
these conventions, the complainant argued that the rules relied upon must
be regarded, in view of the large number and importance of the countries
adhering to those Conventions, as "generally accepted rules" within the
meaning of the Regulation. By initiating the proceeding on the basis of
this allegation also, the Commission considered that the complainant had
established prima facie that the alleged practice was contrary to "generally
accepted rules".

One critic, Alexander, considers that the Commission was wrong
in initiating the proceeding in this case and asserts that equal protection
granted by national law to works of foreign nationals can hardly be
considered as a generally accepted rule. He contends that many copyright
acts discriminate between nationals and foreigners in a way comparable
to that reported about Indonesia; he recalls that under the copyright acts
of the UK, Germany and the Netherlands, works of foreigners are only
protected if the first publication took place within that country or, in the
case of Germany and the Netherlands, if they are published in that country
within 30 days after first publication elsewhere.[48] However, whether this
means that many parties to these convention do not comply with their
obligations and that these should be interpreted in the light of the constant
practices of the contracting parties, or that the complainant and the
Commission misinterpreted these conventions, is a question which may
be left aside. Assuming for the sake of argument that Alexander is right
on the merits, it is enough to state that these arguments are not so manifest
as to rebut the complainant's prima facie case. Such arguments are more
properly dealt with in the investigation itself.

---

[47] Notice of Initiation, *supra* n. 40.
[48] Alexander, *supra* n. 41, at 9.

4.　　Some commentators[49] have raised the question whether a so-called "non-violation nullification and impairement" of GATT benefits[50] could be considered as "a practice incompatible with ... generally accepted rules" within the meaning of the Regulation. This argument is also being put forward by FEDIOL in its appeal against the Commission's refusal to initiate a proceeding against Argentina.

Whether Article XXIII of GATT can be interpreted as establishing a legal obligation for a GATT contracting party not to deny another contracting party's reasonable expectations arising from tariff concessions rather than a right to an offsetting or compensatory adjustment to restore the general balance of advantages can be left aside here. For the purpose of the Regulation it suffices to note that taking action to remedy a non-violation nullification and impairment of GATT benefits is "ensuring the full exercise of the Community's rights with regard to the commercial practices of third countries",[51] a matter for which the Regulation clearly did not provide a right of complaint to the EC industry.

5.　　As indicated earlier much of the discussion on the use of "generally accepted rules" is somewhat of a *faux débat*.

For example, *Unauthorized Reproduction of Sound Recordings in Indonesia* is questioned as being an action that constitutes an undue interference with political decisions which belong to the sovereignty of a foreign state (because Indonesia is not a party to two of the international conventions relied upon).[52] However, not the opening of a proceeding, but the measures the EC would take to remedy the injury caused by "illicit commercial practices" are important for foreign countries. In other words, does it really matter for the rights of foreign countries how the EC defines "illicit practices" under the Regulation?

The definition of "illicit commercial practices" could serve two different purposes, which are not always properly distinguished by some commentators.

One purpose is obvious. It determines the scope of the right of complaint of the EC industry and the powers of the Commission under

---

[49] Hilf and Rolf, *supra* n. 2 at 302–03.
[50] E. McGovern, *International Trade Regulation* 39–41 (2nd ed. 1986).
[51] Council Regulation No. 2641/84, Art. 1 (b), O.J. L 252/2 (1984), *Common Mkt Rep.* (CCH)¶ 3845A.
[52] Alexander, *supra* 1 at 9.

the Regulation. An investigation certainly affects the interests of a third country. The question, however, is whether it affects the rights of a third country. It has been argued that the ability which the Regulation gives to private parties to question the validity of certain foreign legislative acts is a departure from classical foreign immunity law, under which states were only challenged by other states through diplomatic channels.[53] This seems to be based on a misconception of the Regulation. At the investigation stage, the only thing which the Regulation does is to provide for an administrative procedure allowing private parties to show why the Commission should challenge at a later stage a practice of a foreign state. Even if one were to consider this as a private claim against a foreign state, which it is not, the Commission decision to open the investigation after having considered the Community interest can be assimilated to the customary requirement that such a private claim be state-supported. In addition, although this procedure has certain quasi-judicial elements, it only leads to a finding, on the basis of which the Commission will consider whether the matter should be taken further. For this second stage the Regulation provides that measures are only to be decided on after international procedures, "where the Community's international obligations require the prior discharge of an international procedure for consultation or for the settlement of disputes".[54]

Does the definition of "illicit commercial practices" also serve another purpose? It could be argued that it limits the EC's scope of action; in other words that the Council may only take countermeasures against an illicit practice as defined by the Regulation. From an institutional point of view this argument is not convincing: the Regulation does not and probably could not limit the trade policy powers of the Council under Article 113 EEC. Moreover, the *patere legem quam ipse fecisti* argument is excluded by a specific provision.[55] From the point of view of foreign countries, what matters in the end legally is not so much the definition of "illicit practice" as the rule of the Regulation providing for measures "compatible with international obligations and procedures".[56]

---

[53] Zoller, *supra* n. 2, at 231–32.
[54] Council Regulation No. 2641/84, Art. 10 (2), O.J. L 252/5 (1984), *Common Mkt Rep.* (CCH) ¶ 3845K.
[55] Council Regulation No. 2641/84, Art. 13 O.J. L 252/6 (1984), *Common Mkt Rep.* (CCH) ¶ 3845N. which states that the Regulation is without prejudice to other measures which may be taken pursuant to Article 113 EEC.
[56] Council Regulation No. 2641/84, Art. 10 (3), O.J. L 252/5 (1984), *Common Mkt Rep.* (CCH) ¶ 3845K.

E.   Illicit Practice "Attributable" to a Foreign Country

The requirement that the practice be "attributable" to a foreign country does not raise any particular problem when the practice complained of is a measure taken by the State itself, be it a legislative act, a regulation, an administrative order or even a factual situation resulting from the conduct of the authorities in a foreign country. Since the Regulation states *"attributable* to third countries" and does not read *"practices of* third countries", one cannot rule out the possibility that the Regulation can be used where practices of private companies are directly, or to a substantial degree, caused or prompted by government intervention in foreign countries, for example, in the fields of government contracts, price regulations, rules on advertisement, technical standards etc.[57] The issue of the extent to which the Regulation applies to acts of private parties arose in fact in *Unauthorized Reproduction of Sound Recordings in Indonesia,* since the complaint concerned effectively the production in Indonesia of "pirate" sound recordings for commercial purposes. The complaint alleged that "by failing to provide the Community industry with effective protection against unauthorized reproduction of sound recordings Indonesia was in breach both of international law and of generally accepted rules;" the com plaint relied to that effect inter alia on the Paris Convention for the Protection of Intellectual Property, a clause of which obligates the parties to provide other countries of the Union with "effective protection" and "appropriate legal remedies" to counter unfair competition within the meaning of this convention.[58]

This raises the intriguing question to what extent restrictive business practices of foreign undertakings could come within the ambit of the Regulation. Under the EC competition rules as interpreted and applied by the Commission conduct abroad of foreign companies can be caught by these rules whenever that conduct has as its object or effect an appreciable restriction of competition within the EC.[59] As the Commission has made clear, measures resulting from restrictive agreements or concerted practices between undertakings which are merely authorized by the foreign country under that foreign country's law are not for that reason excluded from the application of EC competition rules.[60] Thus the EC competition rules do *not* apply to restrictive business practices of foreign undertakings where they restrict competition and affect EC

---

[57] Steenbergen, *supra* n.2, at 425; acc. Denton, *supra* n. 2 at 9 there should be a "connection to the public law" of the foreign country.

[58] Notice of initiation, *supra* n. 40.

[59] For example, Aluminium from Eastern Europe, O.J. L 92/1 (1985); Wood Pulp, O.J. L 85/1 (1985).

[60] For example, Franco-Japanese Ball Bearings Agreement O.J. L 343/19 (1984).

undertakings on *foreign* markets. Could the Regulation apply where these restrictive business practices are "attributable" to a foreign country? Likewise, could the Regulation apply where restrictive business practices of foreign undertakings restrict competition within the EC but escape from the EC competition rules because they were imposed by the authorities of the foreign country?

By contrast with the situation in *Unauthorized Reproduction of Sound Recordings in Indonesia* there are no international rules that the foreign country would be failing to enforce. Neither the GATT nor any other international instrument contain (substantive) provisions on restrictive business practices.[61] The only exceptions, as far as the EC is concerned, are to be found in the agreements with the EFTA countries (Austria, Finland, Iceland, Norway, Sweden and Switzerland)[62] which contain provisions that mirror the competition rules of the EEC Treaty; were the government of one these countries to approve or compel such restrictive practices incompatible with these provisions, it would expose itself to the risk of a complaint under the Regulation. Otherwise, it is difficult to see how active involvement of a foreign country in restrictive business practices could be considered an "illicit commercial practice" within the meaning of the Regulation. One conceivable exception could arise in a situation where the government of a foreign country would seek to achieve through restrictive business practices, which it would engineer, measures which it could itself not lawfully take under international rules, in particular under the GATT, e.g. restricting foreign purchases of natural resources under conditions that would make them equivalent to prohibited export restrictions within the meaning of Article XI of the GATT.

F.   The Injury Requirement

1.   As in antidumping and antisubsidy cases, injury to the EC industry is a requirement that is part and parcel of the actionable conduct. The procedures established by the Regulations are aimed at "responding to any illicit commercial practice with a view to removing the injury resulting therefrom."[63] In order to be admissible a complaint

---

[61] *Contra* Hilf and Rolf, *supra* n. 2, at 302.
[62] For an analysis see J. Temple-Lang, *European Community Antidumping and Competition Law: Their actual and potential application to EFTA countries*, in *Speakers Notes from the Briefing Day on EEC Competition and Dumping Policies* 40–107 (Z. and L. Sundström (ed.) 1987).
[63] Council Regulation No. 2641/84, Art. l(a), O.J. L 252/2 (1984), Common Mkt. Rep. (CCH) ¶ 3845A.

must contain sufficient evidence of the existence of illicit commercial practices and the injury resulting therefrom.

This requirement has been criticized as unduly restrictive at the stage of the complaint; if the purpose was to allay the concerns of certain Member States who objected to the Regulation's protectionist potential, an injury requirement would only have been appropriate at the stage where at the end of the investigation countermeasures are contemplated.[64] This argument is not convincing. In fact, once the policy decision is taken not to take countermeasures against illicit commercial practices, except when they have caused injury to the EC industry, it is appropriate to require that the complaint allege injury and contain sufficient prima facie evidence which can then be investigated after the proceeding is initiated. This policy choice, which was inspired by a similar requirement to which antidumping and antisubsidy action is subject under the GATT, reflects once again the concern to limit in this Regulation the scope of action against illicit commercial practices at the initiative of private parties.

On this point as well the Regulation is to be distinguished from US legislation, which does not require injury as a prerequisite for investigations and as an element of the practice which it seeks to counteract.

2.	The provisions on injury parallel, as far as possible, those of the EC antidumping and antisubsidy rules.[65] It is to be expected that the practice followed and the experience gained under these rules will be used in investigations and for measures under the Regulation.

In one area the practice followed under the antidumping and antisubsidy rules will be of little help: i.e., where the EC alleges it has suffered injury on export markets. Although evidence can, to a large extent, be found in the accounts of the EC industry at their premises within the EC, for verification of evidence by on-the-spot investigations in the foreign country the Commission depends on that country's willingness to accept such investigations. The usual force of the "facts available" rule might not be as strong as in antidumping and antisubsidy cases, where that rule is internationally accepted.[66]

---

[64] Bronckers, *supra* n. 2, at 228.
[65] For certain differences see Denton, *supra* n. 2, at 10–11; Bronckers foresees a series of difficulties (*supra* n. 2, at 229); only experience will tell whether they cannot be overcome.
[66] See *infra* sec. V(B).

3.   In Aramid Fibre into the US the complainant industry was not yet manufacturing the products on a commercial scale. In fact, it was at the time constructing a 5,000 tonne capacity plant which was expected to be on stream in early 1986. It alleged that the ITC exclusion order would cause material injury through direct loss of sales representing 20% of its production capacity of aramid fibres. It added that being excluded from participating in the technological development of aramid applications in the US would cause a set-back to its world-wide sales position and that the exclusion from the US market would have an indirect impact on its sales position in the EC. The Commission noted that this constituted sufficient evidence to justify initiating a proceeding.[67]

In the investigation the Commission found that actual (limited sale) commercial production by Akzo only started in mid-1986 and concluded that there was no present material injury resulting from the ITC exclusion order. However, it found Akzo's arguments of loss of sales to the US and the EC in the period up to 1990 and beyond convincing and concluded there was a threat of injury.[68] Although the Commission could have been more precise in its decision, the US could hardly have contested the Commission decision on this point, as the ITC itself has found that Akzo's imports into the US had "the tendency to substantially injure an industry, efficiently and economically operated, in the United States".[69]

IV.   COMPLAINT BY EC INDUSTRY

A.   The Role of the Complaint

1.   The Regulation provides that an investigation ("Community examination procedure") is initiated by the Commission "where, after consultation, it is apparent that there is sufficient evidence."[70] The Regulation provides further that "any natural or legal person, or any association not having legal personality, acting on behalf of a Community industry. . . may lodge a written complaint".[71] This somewhat oblique

---

[67] Notice of Initiation, O.J. C 25/2 (1986)
[68] O.J. L 117/18, at 20 (1987).
[69] Certain Aramid Fiber, 50 Fed. Reg. 49,776 (1985).
[70] Council Regulation No. 2641/84, Art. 6(1), O.J. L 252/3 (1984), Common Mkt Rep. (CCH) ¶ 3845F.
[71] Council Regulation No. 2641/84, Art. 3(1), O.J. L 252/2 (1984), Common Mkt Rep. (CCH) ¶ 3845C.

wording, taken over from the EC antidumpting and antisubsidy legislation, means that a complaint is not a *conditiosine qua non:* the Commission may also open a proceeding on a request from a Member State or even on its own initiative.

If the practice under the antidumping and antisubsidy legislation is any guide, it is highly unlikely that the Commission will self-initiate proceedings against illicit commercial practices. On the other hand, once a proceeding is set in motion, the withdrawal of a complaint does not lead automatically to termination. The Community interest may require the pursuit of a proceeding.[72]

2.   In the discussions in the Council leading up to the adoption of the Regulation, several Member States opposed the involvement of private parties in procedures concerning trade practices of foreign countries: they considered that because of their very nature, these matters should be left to governments; they argued that allowing private parties to complain would create expectations that the EC would also take measures to redress these parties' grievances; they felt that a litigation-like procedure would involve too many costs and delays; they feared that it would open the gate to a proliferation of proceedings which would affect negatively the general trade climate and set the EC on a collision course with its trading partners.

These arguments may not appear very convincing to American businessmen and lawyers. They sounded very convincing to the opponents of the proposed Regulation. One should bear in mind that making policy through quasi-judicial process is rather unusual in the EC Member States.[73]

There are at least two reasons why, as a matter of legal policy, the inclusion of a right of complaint for the EC industry is to be welcomed. First, business people are in a much better position than officials to know the practical effects of unfair governmental practices. Second, a formalised complaint procedure, together with presentation of views and conduct of hearings in open proceedings, not only channels and publicises the pressures on the EC institutions to take action against illicit practices,

---

[72] Council Regulation No. 2641/84, Art. 3(4), O.J. L 252/3 (1984), Common Mkt. Rep (CCH) ¶ 3845C.

[73] See Bourgeois, *Les relations extérieures de la communauté européenne et le règie de droit: quelques réflexions,* in *Du Droit International Au Droit De L' Intégration* (Liber Amicorum Pierre Pescatore) 59 at 73–74 (1987) (literature cited).

they also encourage business people who are affected by such practices to make their views directly known that there were trade policy measures to be taken.

At this point the Regulation is the result of a compromise between two opposing views. The right of complaint of private parties, which it establishes, is qualified by certain requirements to be fulfilled by the complainant and by the complaint and is limited in its effects by leaving it to the Commission's discretion to act on the complaint.

B.   Standing Requirements

1.   The complaint may be lodged only on behalf of a "Community industry" defined as *all* producers or producers whose combined output constitutes *a major proportion* of total Community production. They must produce products identical or similar to the product which is the subject of illicit practices or products directly competing with that product. Consumers or processors of such products are specifically included in the definition.[74] Traders are not included.

This standing requirement has been carried over with some changes from the EC antidumping and antisubsidy rules, where it reflects the corresponding provision of the 1979 GATT Antidumping Code and the 1979 GATT Subsidies and Countervailing Measures Code. It has been criticised as restraining unduly the use of the instrument.[75]

The inclusion of this requirement is partly due to the Commission, which proposed it to disarm the opponents. It is also consistent with other Community trade legislation. Above all, it avoids opening investigations which have a financial and political cost, when there is no *prima facie* general material interest at stake.[76]

2.   The Regulation does not define further what is meant by "Community producers".

---

[74] Council Regulation No. 2641, Art. 2(4), O.J. L 252/2 (1984), Common Mkt. Rep. (CCH) ¶ 3845B.

[75] Bronckers, *supra* n. 2, at 228-29, who points to incongruities: If only one put of several manufacturers in the EC exports to a given foreign country where it encounters trade restrictions it could not succesfully lodge a complaint. The proper question, however, is whether the other manufacturers could join in a complaint.

[76] When producers operate on an isolated market within the EC, special provisions apply (Council Regulation No. 2641/84, Art. 2(4)(b), O.J. L 252/2 (1984), Common Mkt. Rep. (CCH) ¶ 3845B.

While it appears obvious from the term "Community producers" that the complainants must have manufacturing facilities in the EC for the product concerned, it is an open question how much manufacturing within the EC is required. This question is not academic in view of the ever increasing international division of labour with the attendant phenomenon of out sourcing.[77]

In practice the Commission could rely on the Community interest clause to weigh, on an ad hoc basis, the interests of a complaining industry with minimal industrial activity within the EC against other interests which would be negatively affected by a proceeding. Legal certainty argues in favor of some official guidelines on this point.

C.   Content of the Complaint

1.   A complaint must contain sufficient evidence of the existence of illicit commercial practices and the injury resulting therefrom. Proof of injury must be given on the basis of the factors indicated in the Regulation.[78]

In practice, as in antidumping and antisubsidy cases, the Commission[79] is willing to assist potential complainants on how to draft a complaint and is willing, without taking an active role, to offer some advice. This informal process obviates the need for formal decisions rejecting complaints that do not meet the formal requirements.[80] Commentators assert that it should be enough for the complaint to state in summary form the subject matter of its complaint supported by available evidence.[81] To the extent that on this point the wording of the Regulation reflects the EC antidumping and antisubsidy rules it requires more than that: it must contain sufficient evidence and not only allegations of illicit practices and injury. There is no sanction against frivolous

---

[77] For example, in Photocopiers from Japan, O.J. L 54/87) an antidumping case, it was found that the value added in the EC by one of the complaining undertakings for some of its photocopiers amounted only to 20–35%. It was nonetheless included in the "Community industry" for the purpose of the complaint and the determination of injury. The regulation imposing definitive antidumping duties is under appeal.

[78] Council Regulation No. 2641/84, Art. 3 (2), O.J.L 252/2 (1984), Common Mkt Rep. (CCH) ¶ 3845C.

[79] Directorate General for External Relations, Trade Policy Instruments Division.

[80] This informal process also allows potential complainants to test the waters and contributes to a filtering out of "bad" cases: there is at least one instance in which a complaint concerning restrictive business practices allegedly actively supported by a foreign government was not lodged after the EC industry had sounded out Commission officials.

[81] Hilf and Rolf, *supra n.* 2, at 305.

complaints and there is a need to ensure, as far as possible, that investigations against States are not initiated on ill-founded complaints.

V.   ADMINISTRATIVE PROCEEDING

A.   Initiation

1.   The proceeding is initiated by the Commission after consultation with Member States representatives sitting in an advisory committee. No votes are taken in the committee on the initiation. The Regulation does not require the Commission to inform or to consult the state whose practice is complained of. In *Aramid Fibre into the US* informal consultations were held with the US Administration; the complainant was informed of the Commission's intention to do so and did not object. This practice was also followed in *Soya Meal from Argentina.*

2.   When it decides to initiate a proceeding the Commission must not only rule on the admissibility of the complaint. The Regulation also requires the Commission to consider whether initiating an investigation "is necessary in the interest of the Community".[82]

In antidumping and antisubsidy matters the Commission and the Council are required to consider the Community interest only when, the investigation being terminated, they are contemplating measures. The intention is obviously to grant the Commission the widest possible discretion in deciding whether or not to open a proceeding. The requirements of the complaint and the rules on standing of the complainant are designed to limit the application of the Regulation to cases of substantive importance. This provision on Community interest is designed to allow the Commission to nip in the bud a case which, in its view, would be controversial and too embarassing for the relations with the foreign country in question or which it would be inappropriate to bring before the GATT.[83] Interestingly, in the US the agency in charge of implementing section 301, i.e. USTR, asserts it has discretion to reject 301 petitions on policy grounds alone, irrespective of the merits of the petition.[84]

---

[82] Council Regulation No. 2641/84, Art. 6 (1), O.J. L 252/3 (1984), Common Mkt Rep. (CCH) ¶ 3845F.

[83] See the distinction between "ordinary non-compliance", "inoperative rules" and "wrong cases" made by Hudec, *GATT Dispute Settlement after the Tokyo round: An Unfinished Business,* 13 *Cornell Int'l L. J.* 145 (1980).

[84] J. Archibald, *Section 301 of the Trade Act of 1974,* in *Manual for the Practice of International Trade Law* VII-5 (1984).

As a practical matter it is important, on account of this as well, for a potential complainant to test the waters with the Commission before embarking on a drafting exercise.

3.   A notice of initiation is published in the Official Journal. The Commission also notifies representatives of the country or countries (i.e. their missions in Brussels) which are subject of the investigation. At this stage consultations may be held with them, where appropriate.[85] Although the Regulation does not require it, the Commission also sends a copy of the complaint to the representatives of the country or countries in question.

4.   A decision on the initiation of a proceeding must be taken "as soon as possible", normally within 45 days of referral; this period may be extended to 60 days in special circumstances.

The Commission considers these time limits as being provided for the benefit of complainants, who may thus waive them. In *Aramid Fibres into the U.S.* and in *Soya Meal from Argentina* the complainants agreed to an extension of the time limit beyond the 45 days, respectively 60 days.

B.   **Conduct of the Investigation. The rules of the Regulation on the investigation are practically the same as those of the EC antidumping and antisubsidy legislation. There is no need to elaborate on these rules as they have been described elsewhere.[86] Only two remarks need to be added.**

First, the Regulation contains a "facts available" clause, as do the EC antidumping and antisubsidy rules. It provides that

When the information requested by the Commission is not supplied within a reasonable time or where the investigation is significantly impeded, findings may be made on the basis of the facts available.[87]

---

[85] Council Regulation No. 2641/84, Art. 6 (1), O.J. L 252/3 (1984), Common Mkt. Rep. (CCH) ¶ 3845F.
[86] Beseler & Williams, Davey, *supra* n. 8. See, also, Van Bael and Bellis, *supra* n. 2.
[87] Council Regulation No. 2641/84, Art. 6 (7), O.J. L 252/4 (1984), Common Mkt Rep. (CCH) ¶ 3845F.

For antidumping and antisubsidy matters the EC can rely for such a clause on internationally accepted rules.[88] To the extent that, contrary to antidumping measures, action will only be taken under the Regulation against a foreign country following consultation with that country or even dispute settlement procedures, this "facts available" clause does not appear to be inconsistent with international law as it stands.

Second, the Regulation distinguishes between "parties concerned" and "parties primarily concerned".[89] From the rule that "parties concerned" have a right to be heard only when they make a written request for a hearing showing that they are a "party primarily concerned by the result of the procedure",[90] it may be inferred that any party showing an interest may make written submissions. Other procedural rights, such as the right to inspect the information made available to the Commission[91] and the right to disclosure,[92] are expressly limited to the complainants, exporters, importers and representatives of the foreign country concerned.

2.   The investigation is to be concluded normally within five months following the initiation; the Commission may extend the period to seven months in view of the complexity of the investigation.[93] In *Aramid Fibre into the U.S.* the proper investigation lasted ten months, and in *Unauthorized Reproduction of Sound Recordings in Indonesia* the whole proceeding was terminated after less than one year.

3.   The proceeding itself must be terminated when it is found that the interests of the Community do not require any action to be taken.[94]

---

[88] Agreement on Implementation of Article VI of the General Agreement on Tariffs and Trade, Art. 6, para. 8, O.J. L 71/90 (1980) (GATT Antidumping Code); Agreement on Interpretation and Application of Articles VI, XVI and XXIII of the General Agreement on Tariffs and Trade, Art. 2, para. 9, O.J. L 71/72 (1980) (GATT code on Subsidies and Countervailing Measures).

[89] Council Regulation No. 2641/84, Art. 6 (5) and (6), O.J. L 252/4 (1984), Common Mkt. Rep. (CCH) ¶ 3845F. The terminology is not consistent: Art. 6, 1 (a) refers to "interested parties".

[90] Council Regulation No. 2641/84, Art. 6 (5), O.J. L 252/4 (1984), Common Mkt. Rep. (CCH) ¶ 3845F.

[91] Council Regulation No. 2641/84, Art. 6 (4) (a), O.J. L 252/3 (1984), Common Mkt Rep. (CCH) ¶ 3845F.

[92] Council Regulation No. 2641/84, Art. 6 (4) (b), O.J. L 252/4 (1984), Common Mkt Rep. (CCH) ¶ 3845F.

[93] Regulation No. 2641/84, Art. 6 (9), O.J. L 252/4 (1984), Common Mkt Rep. (CCH) ¶ 3845F.

[94] Council Regulation No. 2641/84, Art. 9 (1), O.J. L 252/5 (1984), Common Mkt Rep. (CCH) ¶ 3845J.

Although the Regulation does not say so, reasons of legal certainty, even international comity, require that the proceeding be also formally terminated when, following the investigation, no "illicit commercial practice" or no injury resulting therefrom is found. The proceeding may also be terminated, when, following the investigation, the foreign country "takes measures which are considered satisfactory".[95] This course of action was followed in *Unauthorized Reproduction of Sound Recordings in Indonesia.*[96]

In other situations, i.e., pending international consultations of disputes settlements or as long as countermeasures apply, the proceeding remains presumably open, since the Regulation does not expressly provide for termination in such cases. There are good reasons for this in both these situations. In the former situation, international consultations and dispute settlement are part of the proceeding. In the latter situation, it makes sense to avoid a formal reopening in the event it would appear that countermeasures taken do not remove the injury.[97]

The Regulation does not expressly require that the decision to terminate a proceeding be published. As at any rate there is an implicit but clear duty for the Commission to inform the foreign country concerned and the other "parties primarily concerned," there are no apparent reasons why the decision should not be published.

VI.   INTERNATIONAL CONSULTATION AND DISPUTE SETTLEMENT

The regulation provides that "where the Community's international obligations require the prior discharge of an international procedure for consultation or for the settlement of disputes," measures against trade practices may only be decided on "after that procedure has been terminated, and taking account of the results of the procedure".[98]

---

[95] The Regulation itself deviates from this rule, as it provides that measures may be taken under certain conditions after termination of a proceeding without prescribing the initiation of a new proceeding. Council Regulation No. 2641/84, Art. 9 (2)(c), O.J. L 252/5 (1984), Common Mkt. Rep. (CCH) ¶ 3845J.

[96] Commission decision of 11 May 1988, O.J. L 123/51 (1988)

[97] This solution is expressly provided for by the EC antidumping and antisubsidy legislation. Council Regulation No. 2423/88, Art. 7 (9)(b), *supra* n. 8.

[98] Coucil Regulation No. 2641/84, Art. 10 (2), O.J. L 252/5 (1984), Common Mkt. Rep. (CCH) ¶ 3845K.

This provision calls for three brief remarks.

First, the Regulation refers to international obligations that "require" the prior discharge of an international procedure for consultation or for settlement of disputes. Strictly speaking, whether the EC has an international obligation to follow such a procedure is not important.[99] What is meant is that where no measures may lawfully be taken under international law unless there is a prior recourse to such procedures, the Regulation subjects the adoption of measures to this requirement. Although this view does not seem to be shared by some GATT contracting parties, the EC considers that the very existence of the Article XXIII GATT "nullification and impairment" procedure (which provides that the GATT as an organization may authorize the complaining contracting party to take countermeasures) normally precludes the offended party from taking countermeasures on its own, be they reciprocal action or genuine reprisals.[100] In this connection it is noteworthy that in contrast to US legislation, the Regulation does not impose time limits for decisions to take trade policy measures.

For matters not covered by the GATT, e.g. for matters falling under other multilateral agreements or bilateral EC agreements that do not contain any mandatory consultation, conciliation or dispute settlement procedure, the position is different. In such cases the EC could take countermeasures without having recourse to international consultation or dispute settlement procedures.

Second, does the requirement that countermeasures may be taken only when such international procedures are terminated really mean what it says? In the event that, e.g. a dispute settlement proceeding under the GATT or under one of the 1979 Tokyo Round codes is not terminated because the respondent party blocks the adoption of a Panel report, does Article 10(2) of the Regulation imply that the Council would not take any measure? Presumably not, since another provision of the Regulation states that this Regulation "shall be without prejudice to other measures which may be taken pursuant to Article 113 of the Treaty".[101]

---

[99] Hilf and Rolf, *supra* n. 2, at 307.

[100] *Contra*, Zoller, *supra* n. 2, at 240, who relies on general international law and does not mention Art. XXIII of GATT. For a description of this procedure, see E. Mc Govern, *supra* n. 50 at 36 *et seq.* See also E. U. Petersmann, *International and European Foreign Trade Law: GATT Dispute Settlement Proceedings Against the EEC,* 22 *Common Mkt L. Rev.* 441 (1985).

[101] Council Regulation No. 2641/84, Art. 13, O.J. L 252/6 (1984), Common Mkt Rep. (CCH) ¶ 3845N.

Whether measures taken outside of the GATT procedures, in particular the Article XXIII "nullification and impairment" procedure, are to be considered as a breach of GATT is debatable. They raise the issue whether a malfunctioning of the GATT dispute settlement machinery entitles a contracting party to act independently to protect its interests.

Third, such international procedures are only initiated if this is considered to be in the Community interest.[102] This makes clear again that EC action under the Regulation is in the public interest. Even if the complainant has established his "interest to sue"[103] the EC may choose not to pursue the matter or it may pursue the matter partly or from a different angle. Conversely even if the complainant withdraws his complaint, the Commission may continue proceedings in the Community interest.[104]

In *Aramid Fibres into the U.S.* in its decision to initiate GATT dispute settlement proceedings, the Commission explained what elements of the findings resulting from its investigation it considered relevant with respect to "Community interest." After having noted that the previous GATT findings in *Spring Assemblies* did not deal with the question of the compatibility of section 337 with Article III of the GATT, it stated

In view of the foregoing and the past criticisms raised by the Community against certain aspects of Section 337, the Commission considers that it is in the Community interest to initiate international consultation and dispute settlement procedures with a view to achieving the alignment of United States legislation with its international obligation.[105]

Pending the GATT dispute settlement procedure, Akzo and Dupont have agreed to terminate the various civil litigations pending between them. Akzo apparently did not agree to withdraw its complaint under the Regulation. It did at any rate not withdraw it. Even if Akzo had done so, in view of the reasons for which it decided to take the matter up in the GATT, the Commission would not have terminated the proceedings.

---

[102] Council Regulation No. 2641/84, Art. 10(1), O.J. L 252/5 (1984), Common Mkt Rep. (CCH) ¶ 3845K.

[103] Bronckers, *supra* n. 2, at 234.

[104] Council Regulation No. 2641/84, Art. 3(4), O.J. L 252/3 (1984), Common Mkt Rep. (CCH) ¶ 3845C.

[105] O.J. L 117/18, at 20 (1987).

VII. TRADE POLICY REMEDIES

A. "Commercial Policy Measures"

The Regulation provides that "any commercial policy measures may be taken, which are compatible with existing international obligations and procedures" and goes on to list as examples ("notably"):

a) suspension or withdrawal of any concession resulting from commercial policy negotiations;

b) the raising of existing customs duties or the introduction of any other charge on imports;

c) the introduction of quantitative restrictions or any other measures modifying import or export conditions or other wise affecting trade with the third country concerned.[106]

The Regulation does not break new ground: the measures mentioned are measures that the Council is at any rate empowered to take acting under Article 113 EEC. The Regulation's declaratory character on this point is confirmed by another provision stating that the Regulation is without prejudice to other measures which may be taken pursuant to Article 113 EEC.[107]

The EC's potential choice of "commercial policy measures" depends in the end on the interpretation of "commercial policy" within the meaning of Article 113 EEC. As indicated earlier[108] the reach of the EC's powers under Article 113 currently is and will, for some time to come, still be a matter for debate. For the time being it seems, however, safe to predict that, if measures were to be taken, they would be restricted to trade in goods.

B. Aims of Trade Policy Measures

The Regulation makes clear that the aim of possible trade policy measures is to remove the injury resulting from the "illicit commercial practice".[109]

---

[106] Council Regulation No. 2641/84, Article 10(3), O.J. L 252/5 (1984), Common Mkt Rep. (CCH) ¶ 3845K.

[107] Council Regulation No. 2641/84, Article 13, O.J. L. 252/6 (1984), Common Mkt Rep. (CCH) ¶ 3845N.

[108] *Supra* sec. III (C).

[109] Council Regulation No. 2641/84, Article 10(1), O.J. L. 252/5 (1984), Common Mkt Rep. (CCH) ¶ 3845K.

Injury can be removed in a number of ways. Under the EC antidumping and antisubsidy rules this is done by offsetting the foreign producers/exporters' price advantage on the EC market by import duties or by "undertakings" of these producers/exporters or the foreign country concerned to raise the price of exports to the EC or even to cease exports.

As "illicit commercial practices" may also affect EC interests on third country markets or have effects on the EC markets that cannot be readily remedied by raising the prices of imports into the EC, trade policy measures could also be taken with the aim of persuading the foreign country to cease the "illicit commercial practice," i.e. to remove the cause of the injury to the complaining industry. *Unauthorized Reproduction of Sound Recordings in Indonesia*[110] offers a good example. The alleged injury was suffered by the complaining industry in Indonesia (and on third country markets); any trade policy measures against Indonesia would have had to be aimed at persuading it to remove the "illicit commercial practice" itself.

However, even though the trade policy measures may not remove directly the injury suffered by the EC industry, e.g., by raising the price or limiting the imports of the similar or directly competing product that benefits from the "illicit commercial practice" in the exporting country, the trade policy measures may only be taken under the Regulation with a view to remove that practice. As any other measure taken by the EC, it is subject to the principle of proportionality. This implies inter alia that as stated in the preamble to the Regulation, the aim is to "maintain the balance of rights and obligations which it is the purpose of agreements to establish" and trade policy measures under the Regulation should not go beyond this aim.

C.   Substantive International Law Constraints[111]

1.   The trade policy measures that may be taken pursuant to the Regulation must be "compatible with existing international obligations"[112] and the procedures established by the Regulation are overall "subject to compliance with existing international obligations".[113]

---

[110] Notice of initiation O.J. C 136/3 (1987).
[111] For international procedural constraint, see *supra* sec. VI.
[112] Council Regulation No. 2641/84, Article 10(3), O.J. L 252/5 (1984), Common Mkt Rep. (CCH) ¶ 3845K.
[113] Council Regulation No. 2641/84, Article 1, O.J L 252/2 (1984), Common Mkt Rep. (CCH) ¶ 3845A.

One may wonder whether the reference to the EC's international obligations is legally necessary. Since the EC adheres to monism, compliance with international obligations does not depend on a legal act incorporating international obligations in the EC legal system.[114] By referring to these obligations the Regulation expresses or confirms that compliance with them is a legal requirement of EC law itself. From a political point of view, by restraining the scope of action under the Regulation, these express references to international obligations were one of the elements of the compromise on which a qualified majority in the Council for the adoption of the Regulation rested. They were also a way of signalling to the EC's trading partners that, by adopting this Regulation, the EC intended not to depart from these obligations but to reinforce the international rule of law. The question is then what international law constraints there are.

2. This requirement raises some interpretative questions.

A first question is whether, as one commentator suggests,[115] it would limit the EC enforcement to either retorsion or reciprocal action, which do not entail the coercive component that is essential in enforcement matters.

However, measures designed to persuade the foreign country to cease an "illicit commercial practice", assuming that they can be qualified as "reprisals", rather than as retorsions, would presumably not be incompatible with the EC's international obligations. General international law does not prohibit economic coercion and it is only unlawful when prohibited by international agreements.[116] Even the principle of non-intervention in the internal affairs of another state, as expressed in Article 2 of the UN Charter, is not recognized as a customary-law principle prohibiting economic coercion.[117]

A second question then is, whether international agreements, if any, would prohibit or condition recourse by the EC to any of the measures

---

[114] See, e.g., VerLoren van Themaat, *The Impact of the Case Law of the Court of Justice of the European Communities on the World Economic Order*, 82 Mich. L. Rev. 1422 (1984).

[115] Zoller, *supra* n. 2, at 239.

[116] Carreau, *La contrainte économique en droit international*, 1 Rev. Int'l Dr. Econ. 445-75, 462 (1987).

[117] In the case concerning *Military and Paramilitary Activities in and Against Nicaragua*, 1986 I.C.J. 14, the International Court of Justice referred to the suspension of US economic aid to Nicaragua and to the US trade embargo on Nicaraguan products. It stated "that it is unable to regard such action on the economic plane as is here complained of as a breach of the customary-law principle of non-intervention". *Id.* at 126, para. 245.

contemplated by the Regulation. Apart from the various bilateral trade agreements entered into by the EC, the GATT is especially relevant.

Both these bilateral agreements and the GATT contain clauses that prohibit most of the trade policy measures contemplated by the Regulation. These bilateral agreements and the GATT contain a series of escape clauses, but there are doubts whether all of the situations envisaged by the Regulation would be covered by these clauses.

Does this mean that, if and when a situation would arise that is not covered by one of the escape clauses, the various EC bilateral agreements and the GATT are to be interpreted as prohibiting or limiting the right to act against "illicit commercial practices" which the EC has under general international law?

In that event, two hypotheses may occur. The first one is where the "illicit commercial practice" complained of is in breach of the GATT or any of the EC bilateral agreements; in that case recourse should be had to the relevant clauses of these agreements. They contain consultation and/or dispute settlement procedures (supra section VI) and the Regulation provides that trade policy measures may only be decided on "after that procedure has been terminated and taking account of the results of the procedure."[118] The second one is where the "illicit commercial practice" is in breach of other international laws or of "generally accepted principles". Arguably in that case the EC could fall back on general international law and claim the right to take action deviating from GATT or the EC bilateral agreements.

A third question is with whose international obligations trade policy measures must be compatible: only the EC's or also the Member States'? The question is justified since other provisions refer expressly to the Community's international obligations.

However one should interpret the Regulation on this point, there is at any rate under the EEC Treaty itself a general obligation on the part of the EC institutions not to impede the performance of obligations of Member States which stem from a prior international agreement.[119] A potential conflict between Member States' international obligations and

---

[118] Council Regulation No. 2641/84, Article 10(2), O.J. 252/5 (1984), Common Mkt Rep. (CCH) ¶ 3845K.
[119] Attorney General *v.* Burgoa, Case 812/79, 1980 E.C.R. 2787, 2803, ¶ 9, Common Mkt Rep. (CCH) ¶ 8698.

measures taken pursuant to the Regulation appears unlikely as long as such measures will be limited to trade in goods, since there is no room left for independent Member State action in the field of trade policy.

VIII. DECISION-MAKING

A. Introduction

In line with its reaction to the French Memorandum,[120] the Commission sought in its proposal to devise a decision-making procedure that would allow the EC to react swiftly and efficiently. Apart from a "critical circumstances" provision which would have allowed the Commission to take immediate provisional action, it proposed special decision-making machinery: termination of proceedings with or without "undertakings" from the foreign country concerned and commercial policy measures would be decided upon by the Commission with the possibility for a Member State to refer the decision to the Council.[121]

These aspects of the Commission proposal were supported with minor reservations by the European Parliament and the Social and Economic Committee but were predictably among the difficult points of the discussions in the Council. The opposition in the Council resulted from a combination of the traditional tension between the Commission in favour of institutional progress and some Member States which are reluctant to abandon the control they have if matters remain within the Council and the concerns of some of the more liberal Member States which viewed the whole proposal as a dangerous exercise in protectionism.

In order to find a qualified majority in the Council, the Commission had to abandon the "critical circumstances" provision and propose other amendments which shifted the balance more towards the Council.

B. Initiation of a Proceeding and Conduct of an Investigation

1. The assessment of a complaint and the decision to initiate a proceeding are entrusted to the Commission. Before it decides to initiate a proceeding, the Commission is required to consult an advisory

---

[120] *Supra* n. 13.
[121] Commission proposal Article 13. O.J. C 83/6 (1983).

committee, set up by the Regulation, consisting of representatives of each Member State, with a representative of the Commission as chairman.[122] Where necessary, such consultation may be in writing.[123]

The Member States express, through their representatives on the Committee, their opinions on the complaint and on the course of action which the Commission intends to take. No vote is taken. The Commission is not bound by the opinions expressed. The Commission, however, attaches importance to views expressed on behalf of Member States at such advisory committees. Pursuant to internal Commission instructions, these advisory committees must be chaired by a senior Commission official and any draft decision submitted to the Commission, following such consultation, must be accompanied by a report summarising Member States' opinions expressed at such advisory committees.

2.   The conduct of the investigation is also entrusted to the Commission. It carries out this investigation without participation of the Member States, except that it may require their cooperation,[124] and that a Member State, on whose territory checks are carried out, may request that the Commission be assisted by officials of that Member State.[125] The Commission is required to report to the Committee when it has terminated its investigation.[126]

C.   International Consultations and Dispute Settlement Proceedings

Under the Regulation "decisions relating to the initiation, conduct or termination" of international consultation or dispute settlement procedures are taken in accordance with a special decision-making procedure. Under this decision-making procedure, the Commission submits a draft decision to the committee consisting of Member States representatives; after discussions at that committee the Commission

---

[122] Council Regulation No. 2641/84, Article 6, O.J. L 252/3 (1984), Common Mkt Rep. (CCH) ¶ 3845F.
[123] Council Regulation No. 2641/84, Article 5(4), O.J. L 252/3 (1984), Common Mkt Rep. (CCH) ¶ 3845E.
[124] Council Regulation No. 2641/84, Article 6 (1) (c), O.J. L 252/3 (1984), Common Mkt Rep. (CCH) ¶ 3845F.
[125] Council Regulation No. 2641/84, Article 6 (2) (c), O.J. L 252/3 (1984), Common Mkt Rep. (CCH) ¶ 3845F.
[126] Council Regulation No. 2641/84, Article 6 (9), O.J. L 252/4 (1984), Common Mkt Rep. (CCH) ¶ 3845F.

adopts a decision; this decision becomes effective after a period of ten days, if no Member State has referred the matter to Council in the meantime; in the event of the matter being referred to the Council, the Commission decision becomes effective after a period of 30 days, if the Council, acting by qualified majority, has not given a ruling within this period.[127]

The fact that the Commission and the Commission alone is thus deciding on international consultations and dispute settlement concerning "illicit commercial practices" unless the Council acts quickly to the contrary is a significant departure from the usual rather murky and not always expeditious way[128] in which such decisions are otherwise taken: although arguably under the EEC Treaty this should be a matter for the Commission acting alone, the practice has developed to discuss these matters in a Council body consisting of Member States' officials, called the 113 Committee, until some sort of consensus is reached, without formal decisions being taken.

D. Termination of Proceedings

The same special decision-making procedure applies for the decision to terminate proceedings. This is also the case where proceedings are terminated when the foreign country concerned takes "measures which are considered satisfactory".

On this point, the drafting of the Regulation reflects some of the difficult discussions which led to its adoption. Some Member States, which are opposed as a matter of principle to any sort of "voluntary" commitments made by foreign countries with respect to international trade, were reluctant to leave this in the hands of the Commission[129] They and others were of the view that accepting commitments made by foreign countries is tantamount to concluding trade agreements, a matter which under the EEC Treaty is reserved to the Council and may not be delegated to the Commission.[130]

---

[127] Council Regulation No. 2641/84, Article 12, O.J. L 252/6 (1984), Common Mkt Rep. (CCH) ¶ 3845M.

[128] See Hilf and Rolf, *supra* n. 2, at 307.

[129] Yet under the EC antisubsidy rules, proceedings may be terminated after acceptance of a satisfactory "undertaking" from the Foreign country concerned.

[130] This view is apparently not shared by the Court: in *Dürbeck* it is accepted that it was compatible with the principle of proportionality for the Commission to attempt to secure the agreement of exporting countries to a voluntary restriction of their exports before resorting to coercive measures. *Durbeck v. Hauptzollant Frankfurt am Main-Flughafen*, Case 112/80, 1981 E.C.R. 1095, ¶ 39, Common Mkt Rep. (CCH) ¶ 8753. It should be noted that
Continues

Yet an analysis of the rather complicated structure of the Regulation shows that it also leaves it to the Commission to terminate proceedings in this case. Article 9 (2) (a) refers to Article 11, rather than to Article 12 directly, since Article 9 (2) (a) concerns not only "illicit commercial practices" but also "the exercise of the Community's rights". Article 11, to which Article 9 (2) (a) refers, deals with these two different matters and refers in turn to Article 12 for consultations and dispute settlement procedures, while it reserves to the Council the right to take measures of commercial policy, i.e. the sort of measures contemplated by Article 10.

In *Unauthorised Reproduction of Sound Recordings in Indonesia*, the decision to terminate the proceeding in view of certain commitments entered into by Indonesia was taken by the Commission in accordance with the special decision-making procedure.[131] No Member State referred the matter to the Council.

E.   Adoption of Trade Policy Measures

Commercial policy measures, within the meaning of Article 10, are adopted by the Council acting on a proposal from the Commission by qualified majority. The only trace of the Commission's attempts to come to a more expeditious decision-making process on this point also is a time limit. The Council must "act . . . not later than 30 days after receiving the proposal" from the Commission.[132] By "act" the Regulation means that the Council must decide within that time limit, presumably by taking a vote.

Although the Council is presumably prevented by *patere legem quam ipse fecisti* from setting a different time limit on an ad hoc basis, it is not clear what the sanction is when the Council does not respect this time limit.[133]

...under the EC antisubsidy rules, accepting "undertaking" from a foreign country is, subject to certain procedural rules, a matter left to the Commission.

[131] O.J. L 123/51 (1988).

[132] Council Regulation No. 2641/84, Article 11 (2) (b), O.J. L 252/6 (1984), Common Mkt Rep. (CCH) 3845L.

[133] Steenbergen *supra* n. 2, at 432; *accord,* Hilf and Rolf, *supra* n. 2, at 308, who do, however, not exclude an application for "failure to act" under Article 175 EEC.

IX.   JUDICIAL REVIEW

A.   Introduction

The Regulation does not contain provisions relating to judicial protection of the complainant, the foreign country concerned or other "parties concerned". This means that the general rules on judicial review apply. The subject of judicial review of EC trade policy measures has been aptly treated elsewhere.[134] Suffice it to recall that with respect to access to judicial review under the EC legal system the limitations of direct appeal by private parties before the Court of Justice are to a certain extent compensated by the possibility of appeal before courts in Member States; whenever EC trade policy measures are effectively applied by authorities in Member States, the administrative acts of these authorities can be appealed against in Member States' courts which may and, as the case may be, are required to submit questions on the interpretation and on the validity of such trade policy measures to the Court of Justice for a preliminary ruling.[135]

B.   Initiation of a Proceeding

Although there is no judgment of the Court on this point yet, either under the Regulation or under the EC antidumping and antisubsidy rules, it seems safe to predict that the Court would declare an appeal against a Commission decision initiating a proceeding inadmissible.

Under the EC competition rules, whose administrative procedures are comparable to those of the Regulation, it is well established case-law that an action seeking the annulment of the initiation of a proceeding is inadmissible. In *IBM*, recalling its case-law, the Court stated that, in the case of acts or decisions adopted by a procedure involving several stages, an act is open to review only if it is a measure definitively laying down the position of the Commission or the Council on the conclusion of that procedure and not a provisional measure intended to pave the way for

---

[134] J. Temple Lang, *Judicial Review of Trade Safeguard Measures in the European Community*, in 1984 *Fordham Corp. L. Inst.* 641 (B. Hawk (ed.) 1985). See also P. J. Kuyper, *Some Reflections on the Legal Position of the Private Complainant on Various Procedures Relating to Commercial Policy*, [1983] L.I.E.I. 115–29

[135] See, *e.g.* Dürbeck, 1981 E.C.R. 1095, Common Mkt. Rep. (CCH) ¶ 8753 (on the validity of safeguard measures restricting imports of apples); *Celestri v. Ministry of Finance*, Case 172/84, 1985 E.C.R. 963 (on the validity of an antidumping duty).

the final decision; such preparatory acts may be relied upon in an action directed against the definitive act for which they represent a preparatory step.[136]

C. Refusal to Initiate a Proceeding

As indicated above, the issue whether a compainant may challenge the Commission's refusal to initiate a proceeding is currently *sub judice in Soya Meal from Argentina*.[137]

Contrary to the EC antidumping and antisubsidy rules, the Regulation contains an express provision requiring the Commission to verify whether the Community interest calls for initiating a proceeding. Even where the complaint contains sufficient *prima facie* evidence, the Commission may lawfully refuse to initiate a proceeding on the ground that this would not be in the Community interest. The question is still debated whether such a policy decision is open to judicial review. The Community interest requirement for the initiation of a proceeding could also be significant for the legal position of the complainant in general.

In *Fediol I* the Court held that complainants have the right to bring an action against a Commission decision refusing to initiate an antisubsidy proceeding "within the framework of the legal status which the regulation confers upon them", i.e. to defend "a legitimate interest in the initiation of protective action by the Community" as recognized in the EC antisubsidy (and antidumping) rules.[138] It seems that the Court attached importance to the fact that in antidumping and antisubsidy matters the Commission and the Council are required to consider the Community interest only at the end of the investigation when contemplating measures. If this is so, then it could be said that in *Fediol I* the Court held an appeal against a refusal to initiate an antisubsidy proceeding admissible precisely because it construed the EC antidumping and antisubsidy rules as granting to a compliant a *right* to an investigation.[139] It could be argued that there is no such rationale in "illicit

---

[136] *IBM v. Commission*, Case 60/81, 1981 E.C.R. 2639, 10, Common Mkt. Rep. (CCH) ¶ 8708.
[137] O.J. C 96/8 (1987).
[138] *Fediol v. Commission*, Case 191/82, 1983 E.C.R. 2913, ¶ 31, Common Mkt. Rep. (CCH) ¶ 14,013. For a comment, see Bellis, *Judicial Review of EEC Anti-Dumping and Anti-Subsidy Determinations after FEDIOL: The Emergence of a New Admissibility Test*, 21 Common Mkt. L. Rev. 539 (1984).
[139] Hilf and Rolf, *supra* n. 2, at 309, do not consider it as a judicially enforceable right as the decision to open a proceeding is not a "decision addressed to" the complainant. *Contra* Kuyper, *supra* n. 134, at 128.

commercial practices" cases: by expressly referring to the Community interest as a requirement for the initiation of proceedings in these cases, the EC's "legislative branch" excluded precisely a right to an investigation.[140]

Assuming that an appeal by a complainant against a refusal to initiate a proceeding under the Regulation would be admissible, it would not seem that the judicial protection would be of much help to the complainant. As a result of a Court judgment the Commission could be bound to reexamine the complaint if it had infringed the complainant's procedural rights or if it had erred in fact or in law, but it could not be compelled to initiate an investigation if it considered this not to be in the Community interest.

D.   Termination of a Proceeding

Technically a decision to terminate a proceeding is not a "decision addressed to" to any of the parties concerned within the meaning of Article 173 EEC. However, in the light of the Court's case law it would seem that an appeal against a decision to terminate a proceeding by parties to such proceeding is not excluded.

Normally such an appeal would only be brought by a complainant. As *Fediol I*[141] and *Timex*[142] derived a right to bring an action from the specific right of complaint introduced by the EC antidumping and antisubsidy rules, likewise under the Regulation complainants probably have a right of appeal to vindicate "rights which have been recognized specifically"[143] in the Regulation. Once the Commission has recognized a Community interest and has initiated a proceeding, it would seem that a complainant has at least the same *procedural* rights as those recognized in *Fediol I* and *Timex*.

---

[140] According to Hilf and Rolf, *supra* n. 2, at 309, this was apparently done on purpose ("*offenbar bewusst*") as a reaction to the *Fediol I* case.

[141] *Supra* n. 138.

[142] *Timex v. Council and Commission*, Case 264/82, 1985 E.C.R. 849, Common Mkt Rep. (CCH) ¶ 14,143.

[143] This *Fediol I* formula has been extended further in *Cofaz v. Commission*, Case 169/84, 1986 E.C.R. 391, Common Mkt. Rep. (CCH) ¶ 14,284, where, even in the absence of a right of complaint, a party that had been substantially involved in a Commission administrative proceeding on state aids under Article 93 EEC, was found to have a right to appeal against the Commission decision terminating such proceeding; this right of appeal is qualified by the requirement that the applicant's "position on the market is significantly affected by the aid which is the subject of contested decision." *Cofaz*, 1986 E.C.R. at 415, ¶ 25, Common Mkt Rep. (CCH) ¶ 14,284 at 16,763.

In *Fediol I* and *Timex* the Court not only recognized *procedural* rights under administrative proceedings, i.e. a complainant must be able to vindicate by a right of action in the Court, but the Court also recognized complainant's right to challenge decisions on trade policy measures on their merits. As stated in *Timex:*

> the applicant is therefore entitled to put before the Court any matters which would facilitate a review. . . whether or not [the Commission] has committed manifest errors in its assessment of the facts, has ommitted to take any essential matters into consideration or has based the reasons for its decision on considerations amounting to a misuse of powers.[144]

It would appear that not even the Commission's discretion in assessing the Community interest in terminating a proceeding would be completely immune from judicial review.

In *Fediol II*, involving a Commission decision terminating antisubsidy proceedings against Argentina and Brazil, the Court reiterated its stance on the scope of judicial control explained in *Fediol I*. It stated that the applicant's claims, inter alia, relating to the Community interest, should be examined in that framework. As to the merits, the Court referred to the Commission's finding that, since the Brazilian government during the reference period had withdrawn almost entirely the amount of the subsidy complained of, the Community interest did not call for protective measures. The Court held that this appraisal did not exceed the powers conferred on the Commission and could not be considered as being based on considerations amounting to a misuse of powers.[145]

One open question, which may also arise in antidumping and antisubsidy proceedings, is whether a "party concerned" could successfully bring an action for "failure to act" under Article 175 EEC in the event that the Commission would not take any action.

E.   International Consultation and Dispute Settlement

The decision to initiate an "international procedure for consultation or for settlement of disputes"[146] is a preparatory measure,

---

[144] *Timex*, 1985 E.C.R. at 866, ¶ 16, Common Mkt. Rep. (CCH) ¶ 14,143 at 15,782.
[145] Quoting from the French text of *Fediol v. Commission*, judgment of 14 July 1988.
[146] Council Regulation No. 2641/84, Art. 10 (2), O.J.L 252/5 (1984), Common Mkt Rep. (CCH) ¶ 3845K.

not a final decision concluding the proceeding. Like the decision to initiate a proceeding, it is not as such open to review.

In theory, any defects in such a decision may be relied upon in an action directed against either the subsequent decision terminating the proceeding or the decision on trade policy measures. For the purposes of the decision to initiate such international procedures as well the Regulation require the Commission to weigh the Community interest.[147]

Supposing that an appeal against a subsequent decision to terminate the proceeding or against trade policy measures would be admissible, would an applicant have the right to question either the Commission decision to initiate international procedures or the way in which it conducted these procedures? This is disputed. On the one hand, one could accept the principle that the citizen has a right to ensure that the Commission properly uses its discretionary power in this respect;[148] on the other hand, one could argue that once the EC has espoused the complainant's claim, it has become the EC's claim and the EC is free to negotiate about it and, if necessary, to drop it, in whole or in part, without the complainant having any legal remedy whatsoever.[149]

The Court has considered that even the appraisal of the Community interest in antidumping and antisubsidy proceedings is open to judicial review.[150] To extend this to the decision to initiate international consultation and dispute settlement procedures and to the conduct of such procedures does not appear advisable, since it would involve the Court in highly political questions; it does not appear useful since it is hard to see how defects could be remedied.

F.   Trade Policy Measures

The potential range of persons likely to be affected one way or another by trade policy measures is much wider than that found under the antidumping and antisubsidy rules, since the Regulation covers exports as well as imports and covers practices attributable to foreign

---

[147] Council Regulation No. 2641/84, Art. 10(2) juncto (1), O.J. L 252/5 (1984), Common Mkt Rep. (CCH) ¶ 3845K.

[148] "Anspruzh auf ermessensfehlerfreie Entscheidung," Hilf and Rolf *supra* n. 2, at 310.

[149] See Kuyper *supra* n. 134, at 127. *But* see his postcriptum after *Fediol I* at 129; as mentioned sub VII in *Aramid Fibres into the US,* the Commission relied on the Community interest clause and espoused, assuming it did at all, only partly *Akzo's* claim.

[150] Recently, in *Fediol II, supra* n. 145.

countries.[151] Given the multitude and complexity of the situations the following remarks are not intended to cover the whole ground and are no more than tentative.

In addition, one should beware of transposing too readily the case law on antidumping and antisubsidy proceedings to proceedings under the Regulation. The link between the conduct complained of, the measures taken and the applicant appealing against such measures that seems to underlie this case law may not be present in proceedings under the Regulation.[152] Subject to these reservations, the following can be said.

1.   *Complaint*–From *Timex*[153] it may be inferred that the complainant in the administrative proceeding would have a right of action allowing him not only to vindicate his procedural rights but would also be entitled to a review on such questions as whether or not in adopting trade policy measures the Council "has committed manifest errors in its assessment of the fact, has omitted to take essential matters into consideration or has based the reasons for its decision on considerations amounting to a misuse of powers." *Fediol II*[154] confirms that even the appraisal of the Community interest is open to review.

2.   *Foreign Country Concerned*–Normally when adopting trade policy measures contemplated by the Regulation, the Council would have recourse to one of the measures cited by the Regulation. Persons that could be "directly and individually concerned" by such measures are the subjects of the foreign country concerned (producers, exporters) and importers in the EC. If a foreign state wanted to defend its interests before the Court of Justice, it could presumably only do so by intervening in an appeal brought by a party "directly and individually concerned". In *Chris International Foods* the Court granted Dominica leave to intervene in support of applicants.[155] The question whether a non-member State would itself have standing to bring an application for annulment of an EC trade policy measure has not arisen so far. One commentator considers that, presumably, arguments corresponding to those put forward in *Chris International Foods* could be made to show that they have.[156] If, however, the Commission had notified the non-Member State of the initiation of a

---

[151] Denton, *supra* n. 2, at 24.

[152] See also Temple-Lang, *supra* n. 134, at 648–49.

[153] *Supra* N. 5 142.

[154] *Supra* n. 145

[155] Chris International Foods v. Commission, Joined Cases 91 and 200/82, 1983 E.C.R. 417, 419.

[156] Temple-Lang, *supra* n. 134, at 661.

proceeding under the Regulation and that State had failed to participate in the investigation, the Council would probably argue that the appeal is inadmissible.

    3. Producers and Exporters in the Foreign Country–Some commentators consider that the case law on the right of foreign country producers and exporters to bring an action against EC antidumping measures applies to countermeasures taken under the Regulation.[157] It should be added that the Court has so far qualified this right of action in that the actions of applicants must have materially affected the outcome of the procedure leading to the contested measure by providing information, taking part in consultations, producing the goods etc.[158] It is not enough for an undertaking to produce and/or ship the dumped goods to the EC to have a right of action. In *Allied* the Court declared that exporters and producers must be able to establish "that they were identified in the measures adopted by the Commission or the Council or were concerned by the preliminary investigations".[159] "Concerned by" obviously refers to the terminology of the EC antidumping rules and means "directly involved" in the proceeding.[160] To hold otherwise would completely set aside the limits to which the EEC Treaty provisions subject the right of appeal of private parties.

    With respect to producers and exporters of the foreign country, the problem of the link between them, the "illicit commercial practice" of the foreign country (or attributable to it) and the EC trade policy measures would be an important factor on which their right of actions would depend.[161] In the absence of such a link, a situation which is quite conceivable, producers and exporters of the foreign country would not be entitled to lodge an appeal for annulment of the trade policy measures adopted under the Regulation. They would be affected by these measures by reason of the mere fact that they are exporting a product to the EC. This, quite clearly, does not qualify an undertaking to challenge a regulation or another legal act not addressed to it.[162]

---

[157] Hilf and Rolf *supra* n. 2, at 310.
[158] Denton *supra* n. 2, at 26.
[159] *Allied Corporation v. Commission*, Joined Cases 239 and 275/82, 1984 E.C.R. 1005,¶ 12, Common Mkt. Rep. (CCH) ¶ 8869.
[160] Temple-Lang, *supra* n. 134, at 644; *accord* Bellis *supra* N. 138, at 549.
[161] See the hypotheses mentioned by Denton, *supra* n. 2, at 26.
[162] For example, with respect to antidumping measures, Alusuisse v. Council and Commission, Case 307/81, 1982 E.C.R. 3463, ¶ 11, Common Mkt. Rep. (CCH) ¶ 8869

4. Other EC Undertakings–Depending on their nature, trade policy measures may affect a series of EC undertakings other than complainants. In most cases these undertakings will not be able to overcome the hurdle that they are affected by such measures merely because they happen to be importing, buying, selling, processing or consuming the product that is subject to countermeasures. This would not suffice to qualify them to challenge trade policy measures adopted in a regulation or another legal act not addressed to them.[163]

To the extent that it is relevant to measures taken under the Regulation, the case law under the EC antidumping and antisubsidy rules indicates that there may be special circum stances in which such undertakings could bring an appeal against these measures. Here as well, there would at any rate have to be some link between the "illicit commercial practice", the countermeasures and these undertakings. In addition, in this case also, the Council, as a defendant, would probably challenge the admissibility of an appeal by an undertaking that failed to participate in the administrative proceeding.

X.   TENTATIVE ASSESSMENT

The reply to the question raised at the beginning of this paper–is this an exercise in trade policy cosmetics or a genuine attempt at enforcing international law?–can at this stage only be incomplete and provisional. More cases will be needed to resolve some of the outstanding interpretative problems. One should avoid making hasty pronouncements that would be based more on unspoken assumptions and implicit values than on evidence that is up to now insufficient.

It is convenient to make this provisional assessment from a legal, a legal policy and a trade policy perspective.

A.   Legal Perspective

1. The complainant–The position of the complainant might at first blush appear as having more to do with cosmetics than with law enforcement. Even where the complainants manage to clear the hurdle of the standing requirements and convince the Commission that the Community interest calls for initiating a proceeding, they do not have a legally enforceable right to action by the Commission, in the event that

---

[163] See Alusuisse, *supra* n. 162.

the Commission finds an illicit commercial practice and injury to the complainants. Yet once a proceeding is initiated, complainants and "parties concerned" have certain procedural rights that can probably be enforced by the Court. This "procedural due process" should not be underrated: it compels policy makers to listen to and take account of comments made by parties likely to be affected by decisions, over which there is practically no parliamentary control. It is submitted that a reasonable balance is thus achieved. There are indeed sound policy reasons for not going much further. It would not be sensible to create a situation where the Commission or the Council would be legally compelled to take an action that would be favorable to one particular economic sector but could very well be detrimental to wider policy interests. Neither does it appear advisable nor useful to accord to "parties concerned" by proceedings some sort of "substantive due process ". Judicial review over such matters would entail a shift of responsibility from the executive to the judiciary in an area that is normally reserved for the executive and for which the judiciary is ill-equipped.

2. *Enforcement of International Law*–One should bear in mind that when it enacted this Regulation, the Council did not intend to regulate the entire field of the possible EC responses to practices of its trading partners. The administrative procedure and the rules on measures that may be taken in order to enforce international law and generally accepted rules, subject to international obligations and procedures, are there in the event that the EC takes action against illicit commercial practices following a complaint by EC industry. The Council did not say that, where the conditions of this Regulation are not fulfilled, it would not act against practices of its trading partners that affect the EC's interests. Apart from the fact that in the Regulation the Council also indicated how it will act to enforce its rights in other cases, it inserted a "saving clause" stating expressly that the Regulation is without prejudice to other measures which it may take under its trade policy powers. Yet, in setting up this formal machinery to handle alleged breaches of international law or of generally accepted rules, the Council did commit itself to act in that framework in compliance with international rules and procedures.

By expressly including this in a provision of the Regulation, the Council made this into a Community law requirement. This implies that, provided they have locus standi, private parties could as a result of this provision rely on international law to challenge measures taken under the Regulation. The Council could avoid this risk by resting the measures squarely on the "saving clause" stating that the Regulation is without prejudice to other measures, i.e. the provision which makes clear that compliance with international law is not an absolute requirement. While this may be valid under Community law, there may be good political or diplomatic reasons for not taking such a course.

B.　Legal Policy Perspective

The procedural rules established by the Regulation are not cosmetics. The fact that the right of complaint was one of the more contentious elements of the Commission proposal shows that it was not considered by the Council as some political gimmick to appease the business community. In fact, some saw private parties and formal and open procedures in such matters as bulls in a china shop.

It is a piece of "judicialization" of trade policy which is timely and to be welcomed. At a time of considerable interdependency between the EC economy and that of the rest of the world, policy cannot and should not be treated as something quite separate from general economic policy. This implies that the making of trade policy and its implementation should be as open as possible, in line with general economic policy. Appropriate procedures should be followed: (a) that allow those that are affected directly by it to comment; (b) thereby generate and make public as much information as possible on the costs and benefits of trade policy measures, and (c) that imply a duty for policymakers to explain more fully the measures they are taking and the reasons why they are taking them.

In this regard compared to the traditional way in which such matters are treated, the procedures established by the Regulation are, as those under the EC antidumping and antisubsidy rules, a distinct progress. This can be illustrated by comparing *Unauthorized Reproduction of Sound Recordings in Indonesia* and the decision suspending South Korea's benefits from the EC Generalized System of References as a reaction against the discriminatory treatment of EC patentholders.[164] In this latter case there was no investigation and no interested party was given the chance to comment on the measures that were contemplated.

Subjecting both the initiation of proceedings and the opening of dispute settlement proceedings and the adoption of trade policy measures to the express requirement of the Community interest is in the final analysis a wise precaution and does not contradict the "judicialization"

---

[164] Council Regulation No. 3912/87, O.J.L 369/1 (1987).

bearing in mind that findings of the Commission and, as the case may be, of the Council could well be considered by the Court on this point too as being subject to some form of limited judicial review.

C.   Trade Policy Perspective

Some see in the "illicit commercial practices" Regulation a potential protectionist device and a tool to force upon trading partners the EC's own views on how trade should be conducted; they belittle or neglect the reference to the EC's international obligations. Others are skeptical about its value as a trade policy instrument: they view the reference to international obligations and procedures as rendering recourse to the Regulation as virtually meaningless.

If both these criticism are to be believed, in international trade matters one has only the choice between Charybdis and Scylla: having one' interests devoured by one's international obligations or sinking in the whirlpool of arbitrary unilateral action.

However, the straits are not so narrow as to make either of these outcomes inescapable. The evidence there is shows that contrary to the expectations of some, action against illicit commercial practices under the Regulation is not necessarily (another) protectionist device against *imports* into the EC. The case that was settled before a formal complaint was filed and the two proceedings that were initiated so far concern the *export* interests of EC industry; the only complaint that was formally rejected so far concerned imports into the EC.

On the other hand, the action undertaken under the Regulation does not need to reach the international settlement stage to produce results. As shown in one case already,[165] the mere existence of the Regulation, or as shown in *Unauthorized Reproduction of Sound Recordings in Indonesia* the initiation of a proceeding under the Regulation, contribute to solving the problem with which it purports to deal. As further action under the Regulation must comply with international procedures, its effectiveness depends, where the matter is GATT-related, on a proper functioning of the GATT dispute settlement machinery. Against the Council's reference to prior international procedures to act against illicit

---

[165] An Eastern European country stopped selling spirits in a foreign country passing them off as a brand named whisky when a UK producer threatened to file a complaint under the Regulation.

commercial practices, it has been argued that the GATT machinery does not operate satisfactorily. This is undoubtedly correct insofar as this machinery is used to adjudicate disputes. On the other hand, as a system to resolve disputes by negotiation and peer pressure it is rather successful: in fact disputes that are not somehow resolved constitute a minority. The EC has in any event adjusted its policy on recourse to GATT dispute settlement: as from 1986 it started six dispute settlement proceedings against the US, two against Canada and two against Japan. It remains that by subjecting EC action to international procedures as a rule, the Council has given the GATT system a chance. Developments will show whether this was a reasonable chance to take. Assuming that in a given case the GATT dispute settlement machinery works properly and leads to a finding that another contracting party is indeed in breach of its obligations, the reference to international obligation implies further, where a GATT matter is concerned, that normally the EC may only take measures where it has been authorized to do so under Article XXIII GATT. Commentators have been quick to note that up to now there has been only one case in which an "offended" contracting party was authorized to take such retaliatory action against the "offending" contracting party. One should however not too readily conclude that enforcement of the GATT by the GATT does not work. As indicated earlier disputes that are not somehow resolved constitute a minority.

In any event, to the extent that it subjected the EC's action against illicit commercial practices of its trading partners to international law, and in particular where appropriate to GATT, the Council may have engaged either in a "positive sum" or in a "zero sum game": either self-restraint and less efficient and expeditious action will be offset by better bi- or multilateral enforcement of international law to the benefit of all, or it will not, in which case not much damage will be done to the short-term trade interests of the "offending" foreign country but an opportunity to reinforce the rule of law will have been lost. The race is not over yet. Time will tell whether the EC Council bet on the right horse.

13. AN EC PERSPECTIVE
TRADE MEASURES, COMPETITION POLICY
AND THE CONSUMER

The following two contributions concern i.a. the tension between the EC competition and trade policies. The apparent lack of attention to user industries and consumers in EC trade policy decisions has made way nowadays for an analysis of the impact of trade policy measures on these parties. However, when taking measures under either one of these policies, the EC political institutions (the European Commission and, as the case may be, the Council of the European Union) still appear to treat generally these policies as autonomous and separate policies. Where they establish a link between these two policies, it is not readily apparent that they do so thoroughly. A recent example is to be found in a European Commission antidumping regulation on certain graphite electrode systems adopted on 19 May 2004; it rejects an argument about the effect on prices in the EC of the existence and the subsequent end of a cartel.[*] It does refer to a Commission decision under the EC competition rules of 2001 but does not refer to the Commission decision on the electrical and mechanical carbon and graphite cartel of 3 December 2003.[**] The EC courts approach this issue with caution and recycle arguments based on competition policy as being based on trade policy.[***]

---

[*] Regulation (EC) 1009/2004 (OJ 2004 L183/61), paras 77 and 78.

[**] OJ 2004 L125/45.

[***] See e.g. *Extramet* , 1992 ECR I-3813, para 19. The Court of Justice of the EC was faced with the argument that the sole EC producer's refusal to deal was an abuse of dominant position and had caused its EC customer to import from third countries. The Court limited itself to annul the anti-dumping measure on the ground that the injury was self-inflicted. In *Mukand*, 2001 ECR II-2524, the Court of First Instance found that the concerted practice of producers of stainless steel flat products established by the European Commission in a competition investigation had led to cost increases in the EC market for stainless steel bars. The European Commission and the Council of the European Union "ought to have accepted that the anti-competitive conduct of producers of flat products could have had significant repercussions".

Trade policy measures affect the flow or the patterns of trade. Taken at the import side they raise directly or indirectly the price at which imported products compete with the domestic products and/or limit directly or indirectly the quantity of imported goods supplied on the domestic market. Thus some of the competition that would otherwise exist for the like or competing products on the domestic market is restricted or (partially or wholly) eliminated.

To the extent that competition benefits the consumers (either the industry using the product in question or the final consumer) consumers' interests are affected by such trade measures. But consumers may also be more directly affected by trade measures. Trade measures taken at the import-side either consist of a charge levied by the government, a minimum price, or a quantitative limitation. In the first case, the economic agents will as much as possible shift the burden of the charge down the chain to the final consumer: for him the import charge will have the effect of a tax. In the second and third case the minimum price and the restricted supply will normally cause domestic prices to rise; the price-rise will as much as possible be shifted on to the final consumers; the minimum price and the quantitative limitation of imports have for the consumer the effect of a government measure requiring him to pay a subsidy to the domestic industry benefiting from the price increase. It thus appears appropriate to deal separately with the relation between trade policy and competition (I) and with the relation between trade policy and the consumer (II). This paper approaches the topic from a legal point of view and from an EC perspective only. It focuses on anti-dumping measures and countervailing measures against third-country subsidised imports,[1] on safeguard action against imports from third countries, whether they are unfairly traded or not, that may be taken whenever substantial injury is caused or threatened to be caused to Community producers by greatly increased imports,[2] and on measures against illicit trade practices attributable to third countries as they are provided by the so-called "new commercial policy instrument".[3]

---

[1] At present Council Regulation (EC) No. 2423/88 1988, on protection against dumped or subsidized imports from countries not members of the European Economic Community (O. J. L 209/88).

[2] Council Regulation (EC) No. 288/82, on common rules for imports (O. J. L 35/82), as amended by Council Regulation (EC) No. 1243/86 (O. J. L 113/86).

[3] Council Regulation (EC) No. 2641/84 on the strengthening of the common commercial policy with regard in particular to protection against illicit commercial practices (O. J. L 252/84).

I.   TRADE MEASURES AND COMPETITION[4]

Introduction

As indicated earlier, there is a tension between competition policy and trade policy. This appears as stating the obvious. The real world is, however, a bit more complicated.

As far as unfairly traded imports are concerned, anti-dumping and countervailing (anti-subsidy) legislation and legislation designed to counteract other unfair trade practices have to some extent a purpose in common with competition rules: that of eliminating artificial market distortions or their effects.

Moreover, the conflict between trade policy and competition policy should not be overstated. In reality, what governments either attempt or manage to achieve is "workable competition" and "workable free trade".

In addition, competition policy is concerned essentially with competition on the domestic market, trade policy with competition from and on the world market. It may be argued that competition coming from the world market ought not to be treated in the same fashion as competition originating in the domestic sphere. On the one hand, there are no substantive international rules on restrictive business practices and the competitor who comes in from the world market is not necessarily operating in similar conditions as competitors on the domestic market. On the other, the international rules on trade policy accept that business competes world-wide in unequal conditions and their aim is to establish some form of "workable competition" between governmental trade policies. Given this tension, the relevant question is whether and how an appropriate balance is to be struck between the sometimes contradictory requirements of competition policy and trade policy, a policy which in this respect is no different from other regulatory policies involving also departures from the pure competition model.[5]

---

[4] Many of the issues treated in this section have been dealt with in a report submitted by the author at the IBA's 22nd Biennial Conference at Buenos-Aires on September 22, 1988. The report on "Antitrust and Trade Policy: A Peaceful Coexistence? European Community Perspective" has been published in International Business Lawyer, February 1989 at p. 58 and March 1989 at p. 115.

[5] IBA Report *supra* n. 4, *International Business Lawyer*, March 1989, p. 120.

This section deals with the way in which EC law seeks to deal with the tension between the underlying policies and the potential conflict between trade measures and the requirements of competition law (B) and with issues under competition law to which the rote assigned to private parties in trade policy proceedings may give rise (C). Before this, it is appropriate to put these matters in their broader constitutional context (A).

A. The Constitutional Context

1. Competition Policy

(a) A perceptive US observer has noted two differences between the EC and the US in the formulation of what is understood by "competition" policy; first, non-economic political or social values have always played a larger role in EC law than in US law; second, the economics component of competition policy in the two systems now differs considerably given the ascendency of the Chicago school and the general shift in prevailing economic theories in the United States.[6]

There certainly are several explanations. The presence of non-economic components in the EC policy probably reflects some deep-seated philosophical differences with the US. Be it as it may, these non-economic components are relevant for EC competition policy – either in the implementation of that policy (Art. 85 (3) EEC) or when a balance has to be struck between the EC's mandate to ensure "that competition in the common market is not distorted"(Art. 3 (f) EC) and the mandate to conduct other policies –. They are relevant by virtue of the EC "constitution" itself. Competition rules cannot and may not be seen as an isolated part of the EC constitution, and competition policy cannot and may not be conducted as a completely separate policy. These rules and that policy are part and parcel of an array of rules and policies designed to achieve the general aims of EC as set out in its "constitution".

Thus the primary objective of EC competition policy and rules was and still is to prevent the rules on the establishment and proper functioning of the Common Market applying to Member States from being defeated by restrictive business practices. Once the "internal market"

---

[6] B. E. Hawk, "The American (Antitrust) Revolution Lessons for the EEC", 9 *Eur. Comp. L. R.* 53 at 56 (No. 9, 1988).

within the meaning of Article 8 a EEC is established, a shift of emphasis is likely to occur as businesses will lose interest in rebuilding barriers that are no longer useful for their purposes since they will have to confront each other in a single field.[7] Even so, competition rules and policy will remain part of the basic scheme of the EC treaties seeking to achieve the general aims of those treaties by free operation of market forces within the EC.[8]

This basic scheme of the EC treaties, however, does not stand on its own. The ECSC must also safeguard continuity of employment and take care not to provoke fundamental and persistent disturbances in the economies of the Member States (Art. 2 ECSC). The operation of the EEC Treaty is to be accompanied by a progressive approximation of economic policies (Art. 2 EEC) and the conduct of common policies. This implies that in conducting the EC competition policy the Commission cannot disregard other policies.[9] Conversely, this implies that other EC policies must take account of the requirements of competition policy.[10]

(b) Competition Rules and EC Regulation

EC competition rules apply as such only to the conduct of undertakings and not to the Commission and the Council acting in their regulatory capacity.

This, however, does not mean that the EC institutions are completely free to intervene by regulation in the market place producing effects which, if resulting from the conduct of undertakings, would be contrary to the EC competition rules. They may not disregard their mandate to ensure "that competition in the common market is not distorted" (Art. 3f, EEC; comparable language in Art, 3g, ECSC). Commission and Council may thus be put in a position where they have

---

[7] F. Mancini, 'Access to Justice: Individual Undertakings and EEC Antitrust Law - Problems and Pitfalls', 12 *Fordham International Law Journal* 189 at 190 (No. 2, 1989); in the same sense R. Kovar, *Marché intérieur et politique de concurrence*, 15 DPCI 230 at 237 (No. 2, 1989).

[8] This has been repeatedly emphasized by the Court of Justice. *E.g.*: Judgement of 25 October 1977 (Metro v. Commission, case 26/76) 1977 ECR 1875; Judgement of 16 June 1981 (*Salonia v. Poldomani*, Case 126/80) 1981 ECR 1563.

[9] In this sense J.F. Verstrynge, 'Current Antitrust Policy Issues in the EEC: Some Reflections on the Second Generation of Competition Policy', B. Hawk (ed.), 1984 *Annual Fordham Corporate Law Institute* 673 at 678 (Matthew Bender, 1985). For further analysis see R. Kovar *supra* n. 7; for the analysis of some cases, see S. B. Hornsby, *Competition Policy in the 80's; More Policy Less Competition?* 2 ELR 79 (1987).

[10] In this sense, R. Kovar *supra* n. 7 at 238.

to reconcile different objectives set out in the EC treaties and, if need be, to grant priority to one or other objective.

The balancing of the sometimes contradictory requirements resulting from the need to ensure that competition is not distorted and the conduct of other policies is an eminently political task. Yet, in several cases the Court of Justice has been called upon to pass on this question, has not rejected it out-of-hand as a non-justiciable issue, and has marked the perimeter of the discretion of the political institutions.[11] In *Waste Oils* involving EC legislation envisaging the possibility of exclusive zones being assigned to waste-oils collectors, the Court of Justice held that, where they have a restrictive effect on the freedom of competition, the measures provided for by the Council "must nevertheless neither be *discriminatory* nor go beyond the *inevitable restrictions which are justified* by the pursuit of the objective of environmental protection, which is in the general interest" (emphasis added).[12]

2. Trade Policy

The EEC Treaty has vested in the EC institutions the power to establish and conduct a common commercial policy towards third countries (Arts. 3(b) and 113(1) EEC).[13] The EEC Treaty does not specify or qualify this grant of power. It does not provide expressly for any principles or rules, such as the most-favoured nation treatment, non-discrimination of foreign countries or, non-discriminatory competition in international trade transactions between third country citizens and EC citizens.

In the absence of such express principles or rules, attempts have been made in the literature and by parties to Court proceedings to deduce them from the aims of this common policy (Art. 110 EEC).

The literature has, however, generally not managed to infer much more from Article 110 EEC than that the trade policy should be a liberal

[11] For example, Judgement of 18 March 1980 (SpA Valsabbla e. a.; v. Commission, Joined cases 154, 205, 206, 226 to 228, 263 and 264/78, 39, 31, 83 and 85/79) 1980 ECR 907; Judgement of 29 October 1980 (*Maizena GmbH v. Council*, case 139/79) 1980 ECR 3393.
[12] Judgement of 7 February 1985 (*Procureur de la Republique v. ADBHU*, case 240/83) 1985 ECR 538
[13] The position with respect to coal and steel products is unclear, see CD Ehiermann, "The Scope of Article 113 of the EEC Treaty", in *Melanges P. H. Teitgen* 145 (Pedone, Paris 1984).

one, going beyond the requirements of Art. XXIV (5) of the GATT.[14] Views vary as to the binding effect of Article 110 EEC: according to some it lays down a genuine treaty obligation, albeit that it leaves a wide margin of discretion;[15] according to others it is not a normative provision and only a political commitment.[16]

So far, the Court of Justice has not interpreted Article 110 EEC as laying down any general principles which the EC political institutions must respect in the conduct of trade policy or any rules of law against which concrete policy measures may be reviewed.[17]

As far as the nexus with competition policy is concerned, it is at any rate clear that the mandate "to contribute to the harmonious development of world trade by the progressive abolition of restrictions" and the "lowering of customs barriers"(Art. 110) cannot be equated with (contributing to) the establishing of undistorted competition in world trade. To the extent that the EC is a political entity invested as it is with trade policy powers, it is in charge of domestic economic and social interests. Article 110 EEC cannot be decisive for determining the content of the EC's trade policy, which must lake account of the other aims of the Treaties and of other tasks assigned by these Treaties to the EC. In legal terms, therefore, it would appear that with respect to international trade, neither the EEC Treaty provisions on the common commercial policy, nor the Treaties' provisions on competition policy mandate the EC to seek undistorted competition in world trade and to accord in the conduct of its trade policy a *priority* to the objective of ensuring that competition within the EC is not distorted.

---

[14] Vedder in E, Grabitz, *Kommentar zum EWG Vertrag* ad Art. 110 with references to literature (Beck, München, 1986).

[15] For example,Wohlfart-Everling-Glaesner-Sprung, *Die Europäische Wirtschafisgemeinschaft* (Fr. Vahlem, Berlin, 1960).

[16] For example, Megret in Megret, Louis, Vignes, Waelbroeck, *Le droit de la communaute economique européenne*, Vol. 6 ad Art. 110 (ULB, Bruxelles, 1976).

[17] For example, the EMI/CBS cases, i.a. Judgment of 15 June 1976 (*EMI Records v. CBS UK*, case 51/75) 1976 ECR 811; Judgement of 5 May 1981 (*Dürbeck v. HZA Frankfurt*, case 112/80) 1981 ECR 1095.

B.   Trade Measures and the Legal Requirements of Competition Policy

The relationship between trade policy and law and competition policy and law, with a particular emphasis on anti-dumping and countervailing law has been studied mainly in the US. In the EC this topic does not arouse the same interest in academia and in the legal profession.[18] It has been dealt with in the OECD[19] where it has resulted in a Recommendation of the Council.[20]

Although they certainly have points in common vis-a-vis the requirements of competition policy, it is useful to examine separately anti-dumping, safeguard and "new commercial policy" measures. Countervailing, i.e. anti-subsidy, measures are left aside in view of the minor role they play in EC practice.

1.   *Anti-dumping*

(a)   *Two Sides of the Same Coin?*

EC anti-dumping rules and policy have been commented upon, analyzed and scrutinized probably as no other aspect of EC trade policy in the literature. Suffice it to refer to some of the writings.[21]

---

[18] Among the few: J. F. Bellis, *International Trade and the Competition Law of the European Economic Community*, 19 CML Rev. 647 (No. 4, 1979); R. Landslittel, *Dumping in Aussenhandelsrecht und Wettbewersrecht* (Nomos, Baden-Baden, 1987); J. Temple Lang, "Reconciling European Community Anti-trust and Anti-dumping, Transport and Trade Safeguard Policies - Practical Problems" in B. Hawk (ed.), 1988 *Annual Fordham Corporate Law Institute* 7-1 (Matthew-Bender, 1989); P. Vandoren, The Interface between Anti-dumping and Competition Law and Policy in the European Community, (1986) LIEI 1 (No. 2).

[19] OECD, Competition Policy and *Trade Policies, their Interaction* (Paris, 1984).

[20] Recommendation of the Council for Cooperation between Member Countries in Areas of Potential Conflict between Competition and Trade Policies, 23rd October 1986, OECD – Acts of the Organisation – Vol. 26, p. 397 (1986).

[21] J. F. Beseler & A. N. Williams, *Anti-dumping and Anti-subsidy Law: The European Communities* (Sweet & Maxwell, London 1986); I. Van Bael & J. F. Bellis, International Trade Law and Practice of the European Community (CCH, Bicester, 1985); E. Vermulst, *Anti-dumping Law and Practice in the United States and the European Communities* (North-Holland, Amsterdam, 1987); among the numerous articles only the more recent ones: J. Buhart, *Le régime communautaire de l'anti-dumping: vingt ans d'expérience*, 24 RTDE 253 (1988); C. Norall, The New Amendments to the EC's Basic Anti-Dumping Regulation, 29 CMLR 83 (1989); K. Hallbronner and R. Bierwagen, *"Neue" Formen des Dumping und Ihre Regelung im Aussenwirtschaftsrecht der Europäischen Gemeinschaften*, 34 RIW 705 (1988); Vermulst and Waer, *De nieuwe EEG Antidumping Verordening 2423/88: een stille revolutie*, 37 SEW 126 (1989).

Price discrimination and selling at a loss, i.e. the two essential forms of dumping within the meaning of the EC rules, are practices that are prohibited by the EC competition rules under certain conditions. There are at least three situations in which these conditions are met and which resemble dumping.

(1)   price *discrimination* and *predatory pricing* by an undertaking holding a dominant position may be abuse within the meaning of Article 86 EEC. So far the Commission has acted under this Article against predatory pricing in only one case, ECS/AKZO[22] under appeal;

(2)   agreements and concerted practices between two or more undertakings having as their object or effect to *isolate markets* within the EC and horizontal agreements *fixing discriminatory prices* are prohibited per se;

(3)   *price discrimination* between customers in different markets is prevented by the prohibition of exclusive distribution agreements where they impede, in law or in fact, either the re-export of the contract goods by the distributor to other Member States or the import of such goods by third parties from other Member States.

This and other considerations have led some to advocate the replacement of anti-dumping action by the enforcement of competition rules.[23]

Price discrimination and selling at a loss are treated differently under competition law and under anti-dumping law.

–   under competition law, predatory intent in some form is a condition;[24] under anti-dumping law it is not;

–   under competition law, aligning one's price downward to meet a competitor's price is normally a proper conduct; under EC anti-

---

[22] O. J. L 374/85.

[23] Landslittel *op. cit*, n. 18 at 144-145. Similar views have been put forward elsewhere as well: Stegemann, *Anti-dumping Policy and the Consumer*, 19 *JWTL* 466 (1985) al 467. For the US one instead of many Others: Barcelo, *The Anti-dumping Law: Repeal it or Revise it*, 1 *MICH. Y. Intl L.* 53 (1979).

[24] For example, ECS/AKZO *supra* n. 22; abuse of dominant position may also result from "recourse to methods different from those which condition normal competition" (CJEC, Judgement of 13 February 1979, *Hoffmann-La Roche v. Commission*, Case 85/76) 1979 ECR 461.

dumping law the defence of "technical dumping" has so far not been accepted;

— under competition rules, selling at a loss may or may not be prohibited depending on the circumstances; it is at any rate not prohibited merely because it may cause injury to competitors;[25] under anti-dumping rules – apart from the fact that "dumping" does not necessarily imply selling at a loss, it is enough that the export price is below the domestic price – selling at a loss is not permitted in the sense that, when certain conditions are met (substantial quantities, no recovery of all costs within the reference period in the normal course of trade), the exporter will have to set his export price at the (higher) level of the so-called constructed value in order to avoid dumping;

— under anti-dumping law injury to the domestic industry is an essential requirement, under competition law it is not.

In order to understand these differences between them, one should bear in mind that competition rules and anti-dumping rules apply in a different context and have different rationales.

(b) A Different Context

The world market with which anti-dumping rules deal cannot be simply assimilated to the internal market of an industrialized country with which competition rules deal.

The natural defence against dumping in a free market, i.e. shipping the dumped product back to the dumper's home market, may be either impossible or ineffective, as a result of tariff and/or non-tariff barriers. Where the natural defence against dumping is inoperative as a result of restrictive practices on the dumper's market, competition authorities in the country at the receiving end of the dumping will be unable or unwilling to deal effectively with the anticompetitive conduct in the exporting country where that conduct makes the natural defence against dumping impossible. Experience in the EC shows that within a common market price discrimination between markets often requires a combination both of some market power and of governmental measures

---

[25] See ECS/AKZO *supra* n. 22.

that shield market power or that otherwise block the natural defence against dumping. In order to counteract this phenomenon effectively, there is a need for some common rules that apply across national boundaries with respect to restraints of trade by both business and the government and for common institutions empowered to interpret and enforce these rules.

(c) Different Rationales

Authoritative commentators see the rationale of anti-dumping rules in a combination of two elements: preventing a form of unfair competition from having effects within the importing country and eliminating the injury caused to the domestic industry by this form of unfair competition.[26] Anti-dumping measures should not be applied merely as a means of eliminating undesirable competition, or providing unjustified protection to the domestic industry; protective measures should thus be remedial rather than punitive.[27] This view is reflected in the guideline contained in EC anti-dumping rules that the amount of the anti-dumping duty should be less than the dumping margin "if such lesser duty would be adequate to remove the injury".[28]

By contrast, competition rules are designed to protect competition itself, rather than competitors. In its ECS/AKZO decision involving predatory pricing under the EEC competition rules the Commission emphasized that what mattered was not the survival of ECS (AKZO's competitor) as such, but rather the continued competition on the EC market of benzol-peroxide.[29]

(d) Injury Findings

Injury findings in anti-dumping cases are the *"parent pauvre"* in the case law of the Court of Justice as in the literature.[30] Some of the proposals made in the US to follow a competition-based approach[31] and cer-

---

[26] Beseler and Williams *op. cit.* n. 21 at 50-51.

[27] Beseler and Williams *op. cit.* n. 21 at 147.

[28] Regulation 2423/88, Art. 13 (3).

[29] J. L 374/85, para 81.

[30] The only attempt of a thorough analysis known to this author is P. C. Reszel, *Die Feststellung der Schädigung im anti-dumping- und Antisubventionsrecht der Europäischen Gemeinschaften* (Carl Heymanns, Köln 1986).

[31] See e.g. D. P. Wood, *"Unfair" Trade Injury: A Competition-Based Approach*, 41 STANFORD L R 1193 (No. 5, May 1989) and literature cited.

tain of the views put forward in opinions of the US International Trade Commission[32] have so far had no counterpart in the EC.

Competition policy considerations may be relevant for the purposes of injury findings in anti-dumping proceedings mainly in relation to three aspects.

The first aspect is a relatively straightforward one. Where dumped imports undermine a restrictive agreement entered into by the EC industry, this does not constitute injury within the meaning of the anti-dumping rules or injury designed to be remedied by anti-dumping measures. This seems to be at least the position with respect to agreements within the meaning of Article 85 (1) that have not been exempted pursuant to Article 85 (3). In *Certain Sodium Carbonate from the Soviet Union*, the existence of allegedly restrictive agreements between EC suppliers and their customers on dense sodium carbonate was one of the grounds on which it was decided not to take anti-dumping measures.[33] Anti-dumping measures should normally not be taken to protect exempted agreements either, as one of the conditions of the exemptions, i.e. the non-elimination of competition in respect of a substantial part of the products in question (Art. 85(3)(b)), might no longer be fulfilled.

The *second* aspect is more complicated and relates to the following argument: injury resulting to competitors from business conduct that, in the circumstances of the case, is to be considered as normal commercial conduct, should for competition policy reasons not be considered as injury to be remedied by anti-dumping measures. The issue was discussed before the Court of Justice in the *Allied* case;[34] the exporters argued *i.a.* that they had adjusted their export prices to the market prices prevailing in the EC and that this is a normal commercial practice, even if it means selling at a loss in a period of recession. The Court of Justice did not take a position on this argument but annulled the duties on the ground that the regulation did not discuss the question of the amounts of the duties necessary in order to remove the injury.[35] The difficulty with this proposition is that it

---

[32] See e.g. *Certain Red Raspberries from Canada*, USITC Pub. 1707. However, the US Court of International Trade rejected some of these views as being inconsistent with the statute (see *USSX Corp. v. United States*, 682 F. Supp. 552).

[33] O. J. L 48/80.

[34] CJEC, Judgement of 23 May 1985, 1985 ECR 1622.

[35] Whether the Court intended thus to criticize indirectly the injury findings is an open question. In his submissions, *Verloren van Themaat A. G.* took the view that "normal commercial practices compatible with the principle of undistorted competition should...be respected in the implementation of the EC anti-dumping rules".

takes it for granted that competition coming in from the world market is to be treated on the same footing as competition from within the EC. In most situations a case could be made that this should indeed be the approach. It should, however, be examined on its merits in each case.

The *third* aspect is even more complicated. It concerns as much the interpretation of the anti-dumping rules as the relationship with competition rules. In situations were anti-dumping measures that are justified by the need to remove the injury caused by dumping conflict with the EC's mandate to ensure that competition is not distorted within the Common Market, the weighing of the contradictory requirements of both policies and the possible judicial control under the proportionality principle require a more thorough analysis of injury than usual.[36] More recent injury determinations show that the Commission services in charge of trade policy proceedings are aware of this; they also show how difficult it may be to disentangle dumping from other causes of injury to the EC industry.[37] Furthermore the standard used in certain determinations, i.e. the injury caused to 'the most efficient manufacturers";[38] would, if generally applied, go some way towards avoiding tensions with competition policy requirements.

(e) Anti-dumping Remedies

Apart from *Dense Sodium Carbonate from the USSR* referred to *supra*, there are some other cases in which competition policy considerations have played a role when deciding whether or not anti-dumping measures should be taken.[39] An interesting case in this respect is *Glycine*

---

[36] Reszel gives a critical overview of the injury findings *op. cit.* n. 30 at 165–174. See also Vermulst *op. cit.* n. 21 at 640–642. Other legal systems appear to face comparable difficulties in determining the injury to be remedied in practice. See D. P. Wood *supra* n. 31.

[37] *Plain Paper Photocopiers from Japan* (O. J. L 54/87); *Videocassette recorders from Japan and Korea* (O. J. L 240/88); *Dot-matrix Printers from Japan* (O. J. L 130/88); Video cassettes and video tape reels from Korea and Hong-Kong (O. J. L 356/88).

[38] For example, *Electric Motors from Eastern Europe* (O. J. L 280/86, O. J. L 83/87); See also the definition of the representative Community producer in Urea from certain countries (para. 45) (O. J. L 131/87); in *Electronic Typewriters from Japan* (O. J. L 163/85); in calculating the duty to remedy the injury, the Commission disregarded a company because its financial results were heavily influenced by its start-up costs and its minimal turnover in comparison with the other three companies involved.

[39] In *Polyester Fibres from the GDR, Romania, Turkey and Yugoslavia* (O. J. L 103/87), in which no measures were taken, the reduction of the EC's producers' capacity was disregarded for injury findings as it was carried out pursuant to a rationalization cartel exempted under Art. 85(3) EEC. This exemption had been granted taking account i.a. of the fact that other producers and importers held a combined market share of 30 %, of which imports accounted for 10% (O. J. L 207/84).

from Japan.[40] In this case respondents and a major user of the dumped product argued that no anti-dumping duty should be imposed on the ground that only one Community producer and two foreign producers, i.e. the respondents, were supplying the EC market. This competition policy argument was taken into account in determining the extent of the relief granted.

In the same case, competition policy considerations led the Commission to reject the undertakings offered by the exporters. The Regulation imposing definitive duties states in this respect that: 'The decision to impose the same anti-dumping duty on both companies was based on a thorough analysis of the nature of the price undertaking offered and of the glycine market. In a market where only a limited number of companies are competing with each other an alignment of prices resulting from undertakings of the kind offered by the Japanese companies, i.e. to respect the same minimum price, would reduce competition.

This effect, it is considered, would be less likely to occur as a result of the imposition of the same anti-dumping duty, because existing differences in the prices charged in different transactions by the two companies (due among other things to variations resulting from exchange rates, commissions and transport costs) could continue. Furthermore, information with regard to the future role of other Community producers, new entrants or substitute products which could possibly have led to a different conclusion was not available.[41]

(f) Procedural constraints

In some other cases in which competition policy arguments were raised by interested parties, they were not taken into consideration when determining dumping and injury and deciding on anti-dumping measures. While reaffirming that "the purpose of anti-dumping proceedings is not and cannot be to enforce or encourage restrictive business practices", the Commission only indicated that it would review the anti-dumping proceeding on its own initiative, if and when an infringement of EC competition rules was discovered and a proceeding was opened under these rules.[42]

---

[40] O. J. L 218/85.
[41] O. J. L 218/85.
[42] *Ferro-Silico-calcium/calcium-silicide from Brazil* (O. J. L 129/87); in Mercury from the USSR, the Commission merely noted that the anti-dumping proceeding "has no bearing on the investigations being carried out' under EC competition rules (O. J. L 227/87); in the final

continues

There are obvious limitations to the extent to which competition policy considerations can at present be taken account of in anti-dumping proceedings.

First, such proceedings are no substitute for competition policy investigations. Allegations of agreements or practices contrary to Article 85 (1) or Article 86 EEC can neither be taken at their face value nor investigated in antidumping proceedings. It is doubtful whether such allegations can be used in proceedings under competition rules. Clearly, information obtained in antidumping proceedings cannot be used for implementing competition rules.[43] As a rule such allegations can only be taken into consideration once the facts have been established following the proper procedures of competition law or where, at the very least, proceedings were initiated under competition law. Consultations between the relevant Commission departments take place when a competition policy issue is raised in anti-dumping proceedings; they are, however, subject to limitations resulting from the legal duty to protect confidential information and the prohibition to use evidence collected in one type of proceeding for the purposes of another type of proceeding.

Second, anti-dumping proceedings may reveal the existence of situations, which are not in line with competition policy without, however, constituting potential infringements of competition rules. Under the Anti-dumping Regulation as it stands, however, there are no powers enabling the Commission to order an interested party to do something, e.g. to report regularly on its sales or to subject itself to inspections. In a situation such as *Glycine from Japan*, such powers could have been useful.[44] It should be said, however, that if, in such a case, the respondents' r the main users' ear that the complainant would abuse its dominant position would materialize, they could claim 'changed circumstances' and request a review under the Anti-dumping Regulation.

(g) Concluding Remarks

Competition policy aspects have been treated rather infrequently in antidumping proceedings. There are several reasons.

...determination the Council, however, stated that 'if an infringement of Articles 85 and 86 is discovered and a proceeding is initiated, the Commission may review the present proceeding'(O. J. L 346/87).
[43] Regulation 2423/88, Art. 8(1).
[44] O. J. L 218/85.

The 'filtering out' of anti-dumping complaints allows to persuade the EC industry not to file complaints that are presenting obvious risks of a potential conflict with competition rules.

Parties to anti-dumping proceedings seldom raise competition policy arguments and, when they do raise them, they are more often than not unable or unwilling to go beyond mere allegations.[45]

The Commission does not, on its own initiative, investigate in anti-dumping proceedings whether possible infringements of competition rules are involved. Nor does the Commission as a rule examine on its own initiative possible competition policy implications of anti-dumping measures.

The Commission practice to leave it to parties to raise competition law and policy issues is justified. Parties, whose interests are protected by competition rules, can protect them if they choose to defend them in anti-dumping proceedings. Statements made in several cases commit the Commission to review anti-dumping measures if and when an infringement of competition rule is discovered subsequently.

It would be appropriate for the Commission to do likewise even where no arguments had been put forward in the anti-dumping proceeding. This could for example, be the case if, after the adoption of anti-dumping measures, the Commission would find that the complaining EC industry had constituted a cartel and that the anti-dumping complaint had been lodged to seek measures to protect the cartel against foreign competitors. These are "changed circumstances" within the meaning of the review provisions of the Anti-dumping Regulation resulting from information which the Commission itself has collected.

There remains the question whether the Commission should in other cases consider competition policy aspects when adopting anti-dumping measures. To the extent that injury determinations are carefully made, the general practice to limit duties to what is necessary to remove such injury is followed, the position of the import-using industry is taken into account and, where appropriate, existing measures are reviewed, it is doubtful whether systematic competition impact analyses are necessary.

---

[45] See, *e.g. Polyester fibres from USA, Mexico, Rumania, Taiwan and Yugoslavia (O. J. L 348/ 88).*

2.   Safeguard Action

(a)   *The general EC safeguard clause as it appears in the common import regime [46] contemplates a situation:*

–   "where a product is imported in such greatly increased quantities and/or on such terms or conditions";

–   "as to cause or threaten to cause";

–   "substantial injury to Community producers of like or directly competing products".

–   Certain of the procedural rules of the EC Anti-dumping and Antisubsidy Regulation have been inserted in the common import regime Regulation.[47] Safeguard measures are decided normally only following an investigation.[48]

But contrary to the EC Anti-dumping and Anti-subsidy Regulation, the common import regime does not grant the EC industry a right of complaint. An investigation may be opened at the request of a Member State or at the initiative of the Commission.

The opening of the investigation is announced in the *Official Journal* by a "notice of initiation". In that investigation, the Commission is required to examine the trends of imports, the conditions in which they take place and the substantial injury or threat thereof to Community industry resulting from such imports, on the basis of a series of factors.[49] A finding of "substantial injury" or threat thereof resulting from the imports does not suffice. There must also be a finding that the interests of the Community require action.[50]

It is debatable whether under the common import regime as it stands, the Commission may take measures other than quantitative ones.[51] It is clear that other measures, e.g. an import-surcharge, may be taken by

---

[46] Regulation 288/82, Art. 15 (1). There usually are specific "safeguard clauses" for agricultural products whose production and marketing are subject to a "common organization of the markets". Many bilateral trade agreements also contain specific "safeguard clauses".
[47] Regulation 288/82, Art. 6.
[48] Regulation 288/82, Art. 7 (4).
[49] Regulation 288/82, Art. 9.
[50] Regulation 288/82, Art. 15 (1) and Art. 16 (1).
[51] Regulation 288/82, Art. 15 (1).

the Council.[52] In practice, so far only measures of a quantitative nature have been taken.

(b) Injury Findings

In theory, injury findings, in particular, defining the injury that ought to be remedied by a safeguard measure, raise similar issues as injury findings in the context of anti-dumping action. Thus it would seem that where imports would undermine a restrictive agreement entered into by the EC industry, this would not constitute an injury to be remedied by safeguard measures, except maybe where the agreement would have been exempted pursuant to Article 85(3), where the safeguard measure would not lead to eliminate competition (Art. 85 (3) (b)).

In contrast with the situation in anti-dumping cases, injury resulting from business conduct that cannot be claimed to be 'unfair' within the meaning of anti-dumping rules may be remedied under the safeguard clause. Thus, in theory the application of the safeguard clause could interfere much more with the pursuit of the aims of competition policy. This is, however, compensated to some extent by the requirement that the injury be 'substantial'. What 'substantial' is has not been defined but the term indicates at least that the injury threshold is higher than under the Anti-dumping Regulation. The evidence there is in Commission determinations shows that a much higher increase in imports and penetration levels is required.[53]

(c) Safeguard Measures

Safeguard measures as contemplated by the common import regime could have a large impact on competition within the EC: they could indeed in theory involve a complete ban on imports of the "like" product or a "directly competing" product.

In practice, however, the safeguard measures taken so far by the EC, can have had only a limited impact on competition within the EC. They consisted in limiting quantities to be imported, mostly at an amount per year equivalent to the yearly average of quantities imported during the three years preceding the initiating of the investigation. The measures

---

[52] Regulation 288/82, Art. 16 (1).
[53] See e.g. *Tableware from Korea and Taiwan* (O.J. L 369/82); Quartz Watches from the Far East (O. J. L106/84).

did not eliminate competition from foreign competitors. In addition, they were taken with respect to imports in one or two Member States only.

One feature of safeguard measures taken so far may raise concerns from a competition policy point of view: the way in which import quotas are allocated among importers. In one case the Commission made provisions for new entrants[54] In most cases it leaves the allocation to the Member State(s) concerned. Various systems are practised and they all have some disadvantage. Even the auctioning of quotas favoured by some economists could place monopoly power over a product made scarce by public authority in the hands of the highest bidder. Whatever the system the fact that competition is restricted by public authority does not allow private parties to restrict 'the residual field of competition'.[55]

(d) VRA's and VER's

i. Export restraints agreed upon by the exporting and the importing country (Voluntary Restraint Agreements (VRA's)) and export restraints applied unilaterally by the exporting country or the exporters of that country at the request of the importing country (Voluntary Export Restraints (VER's)) raise issues on their own. Export/Import restraints in so-called 'Industry to Industry agreements' are not considered here and neither are VRA's concluded and VER's requested by EC Member States.[56]

According to data compiled by the GATT Secretariat, 61 VRA's or VER's of varying nature in which the EC is involved were in operation between October 1987 and April 1988.[57] These figures do not include the bilateral agreements entered into in the framework of the Multifibre Agreement.

To the extent that they are entered into by the Commission or the Council, or alternatively adopted by a foreign country at the request of the EC, VRA's and VER's in the sense defined above are as such not subject to the EC competition rules. In adopting them, the Commission and the

---

[54] See the measures challenged in CJEC, judgement of 13 May 1971 (*International Fruit v. Commission*, Case 41/70) 1971 ECR 411.

[55] See the *Sugar Cartel* cases, CJEC, judgement of 16 December 1975 (Cöoperatieve Vereniging Suiker Unie e. a, v. Commission, J. Cases 40 to 48, 50, 54 to 56, 111, 113 and 114/73) 1975 ECR 1663.

[56] For some comments, see IBA Report *supra* n. 4 at 118 –119; see, also, M. Matsushita, "Coordinating international Trade with Competition Policy", in E. U. Petersmann and M. Hilf (ed.), *The New Gatt Round of Multilateral Trade Negotiations* at 395 (Kluwer, Deventer, 1988).

[57] GATT, *Developments in the Trading System, October 1987 – April 1988*, Appendix V.

Council have, however, as for other trade policy measures, to take account of the EC's task of ensuring that competition policy is not distorted in the Common Market. If VRA's and VER's entail restrictions of competition within the EC, they are permissible provided that they are necessary for the attainment of trade policy objectives which are in the general interest and that they do not result in the elimination of competition for a substantial part of the EC market.

ii.   Whether and in what circumstances compliance by exporters with such VRA's and VER's can be considered as infringement of EC competition rules requires some further comments. In many, if not in most, instances the exporting country will enforce a VRA or a VER by having recourse to its trade legislation and by imposing export restraints on its undertakings. The Commission has developed some sort of doctrine of foreign sovereign compulsion as a defence in competition policy proceedings.[58] Certain statements, though mostly made in cases where EC undertakings were claiming that EC Member States had pressured them into entering into restrictive agreements or had approved them, indicate that the official sanction of a foreign government will not easily be considered as "foreign sovereign *compulsion*"[59]

Regard should be had to the case-law concerning Member States' intervention. Although the law on Member States' duties under Article 5 EEC with respect to Articles 85 and 86 EEC read in conjunction with Article 3 (f) EEC is in a state of flux,[60] it seems clear that the fact that undertakings meet within a public organization does not remove their agreements from the scope of Article 85(1) EEC, and that agreements fixing a minimum price submitted to public authorities for the purpose of obtaining their approval to make them binding on all traders are caught by Article 85(1);[61] moreover, the Court of Justice has held that Member States may not favour the adoption of agreements, decisions or concerted prac-

---

[58] *Franco-Japanese Ball-bearings Agreement* (O. J. L 343/74).

[59] See *Aluminium Imports from Eastern Europe* (O. J. L 92/85), in which, with reference to the period before the UK's accession to the EC, the Commission did not accept that any encouragement given by the UK Government could be a defence (para 6. 1. 1., para 10. 2); in *Zinc Producer Group* (O. J. L 220/84), the Member State's knowledge of, participation in or approval of price-fixing agreements does not protect their undertakings from the application of the EEC competition rules (para 74).

[60] For an analysis see R. Joliet, National Anti-Competitive Legislation and Community Law 12 *Fordham Int'l* J 163 (1989) with numerous references to legal writings esp. n. 5; See, also, L. Gyselen, *State Action and the Effectiveness of the EEC Treaty's Competition Provisions*, 26 *CML Rev.* 33 (1989).

[61] GJEC, judgement of 3 December 1987 (*BNIC v. Clair*, Case 136/86), 1987 ECR 4789.

tices contrary to Article 85(1) EEC.[62] While EC Member States have a particular duty in this respect resulting from Article 5 EEC Treaty, it can be argued that the Court should reject such a defence by third country undertaking parties to similar practices.

Not only is it likely that the foreign sovereign compulsion will not easily be accepted as a defence. There are also instances where VRA's and VER's are implemented in the exporting country without recourse to public measures imposing restrictions on exporters.[63]

iii.   The fact, however, that a VRA has been concluded by the *Commission* or the *Council* or that a VER has been imposed by a third country at the request of the *EC* should be taken into account. In practice it is hard to see that the Commission would take action against the exporters in question under Article 85(1) if there is no cartel. Even if it did, imposing fines on these exporters would be difficult to justify. This leaves the question of the legality of the exporters' conduct under Article 85(1). Assuming that the restraints imposed directly or indirectly by the EC are lawful, can foreign undertakings that merely comply with such restraints claim immunity from Article 85(1).[64]

The answer is probably yes. The Court's refusal to accept the undertakings' defence of their anti-competitive conduct based on *Member State* action rests in the end on the unlawfullness of the Member State action itself. On three occasions at least the Court of Justice has held that a Member State may not require or favour the adoption of agreements, decisions or concerted practices contrary to Article 85 or reinforce the effects thereof.[65] In other words the underlying rationale seems to be the need to preserve the integrity of Community law and policies.

---

[62] CJEC, judgement of 30 April 1986 (Ministere Public v. Asjes, joined cases 209–213/84) 1986 ECR 1425.

[63] See e.g. the practice in Japan cited by Matsushita *supra* n. 56 at 404-405.

[64] Views differ widely on certain points see e.g. P. Pescatore, "Public and Private Aspects of European Competition Law", in B. Hawk (ed.) 1986, *Fordham Corporate Law Institute* 383 (Matthew Bender 1987); G. Marenco, Competition between National Economies and Competition between Businesses - A Response to Judge Pescatore, 10 *Fordham Int'l L. J.* 420 (1987); P. Pescatore A Rejoinder, 10 *Fordham Intl L. J.* 444 (1987); B. Van der Esch, *Der Stellenwert des unverfalschten Wettebewerbs in der Rechtsprechung des Europäischen Gerichtshofes und der Ver-waltungspraxis der Kommission*, 1988 W&W 563.

[65] CJEC, Judgement of 16 November 1977 (*GB-Inno v. ATAB*, Case 13/77), 1977 ECR 2115; in the *Asjes* case *supra* n. 62; CJEC, Judgement of 21 September 1988 (*Van Eycke v. ASPA*, Case 267/86) 1988 ECR 4769

If this is the case, the same rigour does not seem to be permitted where the EC itself is acting, provided that the restrictions of competition in the EC entailed by such VRA's or VER's can be justified as being necessary to achieve a trade policy aim that is in the general interest.

3. *Action against Illicit Commercial Practices*

(*a*) The 1984 Regulation against illicit commercial practices established 'procedures in the matter of commercial policy which, subject to compliance with existing international obligations and procedures, are aimed at (a) responding to any illicit commercial practice with a view to removing the injury resulting therefrom'.[66]

For an analysis of this regulation reference is made to the literature.[67] The cases in which it has been applied so far have also been commented upon in legal writings.[68]

Only some aspects that may be relevant from a competition policy point of view are addressed here.

(*b*) *The Injury to be Remedied*

The injury to be remedied under the "new commercial policy instrument" may be different from injury within the meaning of the anti-dumping and countervailing rules. For one thing, it may be injury suffered by EC industry on its export markets.[69] The injury that results from a

---

[66] Regulation 2641/84, Art. 1.

[67] Atwood, *The European Economic Community's New Measures Against Unfair Practices in international Trade: implications for United States Exporters*, 19 Int'l Law 361 (1985); Bourgeois and Laurent, *Le "nouvel instrument de politique commerciale": un pas en avant vers l'élimination des obstacles aux échanges internationaux*, 21 Revue Trimestrielle de Droit Européen 41 (1985); Denton, *The New Commercial Policy Instrument and AKZO v. Dupont*, 1 Eur. L. Rev. 3 (1988); Hilf and Rolf., *Das "Neue Instrument" der EG. Eine rechtsstaatliche Stärkung der gemeinsamen Handelspolitik?*, RIW 297-311 (1985); Steenbergen, 125 *The New Commercial Policy Instrument*, 22 Common Mkt L. Rev. 421 (1985); Zoller, *Remedies for Unfair Trade: European and United States Views*, 181 Cornell Int'l L. J. 227 (1985). Comments also appear in M. Bronckers, *Selective Safeguard Measures in Multilateral Relations* 209–40 (1985); I. Van Bael and J.F. Bellis, *International Trade Law and Practice of the European Community*, part IV (1985); Bourgeois, "Rules Against "Illicit Trade Practices"– Policy Cosmetics or International Law Enforcement? "in B. Hawk (ed.) 1988, *Annual Fordham Corporate Law Institute*, 6-1 (Matthew Bender, 1989).

[68] M.I.B. Arnold and M.C.E.J. Bronckers, *The EEC New Trade Policy Instrument: Some Comments on its Application*, 22 JWT 19 (No. 6, 1988); also Bourgeois *supra* n. 67 in Fordham.

[69] As in *Aramid Fibre into the US* (O.J. L117/87) and *Unauthorized Reproduction of Sound Recordings in Indonesia*, (O.J. L. 123/88).

foreign government's action to the EC industry on its home market, may be inflicted by the EC industry's foreign competitors, who derive a competitive advantage from their government's illicit commercial practice, as in anti-subsidy cases, but it may also be directly inflicted by the foreign government (e.g. government export ban that would be contrary to Article XI GATT). Moreover, the injury to be remedied results from practices 'which are incompatible with international law or with generally accepted rules',[70] while dumping is strictly speaking not a violation of international law.

The balance of interests is somewhat different. It could thus be argued that some of the restrictions on the injury to be remedied in anti-dumping cases do not apply in 'illicit practices' cases.

c.   *The Measures*

According to the Regulation, "any measures may be taken, which are compatible with existing international obligations and procedures",[71] with the aim to remove the injury resulting from the "illicit commercial practice".[72]

Injury can be removed in a number of ways. It could be done as in antidumping and anti-subsidy cases by offsetting the foreign producers/exporters' price advantage on the EC market by import duties. In such cases, there may be situations in which competition policy considerations could warrant that no measures be taken or less strict measures. Either because the injury is suffered on third country markets, because of the nature of the illicit commercial practice or because it has effects that cannot readily be remedied by raising the prices of imports of the relevant product into the EC, trade policy measures would be aimed at removing the cause of the injury, i.e. at persuading the third country to cease the illicit practice itself.[73] If such measures were import restrictions, they could give rise to concerns from a competition policy point of view.

---

[70] Regulation 2641/84, Art. 2(1).
[71] Regulation 2641/84, Art. 10 (3).
[72] Regulation 2641/84, Art. 10 (1).
[73] For example, suspension of the benefits of the EC Generalized System of Preferences, as was done, outside of the "new commercial policy instrument", against South Korea as a reaction against discriminatory treatment of EC patent holders (Regulation No. 3912/87, O.J. L 369/87).

C.   The Role of Private Parties in Trade Policy Proceedings

One of the interesting and fairly novel – in the western-European tradition – features of trade law is the existence of a formal, organized right of complaint for private individuals, triggering an investigation by an administrative agency.

This right of complaint has been held by the Court of Justice to grant complainants certain specific rights, such as "the right to have the complaint considered by the Commission with proper care and according to the procedure provided for", "the right to receive information within the limits set by the regulation" and the right to receive reasons why the Commission decides not to proceed with complaints.[74]

This complaint procedure may raise problems from a competition law point of view.

First, in order to be admissible, a complaint must be lodged by or on behalf of 'a Community Industry. For anti-dumping and countervailing duty purposes this means the Community producers as a whole of the like product or those of them whose collective output constitutes a major proportion of the total Community production of the like product.[75] For purposes of the "new commercial instrument", this means also Community producers who are consumers or processors of the product which is the subject of illicit practices.[76]

In order to lodge such a complaint, which must contain *prima facie* evidence of injury, Community producers, and in the case of "illicit commercial practices" also Community consumers or processors of the products in question, must necessarily exchange information on production, capacity utilization, stocks, sales, market share, prices, profits, return on investment, cash flow, employment.[77] There is little question that the exchange between competitors of most if not all such information which is of a confidential competitive nature relating to individual undertakings would in many cases violate Article 85 (1).

---

[74] Judgement of 4.10.1986 (*Fediol v. Commission*, case 191/82) 1983 ECR 2935.
[75] Regulation 2423/88, Art. 5 *juncto* Art. 4 (5).
[76] Regulation 2641/84, Art. 3 (1) *juncto* Art. 2 (4).
[77] Regulation 2423/88, Art. 5(2) *juncto* Art. 4 (2); Regulation 2641/84, Art. 3(l) *juncto* Art. 8 (1).

Second, in anti-dumping and countervailing cases the lodging by Community producers of a complaint triggers a trade policy proceeding against their foreign competitors, which may be raising rivals' costs and, if it leads to trade measures, will be raising rivals' costs. In illicit practice cases the complaint is directed against the action of a foreign country, it may, nonetheless, have a similar effect. As appears from the Commission's decisions taken under Article 85 EEC collusive practices of undertakings, which make it more difficult for third parties to compete with these undertakings, may violate Article 85.

Third, Community producers could conceivably under the cover of a trade policy complaint attempt to protect their collusive market practice or their dominant position or to bring their foreign competitors into line.

EC law has so far not generated a theory comparable to the US *Noerr-Pennington* doctrine.[78] According to this doctrine set out in the US Supreme Court opinion in two distinct cases,[79] there is no anti-trust violation in a company merely petitioning for import relief even if relief would effectively create monopoly power for that company. It would seem, however, that under EC law as well preparing and lodging a trade policy complaint could not in itself be considered as a conduct prohibited by competition rules. *First*, the relevant trade policy regulations themselves provide that this is the proper way to initiate trade policy proceedings; in practice it is the only way. *Second*, agreements of Community producers with their foreign competitors to prevent dumping have been held to be contrary to EC competition rules;[80] if EC law were to treat preparing and lodging of trade policy complaints as being contrary to those competition rules, it would put undertakings in a Catch-22 situation.

However, although so far there are no Commission decisions or case law on this point, the immunity from competition rules is limited by

---

[78] The CJEC's judgement in BNIC/Clair (1985 ECR 391) is at any rate not a rejection of a Noerr-Pennington like doctrine: R. Joliet, *supra* n. 60 at 179. Such a doctrine has been advocated on the basis of freedom of speech! J. Temple-Lang, *Trade Associations and Self-Regulation under EEC Antitrust Law*, in B. Hawk (ed.), 1984, *Annual Proceedings of Fordham Corporate Law Institute* 605 at 649 (Matthew Bender, 1985).
[79] *United Mine Workers v. Pennington*, 381 U.S. 657 (1965); *Eastern R.R. Presidents Conference v. Noerr Motor Freight*, 365 U.S. 127 (1961); for a discussion, see D.E. Rosenthal, Antitrust Risks in Abusing the Import Relief Laws, (1982) Rev.s, dr. *int'l* concurr. 31 (No. 14).
[80] *Zinc Producer Group* (O.J. L 220/84); *Aluminium Imports from Eastern Europe* (O.J. L 92/85).

the requirements of preparing and lodging a complaint. Conduct that would go beyond these requirements could be caught by Article 85 or Article 86 EEC. If, e.g. undertakings, holding alone or jointly a dominant position within the EC, were to threaten foreign competitors with the lodging of a trade policy complaint in order to obtain some arrangement about prices or quantities, such conduct would quite likely constitute an infringement of EC competition rules, even if all objective conditions for the imposition of trade measures were fulfilled.[81] Other collusive conduct of undertakings, such as agreeing not to lower prices in the face of their foreign competitors' prices in order to improve their case for trade measures, would probably also be caught by EC competition rules.

Apart from this general proviso, some specific issues need to be addressed.

1.   *Disclosure of Complaints*

The lodging of a trade policy complaint, if advertised, is likely to have an effect on the market. It may have a chilling effect, but it may also entice foreign competitors to increase their exports to the largest possible extent before they are hit by trade measures. In order to avoid such disruptive effects and in line with a recommendation of the GATT Committee on Anti-dumping Practices, the EC Commission services in charge of handling trade policy complaints have been instructed not to disclose the fact that an anti-dumping or an anti-subsidy complaint has been lodged. The representatives of EC Member States in the committees that are consulted before the initiation of a proceeding, are under a similar duty. Apparently no such instructions exist with respect to 'illicit practices' complaints. Normally the existence of a trade policy complaint is made public only in the notice of initiation of a proceeding published in the *Official Journal* once the complaint has been found to be admissible.

No specific rule exists for the complaining industry itself. It is an open question whether and, if so, under which circumstances the complaining industry could incur any liability under EC competition rules if it were to advertise its complaint before the Commission acted upon it.

---

[81] P. Vandoren, *supra* n. 18; see also J. Temple-Lang, *supra* n. 18 at 7–27.

2.   *Vexatious Complaints*

EC trade law does not contain any rule with respect to vexatious complaints. Nor is there any other EC rule providing for measures against such complaints in administrative proceedings before the Commission.

There is, however, a double precaution against such complaints. Both the Anti-dumping and Antisubsidy Regulation and the "New Commercial Policy Instrument" Regulation require that complaints contain "sufficient *prima facie*" evidence of the existence of dumping, subsidy or an illicit commercial practice and of injury or threat of injury resulting therefrom. Complaints that do not contain such evidence are to be rejected as inadmissible. In addition, and as a result of this requirement, the practice has developped for potential complainants to test the waters with the Commission services in charge of handling trade policy proceedings and to seek the advice of these services on draft complaints.[82] More than half of potential anti-dumping complaints are filtered out: at least some of these draft complaints could be considered as potential vexatious complaints.

3.   *Selective Complaints*

Selective complaints, i.e. complaints that seek trade measures against imports from certain countries only, may raise problems not only from a trade policy but also from a competition policy point of view. The non-inclusion of certain foreign competitors may be linked to the existence of an agreement or concerted practice between the complainant EC industry and their foreign competitors who were left out of the complaint.

There is obviously no easy solution to such a situation.[83] Most of the time where potential complainants seek unofficially the advice of the Commission services in charge of trade policy proceedings, their attention is drawn to the need to include dumping from all sources. If it appears after the initiation of a proceeding that the complaint is "selective", the

---

[82] A practising lawyer who is very familiar with EC trade proceedings describes one of the officials responsible for filtering out anti-dumping complaints as "playing the role of St. Peter in determining which candidate should be admitted after sceptical scrutiny to the next stage". I. Forrester, *EEC Trade Law and the United States* in B. Hawk (ed.), 1987 *Annual Proceedings of Fordham Corporate Law Institute*, 469 at 496 (Matthew & Bender, 1988).

[83] For example, an anti-dumping could be made only against the exporter who refuses to join a cartel or does not comply with the conduct agreed. In such a case the exporters not complained against will presumably *not* be dumping.

extension of the proceeding to other exporters may be decided at the request of the reluctant complainant or, failing such request, on the basis of information submitted by a Member State showing sufficient evidence of dumping by exporters left out of the complaint.[84] Failing this, the Commission could extend the proceeding at its own initiative. If these other exporters are not included, presumably the Commission would limit the relief granted to the complainant taking account of the other imports which the Commission has reason to believe are also dumped.[85]

This problem is not likely to arise very often under the "new commercial policy instrument" in view of the nature of foreign *governments'* actions which it seeks to counteract.

4.   *Withdrawal of Complaints*

The withdrawal of a complaint does not bring about the automatic termination of a trade policy proceeding once initiated. The Commission may terminate the proceeding, unless such termination would not be in the Community interest.[86]

Consequently, where it would appear that complainants had somehow used proceedings to persuade their foreign competitors to enter into an agreement with them that could run counter competition rules, the Commission may, and almost certainly will, disregard a withdrawal of the complaint and continue the proceeding.

II.   TRADE MEASURES AND THE CONSUMER

In dealing with this topic, this section first dwells on some general legal policy considerations, second attempts to analyze it in the light of EC law as it stands.

A.   The Consumer: Relevant or Not?

The term "consumer" is ambiguous. It may refer to the final consumer, it may also refer to the manufacturer who uses the imported

---

[84] In *Tube and Pipe Fittings* the complaint lodged by a trade association against imports originating in three countries was supplemented by a complaint against imports from a fourth country (O.J. C 77/85).

[85] For example, in *Unwrought Nickel from the USSR* the preliminary determination took account of price information and official statistics showing that imports from the USSR undercut by 7% other low-priced third-country suppliers; the provisional duty on imports from the USSR was limited to 7%, their average dumping margin being 40% (O.J. L 159/83).

[86] Regulation 2423/88, Art. 5 (4); Regulation 2641/84, Art. 3 (4).

product as an input ("processor", "import-user"). Vis-à-vis trade policy in general the "consumer" is in the same position as vis-à-vis any other policy. To the extent that it is accepted that as a rule the protection of the consumers' interests is a matter to be left to the operation of the ballotbox,[87] one may wonder why there should be special arrangements for consumers with respect to certain trade policy measures. The issue has nonetheless arisen. Two series of arguments have been put forward.

A first series of arguments derives from general policy concerns. They are inspired less by the protection of the consumer as such than by general economic or political considerations. They start from the premise that trade restrictions have effects similar either to a tax or to a subsidy that the government obliges consumers to pay to a domestic industry. They lead to the suggestion that the impact on the consumer should be assessed before trade restrictions are imposed. This economic argument is that in so doing the cost of protection would become transparent, this transparency in turn would lead to less protection and thus to an improvement of the general welfare.

This economic argument seems to be the underlying rationale of various acts of OECD,[88] and the "check-list" on which it recommended to evaluate trade and trade-related measures. This is also the reason why the *Leutwiler Report* advocated the introduction of a "protection balance sheet" allowing periodic appraisal of existing measures and informed judgement on proposed new measures.[89] The political argument is that this transparency would compensate for parliaments' unawareness of or benign neglect for the governments collecting hitherto hidden taxes or granting hitherto covert subsidies. Parliamentary democracy is no guarantee against "government failure" as seen by economists. As has been pointed out, the historical lesson drawn from the US Smoot-Hawley Tariff Act was that neither the vesting of all trade policy powers in the US Congress, nor the electoral constraints on government were sufficient

---

[87] The EC has passed that stage: Council Resolution, of 15 December 1986, on the integration of consumer policy in other Community policies (O.J. C 3/87).
[88] Recommendation of the Council for Cooperation between Member Countries in Areas of Potential Conflict between Competition and Trade Policies (23rd October 1986), OECD-*Acts of the Organisation* - Vol. 26, p. 397; Resolution of the Council concerning the Report on International Trade and the Consumer - Action taken to give effect to the OECD Checklist and to the Recommendation of the Committee for Consumer Policy (18th September 1987), *OECD -Acts of the Organisation* - Vol. 27, p. 423.
[89] GATT, *Trade Policies for a Better Future* (Geneva, March 1985) p. 35.

guarantees to prevent political log-rolling among organized interest groups seeking protection.[90]

The second series of arguments refers to the position of the consumer as such in the procedures followed by governments when taking protective measures. It starts from the finding that for whatever reasons governments have for many types of restrictive trade measures thought it fit to establish procedures allowing for domestic industry to lodge formal petitions or complaints triggering an investigation by the government and for interested parties to make their views known in the course of such investigations leading up to trade policy measures. Since the domestic industry and the foreign exporters, and, as the case may be, the importers are directly affected by eventual trade restrictions, it is appropriate, even legally necessary, that they be given the opportunity to comment before measures affecting them are taken.

With respect to the position of consumers, there are two opposing views. According to a first view, consumers' interests should not be considered. Consumers are not directly affected by trade measures and should thus not be given the opportunity to comment and when taking trade measures, governments should not take consumers' interests into consideration. To support this view, it is argued that to do otherwise, when applying legislation against unfair trade practices, would make the degree of protection of domestic industry against such practices dependent on the extent to which consumers would be affected by trade measures against such practices; this would lead to discriminations between domestic industries.[91] In addition, the purpose being to prohibit or to prevent unfair trade practices, consumers' interests would be as irrelevant as they are for example, when applying legislation on the protection of intellectual property.[92]

According to the second view, consumers ought to be given the opportunity to comment and their interests should be taken into consideration when taking trade measures. One of the reasons why procedural rules allowing for representation of various interests have been established for many types of trade measures is that such rules are a sort

---

[90] E.U. Petersmann, *Strengthening the Domestic Legal Framework* in E.U. Petersmann and M. Hilf (eds.), *The New GATT Round of Multilateral Trade Negotiations*, 33 at 53 (Kluwer, Deventer 1988)

[91] *Financial Times*, 14 March 1989, Letter to the Editor from M. Bronckers, A. Hoogakker and R. Quick.

[92] Financial Times Letter to the Editor *supra* n. 91.

of substitute for the absentee legislator: in many cases trade legislation is of necessity vague and general and such procedural rules serve to check the governments' unavoidable discretionary powers. To that extent there is no reason why consumers should not be given the possibility to intervene in administrative proceedings and why governments should not be mandated to take their interests into consideration when taking trade measures. Consumers are obviously affected by trade measures. When the "consumer" is a domestic industry using the imported product, most of those that take the first view must recognize this much and admit an exception to their view: they accept that the position of this type of "consumer" must be taken account of. It is true that the industry using the imported product and the final consumer of such product are not in exactly the same position. The industry using the product has no choice: if it is to stay in business it must keep on buying the product, either the imported one or the domestic one, whatever the price. The final consumer normally has a choice: he can stop buying the product and go on living without it. The question then is whether this suffices to consider that consumers are not directly affected by trade measures and to hold that there is no need for governments when adopting such measures to take consumers' interests into consideration. If the consumers' interests are weighed in competition policy proceedings, why shouldn't they be in trade policy proceedings?

The second view does not accept that consumers' interests are irrelevant when implementing legislation against unfair trade. *First,* trade restrictions affect the whole economy; it does not appear inappropriate to allow the degree of protection of the domestic industry to vary in function of other considerations than the injury suffered by that industry, taking the attending consequence in stride that in some cases the injury to the domestic industry will be remedied in full and in other cases not. That a given trade measure would impose on the consumers a disproportionate burden is a consideration as respectable as other public interest considerations. *Second,* the advocates of the first view seem to miss the point that, under the law as it stands, generally trade measures are taken not against unfair trade practices *as such* in order to prevent or prohibit them but to remedy the injury that they cause to the domestic industry.

B.   The Position under EC Law

It is convenient to distinguish two aspects: the procedural rights of the consumers in the administrative procedures of trade legislation on the one hand, the relevance of consumers' interests when adopting trade measures on the other.

1.   *Consumers in Administrative Proceedings*

(*a*)   The procedural rules of the investigation under the common import regimes for purposes of safeguard measures and those laid down under the 'new commercial policy instrument' are modelled on the procedural rules of anti-dumping and countervailing investigations. There are variations, but as far as the definition of 'interested parties'(or 'parties concerned') is concerned there are no material differences.

(*b*)   *The following procedural rights can be distinguished:*

–   the right to make written submissions[93]

–   the right to inspect the information made available to the Commission[94]

–   the right to an oral hearing[95]

–   the right to a disclosure[96], i.e. the right to be informed of the measures contemplated and of findings and conclusions on which they are based

–   These are the rights as laid down by or resulting from the legislation. They imply corresponding duties for the Commission, such as the duty to consider the submissions with proper care and according to the procedure provided for.[97]

Other procedural rights may be derived from general principles of law, relied upon by the Court of Justice in reviewing the exercise of the

---

[93] Regulation 2423/88, Art. 7 (1) (a); Regulation 288/82, Art. 6 (1) (a); Regulation 2641/84, Art. 6 (1) (a).

[94] Regulation 2423/88, Art. 7(4) (a); Regulation 2641/84, Art. 6 (4) (a).

[95] Regulation 2423/88, Art. 7 (5).

[96] Regulation 2641/84, Art. 6 (5); Regulation 2423/88, Art. 7 (4) (b); Regulation 2641/84, Art. 6

[97] Cf. CJEC, Judgement of 4,10.1986 (*Fediol v. Commission*, case 191/82, 1983 ECR 2935); although this case concerned complainant's rights, the reasoning of the Court of Justice applies *mutatis mutandis* to other parties.

Commission's discretionary powers, such as principles of sound and proper administration.[98]

(c)   The Beneficiaries

Under the various regulations, the right to *inspect* the information made available to the Commission exists only for defined categories of parties:

- — in anti-dumping and countervailing proceedings as well as in proceedings under the "new commercial policy instrument": the complainant, the importers and exporters known to be concerned and the representatives of the exporting country.[99]

- — in safeguard proceedings: no right to inspect the information is provided for. Likewise the right to a disclosure is granted only to defined categories of parties:

- — in anti-dumping proceedings, the exporters and the importers (in countervailing proceedings also the representatives of the exporting country).[100]

- — in proceedings under the "new commercial policy instrument", the complainant, the exporters and importers and the representatives of the exporting or importing country.[101]

- — no right of disclosure is provided for in safeguard proceedings.

The other procedural rights are granted to "interested parties", "interested parties likely to be affected", "parties concerned" and "parties primarily concerned". What is meant by these terms is not defined by the regulations. From the rule that "interested parties" or "parties concerned" have a *right to an oral hearing* only when they make a written request for a hearing showing that they are "an interested party likely to be affected by the result of the proceeding"[102] or "a party primarily concerned by the

---

[98] J. Mertens de Wilmars, *The case-law of the Court of Justice in relation to the review of the legality of economic policy in mixed-economy systems* (1982), LIEI 1 at 9 (No. 1).
[99] Regulation 2423/88, Art. 7 (4) (a); Regulation 2641/84, Art. 6 (4) (a).
[100] Regulation 2423/88, Art. 7 (4) (b).
[101] Regulation 2641/84, Art. 6 (4) (b).
[102] Regulation 2423/88, Art. 7 (5).

result of the procedure",[103] it may be inferred *a fortiori* that any other party showing an interest has this right to submit *written submissions* and that such right is not conditional on that party being likely to be affected or primarily concerned by the result of the procedure.[104]

The procedural rights in trade policy proceedings conducted by the Commission vary: some parties have been given more rights than others. There are objective justifications for such differences. Some parties are more directly affected by the ensuing measures than others. In addition more rights are given in anti-dumping and countervailing and in "new commercial policy instrument" proceedings than in proceedings leading to safeguard measures. In the latter case, it should be pointed out that there is no right of complaint for the domestic industry. This may explain why no right of disclosure has been granted to it either. Similarly, no right of disclosure has been granted to the exporters and the importers. One of the interesting questions is whether, if given the opportunity, the Court of Justice would consider that general principles of law require the Commission in safeguard investigations e.g. to disclose to the domestic industry, to the exporters and to the importers its findings and the measures it contemplates. This in turn depends on whether the domestic industry, the exporters and the importers have standing under Art. 173 EEC to challenge safeguard measures or to challenge the Commission's refusal to take safeguard measures.[105]

(d) The Consumers

Under the legislation as it stands, consumers do not have the right to *inspect* the information available to the Commission as they are not among the categories of parties mentioned by the relevant rules. The legality of the relevant rule of the anti-dumping regulation limiting that right to defined categories of parties is currently *sub judice*.[106]

---

[103] Regulation 2641/84, Art. 6 (5).

[104] Acc. Weber, *Das Verwaltungsverfahren im Anti-dumpingrecht der EG*, 20 Europarecht 5 at 15 1985).

[105] For an analysis, see J. Temple Lang, "Judicial Review of Trade Safeguard Measures in the European Community" in B. Hawk (ed.), 1985 *Annual Proceedings of Fordham Corporate Law Institute* 641 (Matthew Bender, 1986), who considers it unlikely that the domestic industry (at 655), importers (at 657) would have standing, while exporters might have standing in certain circumstances (at 650).

[106] The BEUC (European Bureau of Consumers Unions) is challenging in the Court of Justice the Commission's rejection of its request to inspect the Commission's non-confidential files in an anti-dumping proceeding concerning imports of audio-cassettes and tapes from Japan, Korea and Hong-Kong (*BEUC v. Commission*, case 170/89).

Likewise and for the same reason under the legislation as it stands, consumers do not have a right *of disclosure*.

However, consumers may be "interested parties" or "parties concerned" entitled to *submit their views* and to have them considered with proper care by the Commission. In this connection it is worth mentioning that when the OECD Council recommended in 1986 to use a "checklist" for the assessment of trade policy measures it excluded its application to trade measures relating to unfair trade practices[107] after the EC had pointed out that the proceedings concerning the latter measures were open to users and consumers of the imported products. It would, moreover, seem illogical to hold that consumers may not submit their views in trade policy proceedings, since before adopting measures the Commission, and as the case may be the Council, is bound to consider the Community interest, one of the factors of which is the position of the consumers.

2. *The Community Interest Clause*

(a) The three pieces of trade legislation all subject the adoption of the measures they contemplate to a finding by the Commission, and as the case may be by the Council, that 'the interests of the Community call for intervention'.[108] This clause recognizes that anti-dumping or countervailing action, safeguard measures and measures against illicit trade practices involve not only the interests of the domestic industry, but also other interests.[109]

(b) In its 'Guide to the European Communities' Anti-dumping and Countervailing Legislation' the Commission states that the clause refers to a wide range of factors but that the most important are the interests of the consumers and processors of the imported product and the need to have regard to the competitive situation within the Community market.

Its relevance and its interest for the consumers have been questioned in the literature[110] in view of the absence of any evidence

---

[107] Recommendation of the Council of 23 October 1986, Appendix, OECD - *Acts of the Organisation* – Vol. 26, p. 397.

[108] Regulation 2423/88, An. 11 (1), Art. 12 (1); similar language appears in Regulation 288/82 (Art. 15 (1), Art. 16 (1)) and in Regulation 2641/84 (Art. 10 (1)).

[109] For a comment on the clause in anti-dumping cases see J.HJ. Bourgeois, EC *Anti-dumping Enforcement – Selected Second Generation Issues*, in B. Hawk (ed.) 1985 *Annual Proceedings of Fordham Corporate Law Institute* 563 at 588 seq. (Matthew-Bender 1986).

[110] Stegemann *supra* n. 23.

showing that the final consumers' interests have ever determined the outcome of an anti-dumping proceeding (and in view of the limited number of cases in which the import-using industry's interests have led to terminate a proceeding without measures otherwise more limited measures than would otherwise have been taken).

(c)   *This begs the question why this is so. There are several explanations.*

One explanation lies in the nature of the proceedings. Proceedings, particularly in anti-dumping and countervailing cases, are progressively moving towards adjudicative-like processes. This is evidenced by the fact that in practice anti-dumping and countervailing as well as 'new commercial policy instruments' proceedings are set in motion solely following a complaint by the domestic industry that must make a *prima facie* case, by the increasing number and volume of memoranda being filed, by the ever-growing number of hearings held and by the need perceived by the Commission and the Council to improve the structure and the reasoning of their decisions. Implicitly relying on the principle "tantum devolutum, quantum appellatum" the Commission is, understandably, reluctant to raise in the course of proceedings on its own motion certain issues and arguments which parties or even potential parties to those proceedings do not raise. If considerations relating to final consumers' interests do not appear more often in regulations and decisions concerning trade measures, this is simply because representations dealing with such interests are only occasionally made. The fact is that so far representatives of final consumers have failed to intervene in trade legislation proceedings.[111] The only decisions referring to final consumers' interests[112] concern instances in which exporters or importers took up the consumers' banner. Some explain this consumers' absence by referring to the well-recognized disadvantage of consumers and buyers generally in forming political pressure groups to represent their interests as opposed to more specialized seller interests.[113] This explanation is not satisfactory, in that, in the context of the proceedings in question, consumers' representatives are not called upon to act as political pressure groups but to intervene as parties in quasi-adjudicative pro-

[111] *Except* in *Audio and video tapes from Japan, Korea and Hong-Kong.*
[112] For example, *Dot Matrix Printers from Japan* (O.J. L 130/88), *Video Cassettes from South-Korea and Hong-Kong* para 64 (O.J. 174/89).
[113] Stegemann *supra* n. 23 at 474; in the same sense, BEUC, ACTUALITES/NEWS, Legal Supplement (No. 79, December 1988) p. 8.

ceedings presenting their case, making submissions and presenting evidence; in that event the matter will be investigated further and the consumers' interests will be dealt with in detail in the determinations.

A *second* explanation why consumers' interests have so far carried little weight, if and when they were considered, relates to the balance of interests which the consideration of the Community interest involves. In those cases where the consumers' interests were argued, it was found that the interests of the domestic industry out-weighed the consumers' interests. Such a finding is not surprising when one compares the expected impact of the absence of trade measures on a small number of producers, whose survival may be at stake, to the diffused and marginal impact on a large number of final consumers.[114] Even when the impact on the consumers is not marginal, in particular when trade measures concern consumer products, their effect can be considered to be *proportionately* small in terms of growth rate of consumers incomes: e.g. a 25% anti-dumping duty on a compact disc player, a product, the cost of which would represent 15% of the average monthly income of the potential consumers and which is intended to last 10 years.

In some other cases the Commission and the Council stated that (anti-dumping) measures would in the end benefit the final consumers.[115] Such statements seem to be relying implicitly on the assumption, on which legislation against predatory pricing is premised, i.e. once the foreign producers will have eliminated the domestic industry, they will raise their prices offsetting the short-lived benefit to the consumers in the importing country. Assuming that dumping may be assimilated to predatory pricing, neither the Commission nor the Council indicated, however, on which elements they relied to make these statements.

(d) By way of conclusion, some remarks are appropriate.

First, up to now in trade policy proceedings of the type examined, consumers' interests have carried little weight. This is not because

---

[114] This is obvious in a case such as *Hydraulic Excavators from Japan* (O.J. L 176/85) when one tries to assess e.g. the increase of the cost for the home builder resulting from a 20 % antidumping duty on excavators. It is no less obvious in a case such as *Photocopiers from Japan* (O.J. L 54/87) when no attempts to figure out the price-increase per page copied resulting from a 30% anti-dumping duty.

[115] *Electronic Typewriters from Japan*, para 104 (O.J. L 239/86), *Photocopiers from Japan* (O.J. L 54/87), *Dot Matrix Printers from Japan*, para 120 (O.J. L 130/88); *Video Cassettes from South-Korea and Hong-Kong*, para 65 (O.J. L174/89); *CD Players from Japan and South-Korea*, para 134 (O.J. L 205/89); *Bariumchloride from China and GDR*, para 48 (O.J. L 227/89).

the relevant legislation excludes consideration of these interests, but either because consumers have failed to take advantage of the possibility to intervene in proceedings or because in the balance of interests those of the Community industry outweighed those of consumers. This is not to say that in the future there may not be other cases in which evidence submitted would show that the burden on the consumers would be disproportionate and would require that no trade measures be taken or more limited measures than would otherwise have been taken.

Second, the assessment, where made so far, focuses on static short-term effects. Situations may arise in which a case can be made that the longer-term dynamic benefits of trade measures (better conditions for adjustment of the domestic industry, economics of scale, higher profits allowing for more investment in improved technology) cut-weigh the short-run cost to the consumers.[116]

Third, under the "Community Interest" clause, not only the static short-term cost of trade measures to the consumers or their longer-term dynamic benefits to the Community industry are relevant. Other economic factors could conceivably be included in a cost-benefit analysis of trade measures when they are contemplated by the Commission or the Council.[117] This is a challenge both for the parties arguing their case in trade-policy proceedings and for the Commission in conducting the investigation; this may also be a subject matter for a cost-benefit analysis.

---

[116] See some of the studies referred to by T. Smallbone, *Consumer Interest in Textile and Clothing Policy* in *op. cit.* n. 19,145 at 159 *et seq.*; see the mixed results of Mennes & Kryger analysis of the automobile industry, *ibid.* 112.

[117] See, e.g. some of the other factors analysed in D. Greenaway & B. Hindley, *What Britain Pays for Voluntary Export Restraints* (Thames Essays, Trade Policy Research Centre, London 1985); see, also, R. Blackhurst, *The Economic Effects of Different Types of Trade Measures and their impact on Consumers* in *op. cit.* n. 19 at p. 94.

14. THE WORKING OF EC POLICIES ON COMPETITION, IN-DUSTRY AND TRADE: A LEGAL ANALYSIS

I.   INTRODUCTION

This chapter analyses the working of EC policies on competition, industry and trade from a legal point of view. It comprises three parts. First, the legal framework inside which the three policies are to be conducted is examined, then selected cases exemplifying the interaction or the lack of interaction between the three policies are presented and discussed. The paper concludes with some recommendations to improve the common working of the three policies at the Community level.

For the purpose of this article, the scope and the content of the three policies is to be understood by reference to the relevant provisions of the EC Treaty, namely Article 85 and seq., Article 130 and Article 113, as construed by the Court of Justice and as implemented by EC secondary legislation.

II.   THE LEGAL FRAMEWORK

As understood in this chapter, the legal framework consists of the provisions of the EC Treaty which define the purpose and the content of the three policies, as well as the instruments available for their implementation, together with relevant pieces of secondary legislation adopted by the Community on the basis of the EC Treaty. The legal framework will be analysed from two angles.

First, we will discuss the relationship between the three policies in terms of substance. The two main questions which we will address are:

- whether the EC Treaty, i.e. the Community Economic Constitution, gives equal weight to each of the three policies;

- whether the Treaty or secondary legislation provides for their common working and if so, how and to what extent.

Second and more briefly, we will look at the relationship between the three policies from an institutional angle and examine:

- what is the respective role assigned by the EC Treaty to the Community institutions and the Member States in the implementation of the policies;

- whether Community measures implementing the respective policies are taken according to similar or different decision-making procedures.

These institutional aspects are not without importance if consistency is to be achieved in the implementation of the three policies.

A. The Relationship Betwenn the Three Policies from the Standpoint of Substantive Law

Hereafter, we will consider what the relationship between the three policies is, first according to the "general principles" of the EC Treaty, then according to specific provisions of Community law. The main developments will concern industrial policy and its links with the two other policies. It is only since Maastricht that the main Community Treaty mentions industrial policy.

1. The "principles" underlying the EC Treaty

The common provisions of the Maastricht Treaty, which state in broad terms the objectives of the European Union, do not refer to competition, trade or industrial policy. These three policies appear in Part One ("Principles") of the EC Treaty among the policies and activities of the European Community. Article 3 refers respectively in paragraphs (b), (g) and (1) to "a common commercial policy", to "a system ensuring that competition in the internal market is not distorted" and to "the strengthening of the competitiveness of Community industry".

Although Article 3 taken in isolation sheds no light on the relationship between the three policies, it does shed some light on the content of "industrial policy". Article 3(1) does not use the words "industrial policy" as such, but instead the words "the strengthening of the competitiveness of Community industry". Such words express the objective which the Treaty assigns to industrial policy. They are meaningful in two ways. First, in keeping with the concept of an internal market, industrial policy should aim at improving the competitiveness of the Community's industry as a whole. Second, industrial policy, even if it implicitly refers to industrial competition from third countries, is not to be equated with protection of the Community's industry, but rather, and more positively, with improving its ability to compete.[1] Article 130, the specific industry provision which is examined *infra*, confirms that view.

Following the Maastricht Treaty, a new provision, Article(3a), which refers to economic and monetary union, was inserted among the introductory provisions of the EC Treaty. Paragraph 1 of Article (3a) provides that the economic policy of the Member States and the Community shall be conducted "in accordance with the principle of an open market economy with free competition". This principle is again affirmed in Article 102(a) and in Article 130 of the Treaty.

Taken together Articles 3(g), 3(a), 102(a) and 130 imply that competition policy enjoys a higher status than the two other policies. Admittedly, the principle of free and undistorted competition has essentially a political content. It cannot by itself serve as the basis for the creation of rights and obligations which legal subjects could routinely ask the courts to enforce. Its operative content depends on the specific competition rules provided in Articles 85 to 94 and Community legislation implementing these rules. Nevertheless, the principle of free and undistorted competition as such could influence the interpretation of Community law[2] when there is an actual conflict between competition policy and, for instance, trade policy measures. We refer here to a conflict

---

[1] For a discussion of the link between industrial policy and international competitiveness, see D.B. Audretsch, "Industrial Policy and Industrial Competitiveness", in Ph. Nicolaides (ed.), *Industrial Policy in the Community: A Necessary Response to Economic Integration?*, Martinus Nijhoff, 1993, 68–105 and M. Bangemann, *Meeting the Global Challenge – Establishing a Successful European Industrial Policy*, Kogan Page, 1992

[2] In the past, the Court of Justice did not hesitate to rely on Article 3(f) of the EEC Treaty (now Article 3(g) of the EC Treaty) to supplement or even, according to some authors, to modify the letter of Article 86. See Continental Can, ECJ Feb. 21, 1973, case 6/72, 1973 ECR 244, where the Court said: "The... argument that this provision merely contains a general programme devoid of legal effect, ignores the fact that Article 3 considers the pursuit of the objectives which it lays down to be indispensable for the achievement of the Community's tasks. As regards in particular the aim mentioned in (f), the Treaty in several provisions contains more detailed regulations for the interpretation of which this aim is decisive. But if Article 3(f) provides for the institution of a system ensuring that competition in the Common Market is not distorted, then it requires a *fortiori* that competition must not be eliminated. This requirement is so essential that it corresponds to the precept of Article 2 of the Treaty according to which one of the tasks of the Community is 'to promote throughout the Community a harmonious development of economic activities'. Thus the restraints on competition which the Treaty allows under certain conditions because of the need to harmonise the various objectives of the Treaty, are limited by the requirements of Articles 2 and 3. Going beyond this limit involves the risk that the weakening of competition would conflict with the aims of the Common Market."

between competition policy and trade policy, for in the case of a conflict between competition policy and industrial policy, Article 130 makes clear that industrial policy has to yield.[3]

2. *Specific Treaty provisions and secondary legislation*

(a) *Industrial policy*

i. The "constitutional" constraints: the primacy of competition policy and the non-discrimination rule.

As a result of the Maastricht Treaty, a new provision, Article 130, was introduced in the EC Treaty to specifically deal with industrial policy. The most striking feature of Article 130 is that it leaves no doubt as to the prominent position of competition policy. Not only does Article 130 provide that industrial policy measures must comply 'with a system of open and competitive markets' (a reminder of Article(3a) and 102(a), it also stresses, somewhat emphatically, that it may not serve as "a basis for the introduction by the Community of any measure which could lead to a distortion of competition". The limit thus set to the possible content of industrial policy measures seems sufficiently precise to be justiciable. The words used refer back to Article 3(g) of the EC Treaty ("a system ensuring that competition in the internal market is not distorted"), a provision which is not precise enough to be legally enforceable. But Article 3(g) has received concrete meaning and become enforceable through the rules of competition laid down in Articles 85 to 94, as construed by the Court of Justice and implemented by the Council and the Commission. One may therefore argue that industrial policy measures leading to results inconsistent with competition rules would be invalid under the EC Treaty. In other words, competition rules must be seen as determining the permissible content of industrial policy measures. The extent to which EC competition rules allow the pursuit of the industrial policy objectives listed in Article 130, will be discussed *infra*.

The leading role of competition rules in the industrial policy field is in stark contrast with the limited role given to competition rules in the agricultural sector.[4] This also contrasts with the regime applicable to coal and steel. There, competition rules can in effect be temporarily suspended

---

[3] Cf. *infra*.
[4] See EC Treaty, Article 42, and the recent *Banana* judgment, ECJ October 5, 1994, Case C-280/93, as yet unreported.

in times of crisis through the imposition by the High Authority of production quotas and minimum prices respectively on the basis of Articles 58 and 61 of the Coal and Steel Treaty. The fact that the Coal and Steel Treaty permits the conduct of an interventionist industrial policy explains the debate concerning the question of whether it will be renewed or allowed to lapse in 2002. This also helps to explain why, in a series of cases now pending before the Court of First Instance, steel producers make the argument that the Commission should not interpret and implement Article 65 of the Coal and Steel Treaty in the same manner as Article 85 of the EC Treaty, since the former allows a degree of public intervention in the industry.[5] The argument is that the Steel and Coal Treaty competition rules should be construed in the light of the sectoral and interventionist industrial policy permitted under that Treaty. Article 130 of the EC Treaty makes plain that under the latter the reverse should apply: industrial policy measures need to be consistent with competition rules.

The EC Treaty places another "constitutional constraint" on the conduct of industrial policy. Article 58 of the EC Treaty does not distinguish between companies on the basis of the nationality of the controlling shareholders. Therefore, any company set up in accordance with the laws of a Member State qualifies as a Community undertaking under the EC Treaty and may not be discriminated against. This means that, as the general objective assigned to industrial policy is the strengthening of the competitiveness of the Community's industry, the concept of Community .industry encompasses all firms established in the Community whether controlled by Community or third country interests. All these firms should benefit equally from any industrial policy measure taken by the Community or the Member States.

ii.   Objectives assigned to industrial policy

According to Article 130, §1, the general purpose of industrial policy is to ensure the competitiveness of the Community's industry, as already mentioned in Article 3(e). That goal is to be achieved through the pursuit of four sub-objectives:

- speeding up the adjustment of industry to structural changes;

- encouraging an environment favourable to undertakings, particularly small and medium-sized undertakings;

[5] See O.J. 1994, C 146/10, 12, 14 and 15

- encouraging an environment favourable to cooperation between undertakings;

- fostering better exploitation of the industrial potential of policies of innovation, research and technological development.

As it is readily apparent, the final version of Article 130 does not incorporate the proposals made by some Member States during the Intergovernmental Conference, which would have explicitly linked industrial policy and commercial policy and singled out high-tech industries as deserving special attention or even some measure of trade protection.[6] Some have nevertheless expressed the fear that Article 130 might in some instances be used to implement an interventionist form of industrial policy.[7]

As spelled out in Article 130, both the general and specific objectives of industrial policy seem to have been largely inspired by the Commission Communication of 1990, "Industrial policy in an open and competitive environment",[8] which received the Council's approval.[9] The 1990 Communication, known as the Bangemann Memorandum, is based on the premise that competitiveness and continuous adaptation to industrial change is primarily the responsibility of business firms.[10] In that Communication, the Commission repudiated direct public intervention in industrial sectors, but emphasized the need for a horizontal approach to industrial policy, where the task of public authorities is the creation of a favourable environment for industrial development.[11] [12] In keeping with that approach, the Commission, in a new Communication

---

[6] The legislative history of Article 130 was analysed by the late Emanuele Gazzo in Europe, 6–7, 8, 9 and 10 January 1992.

[7] See the ninth report (1990/1991) of the German Monopolies Commission, summarized in *Europe*, 7 October 1992. As P. Buigues and A. Sapir ("Community Industrial Policies', in Nicolaides (ed.), op. cit. *supra*, 21 at 33), indicate, Article 130 leaves open the possibility of sectoral measures provided they enhance structural adjustments.

[8] COM (90) 556 final.

[9] Doc. 10159/90 (Press 198-G), reproduced in Europe Documents, No. 1667, 7 Dec. 1990

[10] On this new approach, see Ph. Nicolaides, 'Industrial Policy: the problem of reconciling definitions, intentions and effects', in Nicolaides (ed.), op. cit. *supra*, 1 at 11–14.

[11] The European Parliament (see Resolution A3-177/91, O.J. 1991 C 240/213), even though agreeing with the general content of the 1990 Commission Communication, insisted on the need for a more forceful industrial policy, including a more vigorous trade policy.

[12] Previous Commission Communications concerning industrial policy are briefly summarized in the opinion of the Economic and Social Committee on the 1990 Communication, see O.J. 1992 C 40/31.

entitled 'An industrial competitiveness policy for the European Union',[13] now identifies four priorities: the promotion of intangible investment, the development of industrial cooperation, fair competition (internally and externally) and the modernization of the role of the public authorities.

iii.   Instruments available to the Community for the conduct of industrial policy. [14]

Article 130, §3, opens up two different roads for the conduct of industrial policy, one which may be termed the main road, the other which looks like a side road and is rather narrow.

The main road available for the implementation of the industrial policy objectives mentioned in Article 130, §1, is "through the policies and activities the Community pursues under other provisions of the EC Treaty". Indeed, the programmes set out by the Commission in its 1990 and 1994 Communications show that in order to achieve these industrial policy objectives resort has to be made, at one point or another, to almost all substantive provisions contained in the EC Treaty: Articles 85 and 86 (competition rules), Articles 92 and 93 (control of state aids), Article 99 (fiscal harmonization), Article 100 a (legislation concerning the internal market), Articles 101 and 102 (state measures resulting in distortion of competition), Articles 112 and 113 (commercial policy), Article 123 (social adaptation to industrial changes), Article 129(b) (trans-European networks), Article 130(a) and seq. (economic and social cohesion), Article 130(f) and seq. (research and technological development), Article 130(r) and seq. (environment). This is not surprising. Once the objective ascribed to industrial policy is as general as the strengthening of the competitiveness of the European industry, industrial policy extends its scope to all economic and social aspects of European integration.

If industrial policy should normally be implemented through the instruments available under the EC Treaty for the implementation of other policies, Article 130 also provides for a secondary road. The Community may take specific measures on the basis of Article 130 in order to support action by the Member States. But such specific measures require the Council's unanimity, and not simply a qualified majority as some Member States had wished. Unanimity is the safety catch which other Member

---

[13] COM (94) 319 final.
[14] For a review of the budgetary and regulatory instruments of EC industrial policy, see P. Buigues and A. Sapir, op. cit. *supra*, 21–35

States wanted in order to ensure that measures of a protectionist character could not be adopted on the basis of Article 130, without their agreement.

The unanimity required by Article 130 has a rather obvious implication. The pursuit of a sectoral protectionist policy can be more easily attempted through the channel of other Treaty provisions such as Article 113 (which allows the use of trade policy instruments on the basis of qualified or, as will be seen *infra*, even simple majority voting) or Articles 92 and 93 (through possible lax enforcement of the control of state aids by the Commission).

iv.   Industrial policy in relation to other EC policies

Article 130 calls for the Community to take a more active role with respect to industrial policy. The opening sentence of the third paragraph of Article 130 reads: "The Community *shall contribute to the achievement of the objectives set out in paragraph 1 through the policies and activities it pursues under other provisions* of this Treaty" (emphasis added).

The language used in Article 130, §3, seems slightly stronger than the language found in Article 128, §4, concerning culture: "The Community *shall take cultural aspects into account in its action under other provisions of this Treaty*"(emphasis added).

Article 130, §3, ought to be construed as requiring Community institutions to implement other Treaty provisions in the light of industrial policy as defined in Article 130, §1 (see *supra*). However such an obligation which in any event applies within the "competitive perimeter" also defined in Article 130, is not very precise since the objectives of industrial policy are expressed in broad terms. There is a political obligation for Community institutions to pursue these industrial policy objectives through the implementation of other Treaty provisions, and this is indeed what the Commission proposes in its Communications. But such an obligation cannot be seen as justiciable, if by that one means the possibility given to a person to challenge the legality of a Community measure on the grounds that it was taken in disregard of certain industrial policy objectives. Here it is worth observing that the wording of Article 130, §3, is somewhat weaker than that of Article 130(r), §2, whose last sentence, as modified by the Maastricht Treaty, reads: "Environmental protection requirements *must be integrated into the definition and implementation of other Community policies"* (emphasis added).

An obligation so phrased could perhaps be subject to judicial review, if not on substantive, at least on procedural grounds. It is submitted that the legality of a measure taken by the Community, for instance in the field of trade, without giving any regard to environmental protection needs, could be challenged before the Court of Justice by a Member State. This can be linked to the fact that environmental protection needs can probably be more easily identified than industrial policy needs, even though the degree of environmental protection to be achieved in a given case may be a matter for debate.

v.   Brief assessment of the contribution of the Maastricht Treaty regarding industrial policy

The Treaty of Maastricht puts industrial policy on the EC Treaty map. But the new Article 130 does not really add to the powers the Community already held under the EEC Treaty with respect to industrial policy. Indeed, Article 130 refers in the first place to other provisions of the Treaty for the implementation of industrial policy. That essentially corresponds to the situation which existed under the EEC Treaty. Second, Article 130 allows specific measures to be taken subject to unanimous voting in the Council. But previously, the Community could and did adopt specific industrial policy measures on the basis of Article 235 of the Treaty, which also requires the Council's unanimity.[15]

Since it defines in a positive way the purpose of industrial policy, i.e. the strengthening of competitiveness, and stresses the prominent role of competition policy, Article 130 seems designed to curtail rather than to enlarge the margin of discretion that Community institutions hold in the conduct of industrial policy. The main significance of Article 130 is that is clearly invites the Community to follow an integrated approach in the implementation of industrial policy.

---

[15] See for instance Council Decision of 22 July 1993 on an action plan for the introduction of advanced television services in Europe, O.J. L 196/1993; Council Decision of 21 December 1990 concerning the implementation of an action programme to promote the development of the European audiovisual industry (Media) (1991 on 1995), O.J. L 380/90; Council Decision of 27 April 1989 on high-definition television, O.J. L 142/1989.

b.   Trade policy

i.   The Treaty provisions

Articles 110 to 113[16] do not directly deal with the status of commercial policy *vis-à-vis* industrial policy or competition policy. Nevertheless, these provisions contain references to each of the latter.

Article 110 in its second paragraph states that: "The common commercial policy shall take into account the favourable effect which the abolition of customs duties between Member States may have *on the increase in the competitive strength* of undertakings in those States" (emphasis added).

As seen *supra*, the increase in the competitive strength of Community undertakings is now the very purpose assigned by the Treaty to industrial policy. Transposed in the internal market context, Article 110 would stand for the proposition that the positive effects resulting from the establishment of the internal market on the competitiveness of the Community's industry should lead to a more liberal trade policy. Of course, as the Court of Justice has ruled,[17] Article 110 is merely a statement of intent, with no binding effect on the Community.

Article 112, §1, provides for the harmonization of national aid schemes for exports to third countries, "to the extent necessary to ensure that *competition between undertakings of the Community is not distorted*" (emphasis added).

The Treaty thus confirms the functional link which exists between the uniformization of export regimes and undistorted competition in the internal market. But Article 112 too is a mere statement of intent, with no binding effect on the Community legislator. Indeed, export aid schemes, which supposedly were to be harmonized before the end of the transitional period, have not yet been harmonized at the Community level, except to the extent that the Community is party to the OECD arrangement on export credits.[18] That situation is, in part, due to the fact that for some Member States export aids schemes remain an instrument of foreign policy.

---

[16] Article 115 will not be considered here. With the advent of the internal market and the uniformization of import regimes, resort to Article 115 should cease, with the possible exception in cases where "regional" safeguard measures are taken.

[17] See Dürbeck, ECJ, May 5, 1981, Case No. 112/80, 1981 ECR 1095.

[18] The question of export credits is well analysed in M.-L. Hoube-Masse,"*La CEE et les crédits à l'exportation. L'intégration en question*", Rennes, 1992.

From the standpoint of both competition policy and industrial policy, the Community ought to proceed with the harmonization of export aid schemes on the basis of the trade policy provision, Article 113.[19] In case it were not to do so, Article 101 could be viewed as an alternative. However, one should observe that decisions cannot be more easily taken on the basis of Article 101 than on the basis of Article 113: both require qualified majority voting.

Article 113, the main commercial policy provision, states that the external trade regime should be based on uniform principles with respect to imports and exports and it explicitly mentions "measures to protect trade such as those to be taken in the event of dumping and subsidies".

From the standpoint of competition policy and industry policy, it is also quite clear that the uniformization of import regimes is necessary so that firms belonging to a given Community industry are all exposed to a similar degree of competition from outside the Community.[20] Such uniformization is also indispensable if a true internal market is to emerge. As we will see *infra*, import regimes were made (almost) fully uniform only very recently. The difficulties which the Community had to overcome in order to establish common rules on imports illustrate the links between trade policy, industrial policy and competition policy.

ii.   International law

The Community is bound by GATT. Now that the agreement establishing the WTO has entered into force, the Community has to comply with the various multilateral agreements negotiated during the Uruguay Round, which are destined to liberalize international trade.[21] In several respects, these agreements limit the ability of governments to intervene in favour of their domestic industry.

Admittedly, the Uruguay Round negotiations did not result in making significantly more difficult the imposition of anti-dumping du-

---

[19] The Commission has recently presented a draft directive, see O.J. 1994, C 272/2 and *Europe*, 8 September 1994, p. 10.

[20] The influence of imports on competition in the European market is discussed in A. Jacquemin and A. Sapir, *"Competition and imports in the European market"*, in L.A. Winters and A. Venables (eds), *European Integration, Trade and Industry*, London: Cambridge University Press, CEPR 1990, pp. 82-92. See, also, P.C. Padoa's comments, *ibid.*, 92–5.

[21] For the detailed content of these agreements, see P. Demaret, *"Les métamorphoses du GATT: de la Charte de la Havanne à l'Organisation Mondiale du Commerce"*, *Journal des Tribunaux Droit européen*, 1994, p. 121 and seq. and the articles published in *Revue du Marché unique européen*, 1994, No. 4.

ties and the pursuit, through such means, of industrial policy objectives. However, orderly marketing agreements and unilateral trade restrictions which do not conform with Article XIX of GATT of 1947 and the new agreement on safeguards are to be gradually scrapped so that they can be completely eliminated by the end of a transitional period. The extension of a safeguard measure beyond a four-year period is itself subject to the condition that the domestic industry protected by the measure proceeds to adjust to foreign competition. Speeding up the adjustment of industry to structural changes is one of the objectives set by Article 130 to industrial policy. These firm rules have obvious implications for the Community's textile and car industry.[22]

In addition, there is a new agreement on subsidies which provide for much clearer and stricter rules than the Tokyo Round code. The new agreement deals not only with subsidies which directly affect trade (through the boosting of exports or the reduction of imports), but also with subsidies to industrial research and with regional and environmental aids.[23] The European Community (and its Member States) will have to take the new international rules on subsidies into account when they try to achieve industrial policy objectives through the granting and the control of public aids. It should, however, not be too hard for the Community to fulfil its obligations under the agreement on subsidies since the Community exerted a significant influence on the content of that agreement.

The new multilateral rules resulting from the Uruguay Round are not only much more comprehensive than the present GATT rules. They should also be more effective, because of the new rules which will govern the settlement of disputes between members of the WTO. What precedes, however, essentially applies at the international level. The effectiveness of multilateral trade rules within the Community legal order remains limited as a result of the case law of the Court of Justice. In the

---

[22] As the Community invoked the derogations permitted by the General Agreement on Trade in Services, the main provisions of that agreement will not apply to the Community's audiovisual sector. This means that the local content requirement (the European works quota) provided by the TV without Frontiers Directive of 1989 does not have to be eliminated. This could be seen as the implementation by the Community of Article 128, §4 (the "culture provision" of the EC Treaty) in the external field and as a form of industrial policy in the old sense.

[23] In the future aids to the Community's shipyards may have to conform to the new multilateral rules negotiated in the context of the OECD, as indicated in the preamble to Council Directive 94/73, OJ L351/10/1994.

recent *Banana* case,[24] the Court confirmed that GATT rules could neither be invoked by a private complainant, nor by Member States in order to challenge the validity of a Community measure, except if these rules were incorporated into, or specifically referred to by Community secondary legislation.[25]

iii.   The uniformisation of import regimes and the reform of trade policy instruments

•   The completion of the internal market

The manner in which the Community proceeded to subject all imported products to common regimes illustrates the interaction between different policies at the legislative level.[26] At the time the internal market was supposed to be completed, the situation regarding imports was as follows.[27] The importation of products from most third countries was governed by common rules either as a result of autonomous measures taken by the Community or as a result of trade agreements concluded by the latter with third countries. Nevertheless, products imported from a number of third countries (most notably certain imports from current or former state economies as well as Japanese cars) had remained governed by national import rules. Such a situation was obviously inconsistent with the notion of an internal market.[28]

All products imported from third countries are now governed by common rules.[29] But this was achieved only after significant trade-offs were made between internal trade liberalization, external trade protection, industrial policy and competition policy.

•   The debate surrounding the reform of trade policy instruments:

Some Member States (France, Italy, Spain, Portugal and Greece) wanted to link tightly the uniformisation of import regimes, internal trade

---

[24] See *supra note* 2.

[25] Community legislation implementing the Uruguay Round agreements appears in O.J. L349 of December 31, 1994.

[26] For the interaction of the different policies in individual cases, see the second part of the chapter.

[27] For a detailed examination of import regimes on the eve of the completion of the internal market, see E. Völker, *Barriers to External and Internal Community*, Amsterdam, 1993, 62–73, 79–81.

[28] About 6,000 national quantitative restrictions were still in force at the end of 1993.

[29] See Council Regulations No. 517/94, 518/94 and 519/94, O.J. 1994, L67/1, 77 and 89, which were adopted on March 7, 1994.

liberalization and the granting of new competences to the Court of First Instance in the trade field to the reinforcement of trade policy instruments (safeguard measures, anti-dumping duties, "new instrument"). They wanted to speed up the adoption of trade protective measures and to give more power to the Commission. The Commission itself submitted to the Council a draft regulation which would have made the Commission responsible for taking final decisions in all matters relating to trade protection, unless overruled by a qualified majority in the Council.[30] Such reform was opposed by the United Kingdom, Germany, The Netherlands, Denmark and Luxemburg, Belgium standing in the middle.[31] The Commission also proposed to give to Community industries the right to lodge complaints with respect to safeguard measures, similar to the right of complaint which exists in dumping cases.[32] This proposal raised the fear that the number of safeguard measures would increase as a result.[33]

Despite the opposition of the United Kingdom, a deal was eventually struck.[34] It provided for the elimination of all remaining national quantitative restrictions and the adoption of new rules on imports.[35] But, in exchange, stricter deadlines were set for the conduct of anti-dumping investigations.[36] Moreover, anti-dumping duties imposed by the Commission now become definitive if confirmed by a simple majority in the Council,[37] instead of by a qualified majority as previously required. The adoption of anti-dumping duties thus can no longer be prevented by a blocking minority in the Council. The new rules are generally seen as making the imposition of anti-dumping duties easier than before. However, such a view in a sense prejudges the Commission's future attitude towards dumping. Indeed, to consider that simple majority voting in the Council will lead to an increase of successful anti-dumping applications rests on the rather intriguing premise that the Commission is intrinsically more favourable to trade protection than the Council.

The Community's industry did not receive the right to lodge complaints with respect to safeguards. Moreover, safeguard measures will

---

[30] See O.J. 1992, C 181/9.

[31] See *Europe*, 30 December 1992.

[32] See O.J. 1993, C 328/8.

[33] See *Europe*, 29 and 30 December 1993.

[34] See *Europe*, 9 February 1994.

[35] See Council Regulations Nos. 517/94, 518/94 and 519/94, O.J. 1994, L 67/1, 77 and 89. Regulation 518/94 has now been replaced by Regulation 3285/94, OJ L 349/53/94.

[36] See Council Regulations No. 521/94, O.J. 1994, L 66/, modifying Regulation 2423/88 now replaced by Regulation 3283/94, OJ L 349/1/1994.

[37] See Council Regulations No. 522/94, O.J. 1994, L 66/10, modifying Regulation 2423/88 now replaced by Regulation 3283/94, OJ L 349/1/1994.

normally continue to require the consent of a qualified majority of the Member States in order to be adopted by the Council or to remain in force where they are taken by the Commission.[38] More complicated rules apply to the textile sector.[39]

- The "interests of the Community" and the competition policy factor

That the rationale underlying, respectively, anti-dumping legislation and competition rules differs, is a well-known fact. Anti-dumping legislation provides for measures to counteract price discrimination and sales below cost which would not be unlawful under competition rules. Indeed, the latter prohibit only predatory pricing. This, however, does not mean that anti-dumping legislation should be systematically implemented in a manner which would contradict competition policy rules and objectives.

Community anti-dumping legislation, as well as legislation regarding safeguards, have now for many years included provisions which refer to "the interests of the Community". From the standpoint of competition policy, such a reference becomes meaningful only if the Commission or the Council, as the case may be, is obliged to consider separately from the interests of the domestic industry, the interests of consumers and industrial users and more generally the market competitive situation. As argued *infra*,[40] the Community interests should, in our view, be understood as requiring that Community trade measures never result in the elimination of competition in respect of a substantial part of the relevant Community market.

As it stood until the end of 1994, Community anti-dumping legislation provided that definitive duties could be imposed if a Community industry was injured and "where the interests of the Community so required".[41] The latter were not precisely defined. The Commission acknowledged that among these interests the most important were "the interests of the consumers and processors of the imported product and the need to have regard to the competitive situation within

---

[38] See Regulation No. 519/94, Articles 14 and 15; Regulation No. 519/94, Articles 15 and 16.
[39] See Regulation No. 517/94, Article 25, paras 3, 4 and 5 which provide for different procedures.
[40] See the developments concerning the limits set by competition rules on the conduct of industrial and trade policy and the second part of this chapter.
[41] See Regulation No. 2423/88, Art. 12§1.

the Community market'.[42] However, in practice, the interests of consumers and the competition policy factor did not play a significant role in anti-dumping proceedings.[43]

• The new anti-dumping legislation

The new anti-dumping regulation in force since 1 January 1995[44] defines in Article 21 what the Community interest means and describes how it should be assessed.[45] There now is an explicit reference to the interests of users and consumers. In addition, a procedure is established whereby the parties representing all the different economic interests at stake can be heard and can comment on each other's views.[46] Article 21 specifically states that: "measures, as determined on the basis of the dumping and injury found, may not be applied, where the authorities, on the basis of all the information submitted, can clearly conclude that it is not in the Community interest to apply such measures".[47]

The new provision should give a stronger voice to consumers and industrial users in anti-dumping proceedings and its implementation could be subject to judicial review in so far as compliance with procedural requirements is concerned. Whether it will bring changes in the material outcome of anti-dumping proceedings is another matter. For reasons stated elsewhere,[48] the injury caused by dumped imports tend to loom larger, in most instances, than the loss which consumers or industrial users may suffer as a result of anti-dumping duties. Moreover, it should be pointed out that the new regulation provides that, in determining where the Community interest lies, special consideration shall be given to the need to eliminate the trade distorting effects of injurious dumping and to restore effective competition.[49] This flies in the face of logic: the analysis of the Community interest comes after dumping and injury findings and

---

[42] On this point, see J. Bourgeois, "Trade Measures, Competition Policy and the Consumer", in Demaret, Bourgeois and Van Bael (eds.), *'Trade Laws of the European Community and the United States in a Comparative Perspective', Story Scientia*, 1992, 227 at 257.

[43] For a detailed review of past practice, see J. Bourgeois, op. cit. *supra*, and Van Bael and Bellis, *Anti-Dumping and other Trade Protection Laws of the EEC*, CCH 2d, ed. 1990, §311.

[44] Council Regulation No. 3283/94, O.J. L 349/1/1994.

[45] Council Regulation No. 3284/94, O.J. L 349/22/1994, which concerns subsidized imports, contains a similar provision.

[46] See Article 21§§2 to 5.

[47] See Article 21 §1.

[48] See J. Bourgeois, op. cit. *supra*, at 257-8.

[49] See Article 21 §1.

the rationale of the regulation is precisely to eliminate the effects of dumping and "to restore effective competition"; the "Community interest" is a corrective that refers to other interests.

In addition to mentioning the interests of the consumers and the users, which normally benefit from competition between foreign and domestic firms, the new anti-dumping regulation attempts to reconcile trade policy and competition policy in other ways. In two instances, it refers to restrictive trade practices which may occur in the context of dumping. The first relates to injury determination. Among the known factors other than the dumped imports, which the authorities are invited to consider when deciding whether the Community industry is injured as a result of the dumped imports, are "trade restrictive practices of and competition between the foreign and Community producers".[50] The second instance concerns price undertakings. These should not be accepted if they were likely to lead to anti-competitive behaviour.[51] In both instances, the language used is not of a mandatory character. In practice, much will hinge upon whether the Commission takes an active role in order to identify possible anti-competitive behaviour in the context of anti-dumping proceedings.[52]

- Safeguard measures

The interests of the Community are also mentioned in the regulations dealing with safeguard measures. But, contrary to what was done in the context of dumping and subsidized imports, the relevant provisions here were not made more explicit when new legislation was adopted at the end of 1994[53] and no explicit reference to competition policy is to be found.

In the context of safeguard measures, the meaning of the concept "the interests of the Community" varies. At times, the interests of the Community seem to mean something distinct from the interests of the domestic industry which suffers from foreign competition.[54] At times, the interests of the Community appear merely to coincide with the interests

---

[50] See Article 3§7. The new regulation concerning subsidized imports contains a similar provision.
[51] See Article 8§3 read in combination with the Preamble. The new regulation concerning subsidized imports contains a similar provision.
[52] See the third part of this chapter for recommendations in that regard.
[53] See Regulation No. 3285/94, O.J. L 349/53/1994, which replaces Regulation No. 518/94.
[54] See Regulation No. 3285/94, Article 17 ("where the interests of the Community so require").

of the domestic industry.[55] At times, the 'economic interests' of the Community are mentioned as an alternative to the injury requirement.[56]

• The industrial policy factor

The insistence of some Member States that the imposition of trade protective measures be facilitated as a counterpart to the completion of the internal market was inspired by industrial policy motives not devoid of certain protectionist overtones. Since anti-dumping duties can be used, consistently with Article 113 of the EC Treaty, as an industrial policy tool, it is important to stress that they may now be adopted (the Commission willing) with the consent of a simple majority of the Member States. This should be compared with the unanimity required by Article 130 for the adoption of specific measures.[57]

Regulations 518/94 and 519/94 explicitly refer to the industrial policy measures that the Community has taken or might take in order to offset the consequences resulting for certain national industries from elimination of national quantitative restrictions.[58] In the textile sector, together with the adoption of the new import rules, the Council, acting on a Commission proposal, decided to give financial help to Portugal to restructure its textile industry (to the amount of 400 million ECU). Portugal was considered as a special case in view of the importance of the textile sector in its economy. Other Member States made similar aid requests, but without success.[59]

This is an example of a type of complementarity between trade and industrial policies, which in the proper circumstances ought to be followed more frequently by the European Community. There may in fact be more cases in which, with a view to which in the taking account of the needs of EC industries in their competitive relations with outside suppliers, this type of measures, USA are qualified as import adjustment assistance, could be used as an alternative to the classical import

---

[55] See Regulation No. 3285/94, Article 16§ 1 and Regulation No. 519/94, Article 15§ 1 ("in order to safeguard the interests of the Community").

[56] See Regulation No. 517/94, Article 11§2 ("or where the economic interests of the Community so requires").

[57] See *supra*.

[58] The preambles of the two Regulations state that "the economic and industrial repercussions of their elimination have been or can be taken into account in the Community's horizontal policies for the market concerned".

[59] See *Europe*, 16 December 1993.

restrictions.[60] Such measures should obviously comply with the principles underlying the EC Treaty provisions on state aids.

• The EC-Japan car arrangement

Through the Commission, the Community negotiated with Japan an arrangement which defines the acceptable level of car imports from Japan into the Community until 1999. Such an arrangement was indeed indispensable for the completion of the internal market. This arrangement, even more than the autonomous import regimes just discussed, entailed a balancing act between internal trade liberalization, trade protection and competition policy. As indicated in the second section of the chapter, certain features of the arrangement seem to run afoul of Article 85, while others are inconsistent with the concept of an internal market and probably also with Articles 6 and 58 of the EC Treaty combined. The arrangement concerning Japanese cars is the most vivid illustration of the pursuit of a sectoral industrial policy objective through a trade instrument.

(c) Competition policy

As indicated above, the EC Treaty recognizes the primacy of competition policy over other EC economic policies in general and over industrial policy in particular. The legal and practical implications of the higher status conferred by the Treaty to competition policy depend on the content given to EC competition rules by the EC Treaty, the Court of Justice, the Community legislator and the Commission. Competition law cannot be examined here in any detail. It is at any rate one of the most developed and most extensively studied areas of Community law. Significant competition cases involving industrial and/or trade policy issues are surveyed in the second section of this chapter.

Hereafter, as part of our examination of the legal framework within which the three policies are to be implemented, only two related questions need to retain our attention. First, do competition rules set precise limits on the conduct of either industrial or trade policy? Second, can industrial or trade policy considerations be taken into account in the conduct of competition policy?

---

[60] An illustration of other possible alternative measures is the suggestion aired by some members of the Commission to rely on a form of import adjustment assistance rather than on a genuine quota system of European audiovisual production

i.   Limits set by competition rules on the conduct
of industrial and trade policy

There is a first and obvious limit. In order to achieve certain industrial or trade policy objectives, neither the Community nor the
Member States may resort to or allow the use of instruments or practices
which are forbidden under EC competition rules. For example, the
Commission may not induce Community firms and third country
competitors to enter into a restrictive trade agreement forbidden under
Article 85 by arguing that such an agreement would serve the same ends
as a safeguard measure or anti-dumping duty. Nor may the Community
or the Member States provide for the setting up of a cartel or permit the
flouting of block exemption regulations in order to police or to comply
with orderly marketing agreements concluded with a third country.
Similarly, a merger which would, on its face, create a dominant position
in the meaning of the Merger Regulation cannot be allowed under the
pretext that such a merger is needed in order to strengthen the
competitiveness of a Community industry.

But, in our view, competition rules set another limit, which could
be called the outer limit, on what can be done by the Community under
the heading of industrial or trade policy. That limit results from Article
85, §3, Article 86, as construed by the Court of Justice in Continental Can,[61]
and the Merger Regulation. Even though Article 85, §3 allows certain
restraints on competition, these may never have the effect of "eliminating
competition in respect of a substantial part of the product in question". In
Continental Can, the Court of Justice construed Article 86 in the light of
the rule laid down in Article 85, §3(b). The same idea underlies the Merger
Regulation which in Article 2, §2, outlaws mergers which "create or
strengthen a dominant position as a result of which effective competition
would be significantly impeded in the common market or in a substantial
part of it". That competition may not be restricted beyond a certain point,
as determined in Article 85, §3(b), Continental Can and the Merger
Regulation, should be the minimal substantive content given to the
principle of undistorted competition, which is proclaimed by Articles 3(g)
and 130 of the EC Treaty. We submit that the principle according to which
competition may not be eliminated in respect of a substantial part of the
relevant market is to be viewed as a general principle of Community law
and that, as such, it ought to bind Community institutions not only when

---

[61] See *supra* note 2.

they apply the competition provisions of the EC Treaty, but also when they take measures implementing other policies.

We would thus suggest that in the conduct of industrial or trade policy, the Community may not take measures whose effect would be to eliminate competition to a significant degree in a substantial part of the internal market. Such a principle has practical implications in those cases where measures taken by the Community are not by themselves technically inconsistent with Articles 85 or 86 or the merger regulation. A possible example arises where a safeguard measure or anti-dumping duties severely reduce foreign competition on a Community market dominated by one or two domestic firms. Such trade policy measures are, in our view, inconsistent with the EC Treaty. Compliance with the principle that competition may not be substantially impeded as a result of measures taken by the Community can be subject to the control of the Court of Justice, in the same way as the implementation of Article 85, §3(b), Article 86 or Article 2, §2 of the Merger Regulation is reviewable by the Court of Justice.

Assuming the primacy of competition rules as construed here, is accepted, there remains ample room for the implementation of trade and industrial policy. Indeed, from a legal point of view, the primacy of competition policy only implies that the Community may not violate its own specific competition rules and that, in addition, it may not take measures whose effect is to significantly distort competition in the internal market. Beyond that, the primacy of competition policy is essentially of a political nature and cannot be translated into sufficiently precise norms of conduct to become operative.

ii.   Integration of industrial or trade policy objectives in the competition policy field

Within the limits just discussed, industrial and trade policy objectives can be taken into account in the course of implementing competition rules. Actually, competition rules as they stand, represent an essential tool for the conduct of industrial policy as defined in Article 130 of the EC Treaty.[62]

For instance, Article 85, §3 and the system of block exemptions may be used, and have already been used at one time or another, by the

---

[62] The point is stressed in Bangemann, op. cit. *supra*, at 26–37

Commission in order to promote each of the four sub-objectives assigned to industrial policy by Article 130.[63] In addition, regulations have been adopted to define how competition rules are to be implemented in specific sectors such as insurance, air or maritime transport. In defining such conditions and in particular ceilings of intensity of state aids the Commission is necessarily making industrial policy choices. The Commission guidelines concerning the application of competition rules to the telecommunication sector[64] can also be viewed as a kind of industrial policy exercise within the boundaries of competition policy. The same observation applies to the directives concerning the telecommunication sector adopted by the Commission on the basis of Article 90, §3.[65] As these directives are intended to open up national markets, which until recently had remained sheltered from competition, they certainly contribute to the strengthening of the competitiveness of the Community's industry, the main objective of industrial policy. To the extent that industrial policy objectives of a general character, such as those listed in Article 130, play a role in the application of competition rules, the practice of issuing regulations, directives or guidelines ought to be encouraged for the sake of legal security.

The control of state aids by the Commission on the basis of Articles 92 and 93 is another competition policy instrument which can and often does serve as an instrument of industrial policy.

Articles 92, §3(c) and (d) concern respectively aids to facilitate the development of certain economic activities or of certain economic areas and aids to promote culture and heritage conservation. Such aids may be considered to be compatible with the Treaty 'where such aid[s] do not adversely affect trading conditions to an extent contrary to the common interest'. In other words, a balance needs to be struck between a certain degree of distortion of competition and the possible positive effects resulting from the aid. That provision, which has given rise to an extensive case law, reveals somewhat paradoxically, as does Article 85, §3, that if ever industrial policy may lead, consistently with the Treaty, to a certain degree of distortion of competition, it is only on the basis of the Treaty competition rules that such a result can be achieved. In particular cases the granting of state aids may even be needed in order to correct certain market deficiencies, as the EC argued with respect to Airbus in the dispute

---

[63] See *infra* part II.
[64] See O.J. 1991, C 233/2.
[65] See Directive 88/301, O.J. 1988, L 131/73, and Directive 90/388, O.J. 1990, L 192/10, as modified by Directive 94/46, O.J. 1994, L 268/15.

with the US However, as explained above, this distortion of competition may never result in competition being eliminated in a substantial part of the relevant market.

The Commission has issued guidelines or codes where it defines, sometimes with great precision, the conditions which horizontal aids (such as aids to small and medium-sized firms, aids for the protection of the environment and aids to research and development), regional aids or sectoral aids (such as aids to the automobile, the synthetic fibre or the textile industry) have to meet in order to be consistent with Article 92. As industrial policy considerations necessarily influence the attitude of the Commission in the field of state aids, it is again better from the standpoint of legal security that that attitude be known in advance rather than *ex post facto* as a result of individual decisions, which are more easily influenced by political pressure from Member States.

Article 2, §2 of the Merger Regulation adopted in 1989 makes incompatible with the Treaty concentrations with create or strengthen a dominant position as a result of which effective competition would be significantly impeded in the common market or in a substantial part of it. As such, the Merger Regulation does not empower the Commission to clear a concentration which creates a dominant position and significantly impedes effective competition on the grounds that it produces offsetting efficiency gains and that it would reinforce the competitiveness of European firms.[66] When competition is significantly impeded, other economic factors, which can be taken into account in the context of Article 85, §3 (within the limit defined by Article 85, §3(b)), become irrelevant. The comparison between the final version of the Merger Regulation and an earlier draft is revealing in that regard.[67] The lack of an explicit reference to industrial policy considerations, distinct from competition policy considerations, has been criticized by some, including the European Parliament, [68] after the de Havilland decision.[69]

---

[66] See A. Jacquemin, "Horizontal concentration and European merger policy", *European Economic Review* 34, 1990, 539–549 who, however, observed that: 'It is hard to believe that, in practice, such a strict policy will be fully implemented and that the role of potential dynamic efficiency gains will be ignored. A danger is that, instead of an explicit cost-benefit analysis, surreptitious compromises would be sought within the Commission." Recent merger cases seem to bear out that observation, see *infra*.

[67] See A. Pappalardo, "*Le règlement des concentrations*", R.I.D.E., 1990, p. 24.

[68] See Resolution on the de Havilland affair, O.J. 1991, C 280/140; see, also, L. Idot et C. Moège, "*Faut-il réviser le règlement sur le contrôle des concentrations? Brefs propos sur l'affaire de Havilland*", Ed. Techniques, Europe, January 1992, p. 5.

[69] O.J. 1991, L 334/2.

However, the Merger Regulation provides for a full economic assessment of a concentration in order to determine whether it creates or strengthens a dominant position that would significantly impede competition. As pointed out by Ehlermann,[70] the Commission has a margin of discretion when it makes that assessment. Indeed, the regulation allows for some flexibility since it implies that the creation of a dominant position does not automatically result in "effective competition being significantly impeded". The Commission, which is a political body, where votes are taken, has recently made use of that margin of flexibility in the Tubes case.[71]

One should add that the Merger Regulation authorizes the Commission to attach to its decision conditions and obligations which the undertakings concerned have to fulfil if the concentration is to be cleared.[72] There too, the Commission enjoys a degree of discretion which it can use to directly influence the structure of a Community industry.[73] As acknowledged by Ehlermann: *"néanmoins, il faut reconnaître que la pratique des engagements est délicate et que le reproche du 'mécano-industriel' est sérieux"*.[74]

B.   The Relationship Between the Three Policies from an Institutional Standpoint

In the trade field, the Community is exclusively competent to act, at least with respect to trade in goods. In the competition field, the Community, even though it shares power with the Member States, is the leading actor. Industrial policy is, as Article 130 clearly indicates, a field where Member States and the Community share responsibilities. When the Community is competent, one, two or three institutions, i.e. the Commission, the Council and the Parliament, may intervene, depending on the policy which is implemented and the legal basis to which the implementing measure refers. The plurality of actors raises the question of whether the three policies can be implemented in a consistent manner

---

[70] *Deux ans d'application du contrôle des concentrations: bilan et perspectives"*, *Rev. Marche commun et de l'Union européenne*, 1993, p. 245–7.
[71] That case is discussed in the second part of the chapter. See also for an application of the failing company defence in the context of mergers, Kali and Salz, O.J. 1994, L 186/38,
[72] See Merger Regulation, Article 8, §2.
[73] For a recent example, see Kali and Salz, cited *supra*.
[74] Cited *supra*, at p. 247. For critical comments regarding the Commission's practice, see I. van Bael, "Two years of Community Merger Control", in Campbell and Flint (eds), *1993: The European Market: Myth or Reality*, Kluwer, 1994, 53, at 65–6.

first by the Community itself, acting alone, and second by the Community and/or the Member States when the latter share powers with the former.

1. *The Community Level*

At the Community level, the question of consistency arises not only with respect to the implementation of the three policies, but also and more fundamentally with respect to the implementation of industrial policy as such. As we have seen *supra*, under Article 130, industrial policy is to be implemented through many different Treaty provisions. Specific measures, based on Article 130 itself, are taken by the Council acting unanimously, the Parliament simply being consulted. Thus, each Member State enjoys a veto power and this may have practical consequence as was shown in the case of HDTV.[75] But as a rule the industrial policy objectives are to be implemented on the basis of a series of other Treaty provisions. If, for example, a measure is based on Article 100 A, the internal market provision, it will require the approval of only a qualified majority of the Member States, but also the approval of the Parliament. It should be observed that the Parliament seems at times favourable to a higher degree of public intervention in industry than the Council (or at least than a blocking minority of Member States in the Council). In the field of research and development, framework programmes are adopted by the Council acting unanimously, with the Parliament's approval, whereas specific programmes are adopted by the Council acting by a qualified majority, the Parliament being merely consulted.[76] Where the pursuit of industrial policy objectives requires the harmonization of national tax laws, the Council act unanimously.[77] Still other decision-making procedures apply to decisions taken in relation to the European Social Fund[78] or to Economic and Social Cohesion.[79]

In the trade policy field, decisions are taken, as seen above, by the Council acting by a qualified majority or, with respect to dumping by

---

[75] See Council Decision of July 22, 1993, O.J. 1993, L 196/48, concerning the Community funding needed to facilitate the introduction of HDTV in Europe. That decision, taken before the Maastricht Treaty came into force, was based on Article 235. The United Kingdom, by using its veto power, was able to obtain a sizeable reduction of the funding which had been initially proposed.

[76] See Article 130(i) of the EC Treaty.

[77] See Article 99 (indirect taxes) and Art. 100 (direct taxes).

[78] See Article 125 of the EC Treaty.

[79] See Articles 130(d) and 130(e).

a simple majority. The Parliament has a significant role to play only when a trade agreement is sufficiently important to come within the scope of Article 228, §3.

In the competition field, the main and often unique actor is the Commission, as it is specifically entrusted with the task of implementing Article 85 (and most notably Article 85, §3), Article 86, the merger regulation and Articles 92 and 93. Moreover, the Commission possesses autonomous legislative powers under Article 90, §3. It also legislates extensively on the basis of delegation from the Council.

From this brief survey, it clearly emerges that if either industrial policy (seen in isolation) or the three policies are to be implemented by the Community with any measure of consistency, the burden is on the shoulders of the Commission. The Commission is always present, whatever the policy implemented or the legal basis used, at least at the proposal stage. The unifying role of the Commission is particularly crucial since the Council, when it does intervene in order to implement the different EC policies, does so in different settings and under the influence of different national ministries. By contrast, the composition of the Commission, which is stable, should help it in the task of developing a consistent approach for the implementation of the three policies. Whether the Commission is always successful in that respect is examined in the second part of this chapter.

2.   *The Community and the Member States*

The question of consistency here mainly concerns the implementation of industrial policy to the extent that it is distinct from trade and competition policy.[80] There is a need for coordination since Member States are responsible for the financing of most measures affecting the Community's industry. Here again the natural coordinator can only be

---

[80] In the trade policy field, the question of consistency arises only in those areas where Member States have not yet relinquished their powers, such as export aid schemes, see *supra*. In the field of competition policy, the question of consistency arises to the extent that national courts are competent to apply Article 85, §1 and that national competition authorities implement competition rules which may differ from EC competition rules. See J. Bourgeois, "EC Competition Law and Member State Courts", in 1993 *Fordham Corporate Law Institute* (B. Hawk (ed.) 475 at 494–5 (New York, Transnational Iuris Publications, 1994) and J. Bourgeois, 'Cooperation between National and Community Authorities: a Role for Subsidiarity?" Liège Conference, November 1993, *Le droit communautaire de la concurrence et son influence sur les droits des Etats membres et des Etats tiers* (forthcoming). In the merger field, the question of consistency is also raised by the fact that below a certain threshold national authorities are exclusively competent.

the Commission and the EC Treaty indeed confers that role on the Commission.

The Commission is, under Articles 92 and 93, given the task of controlling state aids. It would of course be advisable that aids granted through the Community structural funds be subject to the same control as state aids under Articles 92 and 93.

Under Article 130, §2 and Article 130(h), the Commission is invited to take any useful initiative to promote the coordination of the action of the Member States and the Community respectively in the industrial and research and development area.

Finally, under Article 169, the Commission may challenge industrial policy measures taken by a Member State in violation of the EC Treaty.

Outside the EC Treaty framework, the Commission is also increasingly invited, with the approval of the Court of Justice, to coordinate the action of the Member States in differents areas of intergovernmental cooperation, including sometimes cooperation involving third countries. The true limiting factor which the Commission faces in its role of coordinator is its lack of resources.

III.   SELECTED CASES

The purpose of this section is to examine, by reviewing a number of selected cases, whether and how the Commission and, as the case may be, the Council take account in practice of the relationships between competition, industrial and trade policy. To have a more complete picture, where appropriate and in so far as the issue of such relationships was put before the Court of Justice and the Court of First Instance of the European Communities, the stance taken by them will also be considered.

The cases are presented under the heading competition or that of trade policy depending on the qualification given by the Commission or as the case may be, by the Council, either expressly or implicitly by relying on the powers conferred in the relevant area to the EC.[81] In some in-

---

[81] There are no meaningful cases which, up till now, are qualified in legal terms as industrial policy. This does not mean that industrial policy considerations are totally absent in competition policy and in trade policy decisions. Such considerations will be referred to where appropriate.

stances the cases are presented under a joint heading where the matter happened to be treated under two distinct policies.

A.   Competition Policy Cases

1.   *Rules applying to undertakings*

In relation to industrial policy:

A good starting point is the 1968 Commission Notice on Co-operation Agreements[82] intended to give guidance to industry as to a range of horizontal agreements against which the Commission would not object under Article 85.

The main emphasis lies on research and development agreements, specialization agreements, joint ventures and latterly restructuring arrangements. Many other types of agreement have subsequently been investigated and cleared.

In respect of production and the introduction of new technology, the Commission's policy is to permit agreements to cooperate in manufacture, or in joint research and development, that seem genuinely likely to lead to better use of resources, such as rationalization of production, the achievement of economies of scale, or the faster, or more effective, development of new products, particularly where the undertakings concerned are likely to be better able to compete with third parties. Thus, even undertakings with a substantial market share or a large turnover may benefit from exemption under Article 85(3). This is likely to be so, particularly, in capital-intensive industries where restructuring[83] or specialization[84] is necessary to remove excess capacity, or in industries where the capital costs[85] or the technical difficulties[86] of developing new products are such that even large undertakings need to cooperate to produce the desired results, particularly bearing in mind

[82] Commission Notice of 21 July 1968, OJ (1968) C 75/3. See also XXIIIrd Report on Competition Policy (1993), para. 157: 'The Commission considers that, far from being the direct opposite of industrial policy, competition policy is an essential instrument, with clear complementarity between the two policies'
[83] For example, *Synthetic Fibers*, OJ L 207/1984; *BPCL-ICI*, OJ L 212/1984; Eni-Montedison, OJ L 5/1987; *Enichem-ICI, OJ L 50/1989.*
[84] For example, *Lightweight Paper, OJ L 182/1972.*
[85] For example, Rockwell-IVECO, OJ L 224/1983; *Carbon Gas Technology OJ L 376/1983; KSB-Goulds-Lowara-ITT, OJ L 19/1991.*
[86] For example, *Vacuum Interrupters, OJ L 383/1980; GEC-Weir, OJ L 327/1977; Optical Fibers, OJ L 236/1986.*

that many EC undertakings have not yet attained the scale of their American and Japanese competitors.[87]

The main types of agreements cleared by the Commission under Article 85(3) with the aim of promoting a particular EC industrial policy objective are the following.

- Research and Development Agreements

Given the relatively fewer resources devoted by EC undertakings to R&D compared to Japanese and the US undertakings, and their fragmentation, the Commission is generally prepared to encourage joint ventures which promote R&D. The encouragement of such cooperation now is one of the aims of the Community under Article 130(f) of EC Treaty. Already in 1980 the Commission stated that: "The introduction of new processes and products on the market stimulates competition within the common market, and helps to strengthen the ability of European industry to compete internationally",[88] after having pointed out in 1984 that its policy is "to seek the best possible balance between on the one hand a reinforcement of the competitivity of European industry and on the other hand the maintenance of workable competition".[89]

The favourable attitude towards restrictive agreements in the field of research and development in particular is reflected in the 1984 Block Exemption Regulation on certain joint research and development agreements[90] and the 1993 block exemption of such agreements for joint ventures to market the products resulting from the joint research and development.[91]

- Specialization agreements

The Commission has stated that: "Such agreements do... provide a means of obtaining a specialization which contributes to lower costs by the setting up of long production runs and a better utilization of available production capacity by the concentration of effort on a limited number of products".[92]

---

[87] For example, *Alcatel Espace-ANT, OJ L* 32/1990; *Ford-Volkswagen, OJ L* 20/1993.
[88] XIVth Report on Competition Policy (1985), para. 28.
[89] XIIIrd Report on Competition Policy (1984), para. 42.
[90] Regulation 418/, OJ L 53/1995.
[91] Regulation 151/93, OJ L21/1993.
[92] Ist Report on Competition Policy (1972), para. 27.

The basis of specialization agreements is the agreed allocation of production between the parties, accompanied by mutual obligations on each party to supply the other exclusively with the products in which it specializes for sale in the territory of the other party. In this way the parties are usually able to rationalize their production and achieve economies of scale while continuing to offer to third parties the same, or a wider, range of products often at more competitive prices. However, cooperation of this kind between enterprises of a certain size restricts competition within the common market.

The essential condition for granting exemption is that the specialization will not compromise the effectiveness of competition in such a way that the parties to the agreement can utilize the savings in costs for their exclusive profit instead of sharing them fairly with customers.

The two main issues for the Commission are whether the advantages of the agreement outweigh the disadvantages and whether the restrictions in the agreement are indispensable to the attainment of its objectives.

Favourable results from the point of view of the economy as a whole can be obtained by means of specialization agreements, especially where such cooperation enables small and medium-sized undertakings to work more rationally and increase the productivity and competitiveness on a larger market.

• Restructuring agreements

Certain EC industries are affected by chronic over-capacity as a result of changes in market demand. The Commission considered it as one of its general objectives to enable structural over-capacity to be eliminated so as to allow the industries concerned to recover profitability.[93] The classic illustration of this policy has been the Commission's approval of restructuring agreements in the petrochemical industry and its approval of the Synthetic Fibres and Stichting Baksteen crisis cartels.[94] However, exemption of specific restructuring agreements within an in-

---

[93] XXIst Report on Competition Policy (1992), para. 207 et seq.
[94] *Synthetic Fibres, OJ L* 207/1984. The Commission also indicated its preparedness to authorize crisis cartels for the zinc smelting industry (Commission Notice ZINC SHUTDOWN AGREEMENT, OJ C 164/1983); however, the zinc producers decided shortly thereafter that a crisis cartel was unnecessary (XIIIth Report on Competition Policy (1984), para. 58); STICHTING BAKSTEEN, OJ L 131/1994.

dustry subject to serious over-capacity does not give general protection to the industry to indulge in anti-competitive practices.[95]

• Production joint ventures (primarily as regards to high-technology)

In a number of important high-technology sectors EC undertakings are at a substantial technological disadvantage. The Commission has therefore favoured joint ventures between EC undertakings and non-EC undertakings, particularly from the USA and Japan, where the non-EC undertaking transfers important advanced technology. This has been a permanent feature of the EC competition policy beginning with early decisions such as De Laval Stork.[96] However, the increasing recognition of the relative disadvantage of EC undertakings in the high-technology sector has led to an arguably more flexible Commission approach where EC undertakings seek to obtain advanced technology from overseas as in the Optical Fibres, the Olivetti-Canon and the Olivetti-Digital Decisions.[97]

• Energy Sector

The application of competition rules in this area is relatively new and the issue of priority in any potential policy conflicts between the internal market and the competition rules is only beginning to be addressed.

---

[95] See Commission Decisions: POLYPROPYLENE, OJ L 230, 1986; PVC, OJ L 74/1989; LdPE, OJ L 74/1989. See Bellamy and Child, *Common Market of Competition*, 4th ed. (Sweet & Maxwell, 1993), footnote 14.

[96] DE LAVAL-STORK I, OIL 215/1977.

[97] "The agreements enable several European companies to produce a high-technology product with significant advantages over traditional cables in the Community and promote technical progress in relation to both optical fibres and optical cables. Moreover, the joint venture facilitate a more constant and rapid transfer of Coming's technology that would otherwise be possible. The concurrent introduction of Coming's most up-to-date technology in the common market is essential to enable the European companies to withstand competition from non-Community producers, especially in the USA and Japan, in an area of fast-moving technology. A partial or total divestiture would destroy such benefits for the European companies which would then risk becoming uncompetitive on the EEC and world markets. The joint ventures give rise to important benefits for European industry which can be maintained only by the continued participation of Corning". OPTICAL FIBRES, OJ L 236/1986, para. 59. Similarly, in OLIVETTI-CANON, OJ L 52/1988, para. 54, the Commission stated: "It is reasonable to expect that the combination of this technology with that of an also R&D oriented EEC undertaking will contribute to improving the technological patterns of the EEC industry and ultimately its competitivity".

In its Decision of 22 December 1992 approving the Jahrhundertvertrag, the Commission again confirmed the applicability of competition rules in the energy sector: the energy market must not be excluded from competition and, against the background of further development of the internal market, restrictive measures must be limited to what is necessary to guarantee basic security of supply.[98]

As regards the Nuclear Energy Sector, the Electricity Sector and the Oil Sector in granting exemption under Article 85(3) the Commission has always attached much weight to security and independence of supply.

CASE 1   Becton Dickinson / Cyclopore

Cyclopore is a Belgian-based undertaking with close links to the UCL; it produces membranes based on a patent licence granted by UCL. Becton Dickinson is a US medical supply company which has developed a technique to weld these membranes into tissue culture products.

Under the agreement between these two undertakings Cyclopore grants Becton Dickinson the exclusive worldwide right to manufacture and sell its membranes for as long as Becton Dickinson purchases a minimum quantity, and Becton Dickinson undertakes to purchase exclusively from Cyclopore all its microporous track-tech membranes for use in tissue culture, while Cyclopore undertakes to supply exclusively Becton Dickinson.

After parties agreed to limit the latter obligation for five years, the Commission issued an Article 85(3) comfort letter.[99] The Commission cited this case as a good example of its approach of authorizing agreements involving a restriction of the parties' freedom of action, if such restriction is necessary in order to achieve technological innovation that is beneficial to all.[100]

In relation to trade policy

There are a number of competition policy decisions addressing trade policy issues raised by the parties concerned. They reject the arguments according to which the parties entered into agreements with

---

[98] XXIInd Report on Competition Policy (1993), para. 146. See OLIVETTI-DIGITAL, OJ L 309/1994
[99] XXIIIrd Competition Report (1993), para. 241.
[100] XXIIIrd Competition Report (1993), para. 160.

foreign competitors to put an end to the latter's dumping practice on the grounds that it is not up to private parties to take trade policy measures.[101]

Other trade policy issues relating to the competitiveness of EC undertakings entering into restrictive agreements or engaged in merger operations are addressed from time to time in competition policy decisions. Strictly speaking, taking account of actual or potential competition from third countries could be considered a competition policy exercise. This is true. Much depends, however, on the conclusion one draws. The conclusion that a merger may be cleared because competition from third countries will ensure that the resulting dominant merged undertaking will not be in a position to engage in price maximization is a competition policy conclusion. The conclusion that a merger must be cleared in order to enhance the competitive position of the EC undertakings that merge is an industrial policy conclusion.

CASE 2   The flat panel display case

The Flat Panel Display B.V. joint venture between Philips (80 per cent), Thomson (10 per cent) and Sagem (10 per cent) was established with a view to creating the first EC company capable of producing very large-scale series of Liquid Crystal Display screens.

Initially notified under the Merger Control Regulation, the joint venture was examined under Article 85(1) EC. The Commission did not issue a decision but sent a comfort letter to the parties stating that the conditions for the granting of an individual exemption were fulfilled.

The Commission stated that it "ascertained that the joint venture is going to be means for the parent companies to develop and sustain mass-production in Europe of new high technology products in a field where competition from foreign suppliers (mainly Japan) is strong".[102]

This is an interesting case particularly in the light of the Commission's stated position on anti-competitive agreements in third

---

[101] Certain of these cases have been reviewed by J.H.J. Bourgeois, "Competition Policy and Commercial Policy" in M. Maresceau (ed.), *The European Community's commercial Policy after 1992: the Legal Dimension*, 113 at 121-2 (Dordrecht, Martinus Nijhoff, 1993). For a critique see M.C.E.J. Bronckers, "A Legal Analysis of Protectionist Measures affecting Japanese Imports into the European Community", revisited, in E.L.M. Volker (ed.) *Protectionism and the European Community*, 37 at 81–2 (Kluwer, Deventer 1987).
[102] XXIIIrd Competition Report (1993), para. 215.

countries affecting the position of EC undertakings on the markets of
these third countries. Although apparently it does not intend to apply the
EC competition rules against restrictive agreements in third countries
impeding EC undertakings' access to the markets of these third countries,
as the US Department of Justice announced that it would, it criticized
such restrictive agreements and stated that it would not sit idly by.[103]

CASE 3   The Tubes case

The creation of a joint venture, DMV, by Mannesman, Vallourec
and Ilva to which the stainless steel tube business of the parents were to
be transferred was cleared by the Commission under the Merger Control
Regulation.[104]

The Commission found that the joint venture would increase the
degree of concentration in an already highly concentrated market, the
joint market share held by DMV and Sandvik, the other important player
on the market, amounting to approximately 70 per cent, with none of the
existing competitors holding more than 13 percent.[105]

The Commission also found that this was a case in which a joint
dominant position (DMV and Sandvik) would result, noting that "[t]heir
mutual interdependence thus creates a strong common interest and
incentive to maximize profits by engaging in anti-competitive parallel
behaviour" (para. 129).

Yet the Commission cleared the merger. Ostensibly, the grounds
for doing so are that it did not create a dominant position "as a result of
which effective competition would be significantly impeded in the
common market", the second criterion for assessing mergers. The
Commission considered that the entry by Japanese competitors would
be sufficient to constrain the behaviour of the two market leaders (DMV
and Sandvik) and that it was likely that Eastern European competitors
would significantly enter the market in the near future.[106]

However, press reports suggest that the competition analysis in
the decision, as drafted by DG IV and submitted to the Commission by

---

[103] XXIIIrd Competition Report (1993), para. 107.
[104] Decision of 31 January 1994 (OJ L 102/1994).
[105] Decision, *supra* n. 100, para. 127.
[106] Decision, *supra* n. 100, paras 131 and 132.

Mr Van Miert, concluded that the merger should not be cleared. These same reports indicate that other commissioners took the position that in view of the competition from third country tube manufacturers the merger should be approved. One should think that the competitiveness of the EC industry was the real reason, as the arguments relating to the constraints on the two leaders' behaviour by Japanese and Eastern European competitors do not appear very convincing.

2.   *Rules on state aids*

As indicated in section I of this chapter, Commission decisions declaring state aids "compatible with the common market" under Article 92, (3)(b) and (c), and (partly) (d) involve industrial policy choices. An analysis of individual cases of state aids with a view to determine complementarities and conflicts with other policies is difficult as a result of three factors.

First, in many cases involving individual state aids the industrial policy or trade policy assessments have been made in advance and in the abstract in the "frameworks" and "guidelines" which the Commission issues from time to time defining conditions and "aid intensity ceilings".

Second, there is a fairly important number of cases in which Member States fail to properly and timely notify state aids with the result that Commission decisions do not deal with the merits of such State aids.[107]

Third, there are cases in which the Commission has kept silent. A significant example in this respect is Airbus. After having stated in 1973 that "important projects of common European interest" within the meaning of Article 92 (3)(b) include the manufacture of aircraft and aircraft parts,[108] the Commission has stated very little about state aids to Airbus. In the light of the dispute with the USA this is quite understandable. In addition, as the world market is the relevant geographical market rather than the EC, one could probably argue that state aid to Airbus is beneficial rather than detrimental for competition in view of the competitive structure on the world market of wide-bodied civil aircraft.

---

[107] In the Boussac judgment of 14 February 1990 (*France v. Commission*) ECR 1-307, the Court of Justice has, however, ruled that state aids which have not been notified are not automatically illegal. After taking interim measures, the Commission may order that such aids be recovered only if it concludes that these aids are inconsistent with Article 92.
[108] IInd Report on Competition Policy (1973), para. 100.

CASE 4   R&D support to SGS-Thomson

The French Government's proposed aid towards an R&D programme of SGS-Thomson Microelectronics was submitted to the Commission. SGS-Thompson designed the programme to acquire the key techniques and architectures of semi-conductor products. The total cost of the programme came to ECU 1,261 billion and the French Government intended to award a capital grant of ECU 321 million.

In authorizing this state aid the Commission took account of the EC's current deficit in the output of semi-conductors and of the advisability of strengthening the EC industrial capacity in a sector dominated by Japanese and US manufacturers, SGS-Thomson Microelectronics ranking 13th worldwide in terms of turnover.[109]

This, it is submitted, is a clear case of complementarity of competition, industrial and trade policies.

CASE 5   EUREKA projects

Twenty-nine Commission decisions relating to state aids to EC undertakings participating in EUREKA projects were identified by relying mainly on the RAPID data base. Several of these decisions deal with more than one proposed state aid. They cover a great variety of EUREKA projects from biotechnology to telecommunication, from electronic dictionaries to new materials for car body panels.

These proposed aids could be cleared almost automatically as they met the criteria laid down in, and did not exceed the aid intensity ceilings set by, the Framework for State Aids for R&D.[110]

Some of these state aids were, moreover, qualified as promoting 'the execution of an important project of common European interest' within the meaning of Article 92(3)(b) of the EC Treaty.[111]

For others the Commission expressly referred to the need to ensure the viability of EC industry in the face of international competition[112]

---

[109] Commission press release of 27 July 1994 (IP/94/714).
[110] For example, Italy –Alcatel Italia SpA – Synchronus Digital Hierarchy – press release IP/95/34.
[111] For example, Germany – Jessi Programm – press release IP/94/211
[112] For example, Italy – Computers Integrated Manufacturing for Constructional Steel – press release IP/90/448.

or the aim of improving the competitiveness of EC industry[113] or to the fact that the project "represented a significant step to create a competitive European supply".[114]

B.   Trade Policy Cases

CASE 1   Anti-dumping measures against calcium metal from China and the Soviet Union

The facts in this case are interesting. They are briefly restated here.[115] Following a complaint from Pechiney, the sole EC producer of calcium metal, the European Commission initiated an anti-dumping proceeding which led in September 1989 to the imposition of definitive anti-dumping duties.[116] Calcium metal is used mainly in the metallurgical industry. There are few producers. One of the importers was Extramet who processes the calcium metal into granules of pure calcium.

In the course of the anti-dumping proceeding, Extramet stated that it started importing calcium metal when Pechiney became unwilling to supply it with calcium metal in sufficient quantities. Extramet claimed that Pechiney did so because it wanted to enter itself into the market of granules of pure calcium. Extramet had lodged a complaint with the French Conseil de la Concurrence alleging that this refusal to supply was an abuse of dominant position within the meaning of Article 86 EEC.

During the anti-dumping proceeding Extramet put forward an argument relating to the EEC competition rules, to which the following reply was given: 'The third argument concerns a claim that the Community producer has suffered self-inflicted injury in refusing to supply calcium metal to the importer, who has begun court proceedings in one Member State against the Community producer alleging abuse of dominant position'.

The Commission notes that the Community producer has denied these allegations and that no final judgment has yet been reached in the Court proceedings in the Member State concerned.

---

[113] For example, Italy – Laser Work Station for Surface Treatments – press release IP/90/126.
[114] For example, Italy – Three Eureka Projects – press release IP/89/220.
[115] For a more complete account see Jacobs AG in his submissions to the CJEC in EXTRAMET INDUSTRIE v. EC Council 67 CMLREP 2 619 (1993).
[116] Regulation 2808/89, OJ L 271/1989

The Commission takes the view that the purpose of anti-dumping proceedings is not, and cannot be, to condone or encourage restrictive business practices, and that the initiation of such a proceeding does not therefore deprive an undertaking of its right to initiate proceedings under Articles 85 and 86 EEC, the outcome of which cannot be prejudiced by an anti-dumping investigation. Moreover, if and when an infringement of Articles 85 and 86 is discovered and a decision has been made under Regulation 17, the Commission may review the present anti-dumping proceeding in accordance with Article 14(1) of Regulation 2423/88 (Regulation 2808/85, para. 15).

Extramet subsequently challenged the regulation imposing anti-dumping duties in the Court of Justice. In its submission Jacobs AG addressed the competition argument put forward before the Court of Justice by Extramet and concluded that "the Council failed to give proper considerations to the question whether the imposition of a duty was consistent with the need to avoid the distortion of competition in the Common market".[117]

Regretfully the Court of Justice examined only Extramet's submissions that mistakes were made in determining the injury suffered by Pechiney, in particular that Pechiney suffered self-inflicted injury. It allowed this submission and annulled the regulation on this ground.

Following this judgment the investigation was resumed. This investigation resulted in findings of dumping and injury and in the imposition of anti-dumping duties. Not unexpectedly the investigation focused on the issue of whether Pechiney had contributed to its own injury.

The competition aspect was addressed but discarded in the following terms: "In this context, the Council considered whether the adoption of anti-dumping measures might lead to a situation in which effective competition might be significantly reduced. In view of the fact that supplies were available from the United States of America and Canada, and that the imports from the People's Republic of China and Russia would remain at non-dumped prices, the Council concluded that there was no such danger and that there was need to ensure that the Community industry continued to operate".[118] This is a far cry from the

---

[117] EXTRAMET *supra* n. 115 at 670.
[118] Regulation 2557/94 (OJ L 270/1994) para. 29.

sort of analysis that the Commission usually carries out under the competition rules on possible "barriers to entry".

The end-result is not very satisfactory from a competition law and policy perspective. Had this been a decision under competition rules, conditions would have been laid down and charges imposed.

The Council appeared to be aware of this. It took the unusual step of announcing a review by the Commission after six months 'provided that competition conditions in the sector concerned so require' and of deciding that a review is to be initiated at any rate after one year (para. 31).

CASE 2   Automobiles from Japan

In the arrangement between the Commission and the Japanese government taking the form of parallel statements the Japanese side undertakes to 'monitor' exports from Japan to the EC market in accordance with a forecast level of exports in 1999 (1.23 million), based on the assumption of demand in the EC in 1999 (15.1 million), and to 'monitor' exports to certain individual EC Member States in accordance with specific forecast levels of exports. The EC declared "that the necessary measures will be taken to ensure that the operation of competition law does not constitute an obstacle to the operation of the cooperative measures on the Japanese side". [119]

It is obvious why the Japanese side sought assurances in respect of competition policy. In order to comply with the forecasts for individual Member States the Japanese authorities must impose guidelines on the Japanese manufacturers or, as the case may be, the Japanese manufacturers must prevent sales by distributors and dealers of Japanese automobiles from Member States to a Member State with an individual forecast level when that level is exceeded in a given year. Measures taken to that effect by Japanese manufacturers or their distributors and dealers infringe the EC competition rules and, in particular, provisions of the block exemption regulation for the automobile sector.

When the Commission argued in the Council that the arrangement with Japan should be approved by the Council under the EC's trade

---

[119] Text reproduced in 1992 *Revue du Marché Unique Européen* at 323 (No. 3).

policy powers or that the Council should enact a proper trade policy regulation, the idea was rejected.[120] So far, to the knowledge of the authors of this chapter, no other measure has been taken to resolve the legal conflict between the arrangement and the EC competition rules.

The Commission's uneasiness in this respect is reflected in the position it defended in the Court of First Instance claiming that the EC-Japan agreement was a "commercial consensus".[121] This is also reflected in Mr Van Miert's statement in relation to the draft new block exemption on motor vehicles about the EC-Japan agreement "that we cannot get away from".[122]

OTHER CASES

There are a number of trade policy cases in which industrial policy issues are treated. In fact, eliminating injury resulting from imports, whether considered "fair" or "unfair", could generally be considered as a form of industry policy.

Many anti-dumping regulations consider, either under the "injury" or the "Community interest" heading, the argument that the EC industry must be maintained and its competitiveness protected in the face of unfair imports. This has been contested from time to time in the legal literature. The authors of this report do not share the view that it is legally improper for the EC to consider industrial policy issues when adopting trade policy measures. They are of the view that the purpose of anti-dumping and anti-subsidy action is not primarily to counteract dumping and subsidies as such; it is to eliminate injury resulting therefrom. Moreover, measures are subject to the "Community interest", which is an additional requirement that is separate from the interest to counteract "unfair trade". Obviously, when safeguard measures are taken, it is proper to take account of industrial policy considerations.

This is also the case when legislation is enacted on rates of customs tariffs and on origin rules. However, where the Commission determines

---

[120] In a Resolution of 16 May 1994 (PJ C 149/94) the Council calls upon the Commission to reach a decision quickly on how the Block Exemption Regulation should be applied taking account of "the contribution that the Regulation makes to efficient management of the arrangement between Japan and the European Union on trade in automobiles which should not be weakened in any way" (para. 7)!
[121] Judgment of 18 May 1994 (*BEUC and NCC v. Commission*) 1994 ECR II-289.
[122] *Europe* 25 January 1995, p. 25.

in specific cases the origin of products, a legal issue arises, not because of the fact that legislation on rules of origin may not take account of industrial policy concerns but because of the fact that the delegation of powers to the Commission does apparently not allow the Commission to take industrial policy concerns into consideration.[123]

The question arises, however, whether the European Community could still use origin rules as an instrument of industrial policy or even of trade policy in view of the Uruguay Round Agreement on Rules of Origin. Further to this agreement a harmonization programme is set up based on the principle that "rules of origin should not be used as instruments to pursue trade objectives directly or indirectly" (Article 9(l)(d)).

It should be noted, however, that this agreement does not cover preferential origin rules, such as those that the EC applies to imports from Central European Countries or ACP countries.

C.   Competition and Trade Policy Cases

CASE 1   Ballbearings

In its 1974 Franco-Japanese ballbearings decision[124] relating to an infringement of Article 85(1), the Commission found that the agreement between French and Japanese manufacturers designed to bring the prices of Japanese ballbearings imported into France into line with French manufactured ballbearings infringed Article 85(1) of the EEC Treaty. It held that: "the restriction of competition is especially serious because of the volume of sales on the French ballbearing market, the share of Japanese imports in this market and the position of the undertakings in question on their respective national markets and, for some of them, on the world market in bearings" (para. 35).

The Commission noted that no decision in application of Article 85(3) could be taken since the agreement had not been notified. It added: 'In any case, the Commission does not see how this agreement could produce the favourable results specified in Article 85 (3) and, in particular, allow consumers any benefit' (para. 44).

---

[123] For an example, see CJEC, judgments of 31 January 1979 *(YOSHIDA NEDERLAND v. Kamer van Koophandel)* 1979 ECR 115 and *(YOSHIDA GmbH v. Industries- und Handelskammer)* 1979 ECR 151.
[124] OJ L 343/1994.

In 1976 following a complaint from the Committee of the European Bearing Manufacturers' Associations, whose members were the German, British and French Trade Organizations, the Commission initiated an antidumping investigation which led in 1977 to the imposition of definitive duties whose application was suspended as the four major Japanese producers had signed an undertaking that they would increase their prices.[125]

The preamble of the regulation imposing the anti-dumping duties states, following the recital finding that the dumped imports were demonstrably the principal cause of the material injury suffered by the EC industry, that: "Whereas, in the circumstances, the interests of the Community render necessary the imposition of a definitive anti-dumping duty of 15 per cent on imports of ballbearings and tapered roller bearings of Japanese origin and for the definitive collection of the amounts secured by way of provisional duty in respect of the four major Japanese producers up to the rate mentioned above."

CASE 2   Photocopiers

In August 1983, the Commission initiated an anti-dumping investigation[126] against photocopiers from Japan following a complaint lodged by the Committee of European Copier Manufactures consisting of five EC manufacturers representing a major proportion of Community production of the product in question, Olivetti being one of the complainants. One of the Japanese manufacturers mentioned in the complaint and subsequently found to have dumped was Canon. Provisional duties were imposed in 1986, the Commission having found dumping and injury resulting therefrom.[127] Definitive duties were imposed in February 1987 by the Council, who confirmed substantially the Commission's findings.[128]

Among the various findings and statements made by the EC Institutions two deserve to be mentioned in particular.

First, Rank-Xerox's imports from its affiliate Fuji-Xerox which were sold in the EC represented about 7 per cent of Rank-Xerox's total

---

[125] OJ L 195/1977.
[126] J C 194/1985.
[127] Regulation 2640/86, OJ L 239/1986.
[128] Regulation 535/87, OJ L 54/1987.

sales in the EC.[129] Moreover, Rank-Xerox imported sub-assemblies and components for the low-volume copiers it assembled. It was found that overall, in the reference period, the value added by Rank-Xerox in the EC in the production of these low-volume copiers was between 20 per cent and 35 per cent.[130]

Second, the Japanese exporters had argued that the EC industry was not competitive as a result of the inferiority of EC manufactured machines. The regulation contains in this respect the following statement: 'Submissions arguing that the high share of the market of Japanese exporters was due to the alleged superiority of Japanese manufactured machines over those produced by Community producers were not supported by convincing evidence except in respect of multiple features. As regards the range of machines, the evidence suggests that the Community producers as a whole manufacture as wide a range in terms of copy speed as that of their competitors. With regard to quality and reliability no evidence was produced that indicated that Community machines as a whole were inferior or required more servicing. Nor was there any indication that Community producers' after-sales service was inferior compared with that of their Japanese competitors" (Regulation 535/87, para. 86).

An issue about which no interested party apparently put forward any argument but which the Commission ought arguably to have addressed was that of the competitive situation resulting from the corporate links between Fuji-Xerox and Rank-Xerox. Imposing anti-dumping duties on imports of photocopiers from Japan, while allowing Rank-Xerox to continue to import sub-assemblies and components from its affiliate Fuji-Xerox without anti-dumping duties, certainly changed the competitive position of the Xerox Group vis-à-vis its Japanese competitors on the EC market.

About ten months later, in December 1987, following a notification made to it by the parties, the Commission granted an exemption under Article 85(3) EEC to the Canon/Olivetti joint venture.[131] The Commission described this joint venture as follows: "The scope of OCI is to develop, design and manufacture copying machine products, laser beam, printer product and facsimile products".

---

[129] Regulation 535/87, para. 52.
[130] Regulation 535/87, para. 55.
[131] OJ L 52/1988.

Among the grounds on which the Commission relied to grant the exemption the following one is particularly noteworthy in the light of its finding on the same element in the anti-dumping investigation: "The joint venture enables a transfer of the benefit of advanced technology to Olivetti, a Community undertaking, in markets where technology is of crucial importance".

CASE 3   Soda-Ash

• Anti-dumping measures against soda-ash imports

In 1983, anti-dumping duty was imposed on imports of dense sodium carbonate from the USA and price undertakings from three US companies were accepted.[132] In 1984, anti-dumping proceedings were reopened following a request from the European Council of Chemical Manufacturers Federations; the scope of the existing measures was amended[133] and price undertakings offered by two US companies were accepted.[134]

In 1988, a review of the existing anti-dumping measures was requested by certain US producers and the EC glass industry which claimed that US exporters were no longer dumping. In March 1989, the Commission initiated a review and investigated whether dumping had occurred between 1 December 1987 and 28 February 1989.

• Competition decisions against soda-ash producers

In March 1989 the Commission carried out investigations under the EC competition rules at the premises of EC producers of soda-ash and opened formal proceedings under these rules in February 1990. On 19 December 1990 it adopted a series of decisions under the EC competition rules.

In one of these decisions it found that two EC producers had participated, since 1 January 1973 until at least the institution of the pro-ceedings, in a concerted practice by which they confined their soda-ash sales in the EC to their respective home markets. The Commission or-

---

[132] OJ L 64/1993.
[133] OJ L 311/1984.
[134] OJ L 206/1984

dered the two producers of soda-ash to cease and desist, and imposed on each of them a fine of ECU 7 million.[135]

In a second and third one of these decisions[136] the Commission found that two EC producers of soda-ash occupied a dominant position in the relevant product and geographic markets (70 per cent, viz. 90 per cent) and that they had abused their dominant position by various measures. The Commission ordered them to cease and desist, and imposed a fine of ECU 20 million, viz 10 million. The Commission found that the measures taken by both EC producers to ensure the continuance of their dominant position were aimed in the first place at direct competition from outside the EC (the United States and Poland). It also found that "a major plank" of the commercial policy of one of these EC producers was "to ensure the maintenance of the anti-dumping measures in place against the United States producers of heavy ash as well as the East European light ash suppliers".

For good measure in another one of these decisions[137] the Commission found that the American Natural Soda-Ash Corporation (ANSAC) (a Webb-Pomerane association) membership agreement and related agreements which ANSAC had notified to it infringed the EC competition rules in so far as they related to the EC market. The European Commission ordered ANSAC and its members to refrain from implementing the agreements in the EC.

- • The fate of the anti-dumping measures against soda-ash imports

In the meantime the review proceeding of the existing anti-dumping measures had been going on. On 7 September 1990 the Commission adopted a decision on the matter. It found dumping margins for four US companies ranging from 2.9 per cent to 12.8 per cent. However, it terminated the investigation without imposing anti-dumping measures, having found that the dumping had not caused injury and recognized "that it has not been established that the expiry of the existing anti-dumping measures would threaten to cause serious injury to the Community industry".[138]

---

[135] OJ L 152/1991.
[136] OJ L 152/1991.
[137] OJ L 152/1991.
[138] OJ L 283/1990.

It took the view that there was no "threat of injury": the current level of US exports was very low, and the US producers did not have the proper sales structure needed to increase their sales significantly.

Whether the decision to terminate the review without anti-dumping measures being taken resulted from the anti-competitive conduct of the EC soda-ash producers, the role which anti-dumping measures had played in shoring up the dominant position of at least one of them and the subsequent decisions taken against them under the EC competition rules, is a matter for speculation.

Whereas in some of its decisions under the competition rules relating to the soda-ash sector the Commission refers to existing anti-dumping measures, in its decision terminating the review of the existing anti-dumping measures on soda-ash it does not say a word about its findings under the competition rules.[139] On the face of it, the Commission could, as it did, terminate such review a purely on grounds relating to the Anti-dumping Regulation and did not need to refer to competition law policy considerations. But in this case the tension between the two policies was too obvious to be ignored in substance. It is noteworthy in this respect that in its 1993 review of the EC's trade policy, the GATT secretariat commented on this case as follows: "A recent case in which the EC authorities intervened to restore competitive conditions concerns soda-ash, where domestic producers had sought anti-dumping protection to defend cartel rents against competing imports. The companies involved were convicted under EC competition law and the anti-dumping measures repealed in 1990/91."[140]

This statement has apparently not been contradicted by the Commission in the course of the so-called "review meetings" conducted in the GATT on the basis of this GATT report containing these comments.

This, however, is not the end of the story. In August 1993 following a new complaint from the European Council of Chemical Manufacturers Federations, the Commission initiated yet again an anti-dumping proceeding relating to soda-ash from the USA.[141] It has been reported that

[139] P. Vandoren, "Recent Developments in the Area of the Interface between Anti-dumping and Competition Policy in the EC", (1993) LIEI 21 (No. 1 at 27) finds it surprising that competition considerations were not mentioned in connection with imports from the USA.
[140] GATT, Trade Policy Review Mechanism, European Communities. Doc. C/RM/S/36A p. XII (19 April 1993).
[141] OJ C 213/1993.

this preliminary investigation is terminated and that draft measures are being considered by the Commission. At the time of writing measures have not been taken.

One will have to wait for the publication of a regulation or a decision to know whether the market has changed much in the meantime. That the share of the EC market taken by US producers has increased would not be surprising. As the abuse of dominant position by some of the major EC players consisted precisely in measures designed to keep the US producers out, stagnating sales by US producers would arguably show that the Commission's decisions under the competition rules did not have any effect whatsoever.

Apparently, there has been not much change in the market structure in the EC, except that ICI reportedly sold its soda-ash division to the main Australian producer of soda-ash. Normally, the new owner of ICI's soda-ash division may be expected to want to protect his investment and to refrain from importing soda-ash from Australia into the EC at low prices.

In addition, the acquisition of substantial production capacities in the US by certain EC producers raises yet another competition issue, that is, whether it is appropriate and wise to allow EC producers to strengthen their position on the US market vis-à-vis their competitors by restricting the latter's access to the EC market.[142]

The Commission could, however, once again duck the competition law and policy issue and terminate the investigation without taking anti-dumping measures by relying on the 'Community interest' clause of the Anti-dumping Regulation. In a case such as this there is something to be said for taking account of the interests of the user industry, in particular the glass industry, which offers employment to several times the number of people employed in the soda-ash industry and whose production costs depend significantly on the price of soda-ash.[143]

---

[142] This sort of situation is described in more detail by J. Temple-Lang, 'Reconciling European Community Antitrust and Antidumping, Transport and Trade Safeguards Policies- Practical Problems', in 1988 Fordham Corporate Law Institute, B. Hawk (ed.) 7-1 at 7-41 (Matthew Bender, New York, 1989).

[143] The situation is complicated further by soda-ash imports from Central and Eastern Europe. These imports have increased from 27,000 tonnes to 162,000 tonnes in 1992 and have replaced West European production (FT 6 July, p. 5).

Be it as it may, under the post-Maastricht rules referred to in section I of this chapter competition policy has been given a more prominent function. Taking anti-dumping measures in a case such as this one would appear on the face of it as highly questionable.

IV.   RECOMMENDATIONS

While preparing this chapter, the authors wondered whether as lawyers they ought to put forward recommendations on the proper policy mix the EC Institutions should strive for when taking into consideration the three policy areas within the broadly defined legal mandate set out in the 'constitutional' instruments described *supra* (Section I). In the end they decided to refrain from doing so, mainly for two reasons.

First, they were of the view that the policy choices which decisions on the proper policy mix involve are too dependent on the facts of each case and the economic and policy assessment thereof to be capable of being regulated by substantive norms that would be precise enough to be operational and at the same time offer legal certainty, while being sufficiently durable to be predictable.

Second, they considered that, at any rate, while lawyers may assist policy-makers in their decision-making process, they do so in a legal perspective, while the choices to be made in the matter discussed in this paper are essentially policy choices. There are, however, recommendations to be made from a legal perspective. Such recommendations are of a procedural nature.

First Recommendation

From an institutional and organizational point of view the Commission is, as a decision-making body, in a fairly advantageous position. While in other jurisdictions, e.g. in the USA, policy management is spread over different bodies, each responsible for a given area such as antitrust policy, industrial policy and trade policy, the Commission is as a collegiate body in a position to consider at all times the interrelationships between the various policy areas. As the exclusive source of legislative proposals, at least under the EC Treaty, the Commission is also acting as a collegiate body and here as well it is in a position to consider these interrelationships when working out such proposals and to ensure that these interrelationships are considered when its proposals are discussed in the various "specialized Councils" of the European Union. This requires appropriate internal procedures within the Commission to ensure always that, when a draft decision to be taken within a given policy area is considered, the relationships with other policy areas are taken into account.

There are effectively within the Commission internal procedures requiring the input of *"services associés"* and of *"services consultés"*. There also are the Chefs' meetings. However, from the cases examined in this report one is bound to conclude at first blush either that these procedures and machinery are inadequate or that they do not function properly.

The first recommendation is thus that the Commission adopt internal procedures ensuring that generally when the responsible DG submits a draft decision, say in the competition area, there is a genuine input of the DGs in charge of say industrial policy and trade policy and conversely.

The objections which are from time time put forward against this are not convincing

The first objection has to do with the legal limits on the use of information collected and the rules on professional secrecy. Under the legislation as its stands[144] information collected by the Commission in competition investigations, i.e. in trade policy investigations, may be used only for the purposes of the enforcing competition rules, (trade policy rules) and, as the case may be, only for the purposes of the relevant investigations; moreover, the Commission and its officials may not disclose information acquired through these investigations of the kind covered by the obligation of professional secrecy. This, however, should not impede the Commission and its officials from taking account of the interrelationship between different policy areas when considering measures in a given policy area.[145] The Commission and its officials are not under a legal duty to initiate a competition policy investigation when, in the course of a trade policy investigation, they are made aware of a possible infringement of competition rules, and conversely. The involvement of officials in charge of trade policy when competition policy measures are prepared, and conversely, does consequently not put them

---

[144] In the competition policy area: Regulation 17/62, Article 20 and Regulation 4064/89, Article 17; for the anti-dumping and anti-subsidy area: Regulation 2423/88, Article 8(1), now Regulation 3283/1994, Articles 7(1) and 9(4) and Regulation 3284/94, Articles 9(1) and 11(6), both OJ L 349/1994.

[145] Ace. Jacobs AG in his submissions in EXTRAMET n. 24 at p. 669.

in a situation of conflicting duties. In addition, when in a competition case trade policy implications are considered this does not turn a competition case into a trade policy case. The subject matter is and remains enforcement of competition rules.

The second objection concerns the limited scope of the examination of issues relating to a given policy in the framework of an investigation relating to another policy. It has been argued, e.g. that the Commission could not investigate fully a competition matter arising in an anti-dumping investigation.[146] However, *"le mieux est l'ennemi du bien"*: what is required is that the Commission does not disregard considerations of competition policy in an anti-dumping case. To that purpose the Commission does not need to embark on a fully-fledged competition investigation.

The third objection is that in a case pertaining to a given policy area and therefore allocated to the DG in charge of that policy undue consideration would be given to other policies as a result of interference by other DGs. While "undue consideration" is to be avoided, the present situation in which apparently the Commission's left hand too often ignores what the Commission's right hand is doing is a cure worse than the disease. Moreover, as far as consideration of competition aspects is concerned, the objection has little legal merit in view of the prominence now conferred to competition policy by Article 130 of the EC Treaty.

Second Recommendation

The Commission does not investigate on its own initiative whether possible infringements of competition rules in trade proceedings are involved. Nor does it, as a rule, examine on its own initiative possible competition policy implications of trade policy measures. In competition policy proceedings the Commission follows a similar approach as far as trade policy issues are concerned. In proceedings in both these areas the Commission practice is to leave it to parties to raise issues pertaining to the other policy area.

One of the authors of this chapter has in the past raised doubts about the need of systematic competition impact analyses in anti-dumping case, to the extent that injury determinations are carefully made, the general practice to limit anti-dumping duties to what is necessary to

---

[146] Argument put forward by the defence in EXTRAMET n. 115 at p. 669.

remove such injury is followed, the position of the import-using industry is taken into account and, where appropriate, existing measures are reviewed.[147] This author is bound to recognize, however, that these qualifications, while allowing account to be taken of the interests of parties as they are protected by competition rules, do not exclude the risk that competitors of the parties involved in such proceedings may be affected, nor the risk that the exporters and importers refrain from raising competition policy issues in view of a deal they may want to make with the complainant industry. In the final analysis not only the interests of competitors and users are matters of concern but also the maintenance of competition as such.

Thus the Commission ought not to leave it to parties in proceedings in a given policy area to raise issues relating to other policy areas but should examine such issues on its own initiative.

In competition investigations, at least those relating to agreements and concerted practices, this may give rise to a problem, to the extent that examining industrial and trade policy implications would, under the traditional interpretation of Article 85(1) EC, only be relevant for Article 85(3) EC purposes. Under the rules as they stand,[148] Article 85(3) individual exemptions may only be granted in respect of agreements which have been specifically notified for the purpose of seeking an exemption. One could argue, however, that this rule may be set aside in appropriate cases and exemptions thus be granted in the Community interest rather than in the interest of the parties to such agreements.

Third Recommendation

"Justice must not only be done. It must also be seen to be done."

In trade policy decisions most of the existing legislative instruments require the Commission and, as the case may be, the Council to consider whether the "Community interest" calls for intervention. The "Community interest" clauses remain the *"parent pauvre"* in trade policy investigations and in the decisions taken following such investigations.[149]

---

[147] J.H.J. Bourgeois, "Trade Measures, Competition Policy and the Consumers', in P. Demaret, J. Bourgeois and I. Van Bael (eds) *Trade Laws of the European Community and the United States in a comparative Perspective* at 241 (Story-Scientia, Brussels, 1992).

[148] Regulation 17/62, Articles 4(1), 5(1) and 25.

[149] For example, with respect to consumers' interests, see J.H.J. Bourgeois, *supra* n. 1472 at 258.

Competition policy decisions, i.e. the formal ones, not the comfort letters, are more explicit and better drafted in this regard if and when they address issues relating to other policies.

The third recommendation is consequently that not only issues relating to the other policies be examined in investigations relating to another policy but also that these issues, their assessment and the conclusion reached be clearly reflected in the text of the decisions.

15. EC TRADE POLICY MEASURES –
THEIR COSTS AND BENEFITS

I. INTRODUCTORY REMARKS

Trade policy measures are as a rule taken by governments in order to secure some economic benefits. Governments may also take such measures to further broader trade policy aims and even political aims: measures against imports coming from a given country help to persuade that country to open its own market; certain trade protection measures act as a safety valve, allowing to ward off pressures for more drastic trade protection measures; in certain cases governments consider it expedient simply to bow to pressure from politically powerful sectors; governments from time to time use trade policy measures as economic sanctions against certain countries.

The purpose of this paper is to draw attention to the economic aspects of European Community (hereafter, the EC) trade policy measures. The examination of these economic aspects – conveniently but improperly called cost/benefit analysis – covers three different elements: the cost/benefit of trade policy measures to the EC economy as a whole; the related aspect of their economic effects, on the importing and the exporting industry, both in the EC and in the foreign country; and on EC producers; and the cost to EC producers of obtaining relief under EC trade policy rules and the cost to foreign producers of defending themselves under these rules.

Before dealing with the cost/benefit analysis proper it is useful to recall briefly the relevant aspects of the main EC trade policy instruments.

II. EC TRADE POLICY INSTRUMENTS

Quite a few governmental measures, while not having the object of controlling imports or exports, may have such effect. This is the case i.a. for technical regulations and standards, "buy national" policies in government procurement, subsidies to domestic producers, inadequate protection of intellectual property and comparable rights and discriminatory taxation. The EC and its Member States have their share of such measures.[1] These are not addressed in this paper, which only deals with straightforward, classical trade protection instruments.

These instruments are: customs duties, quantitative restrictions, safeguard action, antidumping and (subsidy) countervailing duties and measures against "barriers to trade" maintained by foreign countries.[2]

A.   Customs duties

Customs duties are a cost to importers, as are the formalities involved in clearing customs. However, as a result of both their fairly low level and their across-the-board reductions in the Kennedy and Tokyo Rounds of GATT multilateral trade negotiations, EC customs duties normally no longer function as an instrument to protect particular industries.

There is one exception to this. In the past the EC managed not to "bind" its customs duties in the GATT for a series of agricultural products. It has now done so when transforming its system of variable levies into tariffs. These tariffs are high and could have the same effect as quantitative restrictions when world market prices attain a certain level. Moreover, it has been argued that the system of tariff quotas on imports of bananas also operates as a quantitative restriction.

Suspensions of customs duties are being used to improve the supply situation of the EC industry.

Under the EC's Generalized System of Preferences, customs duties may be wholly or partly suspended on imports of developing countries. This may be of interest to certain sectors of EC industry that source components or even manufacture finished products in these countries.

Moreover, the EC has a host of preferential agreements with other countries providing for customs duty free access.

Except for some specific measures provided for by the EC Customs Code, there are no procedures granting private parties the right to petition for a reduction or an increase of customs duties.

---

[1] See, e.g. the EC and Member States sections in USTR, *1995 National Trade Estimate Report on Foreign Trade Barriers* and in *MITI 1996 Report on the WTO Consistency of Trade Policies by Major Trading Partners.*

[2] The procedure to suspend provisionally the "release for free circulation" of counterfeit goods is not dealt with in this paper.

B.   Quantitative restrictions

Quantitative restrictions as a trade policy instrument are no longer a feature of EC trade policy. In fact, they never were. In the past, rather than adopting quantitative restrictions itself, the EC allowed its Member States to keep certain such measures at the national level. They were all abolished in 1994.

There are two exceptions. First, as other countries, the EC, as a party to the Multifibre Agreement, introduced quantitative restrictions for textile products covered by that agreement. These restrictions are to be phased out under the World Trade Organization (hereinafter: the WTO) Agreement on Textiles and Clothing. Second, when it abolished the remaining quantitative restrictions in 1994 which it had allowed Member States to keep, the EC introduced at EC level such measures against imports from China of gloves, footwear, tableware, ceramic tableware, glassware, radios and toys.[3]

In the past, the EC and many other countries bypassed the GATT prohibition of quantitative restrictions and the GATT rules on safeguard action by so-called Voluntary Restraint Agreements (VRAs) or Voluntary Export Restraints (VERs) it managed to obtain from exporting countries. These may no longer be taken nor maintained under the WTO Agreement on Safeguards. Existing VRAs and VERs must be phased out by 1998. The EC managed to negotiate an exception to this for its VRA with Japan on automobiles which will terminate by 31 December 1999.

C.   Safeguard action[4]

EC trade rules provide that

> "[w]here a product is imported into the Community in such greatly increased quantities and/or on such terms or conditions such as to cause, or threaten to cause, serious injury to Community producers"

the European Commission may establish an import quota. Such safeguard measure applies for a period not exceeding four years. The

---

[3] Cases are pending in the Court of Justice and the Court of First Instance of the European Communities challenging the legality of the quantitative restrictions on toys.
[4] The relevant regulations are : Regulation 3285/94 (OJ 1994 L 349/53) and Regulation 519/94 (OJ 1994 L 67/89) applying to State-trading countries.

period may be extended if it is determined that the measure continues to be necessary to prevent or remedy serious injury and there is evidence that EC producers are "adjusting".

There is no procedure granting private parties the right to petition the European Commission to take a safeguard measure. Relying on the wording of the Regulation on Common Rules for Imports which provides that the European Commission takes safeguard action at the request of an EC Member or on its own initiative, the European Commission routinely turns down petitions from EC producers. The only possibility left to EC producers is to act through an EC Member State.

D.   Antidumping and Countervailing Duties[5]

The phenomenon with which antidumping duties and countervailing duties deal is different. The former ones address "dumping" by exporters that sell export to the EC at a price lower than the price they charge on their domestic market; the latter ones address subsidies granted in the exporting country on products that are exported to the EC.[6] However, many of the conditions and the procedure for taking these measures are identical. It is consequently convenient to consider them together.

There are certain features which distinguish antidumping and countervailing duties from the trade policy instruments which have been mentioned earlier.

First, antidumping and countervailing duties may be targeted against imports from particular countries. When using these instruments, a WTO Member, such as the EC, is not obliged to comply with the principle that WTO Members may not be discriminated against.

Second, the EC imposes such duties following a complaint from EC producers and only following such complaint.

Third, antidumping duties are by far the most frequently used EC trade policy instrument. In the past ten years less than ten safeguard

[5] The relevant current regulations are Regulation 3284/94 (protection against subsidized imports) (OJ 1994 L 349/22) and Regulation 384/96 (antidumping) (OJ 1996 L 56/1).
[6] Note: there is a specific regulation providing for the possibility to impose an "injurious pricing charge" on the builder of any "injuriously priced vessel" (Regulation 385/96, OJ 1996, L 56/21); there also is a specific regulation against unfair pricing practices in maritime transport (Regulation 4057/86).

measures have been taken. However, the abolition of EC Member States quantitative restrictions and the legal impossibility of using VRAs and VERs may in the future lead to an increase in safeguard measures. By contrast, in the period 1989–1994 alone 446 antidumping and countervailing investigations have been initiated and on 31 December 1993 53 regulations imposing antidumping or countervailing duties were in force.

1   Complaints

Complaints are filed by a "Community industry", i.e. by at least a major proportion of the EC producers of the "like product". The complaint must contain sufficient evidence of dumping or subsidies and of injury resulting from it to EC producers.

2   Investigation

Like safeguard measures, antidumping duties and countervailing duties are imposed to remedy injury or a threat of injury to EC producers caused by imports. Although in the case of dumped and subsidized imports the injury must be "material" while in the case of other imports the injury must be "serious", the investigation of such an injury is carried out along similar lines and is assessed in relation to of the same factors. In this respect, the involvement of EC producers is similar for the three trade policy instruments. They are requested to respond to fairly extensive questionnaires and are subject to on-the-spot investigations by European Commission officials. Contrary to what may happen in an investigation under the EC competition rules, the EC producers' refusal to cooperate does not expose them to fines and penalties. However, such refusal to cooperate will be regarded as evidence that they did not suffer injury with the consequence that no antidumping or countervailing duties will be imposed.

A refund by exporter to cooperate exposes them to the risk that findings will be made on the basis of "the evidence available", i.e. in most cases the data submitted by the complainants.

3   Measures

Findings of dumping/subsidy and of injury resulting therefrom lead to the imposition of antidumping or countervailing duties, provided that action is required in the (public) EC interest. Such duties come on top of customs duties and are collected in the same way.

E.   Measures against "Trade Barriers"

In December 1994 the European Community enacted the so-called "Trade Barriers" Regulation[7] thrown by its acronym TBR. This piece of legislation lays down a new procedure whereby the "EC Industry" and EC enterprises can request the EC to act internationally to obtain enforcement of international trade rules where foreign countries adopt or maintain barriers to trade.

1.   *Trade Barriers*

By trade barriers the Regulation means "any trade practice adopted or maintained by a third country in respect of which international trade rules establish a right of action" on the part of the EC. This covers violations by a Member of the WTO of its obligations, but also situations or trade practices which, while not violating a WTO rule, are nevertheless harmful and may give rise to a so-called "non-violation" complaint in the WTO. Violations of bilateral agreements between the EC and a foreign country are also included in this definition.

The TBR also applies to transfrontier services which do not involve the physical movement of persons, as well as to intellectual property rights, where the violation of such rights has an impact on trade in goods between the EC and a foreign country.[8]

This instrument is designed to complement existing trade policy instruments (such as antidumping and countervailing duties, safeguard action). It differs from the other EC trade policy instruments in that it applies to a wider range of situations: it is not limited to the defence against

---

[7] Regulation 3286/94 (OJ 1994 L 349/71). For further reading : *European Commission, What is the Community's Trade Barriers Regulation? Opening New Trade Opportunities for European Businesses* (OOPEC, Luxembourg, 1996); see also A. Stewart, *Market Access: A European Community Instrument to Bread Down Barriers to Trade*, 2 Int'l T. L. Reg. 121 (1996).

[8] This partial coverage by the TBR of the WTO General Agreement on Trade in services and the WTO Agreement on Trade-related Aspects of Intellectual Property Rights results from the fact that these agreements where entered into by EC Member States alongside the EC in line with Opinion 1/94 of the Court of Justice of the European Communities. For a comment, see J.H.J. Bourgeois, *The EC in the WTO and Advisory Opinion 1/94: An Echternach Procession.* 32 CML Rev. 763 (1995).

imports; it is not primarily intended to result in measures imposed at the EC borders but rather to induce or compel foreign countries to lift their barriers to trade.

2. Complaints

The European Commission will initiate an "examination procedure" following a complaint. The conditions which complaints must fulfil differ according to the situation which they address.

Where barriers to trade of a foreign country result in an effect on the EC market, a complaint may be lodged by a "Community industry" which must show that it suffered "material injury" as a result of the obstacle to trade. "Community industry" means as a rule producers accounting for a major proportion of total EC production of identical, similar or directly competing products, or an industry consuming or processing the product affected by the trade barrier.

Where barriers to trade of a foreign trade result in an effect on the market of a foreign country, a complaint may be lodged by an enterprise "directly concerned by the production of goods ... which are the subject of the obstacle to trade". Such enterprise must show that it has suffered "adverse trade effects" which have a material impact on the EC economy, a region of the EC or a sector of economic activity in the EC.

The instrument could thus be used where a trade barrier prevents trade opportunities from arising (e.g. where the supply of parts, components or raw materials to EC firm is affected, where trade flows are diverted or where EC firms are prevented from selling into foreign markets).

3. The possible results of a complaint

Once initiated the "examination procedure" can lead to any of the following results.

- the foreign country concerned takes on its own the steps to eliminate the "adverse effects" or the "material injury" complained of; the European Commission suspends the procedure and monitors the implementation by the foreign country of the measures;

- the foreign country seeks an amicable solution, which may be reached independently of an international dispute settlement procedure or may be the result of such procedure; or

- where the international dispute settlement procedure results in a decision in favour of the EC, the foreign country may accept this result and abolish or modify the trade barriers; if not, the EC may adopt a trade policy measure, provided in where the WTO Agreement applies, that the EC has been authorized by the WTO Dispute Settlement Bodo to do so.

III.   THE COST/BENEFIT OF EC TRADE POLICY MEASURES

As already indicated an analysis of economic aspects of EC trade policy measures covers three different elements: the cost/benefit to the EC economy as a whole; the related aspect of their economic effects on the importing and the exporting industry and on the EC producers; and the cost to EC producers of obtaining relief under EC trade policy rules and the cost to foreign producers of defending themselves under these rules.

No attempt has been made to address in this paper the cost to foreign exporters. In theory, the economic effect of EC trade policy measures on foreign exporters and the economic effect thereof on EC producers are roughly the two sides of the same coin. How foreign exporters react to that economic effect depends on a variety of factors. They may shift the cost of EC trade policy measures forward to their customers in the EC. They may also absorb this cost or agree with their importers in the EC that they will bear the cost of the EC trade policy measures.[9]

In the context of EC trade rules, the question about costs and benefits is perfectly justified in legal terms. In certain jurisdictions, e.g. in the US, as far as antidumping and countervailing duties are concerned, a finding of dumping/subsidy and of resulting injury to domestic producers leads automatically to the imposition of duties. The US Congress has made a conscious policy choice to provide remedies whose benefits accrue to producers, whose costs are borne by consumers and whose welfare costs may outweigh the benefit to domestic producers. The EC "legislator" has

---

[9] The EC has included in its Antidumping Regulation a provision requiring that antidumping duties lead to "movement in resale prices or subsequent selling prices" in the EC (Art. 12).

not made such a conscious initial policy choice. A finding that the substantive conditions for safeguard action are fulfilled, a finding of dumping/subsidy and resulting injury to domestic producers or a finding that a trade barrier causes injury do not lead automatically to the imposition of measures. In each case the finding needs to be made that such measures are in the public EC interest, which could arguably be a form of cost/benefit analysis.

Regretfully, so far, with the exception of certain analyses made by Prof. Messerlin[10] and a study carried out in 1991 for the European Parliament[11], all limited to antidumping policy, there appears to be no overall study analyzing the economic impact of EC trade policy measures.[12]

Although there were rumours of a study in 1995, in the wake of the publication in 1995 of the "Carla Hills" study in the US[13] it is unknown whether and when the European Commission will have the cost/benefit analysis study made. The study carried out *sine ira et studio* by a group of independent experts at the request of OECD under the chairmanship of Prof. Wilig in 1992 on antidumping and competition is still to be published. It probably appears too controversial to government official of Member States.[14]

Recommendations to systematically evaluate the costs and benefits of trade policy measures before they are taken have been made in the past within the GATT framework, i.e. the *Leutwiler Report*[15], within the OECD[16] and also within the EC, i.e. the *Molitor Report*[17]. So far, these recommendations have not been followed.

---

[10] *The EC Anti-dumping Regulations: A First Economic Appraisal 1980-1985*, 125 WW Archiv 3 (1989); *Antidumping Regulation or Pro-cartel Law* 13 World Economy 4 (1991).

[11] *European Parliament, Directorate General for Research. The Economic Impact of Dumping and the Community' Anti-dumping Policy, Economic Series E-1* (Luxembourg, 1993).

[12] The OECD study of 1986, *International Trade and the Consumer* (Paris, 1986) is either more general or contains studies on certain sectors; see also *Greeneway and Hindley, What Britain Pays for Voluntary Export Restraints* (Thames Essay. No 43, 1985).

[13] USITC, *The Economic Effects of Antidumping and Countervailing Duty Orders and Suspension* Agreements (investigation No 332-344, June 1995).

[14] *Attack on Antidumping Law Sparks OECD Row*, Financial Times, September 2, 1995.

[15] Trade Policies for a Better Future (GATT, Geneva, 1985).

[16] OECD, *Competition and Trade Policies: Their Interaction (OECD, Paris, 1984).*

[17] *European Commission, Report of the Group of Independent Experts on Legislative and Administrative Simplification* (1995) COM (95) 288.

Politicians do not like cost/benefit analyses. *Ex-ante* analyses are seen as limiting their discretion. *Ex-post* analyses may show that their decisions were misguided or inefficient. Their officials consider cost/benefit analyses either as not convincing or, where they are correctly carried out, as too complicated. The officials may have a point.

In their seminal study[18] in which they developed a model designed to quantify welfare effects of the lifting of trade barriers, Hufbauer and Elliot identify the following effects: the gain of consumer surplus resulting from changes in prices and quantities due to liberalization; the partial offset thereof by a loss in producer surplus in the market for the domestic substitute, where prices and output both fall; the loss of revenue for the government if the trade barrier is in the form a customs duty; and the efficiency gain resulting from a better allocation of resources. Hufbauer and Elliott base their model on a partial equilibria analysis, for which they had to make assumptions. These assumptions are: the domestic good and the imported good are imperfect substitutes; the supply schedule for the imported good is flat (perfectly elastic); the supply schedule for the domestic good is upwardly sloped (less than perfectly elastic); and all markets are perfectly competitive. This shows that in order to be reliable a cost/benefit analysis must be based on a careful review of each product market concerned, taking into consideration its specific attributes. Although time consuming and complex such analysis does not, however, create unsurmountable difficulties. In this respect EC trade policy officials in particular could learn a thing or two from their colleagues dealing with merger control.

A.   Customs Duties

1.   *Welfare effects*

The cost which the existing customs duties represent for the EC economy is difficult to assess. The aggregate amount of customs duties to be collected in 1996 is estimated in the 1996 budget of the EC at 14,281,000,000 ECU. This, however, is not the proper measure of the so-called consumer surplus losses. While these customs duties keep the price of imports in the EC market higher than they would be in the absence of such customs duties, this does not tell the whole story. As in the case of other trade policy instruments much depends on factors such as the supply

---

[18] *Measuring the Cost of Protection in The United States* (Institute of International Economics, Washington, D.C., 1994).

elasticity of imported and domestically produced goods and the degree of competition of the markets. Moreover, the consumer surplus loss is not the only element of a cost/benefit analysis. As a result of customs duties, the prices EC producers get for their products are normally higher. Thus, customs duties mean revenue for the EC.

2. *Economic effects on EC producers*

As to the economic impact on EC producers and exporters, while there are a number of overall studies, there appear to be practically no published analyses of the economic impact of EC customs duties on specific sectors of industry.

3. *Cost of relief and defence*

As there are no formal procedures involving private parties in connection with the level of customs duties, the cost for the EC industry of seeking relief and the cost for foreign exporters of defending their interests is difficult to estimate.

B.   Quantitative restrictions and safeguard action

1.   *Welfare effects*

There is little published evidence on the welfare effects of quantitative restrictions in the EC, which mostly take the form of VRAs or VERs, and of safeguard measures.

According to a 1991 analysis the economic costs to EC consumers of the VERs on Japanese cars exceed the gains to European producers by 5 billion ECU per year and the replacement of a VER by an "equivalent" tariff would provide a net gain of 3.6 billion ECU. Therefore, the greater part of the cost of the VER is the excess cost associated with its anticompetitive effects.[19]

---

[19] A. Smith and A.J. Venables, *Counting the costs of VERs in the European Car Market* in E. Helpman and A. Razin (eds), *International Trade And Trade Policy* 187–220 (MIT Press, Cambridge Mass. 1991), cited by P. Holmes and A. Smith, *Automobile Industry* in P. Buigues, A. Jacquemin, A. Sapir (eds) *European Policies on Competition, Trade And Industry* 125–159 (Edward Elgar, Aldershot, 1995).

2. Economic effects on EC producers

Similarly there is no published evidence on the economic effects of such measures on the EC producers themselves.

The VER on footwear led, not surprisingly, to reduced competitive pressures and higher prices by the EC manufacturers.[20]

With regard to the effects on the EC automobile industry of the Japanese VER, the jury is still out. One may wonder whether the most important issue is trade protection. The issue probably is whether the EC producers will be able to respond to Japanese makers that successfully produce in the EC.

3. Cost of relief and defence

As already indicated there is no formal right for the EC industry to petition the European Commission.

However, the relevant regulation provides that safeguard measures can only be taken following an investigation by the Commission which connects the imports and the injury to the EC producers. EC producers, importers, industrial users, and also consumers may have an interest in cooperating with the Commission. Interested parties also have a right to be heard. Cooperating in the Commission investigation essentially means supplying data on the factors which the Commission considers relevant. For importers this implies gathering detailed data on such matters as import trends (quantities over the last three years; increase, if any, in absolute terms or relative to consumption) and import prices (average prices on importation, prices relative to EC producers' prices).

For the EC producers this involves gathering detailed data on production, sales, market shares, financial results and employment. Normally, EC producers will rely on a trade association to collect and aggregate all the data which, however, will have to be provided by the individual member companies.

If this work is entrusted to an outside consultant the fee may vary from about USD 20,000 to about 60,000. In the course of the

---

[20] L.A. Winters, *Integration. Trade Policy and European Footwear Trade* in L.A. Winters (ed.), *Trade Flows and Trade Policy After* 1992 (Cambridge University Press, Cambridge, 1992).

investigation and at hearings both importers and EC producers would be well advised to rely on the assistance of lawyers. Although the proceedings are quite informal, legal issues are playing an increasingly important role. Lawyers' fees vary and much depends on the amount of work to be done which varies from case to case. Such fees range from USD 3,000 to 50,000.

C.   Antidumping and countervailing duties

1.   *Welfare effects*

The study commissioned by the European Parliament[21] does not really attempt to measure the welfare effects of EC antidumping measures. It limits itself to assessing the impact of these measures on prices, competition, trade, Community producers and their employees, industrial purchasers, consumers, exporters and the overall (Community) public interest.

On the issue of prices, it reviews estimates made in a 1990 working paper by the UK National Consumer Council on Consumer Electronics and the EC's Anti-dumping Policy and concludes that such estimates, which the UK National Consumer Council considers itself as "little more than a guess at rough orders of magnitude", "do demonstrate the potentially very significant impact of anti-dumping duties on prices and costs in the Community" (at p. 161). Yet its review of four cases is rather mixed. In Mini Ball Bearings measures have had some impact on prices. In Plain Paper Photocopiers, the question required more detailed study. In Polyvinyl Chloride, a number of factors suggested that the measures did not have any significant impact on prices. Finally, in Small Screen Colour Televisions, there were indications that EC prices continued to fall, maybe as a result of circumvention by relocating production in other countries (at pp. 162–163).

As far as competition is concerned, the EP study refers to its estimates according to which in 40% of cases there are five or fewer producers in the EC. There is evidently scope for conflict between the EC competition and antidumping policies.[22] It should be noted in passing that it is generally accepted that EC producers may lawfully exchange

---

[21] *Supra* n. 11.

[22] For an analysis of a series of cases, see J.H.J. Bourgeois and P. Demaret, *The Working of EC Policies on Competition, Industry and Trade: A Legal Analysis* in Buigues, Jacquemin and Sapir *supra* n. 20 65–114.

information about their business and their foreign competitors' business for the purpose of drafting an antidumping or a CV complaint.

Looking at trade, while the total value of imports affected by antidumping measures is small (the measures in force in 1991 concern 1.1% of all EC imports), on average imports from countries subject to measures accounted in 1991 for 19 % of all imports of the relevant products, and 35% in the electronics sector. A year after initiation of the average reduction in import volumes from countries investigated was 18%; after three years the reduction was around 35 %. However, imports from other countries rose by 20% in the year following the investigation and by nearly 50% over four years (at p. 166).

The impact on industrial purchasers is not measured in the EP study.

As far as the impact on consumers is concerned, the study notes that the effect of duties in redistributing income from consumers to producers does not represent a net loss of economic welfare to the EC but states that the loss of consumption efficiency should not be neglected as a trivial consideration. The study adds that in cases of predatory dumping low prices in the short term are not generally in consumers' interest, taking into account the increase in prices that follows successful predatory dumping (at p. 169). The problem here is that the EC uses this argument often without ever substantiating that a given case of dumping is predatory and showing that prices would increase.

As already indicated, the provision on "Community interest" should normally mean that a genuine cost/benefit analysis be made. Although there has been same improvement lately, the findings made fall generally short of making such analyses. In fact, very often it is assumed that dumping is found to be detrimental to economic welfare and that the imposition of duties will increase economic welfare.

One last element may be of interest for economies, particularly for ones such as the EC, that are highly dependent on international trade: EC exporters are a major target of antidumping investigation by other countries. Over the period 1980-1989, other countries opened 344 investigations against EC exports, 159 against Japan exports and 144 against US exports.[23]

---

[23] EP study *op. cit.* n. 11 at 158.

2.   *The effect on EC producers*

It is fairly obvious that, by reducing import competition and allowing EC producers to increase sales volumes and/or price, antidumping and countervailing duties normally have a beneficial effect on EC producers of the like product. The question, however, is whether antidumping and countervailing duties that create the producer surplus gain, which is not compensated by the loss of consumer surplus, have effectively contributed to improving the EC producers' competitiveness.

The EP study examines the impact of antidumping duties on the EC producers in four cases. In Mini Ball Bearings there were respectable public interest arguments in favour of antidumping measures: 10 world producers account for 90% of the supply, the barriers to re-entry are high, and the EC cannot afford to risk losing the industry for defence and economic strategic reasons. Yet, antidumping duties have been in place for more than 15 years, Japanese producers may be more cost competitive in certain parts of the market. Chances are that the antidumping measures have not been effective in allowing the EC industry to regain competitiveness (at p. 172).

As seen in Polyvinyl Chloride, until the late 1980's when there was a further surge in imports from Eastern Europe, the EC producers appear to have retained their market share. This may suggest that they did not suffer any long term damage from the dumping. The case for improving antidumping measures to assist the producers to rationalise would seem weak (at p. 173).

The main considerations in the Plain Paper Photocopiers case were about preserving the strategic importance of the technology involved and therefore to keep the structure of the EC industry. It would seem that the measures have affected this structure (at p. 174).

With respect to Small Screen Colour Televisions, the concerns focused on the threat to the viability of EC production and to the development of High Definition Television, the technology of which is said to be linked to the SCTV technology. The question is what is meant by EC production in light of the high degree of mobility of producers in a sector such as this one with non-EC producers establishing production facilities in the EC and EC producers establishing such facilities abroad.

What is totally missing is published evidence on whether antidumping and countervailing duties have improved "the state of the [relevant] industry" when measured by looking at the factors used to assess "injury" (sales, profits, output, market share, productivity, return on investments, capacity utilization, etc.). In other words we do not know how far the relief offered by antidumping and countervailing measures is effective.

3.   *The cost of relief and defence*

The two main private actors in antidumping and countervailing proceedings are the complaining EC producers and the foreign exporters. In countervailing proceedings the respondent is the foreign country that granted the subsidies; however, exporters are practically as much involved in countervailing proceedings as in antidumping proceedings.

The complaint submitted by EC producers must contain sufficient evidence of dumping/subsidy and injury. In practice, the European Commission has become much more demanding than in the past. It puts a questionnaire at the EC producers' disposal. Filling out this questionnaire to the Commission's satisfaction requires substantial information gathering. Even where the necessary information on injury is provided by the EC producers themselves, the cost of preparing a complaint may, as a result of the need to collect information on market prices and production costs in the exporting country, in an average case amount to at least USD 50,000.

After the initiation of the investigation both the exporters and the complaining EC producers are sent an elaborate questionnaire which they are requested to fill out.

Subsequently, after follow-up questions, European Commission officials carry out on-the-spot investigation.

Parties may request to be heard and may make additional submissions.

After provisional duties have been imposed the European Commission is bound to disclose to each party, in detail, the findings it made.

Thereafter, parties again have the possibility to make submissions.

Before definitive duties are imposed, the Commission is bound to disclose the definitive duties it will propose to the Council of the European Union.

All these steps in the proceeding involve costs both for the EC producers and the foreign exporters. Usually the cost to exporters is higher than the cost to the complaining EC producers. These costs may vary considerably from case to case. The cost of the work done in-house by companies is difficult to estimate. It is advisable to both exporters and EC producers that they seek the assistance of a lawyer throughout the proceeding. Lawyers' fees vary in function of the amount of work required. EC producers should expect lawyers' fees in the amount of at least US 50,000 and foreign exporters double this amount.

D.   Measures against Trade Barriers

Proceedings have not yet been initiated under the Trade Barriers Regulation. The cases under the preceding Illicit Trade Practices Regulation do not permit one to say anything meaningful about the welfare effects and the economic impact of the measures taken.

The cost of seeking relief for the EC producers involves the cost of preparing a complaint which should normally be lower than that of antidumping and countervailing complaints.

The costs involved in participating in the proceeding should also normally be less for the EC producers. They should also be less for the foreign producers, as the foreign country will have the burden of defending its "trade barrier".

V.   CONCLUSION

The absence of any cost/benefit analysis by the EC of the trade policy measures it takes is as such to be deplored. Such analysis would force the EC to verify in each case whether the cost of import protection is in fact acceptable. Once it decides to intervene, the EC can use cost/benefit analyses to help it to choose the most appropriate, least costly regulatory instrument. The publication of cost/benefit analyses would inspire more confidence in the decision-making process.[24]

The evidence is insufficient to assess whether the relief granted by the EC trade policy measures has the effect contemplated, i.e. repair the injury caused to the EC producers by the imports.

When seeking relief and when defending one's interests, EC producers and foreign exporters must be prepared to incur costs that are not negligible.

---

[24] Cfr. M.C.E.J. Bronckers, *Rehabilitating Antidumping and Other Trade Remedies through Cost-benefit Analysis*, 30 *Journal of World Trade* 5–27 at 34 (1996).

ABOUT THE AUTHOR

Jacques Bourgeois is partner at Akin Gump Strauss Hauer & Feld LLP where he advises clients on all aspects of European Union law, particularly competition policy matters and international trade issues, including antidumping and anti-subsidy proceedings. Mr Bourgeois represents and assists clients before the European Commission, the Council of the European Union and other EC institutions, and in EU courts. He also advises clients on matters related to the World Trade Organization, has assisted clients in WTO dispute settlement proceedings and has presided over a WTO dispute settlement panel and a panel established under its predecessor organization, GATT.

Prior to his re-entry into private practice in 1991, Mr Bourgeois was a senior official in the European Commission. From 1987 to 1991 he was principal legal adviser of the Commission, where he was in charge of foreign trade policy and, later, antitrust policy. Mr Bourgeois entered the Legal Service of the Commission in 1965 and was responsible successively for questions pertaining to personnel, the institutional domain, the agriculture and fisheries policy, and external relations. From 1983 to 1987 he was head of the Trade Policy Instruments Division in the Directorate General for External Relations, and was responsible for the implementation of the EU's regulations on antidumping and subsidies, as well as for safeguard measures and protection against illicit commercial practices.

Mr Bourgeois is a professor of the College of Europe (Bruges) and was a visiting professor at the University of Michigan Law School in 1976. He was nominated to the Jean Monnet Chair at the University of Bonn during the 1992–1993 academic year.